CEASEFIRE!

Why Women and Men Must Join Forces to Achieve True Equality

CATHY YOUNG

THE FREE PRESS

The Free Press
A Division of Simon & Schuster Inc.
1230 Avenue of the Americas
New York, NY 10020

THE FREE PRESS and colophon are trademarks
of Simon & Schuster Inc.

Designed by Brady P. McNamara

Manufactured in the United States of America
10 9 8 7 6 5 4 3 2 1

Library of Congress Cataloging-in-Publication Data

Young, Cathy.
    Ceasefire! : why women and men must join forces to achieve true
equality / Cathy Young.
        p.   cm.
    Includes bibliographical references and index.
    ISBN 0-684-83442-1
    1. Feminism—United States.   2. Sex role—United States.
3. Equality—United States.   I. Title.
HQ1421.Y58   1999
305.3—dc21   96-49653
                                                                    CIP

This book is dedicated to my parents, Alexander and Marina Young, who showed me that a true and equal partnership between a man and a woman is possible.

The Gender Wars

Modern feminism, until recently at least, promised not to intensify
sexual warfare but to bring about a new era of sexual peace in
which women and men could meet each other as equals, not as
antagonists.   —Christopher Lasch, *Women and the Common Life* [1]

Near the end of the century in which equality of the
sexes became a basic tenet of civilized society, the
best-seller of the decade says that men and women are creatures
from different planets. A state legislature rewrites the text of marriage licenses to warn about domestic abuse, which, sponsors say, is
"a leading cause of death and injury for U.S. women." In a seemingly endless stream of films and books, the war of the sexes rises to the
level of mutual assured destruction. On a television show, actress-
comedienne Janeane Garofalo declares that American women have
been as oppressed as blacks since fat women don't get good movie
roles, and that "everything we eat, sleep, and drink" is about disrespect for women. From some quarters, women are urged to take
offense at male sexual interest; from others, to reclaim their power of
sexual manipulation. Above all, women are urged to get mad: "To be
a woman today is to be angry," a suburban working mom tells a
newspaper.[2]

When I came to the United States in 1980 at the age of seventeen, I was a feminist—before I even knew the word. In the Soviet
Union, where I was born and raised, the official dogma of equality
coexisted with pervasive old-fashioned sexism: catching a husband

was supposed to be a girl's supreme goal; the superiority of the masculine mind was taken for granted by many women as well as men;
too much intellect, ambition, or strength in a woman raised the fearful specter of lost femininity.

As a preadolescent, I began to chafe at these attitudes. My reading
heightened my interest in what used to be called the "Woman
Question." I passionately believed that, as Nora said in *A Doll's
House,* "Before I am a woman I am a human being": what I was and
what I did was not defined by my sex.

This was the feminism that I thought I had found in my adopted
country. My discovery of America was also the discovery of a culture
where female independence was celebrated; where it was not a
compliment to tell a woman she thought like a man; where it was
not beneath a man's dignity to push a stroller; where an easy camaraderie seemed to reign between young men and women on college
campuses.

Despite the occasional article suggesting that maybe equality had
been a foolish idea and that women should go (or were going) back
home, I never saw much of a backlash to worry about in the 1980s.
I was more bothered by what was happening to feminism. In my
college classes, some young women were acting as a volunteer
thought police, ready to pounce whenever a professor imprudently
used the word *mankind*. Antipornography activists seemed to argue
that sexuality itself demeaned women; the concept of rape was being
expanded to include confused, nonviolent drunken encounters.
Many feminists were rejecting autonomy, logic, and objectivity as
"male values."

In the 1990s—after Anita Hill, after Susan Faludi's *Backlash,* after
the "Year of the Woman"—much of what had troubled me moved
from the feminist fringe to the mainstream. Days after the 1992 Los
Angeles riots set off by the acquittal of the white cops in the
Rodney King beating, an ABC News town-meeting discussion of
rape opened with Peter Jennings declaring that "the violence done
to women" was as divisive an issue as racial strife (even if "there have
been no bricks or bullets exchanged on this subject yet") and that,
to illustrate the gender divide, men and women in the audience had
been seated separately.[3] That night, my belief that feminism was
helping make things better between the sexes died.

In *Backlash,* Faludi wrote that feminism is a "simple concept,
despite . . . efforts to dress it up in greasepaint and turn its proponents into gargoyles." Women are people, "just as deserving of rights

and opportunities, just as capable of participating in the world's events" as men. But the gargoyles are real, and the concept is anything but simple.[4]

To some, feminism is about "the belief in women's oppression" here and now; to others, it's about affirming the "different voice" of female values and repudiating such "male" notions as logic, individualism, and pursuit of knowledge and excellence. Maybe it means (according to feminist philosopher Judith Lorber) applying blatant double standards because a woman's mistreatment of a man "redresses [the] imbalance of power," while a man's mistreatment of a woman reinforces it. Maybe, as legal scholar Catharine MacKinnon says, it means "believing women's account of sexual use and abuse by men" and measuring everything by one yardstick: "Is it good for women?"[5]

These ideologies sometimes clash; feminists who focus on oppression have accused "different voice" proponents of validating stereotypical femininity. But they also mesh easily: all reject the principle of equal treatment, either because equal standards are inherently "male" or because one cannot treat oppressor and oppressed as equals. All divide humanity along gender lines.[6]

It's hard to tell why the movement went this way. In fact, it was always pulled in different directions by the belief in equality and female superiority, in individual rights and female community. Naomi Wolf says that "victim feminism" arose in the 1980s because feminists felt so besieged fighting "the backlash."[7] But perhaps it was the reverse: with most battles for equal opportunity won, feminism came to be dominated by other goals and creeds. One could say that the movement had outlived itself and had to justify its existence, or that feminists were frustrated because, with the external barriers gone, women were still held back by more subtle obstacles. Or maybe many feminists realized that equality wasn't what they wanted.

But does feminism matter much anyway? After all, only about a third of American women identify themselves as feminists. The National Organization for Women has 250,000 members; *Ms.* has a circulation of 200,000, while the readership of more traditional women's magazines is in the millions.[8]

And yet "gender feminism," to use the term coined by Christina Hoff Sommers, has had a powerful impact. It has won government backing for programs that give special priority to women's health and girls' educational problems, in response to alleged inequities. It has guided the campaigns against sexual harassment and domestic violence, issues that are real enough but are largely viewed today through the distorting prism of gender politics and bogus statistics. It has helped shape law and public policy in other areas, from rape (where the changes have often gone far beyond correcting traditional biases against women) to child custody (where feminist influence has often reinforced traditional biases against men).

The obscure theories trickle down from the ivory tower and blend into a kind of pop feminism, epitomized by Anna Quindlen's now-defunct column in the *New York Times,* with its twin themes of men's victimization of women and women's superior virtues. Pop feminism also thrives, in a strange cohabitation with beauty-and-relationships fare, in many women's magazines. Readers of *Redbook, Ladies Home Journal,* and *Mademoiselle* are told that male violence is a constant threat, that the legal system is biased against them, that medicine neglects their needs, and that criticism of Hillary Rodham Clinton is driven by hostility toward ambitious women.[9]

Quite a few women who may not call themselves feminists cheer the acquittal of penis slicer Lorena Bobbitt and say, "Well, men have gotten away with abusing women for thousands of years." A woman who has never taken a women's studies course and who has never read Catharine MacKinnon may tell a pollster that it's offensive for a man to talk to a coworker about her sexual attractiveness, or that it's rape if a man "argues with a woman who does not want to have sex until she agrees." Commenting on women's alienation from feminism, journalist Elinor Burkett notes that "it is Roseanne, not Gloria Steinem, who is a heroine to American women." But is that so encouraging, given Roseanne's tirades about how women should kill their husbands more often?[10]

The new feminism appeals to many women by "validating" and giving a larger meaning to their personal problems, and in particular by tapping into their anger at men—which has little to do with politics, patriarchy, or even men being from Mars and women being from Venus. It has to do with the tensions and messiness of intimacy, perhaps exacerbated by rapidly changing expectations and roles. Exasperation with one man is easily projected onto men in general. The same is true of men's anger at women. But these days, male anger is viewed as misogynistic and dangerous. (A *Redbook* writer interviewing an imprisoned serial rapist notes that his rants about men getting "screwed over" by women aren't much different from what she has heard from normal men going through a nasty divorce.) Women's anger, meanwhile, is politicized and sanctioned—

and not just by feminists who argue that "a woman's distrust of any man is a completely rational response to the sustained attack on women perpetrated by both individual men and androcentric systems." A poll in which 42 percent of women agree that "men are basically selfish and self-centered" is presented as evidence of male rottenness, not female chauvinism. One could hardly imagine the reverse.[11]

To some extent, feminism has always politicized the personal, inasmuch as it sought to change relations between women and men. But once, it targeted laws that gave the husband authority over his wife, and later the social norms dictating a woman's place: the assumption that she should subordinate her ambitions to her husband's, that he should have the final say in the household, that sex before marriage was fine for him but not for her.

This critique did not presume male malevolence or female innocence. In his 1869 essay, *The Subjection of Women,* after discussing the husband's formal powers over the person and property of his wife, John Stuart Mill emphasized that he was describing "the wife's legal position, not her actual treatment": "Happily there are both feelings and interests which in many men exclude, and in most temper, the impulses and propensities which lead to tyranny." (Yes, Mill was a man; but his wife and collaborator, Harriet Taylor Mill, took a similar view in her writings.) A century later, in *The Feminine Mystique,* Betty Friedan saw the suburban man as less the oppressor than, in some ways, a victim of the woman who had to derive her identity from her husband and made him "an object of contempt" if he didn't live up to her expectations. Friedan even viewed male hostility toward women with some sympathy, as a reaction to "the devouring wife."[12]

The new feminism, on the other hand, focuses on the evil that men do to women. In 1998, when feminists were criticized for failing to support the women allegedly victimized by President Clinton, Susan Faludi wrote a remarkable article contrasting "real feminism," which is about "becoming equal and mature players in public life," and "girl power," gained by "celebrating yourself, ideally via your injuries, [and] talking about what was *done* to you" (like Paula Jones or Monica Lewinsky). Although her criteria were purely political, it's still a good point. Indeed, critics whom Faludi had ridiculed as "faux feminists" have been saying it for years.[13]

This shift from women's rights to women's wrongs has far-reaching implications, besides making victimhood central to feminism.

Male abuse of women and girls (including acts that Western culture had long abhorred, such as rape, wife beating, and incest) must be redefined as the enforcement rather than the violation of social norms, and interpreted as broadly as possible to maximize the number of victims. Believing specific accusations by one person against another becomes an issue of politics more than fact. Private conduct becomes political (which is, of course, precisely what led Clinton's feminist supporters into a self-created quandary). Indeed, the very concept of privacy becomes suspect, merely a smokescreen for, in MacKinnon's words, "the right of men 'to be let alone' to oppress women one at a time."[14] The evil that women do—to children, other women, men—must be erased. The same people who choke with indignation if someone suggests that women lack the "killer instinct" in the workplace or the military will sneer at the idea that women might be aggressors in domestic violence.

The assumption that the personal is political is deeply entrenched in the gender debates. Even Karen Lehrman, who explicitly asserts in her book, *The Lipstick Proviso,* that the personal is *not* political— that is, not a proper sphere for government action—still believes it's a feminist issue that many women stay in "bad relationships" and let men mistreat them.[15]

Yet deep down, I think, most of us know that the sexes are roughly equal in inflicting personal misery on each other. This may have been true even when men had far more legal power in the home and far more freedom outside it. By focusing on women's private grievances, feminism not only promotes a kind of collective feminine narcissism (which reached its peak after the death of Princess Diana in the rush to turn the unfortunate princess into a symbol for the woes and the victories of the modern woman) but links itself to the myth of female moral superiority and the demonization of men.[16]

And where *do* men fit in? There is much chuckling about white males who feel beleaguered because their power and privilege are eroding. But power and privilege have always been a fairly abstract notion for most men. And today, whatever advantages men may still have, in some ways they have fewer choices than women do: less freedom to choose between traditional and nontraditional roles, to drop out of the workforce, to trade a better-paying job for a more fulfilling one.

Yes, some men miss the old days when girls were girls and men were men. But there are probably far more who are troubled by the sense that they, as men, are under attack and that women want it both ways.

It is widely felt that at the core of today's gender troubles is the fact that women have changed but men have not: they still fail to treat women as equals and to do their share of traditional "women's work." But in some ways, women haven't changed either. Many still want to be protected, even if they also want independence; to marry a man who earns more, even if they also want equal pay; to let their husbands bear the primary burden of financial responsibility, even if they also believe they are entitled to a career. As Katie Roiphe noted in a provocative essay, "We want men to be the providers *and* to regard us as equals."[17]

Sometimes this attitude is expressed openly. In a 1996 article in the campus paper the *Daily Bruin,* UCLA student Jessica Morgan calls it "creative feminism." Women, she asserts, should employ "a combination of feminist ideals and the advantages that come with being female" to achieve their ends: fall back on feminism if they feel sexually harassed but on femininity if they need to use sex appeal to get their way; refuse to defer to men but rely on them to do manly things like squash bugs. "So men are confused, and I say 'good,'" adds Morgan. "The more confused the men of this country are, the easier they are to manipulate. . . . The more easily they are manipulated, the more likely it is that we'll get what we want— whatever it is that we want."[18]

Such frankness may be rare. But a having-it-both-ways philosophy is characteristic of much modern feminism: women are the same as men or different, whichever suits them; sex stereotypes are endorsed if they're positive (e.g., that women are more nurturing than men) and denounced if they're negative (e.g., that women are less intelligent than men). Feminists who resent any suggestion that a mother belongs with her children often insist, when it comes to child custody, that children belong with the mother. Feminists acutely sensitive to bias against women show little concern for bias against men, whether it's the informal leniency accorded female defendants in court or overtly discriminatory draft registration.

Blindness to male disadvantage is hardly limited to feminists. Throughout our culture, women's interests and demands tend to be seen as uniquely legitimate. One can hardly imagine politicians talking about what they've done "for men" the way they talk about doing something for women. Partly it's because of the presumption, rooted in the long history of women's struggle for the most fundamental rights, that women's cause is a just cause. Added to the mix is the traditional paternalism that views women as deserving more protection from harm than men do. The charge that women's lives or health are being jeopardized would have a less powerful effect if one were to substitute the word *people*.

As a result, efforts to right old inequities, real or perceived, may lead to new ones. Men's problems, such as male health issues or boys' educational needs, become invisible or are put on the back burner. Men accused of violence toward a woman may face a virtual presumption of guilt. As men's advocate Warren Farrell points out, the notion that men have all the power and women are powerless (which was never quite true, and is preposterous in America in the 1990s) "makes us fear limiting the expansion of women's power," even when that power becomes unjust.[19]

That is why the alternative to "victim feminism" proposed by Naomi Wolf in *Fire with Fire*—"power feminism" with the slogan "More for women"—won't do. Women don't always deserve more. Moreover, power feminism can mutate into exploitation feminism: grab power whichever way you can. Jessica Morgan's "creative feminist" manifesto is easy to dismiss as one article by one ditzy girl, but it could be part of a mini-trend. A book-length version of the same viewpoint can be found in Elizabeth Wurtzel's 1998 clunker, *Bitch: In Praise of Difficult Women*. (Wurtzel summarizes the "bitch philosophy" as, "I intend to do what I want to do and be whom I want to be and answer only to myself," and imagines that "for men this attitude is second nature.") New York–area attorney Rosalie Osias has gained notoriety by running provocative photos of her leggy self in ads for her law firm and by preaching what she practices: women, kept down by an old boy network, should use sex as an asset. A female newspaper editor opines that if such advice can help women feel better about themselves and get ahead, isn't that "the point of real feminism?"[20]

I don't wish to paint too harsh a picture. Most people's lives remain relatively untouched by politics, gender or otherwise. I feel hopeful when I talk to a young woman who is baffled by the talk of teenage girls' losing self-confidence; when I see dads shopping with their children and overhear two burly fellows in a supermarket discussing baby food brands; when I talk to enthusiastic male fans of the Women's National Basketball Association; when I read about a businesswoman or an astronaut who gives more thought to doing her job than to her gender; when I see women admiring male beauty.

But I also know that all is not well. Too many young women waste their energy on "anger," while others, disgusted by feminist excess, embrace traditionalist views at odds with their own lives. Too many quietly resentful men are walking on eggshells. Too many children are growing up without fathers. *The Rules,* a supremely cynical manual that instructs women how to scheme their way to the altar by mixing old-fashioned coyness with postfeminist independence, lands on the best-seller list, filling the vacuum left by feminism's failure to present a positive vision of love between equals with a pseudo-traditionalist and, at bottom, profoundly adversarial prescription for courtship.[21]

Only a fevered fantasy could conjure up a gender war fought with guns and bricks; parallels between race and sex go only so far. But precisely because there is much more social and personal intimacy between the sexes than between races, ostensibly gentler and quieter gender warfare can inflict deeper wounds and wreak greater havoc. Today the gender police seek to invade male-female relationships at every stage. Marital conflict is redefined as "abuse," which, pamphlets warn, may consist merely of "making you feel bad about yourself." A clumsy advance or an off-color joke becomes "sexual harassment," which in some states children are being taught to recognize as early as elementary school.[22]

Do I still consider myself a feminist? No, if feminism means believing that women in Western industrial nations today are "oppressed" or if it means "solidarity with women," as essayist Barbara Ehrenreich claimed on National Public Radio in 1994. Yes, if it means that men and women meet each other as equals, as individuals first and foremost; if we remember what British philosopher Janet Radcliffe Richards wrote more than fifteen years ago: "No feminist whose concern for women stems from a concern for justice in general can ever legitimately allow her only interest to be the advantage of women."[23]

I still believe the feminist challenge to woman's place was right. I think we can take pride in the fact that a woman is now expected to be her own person and make her own way in the world, and that the public sphere is no longer considered a male domain. Like all other cultural shifts, these changes have not been cost free. But most women (and, I think, most men) don't want to go back, nor should they.

Contrary to some conservatives' claims, the fifties were not an idyll in which women enjoyed respect as homemakers and ample

opportunities if they wanted a career. Employers themselves reported rampant discrimination against women, without risking much
public disapproval, since most Americans did not believe that
women should have equal opportunity in the job market. Many top
colleges did not accept women, and those that did routinely gave
preference in admissions to less qualified men. Young women who
did go to college were often held back by the fear of being too smart
and scaring boys away. Asked to complete a story about a high-
achieving female medical student, they typically produced scenarios
in which the woman suffered a dire fate (death, disability, spinsterhood) or let her grades slip on purpose and focused on helping her
man.[24]

A charge often made against "dissident feminists" like myself is
that we acknowledge past problems only to say that equality has
now been achieved and the women's movement has outlived itself.
Unfortunately, those who make this accusation usually build their
case for continued feminist activism on claims that, as I intend to
show in this book, do not stand up to scrutiny. Girls are *not* silenced
or ignored in the classroom. Medicine has *not* neglected women's
health. Abuse by men is *not* the leading cause of injury to American
women; the courts do *not* treat violence toward women more
leniently than violence toward men. Gender disparities in pay and
job status are *not* merely a consequence of sex discrimination. The
eighties were *not* a "backlash decade" but a time of steady progress
for women and, generally, of strong support for women's advancement. The climate in our society is not one of "cultural misogyny,"
as feminist writer Katha Pollitt asserts, but is far more saturated with
negative attitudes toward men.[25]

Nevertheless, I too believe there is some unfinished business—
besides undoing the harm done by the extremists. We need to reexamine "pro-female" stereotypes and double standards as seriously as
we have reexamined antifemale ones in the past twenty-five years.
We need to determine how, in an era when women participate
equally in the public world, the responsibilities of the home can be
balanced in a way that is fair to women, men, and children. Of
course, these problems must be solved by each couple in its own
way, but society can make it easier, or harder.

I believe we still need a philosophy to guide us on the journey of
an unprecedented transition: a philosophy that is not pro-woman (or
pro-man) but pro-fairness; that stresses flexibility and more options
for all; that encourages us to treat people, regardless of sex, as human

beings. If sentimental traditionalism won't get us there, neither will the gender warfare that would destroy our common humanity in order to save it. I don't know if this philosophy should be called feminism or something else. But the biggest impediment to its development is what passes for feminism today.

PART ONE

Myths of Difference,
Myths of Oppression

CHAPTER ONE

Men Are from Earth, Women Are from Earth

> The first thing that strikes the careless observer is that women are unlike men. They are "the opposite sex" (though why "opposite" I do not know; what is the "neighbouring sex?"). But the fundamental thing is that women are more like men than anything else in the world. They are human beings.
>
> —Dorothy L. Sayers, *Are Women Human?*[1]

A study claiming to shed light on why boys will be boys and girls will be girls sparked a flurry of reaction in 1997. Dr. David Skuse of the Institute of Child Health in London and his colleagues had been studying girls with Turner's syndrome, who have one X chromosome instead of two and have normal intelligence but tend to lack social skills. As *Time* put it, "They butt into conversations. They misread facial expressions, tones of voice, body language. They're insensitive to others' feelings. They act, in other words, a lot like boys."[2]

The scientists found that Turner's girls who got the X chromosome from their mothers, as all boys do, were far more antisocial than girls with a paternal X. This led them to speculate that a social adjustment gene linked to the X chromosome is activated only if the X comes from Dad—and thus is active only in (normal) girls, who inherit one X from each parent.[3]

"Experts Say Men Are Programmed to Behave Badly; 'Social Gene' Makes Lasses Nicer Than Lads," cried the headline in the London tabloid the *Mirror*. "Preposterous," scoffed feminist writer Susie Orbach: "Gender roles are culturally prescribed—they've nothing to do with genetics."[4]

Orbach is no expert on genetics. But, fascinating though Dr. Skuse's hypothesis may be, are those sweeping statements about sensitive lasses and oafish lads grounded in reality?

Actually, Turner's girls act far *worse* than boys. On an index of antisocial behavior reported by parents, the average scores for Turner's girls with a maternal X was 9, out of a maximum 24. Boys, and Turner's girls with a paternal X (who, if the theory is right, should have been as socially skilled as other girls), scored about 4; normal girls scored 2. There was also a good deal of overlap among normal children: three out of ten boys were as nice as five out of ten girls—a difference, to be sure, and maybe a genetic one, but hardly of Mars-Venus magnitude.[5]

The "social gene" brouhaha is all too typical of how we talk about sex difference: biology is everything or nothing; men and women are identical or polar opposites. In a *New York Times* column, conservative writer Danielle Crittenden says that men's "genetic wiring" makes them immune to "the mental strain of walking out the door" suffered by working mothers; irate readers dismiss this as "absurd" and assert that if a woman feels more torn about leaving her baby, it's only "cultural conditioning." Is it so absurd to think that the parent whose body is involved in the birth may have a biological predisposition to be more attached to the baby? On the other hand, a biological predisposition is not a universal imperative. Men unexpectedly thrust into a "Mr. Mom" role because they are out of work when the baby arrives often feel heartbroken when *they* have to walk out the door.[6]

Paradoxically, the two extremes of polarity and sameness are equally entrenched in mainstream culture. The notion that without sexism, half of all CEOs, engineers, and firefighters would be female is matched by the equally pervasive notion that women and men are worlds apart. A story on gender in cyberspace says that women want computers to "meet people's needs" while men want to explore and conquer. In April 1998, the *New Yorker* ran two articles in two consecutive weeks about how women will remake government and business in a collaborative, nurturing, consensus-oriented mold. If the subject is women athletes or chess players, we are told that they are more concerned with teamwork than with winning. Women architects? Unlike men, they place human needs above the ego and "collaboration" above "individual brilliance."[7]

The evidence for all these claims is usually underwhelming. If 58 percent of women and 46 percent of men tend to favor an activist government, that mutates into "fundamental differences" in political values—even though, in the same poll, 44 percent of men and 49 percent of women feel that "government should do more to help needy Americans even it means going deeper into debt."[8]

I have often wondered if I somehow fail to notice supposedly obvious differences between the sexes. Men don't talk to each other about their personal lives? The ones I know seem to know quite a lot about their male friends, and even the ones I hear talking on the train or at the gym discuss not only sports but marriages, kids, and family problems. Men don't ask for directions? When someone asks me for directions, it's usually a man—and it was a woman who refused directions to my house, insisting that she could find it (she was wrong).

I've heard the morality tales about people who think there are no innate gender differences until they have kids, and somehow always end up with daughters who will wear only frilly dresses. Yes, boys play with guns and girls play with dolls, even when parents try to discourage stereotypes. But I also suspect that many parents, even nontraditional ones, are tempted to explain children's behavior in terms of sex rather than individuality. I once heard a mother of four-year-old nonidentical twin girls marvel at how different they were: one affectionate and nurturing toward their baby brother, the other aggressive and often resentful of the attention given the baby. Had the second girl been a boy, this would have been another boys-will-be-boys-girls-will-be-girls litany.

It is sometimes suggested that to deny differences between men and women is a willful blindness to reality.[9] But all those grandiose pronouncements about men and women often seem to be no less at odds with how actual human beings act.

When the women-only sailing crew of *America*[3] raced for the 1995 America's Cup, the media readily picked up team sponsor Bill Koch's favorite theme: women (unlike men) make decisions cooperatively and don't have a problem subordinating their egos to the team. Yet an earlier all-female team, the U.S. Women's Challenge in the 1993 Whitbread race, was plagued by rivalries that prompted ousted skipper Nance Frank to lament, "Basically, there's no difference between men and women."[10]

It's not just in sports that one finds evidence that power struggles and obsession with winning are hardly alien to women—from scientist Margot O'Toole's apparently wrongful crusade to expose senior researcher Thereza Imanishi-Kari as a fraud to a high school student's legal fight to avoid sharing her spot as class valedictorian with another girl who had a near-identical grade-point average.[11]

When *Men Are from Mars, Women Are from Venus* author John Gray took his act to Broadway, a celebrity member of his onstage panel, the supermodel Frédérique, wouldn't play along, declaring, "I relate a lot more to the Martian side." Gray scrambled for a face-saving answer that stood his basic conceit on its head: Women, he said, "are both Martian and Venusian."[12] Yes, and men too.

Feminism's "Different Voice"

It is widely believed that feminism in the 1970s minimized differences between the sexes and exhorted women to be like men. In fact, there was some ambivalence about this from the start. The editors of the 1971 anthology, *Woman in Sexist Society,* proclaimed that women "do not want to be free for ruthless competition" but seek "a place in public life for the values they have been forced to cherish in private." At the time, however, such sentiments were overshadowed by the enthusiasm of women who did want to be free for "ruthless competition." The turning point was the 1982 book, *In a Different Voice,* by Harvard psychologist Carol Gilligan, who challenged the "masculine bias" of psychological theories that regard autonomy as the basis of mature adulthood. According to Gilligan, male moral reasoning is based on rights, justice, and abstract principles, while women's "ethic of care" is based on human needs and connections.[13]

The factual basis for Gilligan's pronouncements was slight. For one, only four of the thirty-two subjects in the study on which *In a Different Voice* was based were male. Besides, as Gilligan's critics have pointed out, she often appears to tailor their comments to a preconceived scheme. When a boy says that a man who can't pay for a drug to save his dying wife should steal it because "human life is worth more than money," he is focusing on an abstract hierarchy of value; when a girl says he should steal it because the wife is "another human being who needs help," she's focusing on human need. In fact, research on gender and moral reasoning offers little if any evidence of a masculine ethic of justice and a feminine ethic of care.[14]

Although many feminists were troubled by Gilligan's validation of traditional feminine virtues, *Ms.* put her on the cover as "Woman of the Year" in January 1984, and the "different voice" soon became the official voice of feminism, especially in academia.[15] Columnists Ellen Goodman and Judy Mann praised Gilligan for vindicating "women's values" and invoked her theories to explain the gender gap: women prefer Democrats because they want a caring government. In 1996, Gilligan was named one of the "*Time* 25"—people who have helped "change the ways we think about ourselves and others."[16]

"Difference feminism" found a great popularizer in linguist Deborah Tannen, whose 1990 book, *You Just Don't Understand: Men and Women in Conversation,* topped best-seller lists for nearly two years. Lively and often amusing, the book tapped into the gold mine of frustrations about intimacy. The promise that everyday misunderstandings could be solved was appealing, as was Tannen's eagerness to blame these conflicts on innocent error. A *Washington Post* reviewer saw the book as a respite from "feminist bashismo."[17]

But Tannen's friendly disposition toward men has its limits (in 1996, she wrote a rather snide essay about how men don't seem to be capable of uttering the words, "I'm sorry"). In her book, she never overtly says that women are better. But when she contrasts male and female views of conversation—"negotiations in which people try to achieve and maintain the upper hand" (men) versus "negotiations for closeness in which people try to seek and give confirmation and support" (women)—how neutral is that? The niceness attributed to women may be a liability in, say, a legal career, but it surely sounds more attractive than one-upmanship.[18]

At times Tannen concedes that she may have slighted female competition and male affiliation. Men's "ritual combat" may foster bonding; women's community "may mask power struggles." Analyzing videotaped conversations between friends, she acknowledges that the most intimate one is between two teenage boys who reminisce about "stay[ing] up all night long . . . just to talk" (which doesn't lead her to reconsider her claim that boys *don't* "just talk"). Tannen notes that the boys sit farther apart and have less eye contact than girls. Her point, however, is not to disparage male intimacy but to explain how stylistic differences may cause women to miss it.[19]

But many of her interpretations are too carefully tailored to the status-seeking man–connection-seeking woman model. Consider the classic scenario in which the woman complains about a problem to get sympathy, the man offers solutions, and she gets upset because giving advice does not establish rapport but puts the giver in a "one-up" position. How does this square with Tannen's claim that men tend to suspect one-upmanship in innocuous exchanges? Isn't it *women* here who seem to see one-upmanship where men, who help each other with problems "by finding a solution or by laughing them off," see helpfulness?[20]

The tendency to put a positive spin on female behavior is most visible in Tannen's discussion of a study of preschool children's conflict tactics by University of Minnesota linguist Amy Sheldon. Two boys fight over a toy telephone, saying nothing more sophisticated than, "It's my phone"; two girls "enact a complex negotiation" over a doll and toy medical instruments. Complex, yes; but not very nice. True, when Elaine has the toys, Arlene asks politely and Elaine compromises ("just use it once"). But after gradually seizing control, the little Machiavellian ruthlessly shuts out her playmate, issues supposedly boy-style harsh commands ("Now don't touch the baby until I get because it IS MY BABY!"), and quashes Elaine's bids to regain some ground ("NOW DON'T YOU DARE!"). Tannen's summary—the girls are "trying to get what they want while taking into account what the other wants"—seems unaccountably benign.[21]

Hard-Wired to Be Different?
"Difference feminists" usually skirt the question of where the difference originates, though Gilligan dances on the edge of arguing that childbearing gives women "easier access . . . to the fact of human connection." This evasiveness has earned them some ridicule. Journalist Robert Wright pokes fun at Tannen for arguing that boys "learn" to jockey for status in their more hierarchical social networks, without explaining "why the boys' groups are always more hierarchical in the first place."[22] (The "always," as we shall see, is quite an overstatement.)

Wright is the author of *The Moral Animal,* one of a spate of books promoting evolutionary psychology (others include *The Evolution of Desire,* by David Buss, *The Red Queen,* by Matt Ridley, and *How the Mind Works,* by Steven Pinker).[23] According to this theory, *la différence* is a product of reproductive strategies that evolved to ensure genetic survival. The male, who can increase his progeny by having many mates, is "programmed" to wander and seek dominance, which ensures access to females. The female, for whom parenthood is time-consuming and who can have the same number of offspring with one mate or fifty, saves her favors for males who have good genes and/or are willing and able to "invest" in her and her young. He looks for youth and attractiveness in a mate (signs of fertility); she looks for status and resources. Even if these patterns aren't relevant in an industrial society, they are hard-wired into our brains by millennia of evolution.

The political implications of this theory can cut both ways. Wright and Ridley invoke it to support affirmative action: since men's advancement is propelled by lust for power, often unrelated to merit, women must be favored "not to redress prejudice but to redress human nature." Others, such as Wayne State University law professor Kingsley Browne, argue that in the light of Darwinian science, male dominance in the public sphere is "natural." And some evolutionary psychologists take issue with the view of women as less power hungry. Primatologist Sarah Blaffer Hrdy points out that female apes compete for status quite aggressively, if less flamboyantly than males.[24]

Our genetic heritage may shed light on many things about men and women, but we should heed philosopher Thomas Nagel's warning against "the ludicrous overuse of evolutionary biology to explain everything about life, including everything about the human mind," particularly since scientific knowledge of how it shapes the human mind is not just incomplete but highly speculative.[25]

There is also much that science has yet to learn about hormones and brain organization, two other hot areas of research on innate sex differences. Some of that research casts doubt on the proverbial link between testosterone and aggression.[26] Findings of "masculinized" behavior, such as increased play with "boy" toys, in girls exposed to high prenatal doses of male hormones (androgens) are not unambiguous: thus, androgenized girls don't show elevated levels of physical aggression or rough-and-tumble play. In another study, contrary to the researchers' expectations, girls with twin brothers, who have some exposure to androgens in the womb, exhibited no unusually tomboyish behavior, while girls with an older brother did.[27]

Nor does magnetic imagery brain research lend itself to simple conclusions. In the much-publicized Yale study in which men and women used different parts of the brain when picking rhyming word pairs, over 40 percent of the women—eight out of nineteen—thought like a man, so to speak, but no men showed a female pattern. Could it mean that women are less rigidly sex typed? Maybe. Except that in another brain scan study, from the University of

Pennsylvania, which found some differences in brain metabolism, a third of the males and only four of the twenty-six females had "cross-sex" brain patterns.[28]

Meanwhile, there has been an explosion of media interest in sex difference research. "Why Are Men and Women Different?" asks the cover of *Time,* while *Newsweek* offers "The New Science of the Brain: Why Men and Women Think Differently." In 1995, ABC aired a special, "Boys and Girls Are Different: Men, Women, and the Sex Difference," reported by politically incorrect gadfly John Stossel and billed as a provocative challenge to feminist taboos.[29]

Unisex feminism certainly has its inanities and its Know-Nothing zealotry, aptly dubbed "biodenial" by Daphne Patai and Noretta Koertge. Feminist biologist Anne Fausto-Sterling (undaunted by revelations that the prowess of East German women athletes, which she had touted to disprove the "naturalness" of the sex gap in physical strength, was due to steroids) argues that the very idea of two sexes is a cultural construct, since babies with genital or chromosomal abnormalities are neither male nor female. Some women scientists report pressure to stop or bowdlerize their sex difference research. On the ABC program, Bella Abzug and Gloria Steinem dismissed this work as "poppycock" and "anti-American crazy thinking."[30]

Yet the fascination with *la différence* can make truth a casualty too. Take an oft-cited study in which one-year-olds were separated from their mothers by a barrier. "Most boys try to knock the barrier down," Stossel said. "Most girls just stand there and cry for help." What a depressing image of feminine passivity! But when Stossel added that his crew tried to tape such an experiment and "saw only the exceptions"—boys crying, girls struggling to get out—I was sufficiently intrigued to look up the original 1969 study.[31] In fact, the girls cried almost twice as long as the boys, and more boys wandered to the ends of the barrier where it was latched to the wall, which was taken to mean that they were trying to solve their predicament. But ten years later, the lead researcher, Dr. Michael Lewis, published a more detailed analysis of these data, along with a follow-up study of the children one year later. One-year-old girls, it turns out, pushed at the barrier as much as boys did, and tried to open the latches *more* often; the boys who moved to the end of the barrier mostly just stood there. At two years old, girls were no weepier than boys and were far more active problem solvers: over 20 percent of them got out, compared to 7 percent of the boys.[32]

The truth is that much in the nature-versus-nurture debate remains unresolved. Thus, there is strong evidence that mathematical ability is influenced by biology. But other findings—for instance, that girls' math and science achievement drops in adolescence only if their parents hold traditional sex-role beliefs—suggest that it's too early to dismiss cultural factors.[33]

One would have to be very unobservant or very stubborn to deny that some traits are more common in one sex or the other. But as Stossel noted, "individual differences are often much greater than the differences between the sexes." Unfortunately, his own comments about how we are "biologically hard-wired to be different" seemed to leave little room for individual variety, as did all the footage of girls playing with tea sets and boys with swords.

It's all very well to make fun of feminists whose denials of the boyness of boys and the girlness of girls are blown away at Christmas, when girls want Barbies and boys want guns. Actually, letters to Santa paint a more nuanced picture. Bikes, roller skates, radios, and clothes are universal favorites; so are pets. About a third of requests for computers and video games come from girls, who often show highly eclectic tastes: "roller skates, basketball, football, makeup, earrings"; "Barbie and a soccer ball"; "nail polish and Legos." Boys are more unanimous in their preference for athletic fare and weaponry, but they also want stuffed toys: Tickle Me Elmo was a universal favorite in 1996. Martial Power Rangers, violent "Goosebumps" books, and cuddly Beanie Babies have cross-sex appeal.[34]

The boys with swords and the girls with tea sets are real enough. But we shouldn't forget the other half of the picture: the girls I see in my suburban neighborhood playing baseball or kicking a soccer ball around the supermarket; the boys who care tenderly for a puppy or kitten; the girls who make up at least a third of the contestants in soapbox derby races.[35]

Measuring Gender Gaps: Myths and Facts

Much as they diverge ideologically, difference feminists and biological determinists have something in common: a propensity for sweeping statements based on modest evidence. The 1969 study that created the myth of girls crying helplessly when placed behind a barrier and boys trying to get out is one example.

Today the generalizations remain as broad. Tannen cites a finding by developmental psychologist Campbell Leaper that five-year-old girls interact "in a 'mutually positive' manner," while boys "exhibit 'negative reciprocity' by which one boy tries to control and the other withdraws." In fact, Leaper found virtually no sex differences among children ages four to six. Between ages six and nine, the boys were a bit less cooperative and the girls noticeably more so: 42 percent of their exchanges were "mutually positive" compared to 21 percent of the boys'. But even older boys collaborated much more than they sought to dominate and exhibited very little "negative reciprocity."[36] Tannen summarizes a study of gender dynamics in groups of college students, as "The men tended to set the agenda by offering opinions, suggestions, and information. The women tended to react, offering agreement or disagreement." But "agenda-setting" remarks accounted for 55 percent of the men's speech and 45 percent of the women's (and women talked more overall).[37]

On the other side of the political spectrum, Kingsley Browne speaks of "substantial evidence for sex difference in the spontaneous emergence of leaders." His source is a meta-analysis of studies showing that overall, in small groups working on a task, men emerged as leaders all of 58 percent of the time. The difference was largest in laboratory studies and barely present in natural settings (mostly college students working on class projects). Male leadership was also most likely in groups that met for less than twenty minutes; the division was close to fifty-fifty if there was more than one meeting. In other words, the more the conditions of the study resembled the real world, the smaller was the difference.[38]

Even science reporter Deborah Blum, whose charming book, *Sex on the Brain,* judiciously avoids the extremes of "biodenial" and biological determinism, sometimes lapses into dubious generalizations about sex differences, such as the assertion that women are more empathetic than men. In fact, for children and adults alike, the female edge in empathy is quite large when measured by subjects' ratings of themselves but nonexistent or minimal when one looks at nonverbal reactions to another's distress, from changes in blood pressure to facial gestures, or at actual compassionate behavior.[39]

There is also the issue of within-sex variation: most psychological sex differences are in the small-to-moderate range, meaning that the distribution of a trait or behavior between the sexes is somewhere between 52–48 and 66–34. Sometimes the research partly corroborates the stereotypes, but many pieces of the puzzle don't fit into the Mars-Venus schemes promoted by difference feminists, biological determinists, or both. Consider the claim central to Deborah Tannen's work: the social world of boys is hierarchical and concerned with power, that of girls egalitarian and concerned with intimacy.[40]

One study in which same-sex pairs of preschoolers were observed in the playground seems at first glance to back Tannen: boys used "heavy-handed persuasion"—physical force or threats— in 22 percent of their conflicts, compared to 9 percent for girls; the percentages were reversed for "conflict mitigation." Yet both sexes settled about two-thirds of their conflicts by "moderate persua- sion" (which included giving orders). And "conflict mitigation" did not always denote Gilliganian concern with relationships: it included indirect displays of anger, such as staging a fight between disputed dolls, and the "male" tactic of walking out of a conflict situation.[41]

There is evidence that in dealing with conflict, girls are some- what more concerned with maintaining relationships and boys with asserting control.[42] But plenty of research casts doubt on beatific visions of warm, egalitarian girls' communities, as does, of course, the personal experience of anyone who has been a girl. True, boys' power contests are more often expressed in physical aggression, while girls often employ the stereotypical feminine weapons of social ostracism and rumors. But according to behavioral scientist Diane Jones, "competition and asymmetric relationships are as much a part of female groups as male ones."[43]

University of Wisconsin psychologist Betty Black observed preschoolers in small groups after finding out through a confidential survey which children were liked and disliked by their peers. Despite some differences (boys talked about themselves more; girls were more likely to elaborate on a playmate's idea), popular boys and girls had much more in common with each other than with unpopular kids of their own sex. Moreover, behavior that Tannen sees as typical of boy culture—giving orders, grabbing center stage—was treated as undesirable in the social networks of both sexes.[44]

Observations of children playing board games in same-sex pairs have found surprisingly few differences in combativeness or willing- ness to compromise. In one such study, boys engaged in slightly more one-upmanship (bragging or put-downs) but also showed more of what Tannen calls "one-downmanship": complimenting the opponent or disparaging oneself.[45] In a more intriguing experiment, preschoolers in single-sex groups of four were given a film viewer designed so that a child could watch a cartoon through an eyepiece only if two others cooperated by turning a crank and pressing a switch. There was much more playful pushing and hitting among boys. But the girls weren't shy about giving orders, using put-downs, or physically interfering with another's attempt to watch, such as blocking the viewer. Moreover, girl groups tended to have "a single dominant individual," while boys showed "more equal participation" in viewing. And the alpha females did not get to the top by being nurturing: they gave commands, hit, and disrupted others' viewing much more often than other girls.[46]

The picture is equally complex when it comes to other truisms:

• *Men are competitive, women cooperative.* In a survey in Minnesota schools in the early 1980s, 45 percent of students who scored above average on competitiveness were female. Kingsley Browne cites this study as proof that "competition . . . is a more unalloyed positive experience for boys." But being highly competitive had drawbacks, such as feeling too pressured, for young children of both sexes. By high school, this pattern disappeared for boys and *almost* disappeared for girls, and more competitive girls had a stronger sense of self-worth.[47]

A few years later, another study found that when high school athletes rated the importance of various goals that sports should accomplish, girls emphasized teamwork somewhat more than boys did, while the reverse was true for winning and learning to be tough. Yet both sexes ranked cooperation first, followed by fitness, self-esteem, character building, and finally competition.[48]

None of this suggests differences "broad enough to be considered a world view," as one team of psychologists put it—after finding that when college students were asked to evaluate various traits on a scale of one (very bad) to five (very good), women's ratings of such qualities as "compassionate," "sympathetic," and "sensitive to the needs of others" were about 10 percent higher than men's.[49]

• *Men are autonomous, women "relational."* A 1971 study did find a dramatic gap: 80 percent of women but only half of the men defined their identity in terms of interpersonal connections. By the 1980s, this difference had all but vanished. When San Francisco State University English professor Jo Keroes analyzed student essays on personal dilemmas they had faced, she expected men to focus on self-determination and women on relationships, but "autonomous" themes prevailed for both sexes. Another study was construed by its authors as supporting Gilligan's thesis since college women scored higher on "intimacy" than on "autonomy"—but so did the men.[50]

• *Girls are more docile than boys.* In a study that had parents evaluate children's temperament, 60 percent of kids in the "most difficult" quartile were boys, surely not enough to suggest a fundamental difference, though perhaps enough to convince many parents that boys are "wired" to be more obstreperous. The imbalance is greater at the extreme end: in one sample of nearly six hundred children, one in eighteen boys but one in forty-five girls were classified as "angry/defiant" and socially withdrawn. On average, however, most investigations show surprisingly few sex differences in obedience, as reported by parents or observed by researchers. Interestingly, schoolteachers perceive boys and girls as equally argumentative, though they describe boys as being more likely to fight and get in trouble.[51]

It is also interesting to note that although parents overall do not treat boys and girls very differently, it appears that male toddlers to this day receive somewhat more positive feedback when they act aggressively.[52]

• *Men don't share their feelings (especially not with other men).* When scholars Kathryn Dindia and Mike Allen analyzed more than two hundred studies on self-disclosure, they found that although the stereotypical differences existed, they were not nearly as vast as one might expect: "If approximately 45 percent of men would disclose a particular item, approximately 55 percent of women would disclose the same information." Subsequent research supports this conclusion.[53]

Researchers Steven Duck and Paul Wright even question the cliché (promoted by men who write about men's faults for women's magazines) that women have intimate friendships while male buddies just do things together. Both sexes, they say, "are attuned to caring, supportiveness" and other emotional aspects of friendship. Ironically, Duck and Wright admit to helping perpetuate "the fashionable dichotomy" in their earlier work; for instance, reading much into the finding that women's meetings with friends were usually spontaneous and men's were more often planned, on the basis of a 10 percent gap.[54]

In the late 1970s, sociologists Lucile Duberman and Lynne Davidson queried young single men and women about their conversations with their best friends of the same sex and concluded that it was wrong to stereotype female friendships as focused mainly on personal talk. Although 38 percent of the conversations women reported were personal, 33 percent were on topical subjects—the news, work, movies. The authors seemed less interested in debunking stereotypes about men, who were described as relating "primarily on a topical, more external level": 60 percent of men's reported conversations were "topical" and 30 percent were "personal." Yet most men did talk to male friends about personal matters, and a sizable minority considered such exchanges essential to the friendship. And there's the issue of interpretation. When a man says, "We talk about sex, horses, guns, and the army," is this impersonal "topical" conversation as classified by Duberman and Davidson, or possibly quite personal? Does all this suggest, as the authors claim, that "men, unlike women, feel the need to guard against self-exposure and vulnerability"?[55]

• *Men deal with stress by trying to solve the problem, women by brooding or seeking emotional support.* Actually, both women and men take the problem-solving approach most often, followed by seeking support and then by emotional responses such as self-blame and distraction. Are there differences? Yes, some. In one study, men reported using problem solving as the coping technique of first resort 56 percent of the time in recent stressful situations, compared to 44 percent for women. But for both women and men, other methods lagged far behind.[56]

And the famous you-just-don't-understand scenario, where she complains about a problem to get sympathy, he offers a solution, and she gets upset? Tannen's evidence for this archetypal misunderstanding consists entirely of anecdotes, obviously meant to inform us with a flash of recognition. But while it did just that for one of my male friends, another recalled Tannen vignettes in reverse when *he* sought sympathy from women who "snapped into an 'I have to give advice *right now*' mode." And for one woman, the recognition involved herself in the "male" role of would-be problem fixer when talking to her mother.

Had Tannen wanted to cite research, it might have been difficult. Several studies that look at "nurturant" and "problem-solving" responses to another's distress have found slight differences—but no evidence of a gender gap that requires self-help books to bridge it.[57]

Sex, Lies, and Evolution

> Sex is fine with someone you love.
> Sex is fine, period. Get it while you can.

How many college age men and women would you expect to agree with each view? To hear comedians like Jay Leno or Bill Maher of *Politically Incorrect,* one would assume that 95 percent of young men would endorse the second statement and the remaining 5 percent would be lying, while 95 percent of young women would endorse the first statement and the remaining 5 percent would say that even with someone you love, it's still kind of icky.

But in one survey in the 1990s, 38 percent of college boys voted for love and 44 percent of the girls voted for sex. In another, only 46 percent of young men (and 23 percent of young women) disagreed with the statement, "I would probably not have sex with someone until I'm sure that I love the person."[58]

Comedians are in the business of exaggerating stereotypes for effect. But they are hardly the only ones who tell us that, in the words of sociologist John Gagnon, "men and women live in different sexual worlds."[59]

According to a 1994 article in the *New York Times,* when it comes to sex in the movies, gentlemen prefer nude blondes and graphic sex with a dash of violence, while women like "flirtatious glances" and steamy kisses. An informal survey of filmgoers about their favorite sexy scenes was cited to support this idea—except that the survey *didn't* support it. None of the men's choices featured a nude blonde. At the top of their list was Sharon Stone's hardly explicit no-underwear scene from *Basic Instinct,* followed by a fully dressed Michelle Pfeiffer slinking around on a piano in *The Fabulous Baker Boys.* The most graphic scenes, such as the kitchen-counter coupling in the remake of *The Postman Always Rings Twice,* were on the *women's* top ten, led by a scene of violent lust: William Hurt in *Body Heat* smashing a window to get to Kathleen Turner.[60]

In the *Ladies Home Journal,* Leslie Bennetts writes that judging by how women's and men's magazines treat sex, we are hardly from the same galaxy: the former focus on romance and pleasing a mate ("Drive Him Wild in Bed!"), the latter on pleasure and adventure ("Infidelity: It's in Our Genes"). But Bennetts stacks the deck with family-oriented publications like *Redbook* on one side and the likes of *Playboy* on the other, and never mentions that even *Redbook* is preoccupied with more and better orgasms. Women's magazines with a mostly single readership careen from overstating women's linkage of sex and romance to cheerleading for libertinism. *Elle* proclaims that women too have evolutionary reasons to fool around. A 1995 piece in *Cosmopolitan* titled "To Cheat or Not to Cheat" emphasizes the pros; a 1996 article by the same title in *GQ,* the cons.[61] *New York Times* columnist Maureen Dowd links a *Newsweek* cover on adultery to a general theme of "men behaving badly." Yet survey data quoted in the magazine story show that among married people under age thirty-four, wives are now *more* likely to cheat.[62]

What does the research tell us? In the National Health and Social Life Survey, on which the much-publicized 1994 book *Sex in America: A Definitive Survey* was based, one in four women under twenty-five, one in five women in their thirties, and about one in three men in all age groups held a "recreational" view of sex. The most common outlook for both sexes was "relational," linking sex to emotional intimacy but not necessarily marriage.[63]

Other studies point both to undeniable gender gaps and to much common ground:

• Among university students surveyed in the 1980s, 61 percent of women but only 20 percent of men considered emotional closeness to be a prerequisite for sexual arousal. However, 44 percent of the women (and 60 percent of men) admitted being sexually attracted to others while involved with a steady partner, and nearly a quarter said that being in a relationship gave them *more* of a roving eye (as did 42 percent of men).[64]

• When respondents in another survey were asked to pick ten out of forty-eight wishes—from world peace to wealth to going to heaven—that they would most want fulfilled, sex "with anyone I choose" was selected by one in seventeen women and one in four men. Yet the wish that got the most votes from both sexes—73 percent of the women and 58 percent of the men—was "to deeply love a person who deeply loves me."[65]

• In a survey at a private college in California conducted by anthropologist Michael Mills, 30 percent of female students and only 9 percent of the men claimed that they wouldn't be interested in a purely sexual relationship relationship with anyone. But only 19 percent of the men (and 3 percent of the women) were certain that they would avail themselves of an opportunity for no-strings sex with an attractive stranger with no risk of adverse consequences; one in five women, and one in three men, said they would "probably" do so.[66]

Evolutionary theorists chuckle over an experiment in which students on college campuses were propositioned by a reasonably good-looking stranger of the opposite sex: three out of four men, and not one woman, said yes. Yet this situation bears little resemblance to real life; we don't know how many men even thought the offer was for real. (In the more natural setting of singles bars, nearly all men interviewed claim to have turned down a sexual opportunity at least once.) And one of the campus experiments had a curious follow-up. Research assistants called a few unattached friends and asked if they would like to go to bed with a fictitious friend— described as warm, sincere, attractive, and great in bed—who was in town and looking for a good time. This time, infidelity was not an issue, and the men didn't have to worry about the woman's being a psycho; yet half of them declined, mostly, they said, because they didn't know her well enough.[67]

Why would men be less willing to accept a third-party offer of a "sure thing" than a direct invitation? Could it be that a man who is propositioned is not only tempted by the sexual opportunity but flattered because a woman who, he presumes, would not have sex with just anybody has singled him out—while a woman who is looking for "just anybody" is not as attractive? Could it be that they feel it's unmanly or ungentlemanly to say no? This explanation is bolstered by studies of men's unwanted sexual experiences. In one recent campus survey, one in four men reported being pressured into sex by a woman, and one in five said that they had "felt sexually taken advantage of."[68]

Clearly, gender differences in sexual attitudes and behavior are much more dramatic than in virtually any other area, be it moral reasoning, emotional expression, or competitiveness. Whether that's due to nature or culture, or both, is another matter. It is surely rather overconfident to discount biology out of hand, as do, for example, the authors of *Sex in America,* who flatly state that there is "no reason to believe these differences . . . reflect some sort of genetic imperative."[69] Indeed, it would be strange if a physical distinction as basic as childbearing had no effect on men's and women's attitudes toward sex. In this area of human behavior, evolutionary logic makes the most sense.

But any theory that reduces human motivation to a mechanism that works independently of conscious intent can lose touch with reality. Robert Wright asserts that in casual sex, "the worst likely outcome for the man (in genetic terms) is that pregnancy would not ensue"; never mind that in real-life terms, the worst likely outcome is that it *would*. That the human animal has looked for ways to separate sex from procreation since the dawn of history somehow never comes up.[70]

At times, Wright's efforts to patch logical holes in the theory aren't very helpful. When Wright explains why it makes "genetic sense" for a man to dump an aging wife (he can remarry and father more children, whether or not he wants any), he also has to explain why it doesn't matter that women dump their husbands: there is "no Darwinian force *driving* them to leave," and even if a woman seeks a divorce, "that doesn't mean *her* genes are ultimately the problem."[71] That certainly clears everything up.

Or else inconvenient facts are mostly ignored. In one of his studies, David Buss, University of Michigan professor and leading evolutionary psychologist, stresses that among newlyweds, the wife's marital discontent is most consistently related to the husband's sexual aggressiveness and the husband's discontent to the wife's sexual withholding—though these problems came up, he admits, less often than he expected. But he skips over another finding: *wives' discontent was also linked to sexual withholding by husbands.* In fact, for every wife griping about a husband's sexual demands, two complained of his insufficient ardor. (It's worth noting that in another study of soon-to-be-married couples, 17 percent of women and 10 percent of men said that their partner had pressured them into unwanted sexual activity.)[72]

It also seems that, as evolutionary theory would predict, men are more distressed by a woman's sexual infidelity (a threat to paternal certainty) and women by a man's emotional attachment to another woman (a threat to resources). But that doesn't explain why anywhere from a sizable minority to a slight majority of men find emotional infidelity more distressing—or why more women say that they would consider divorce if their spouse had a one-night stand with a stranger.[73]

What's more, clichés of randy males and coy females are now challenged by many evolutionary psychologists. Wright devotes four pages to Darwinian reasons for females to play the field, speculating that our foremothers may have been by turns wanton and virtuous—but forgets all about that when he gets around to the social implications of the "new science of the human mind and treats women as simply monograms." Sometimes the theorists can't seem to decide whether men have strong incentives for monogamy or, in Wright's words, "giving men marriage tips is . . . like offering Vikings a free booklet titled 'How Not to Pillage'"; whether "women as well as men have short-term mating within their strategic repertoire" or "sex *as an end in itself* is unlikely to constitute an evolved desire in women"—statements Buss makes in a single article.[74]

Differences in attitudes toward sex may have biological aspects for which one needn't reach back into prehistory. A woman who has sex with a stranger is more vulnerable not only to violence but to disease, concerns that play a major role in women's qualms about casual sex. Women who aren't on the pill risk pregnancy, and few relish the prospect of abortion. A woman's sexual pleasure tends to be more dependent on her partner's sensitivity; she may not want him to stick around long enough to play Dad, but at least long enough to give her an orgasm. If she wants children, declining fertility makes it more urgent for her to find a steady mate.[75] Indeed, "reproductive strategy" may involve more conscious calculation than sociobiologists allow. In some cultures, it has been chic for men to have older mistresses while seeking young brides. This makes sense if the goal is to reduce chances of pregnancy in affairs and increase them in marriage. It is far less clear that sexual choices are controlled by instincts so deeply "wired" into us as to be resistant to change in circumstance.

Did women evolve to value a man's status over his looks? Maybe. But even before feminism, their pin-ups were handsome movie stars, not wrinkled millionaires, and successful women may place more importance on male beauty. Did men evolve to put little value on women's income? Maybe. But they were hardly indifferent to it in societies where a dowry was the norm. Does nature dictate that power will enhance older men's sex appeal? Maybe. But some powerful middle-aged women (like lawyer Leslie Abramson, described as "dominatrix-like" in *Playboy,* and even Margaret Thatcher in England) can become sex symbols of sorts. In Hollywood, the trend of high-status older women taking up with downwardly mobile young studs, which sociobiology cannot explain, has spread from movie stars like Elizabeth Taylor or Glenn Close to rich divorcées. If successful women in business and politics have yet to join in, it may be because they have to be more concerned about their image.[76]

Wright himself stresses that "the human brain is a pretty flexible thing." Thus, conceding that male insistence on female chastity varies greatly from culture to culture, he insists only that "the flexibility is bounded": few men will marry a woman who is intent on "sleeping with a different man each week."[77] Granting this unremarkable fact, how many women would want a husband with a habit of sleeping with a different woman each week?

Men and women do live in the same sexual world after all, even if men spend more time on some of its continents and women on others. It's not that women want intimacy and men want casual sex; both believe that sex in a loving relationship is best, but men are considerably more willing to settle for sex without one. (The gender gap in fantasies about strangers is far smaller.) Men think about sex more than women do, but women are hardly unperturbed by sexual urges.[78]

The urge to magnify tendencies into absolutes is especially strong in sexual matters, and social constructionists are as guilty as biological determinists. Discussing men's and women's erotic tastes in *Sex in America,* the authors minimize biology but maximize difference: "soft, hazy, romantic" female fantasies versus the "body parts and sex acts" of the male imagination. In the strangest logical leap, after reporting that 81 percent of women under age forty-five, compared to 93 percent of the men, find it appealing to watch their mate undress, they launch into an earnest analysis of "cultural forces" that discourage female interest in male nudity and "encourag[e] exactly the sort of responses that we saw."[79]

Two Sexes, One Planet

Clearly, the way we think about differences and similarities between the sexes has major consequences. If there is no innate sex difference in ability or inclination to be a physicist or engineer, women's underrepresentation in these occupations proves that they are held back by discrimination or social pressure. If there is a difference, one could still call for special programs for girls, perhaps at the cost of steering some away from fields that suit them better. Or one could just focus on equal opportunity, even if, when the dust settles, women make up 30 percent of engineers (as psychologist Janet Hyde estimates from spatial ability tests) or fewer.[80]

But that would never do for the equality *über alles* school. When, on his "Boys and Girls" special, John Stossel asked Bella Abzug if gender equality meant equal numbers in every field, she fired back, "Fifty-fifty—absolutely."

If this notion of equality is misguided, clinging to it can lead us to see sexism where there is none and pursue coercive social engineering—or even imperil lives, as when fire departments' fitness standards are lowered to accommodate women. (When asked about this, Gloria Steinem suggested that firefighters shouldn't have to carry people out of buildings: it's better to drag them "because there's less smoke down there.")

Yet assumptions based on seemingly solid data about sex differences can miss the mark. In *The Female Woman,* a 1973 critique of "Women's Lib," Arianna Stassinopoulos (now Arianna Huffington) predicted that equal opportunity without artificial parity would lead to "a small rise in the numbers of women accountants, engineers or geologists but a big rise in the numbers of female physicians, psychiatrists, lawyers, clergymen." So far, she has been correct about engineers and geologists, but in 1993, about half of accountants in the United States were female.[81]

The history of Title IX, which bans sex discrimination in school athletics, illustrates the difference between equity and numerical equality. The 1972 law has opened up unprecedented opportunities in sports for girls and women. Even today, there are Title IX lawsuits directed at fairly glaring injustices, such as girls' softball teams' being denied access to the best public playing fields due to a seniority system which gives preference to boys' teams because they were there first. But the law has also been interpreted so as to require that similar proportions of male and female college students be involved in varsity sports even if fewer women are interested. To comply with this vision of equality, excellent men's sports programs are being dismantled, with the result that a male student who wants to participate in sports has less opportunity to do so than his female counterpart.[82]

But conservatives who rightly criticize this trend sometimes seem to assume a static gender gap in interest in athletics. In fact, girls' enthusiasm for sports has skyrocketed; so say not just statistics (girls now make up about 40 percent of high school athletes, up from 5 percent in 1971) but men who coach children's teams and music teachers who complain that girls as well as boys now skip piano lessons for basketball practice.[83]

Ironically, even as we learn more about the biological roots of sexual identity, we see fewer sexual divisions. A 1997 report that shot down a favorite social constructionist fable—about a baby boy who lost his penis in an accident, was raised as a girl, and became a well-adjusted female (in fact, "she" hated dresses, tried to urinate standing up, and eventually, after learning the whole story, had "herself" surgically turned back into a man)—ran in *Newsweek* right next to an article on the dramatic rise of women's ice hockey.[84]

In England, psychological tests show that sex differences found among older people on such items as, "I often try to get my own way regardless of others," do not hold for those under thirty—perhaps due less to changes in personality than to younger women's greater candor about such traits. American women have become more assertive players in financial markets, shedding their traditional risk aversion; on the darker side of risk taking, they are catching up with men in pathological gambling and in drug and alcohol abuse.[85]

Most scientists who study the biology of sex differences agree that nature and nurture interact in complex ways. The link between biology and behavior may be a two-way street: our activities and environment can alter brain organization and hormonal makeup, creating, as science writer Deborah Blum puts it, "a self-reinforcing feedback loop." If, as Kingsley Browne suggests, it's "adaptive" for a child to imitate same-sex models, girls surrounded by images of strong women, from athletes and political leaders to television and film characters, will probably grow up different from earlier generations.[86]

One way to inject common sense into this debate is to shift the focus from groups to individuals. Otherwise, "difference talk" has its dangers. A boy will do better on a math test than a girl 63 percent of the time, whatever the reason.[87] But if you automatically assume that a male is better at math than a female, whether in hiring someone or helping a student make a career decision, you'll be wrong nearly four out of ten times.

Professor Browne wonders why "a tendency for men to exhibit male traits and for women to exhibit female traits is inferior to a situation in which the traits are distributed at random." In a sense, he is right: if women make up 63 percent of people with one trait and 33 percent of those with another, it shouldn't be a problem. But if these unevenly distributed qualities are designated as male and female with no quotation marks, people may be hindered from developing or acting on "cross-sex" traits, particularly when we have feminists mocking women who prize "linear thinking" as "male identified" and conservatives warning that a marriage that strays from sex-appropriate roles is all but doomed to misery.[88]

Such assumptions may also cause people to be judged, perhaps unconsciously, by sex-based generalizations. Men get 40 percent more speeding tickets when speed is measured by radar but *250 percent* more when the judgment is made by an officer's naked eye— partly, perhaps, because of chivalry, but also because the real gender gap in speeding is reinforced by the stereotype.[89]

That men are more likely to think and act in some ways and women in others, and that every man or woman should be treated as an individual, are two ideas we ought to be able to hold at the same time. This means avoiding comments like, "Each sex seems to have a different definition of what constitutes success in life." Sexes don't have definitions of success; people do. It means that, questioning the overuse of the attention deficit hyperactivity disorder (ADHD) label for unruly male children, we should beware of generalizing about normal "boyhood" or exaggerating girlish docility. But it also means not crying bias when women make up 51 percent of university students but "only" 38 percent of varsity athletes, which no more proves inequity than does the overrepresentation of girls in high school student government. It means accepting that in a nonsexist society, most corporate executives may be men and most "primary caregiver" parents may be women.[90]

Such an approach also negates arguments for including women in various fields on the basis of their special strengths, given how unpredictably these strengths are distributed. Robert Wright suggests that affirmative action should be based on the premise that women are less prone "to sacrifice the organization's welfare to personal advancement," and hence good for business. But the world is full of women looking out for Number One, and they would be far quicker than their meeker sisters to reap the benefits of quotas. Women managers may not even be more sympathetic toward employees' family problems.[91]

Just as specious is the notion that women *as women* have something unique to contribute to human understanding. A woman who criticizes individualism, competition, technology, or the elevation of reason over feeling will be in agreement with plenty of men, from Rousseau to Tolstoy to Marcuse. Rachel Carson, sometimes cited as a female voice affirming an organic vision of the sanctity of life, drew her inspiration from Albert Schweitzer, unmistakably one of the Y chromosome set. Carol Gilligan offers an "ethic of care" as a challenge to a "masculine" ethic of rules, but Jimmy Stewart said it before in Frank Capra's *Mr. Smith Goes to Washington:* "I wouldn't give you two cents for all your fancy rules if behind them they didn't have a little bit of plain, ordinary kindness and a little lookin' out for the other fella." The authors of the academic feminist bible, *Women's Ways of Knowing,* unwittingly hint that there is nothing uniquely female about "women's ways," pointing out that "subjective knowledge and intuitive processes" are esteemed in many non-Western cultures (which, one might add, are not too female friendly) and were prized by such great Western philosophers as Spinoza and Henri Bergson.[92]

Given the range of "male" and even "white male" thought, it's unlikely than women can produce ideas entirely free of its influence; indeed, it would be ludicrous for women to deny themselves that heritage. For the "difference feminists," it's a major inconvenience. Describing an "ethic of inseparability" expressed by a character in Alice Walker's *The Color Purple,* feminist philosopher Catherine Keller notes its kinship to the "process-relational metaphysic" of Alfred North Whitehead—only to rebuke herself for such a "turn for legitimation to the male philosopher" and appeal to the female authority of Carol Gilligan.[93] Worse, "difference feminism" can turn into a new straitjacket for women: both Gilligan and the authors of *Women's Ways of Knowing* disparage women who see "male" individualism or rationality as liberating.[94]

The "difference feminists" are not traditionalists; they seek not to validate domesticity but to remake the larger world in a "female" image, in some ways a more radical agenda than entering it on the same terms as men. Still, neofeminism does bear a strong resemblance to paleosexism, as we see when women's studies professors proclaim that a female voice must counter the "Western male tradition" of mastery and transcendent truth by celebrating "the small nurturing things that women do."[95]

Indeed, the feminists who argue that the "male" model of learning is ill suited for women echo some 1950s academics who envisioned a curriculum for future housewives, based on the feminine sense of "intangible qualitative relationships," "the intuitive," and "the emotional" rather than masculine "egotistic individualism," "abstract construction," and "quantitative thinking." This feminine curriculum, one such educator wrote, would shun "flamboyant" fine art for ceramics and textiles. Today, Peggy McIntosh of the Wellesley Center for Research on Women warbles about incorporating "quilts, breadloaf shapes, clothing, pots," and the like into the study of art.[96]

The trickiest part, perhaps, is applying an appreciation of sex difference and individual difference to personal life. If one in three young men and one in five young women think sex just for fun is great, that's enough of a gap for many girls who want love to run into boys who want a romp; that's one reason generalizations strike a chord. But it is also in the area of love and sex that we run the greatest risk of not seeing the individual behind the stereotype.

Life confounds all dogmas, whether of sameness or difference. A very "eligible" man I know broke up with a woman he had been seeing because he wanted marriage and she, a divorced mother with a good income, wanted to just go on dating. A woman I know was once with a man who stopped in the midst of heavy petting because he was troubled by her seeing other men and wanted "a real girlfriend." (One of life's little jokes, it seems, is that girls who want to have fun keep running into boys who say things like, "I feel like you're just using me.")[97]

Some argue that the abandonment of traditional wisdom about masculine and feminine nature has misled many women into thinking they could sleep around with no painful emotional consequences. But some men, too, have overestimated their ability to separate sex and love. And if ignoring traditional wisdom about what men and women want can cause trouble, so can relying on it, as this story from a collection of college students' sexual autobiographies illustrates:

> She was the one who hinted around to have intercourse. . . . I told her that I didn't want to marry her and she said she had no intentions of marrying me either. . . . I was afraid if we had sex she would never let me go. I was wrong! In fact, one month later she broke up with me and it was me who was running after her.[98]

Likewise, the male-fear-of-commitment cliché may be an excuse for many women to avoid confronting *their* commitment anxiety. So concluded two people who helped propagate the cliché—Steven Carter and Julia Sokol, authors of the 1984 best-seller *Men Who Can't Love*, whose 1993 follow-up was titled, *He's Scared, She's Scared*. Some female commitment avoiders are those who complain the loudest about commitment-phobic males, and keep selecting the wrong men and rejecting the "good" ones. Others act much like men with cold feet. What prompted Carter and Sokol to write the second book was the letters from men who had been on the receiving end of the behavior described in *Men Who Can't Love*.[99]

While a *Redbook* survey of wives in their twenties and thirties lends some support to the cliché of the husband who won't talk or listen—about one-third mentioned this as a cause of marital discord—nearly one in five said their own failure to communicate was an issue. Men apparently agree. In an unscientific survey asking them what their mate could do to improve the relationship, "communicate more" and "listen more" were high on the list. And studies show that while the classic pattern in which the wife brings up a problem and the husband withdraws is more typical, it's reversed more than a third of the time.[100]

One could point to the popularity of *You Just Don't Understand* or *Men Are from Mars, Women Are from Venus* as proof that male-female conflicts stem from living with a member of a different species whom we mistakenly treat as one of our own. But does it prove much beyond the fact that intimacy is messy and complicated? Don't mothers and daughters, fathers and sons, siblings, same-sex lovers feel at times that they must cross a labyrinth to reach one another? Mars-Venus advice promises a quick fix: you just pull out the blue file marked "men" or the pink one marked "women" instead of trying to deal with the other person's unique qualities or your own inadequacies.

For most of us, romance thrives on the erotic tension of *la différence*. Does this require distinct roles? In the 1996 best-seller *The Rules,* Ellen Fein and Sherrie Schneider insist that the man must pursue and "take charge," while the woman must be coy and demure, forbidden not only to talk to a man first but to smile at him or make eye contact.[101] The appeal of this message is hard to gauge: a year after the *Rules* hoopla, 85 percent of single women agreed that it's "totally acceptable for a woman to ask a man out on a date," as did 93 percent of men. This does not mean that they want the sexes to be interchangeable. One can relish small courtship rituals that symbolize sexual distinctions, yet reject rules that reduce women to pliant damsels or men to manipulated prey. (As writer Nancy Friday says, "I like having my chair pulled out for me, but I also like paying for a man's meal.") Who says you can't have charm and mystery, *and* ask a man to dinner?[102]

In part, the fascination with difference is a justified response to the excesses of unisex feminism. Only in women's studies can a utopia where gender matters no more than eye color hold any appeal. Sexual differentiation in some sense is a profound human need. The idea of a child being raised as an "X," its sex known only to the parents—the premise of a story by Lois Gould published in an early issue of *Ms.*—is likely to strike us as sick.

This has nothing to do with believing that how people think and act should be determined by gender. Once, watching a TV interview with the Italian journalist Oriana Falacci, it occurred to me that here was a woman who had led a "male" life of work and danger and expressed her feelings sparingly and who was, beyond any question, womanly. The magic of sexual difference is precisely that it is a *je ne sais quoi,* more a chemistry or an aura than a set of qualities that can be put into words.

Some people, fed up with the strange creed that simultaneously holds that women and men are the same *and* that women are innocents and men are beasts, welcome the message that we should accept our differences and be tolerant. But an armistice in the gender wars is unlikely to work if it focuses on acceptance of collective but not individual differences. A world divided into pink and blue would be only marginally less oppressive than a world of khaki uniforms.

CHAPTER TWO

The Mommy Wars and the Daddy Track

"She was not ashamed of what she wanted, even though it was traditional," a former roommate at Bryn Mawr College said of Stefanie Rabinowitz—the first in their group to get married and have a baby—as friends mourned the death of the young mother murdered in her suburban home days before her daughter's first birthday in May 1997. It says a good deal about campus politics that being traditional was something to be ashamed of at Bryn Mawr. But it says more about our times that Stefanie Rabinowitz could be seen as "traditional." The woman described by a friend as "very much into having just had a daughter" was also an attorney who had returned to her job with a Philadelphia law firm after maternity leave.[1]

On a happier note that year, the inaugural season of the Women's National Basketball Association saw star player Sheryl Swoopes of the Houston Comets return to the court six weeks after giving birth to a baby boy, while her husband, Eric Jackson, who sat in the stands cradling little Jordan in his lap, had put his career in football on hold. "This is my job; my son is my life," he told the *New York Times.* "My wife has the perfect opportunity, and it pays well. I have no problem with that."[2]

The influx of mothers into the labor force has been one of the most dramatic social changes of the second half of our century. In 1960, fewer than one in five married women with children under age six were working for pay. By 1995, more than three out of five were employed and two out of five worked full time (more than three-quarters of mothers with school-age children were employed).[3]

Early on, when feminists exhorted women to join men in the larger world, they seemed to give little thought to the question of who would take over women's traditional tasks at home—in particular, the care of children. In *The Second Sex,* Simone de Beauvoir curtly stated that in a "properly organized society . . . children would be largely taken in charge by the community." The ideologues of "Women's Lib" in the 1970s had similar ideas: Kate Millett scorned the nuclear family as "self-centered" and "inefficient."[4]

Even Betty Friedan, who stressed in *The Feminine Mystique* that rejecting domesticity did not mean abandoning home or children, gave short shrift to practical solutions. In fact, she seemed to suggest that combining motherhood and work wouldn't be all that hard if women ran their households more efficiently or hired better help (though she also saw part-time work as a good way for women with young children to retain their commitment to a career goal).[5] By 1981, when Friedan urged feminists to incorporate family issues into their agenda in *The Second Stage,* it was clear that the balancing act had not turned out to be so easy. The plight of women who wanted to "have it all" and ended up doing it all became a familiar theme: "We've won the right to be exhausted," sighed feminist novelist Erica Jong.[6]

Even those most supportive of women's career gains have voiced anxiety about the parental time deficit in two-earner couples.[7]

Recently, liberals and centrists as well as conservatives have affirmed the importance of strong family structures. But the role of women in these structures remains the subject not only of disagreement but of confusion.

Thus, Dana Mack, a scholar with the Institute for American Values, writes in *The Assault on Parenthood* that what she calls "the New Familism" is found less in a return to full-time mothering than in "increasingly inventive ways parents combine work and parenting," from telecommuting to tag-team arrangements between parents working different shifts. Elsewhere in the book, however, Mack asserts that "the overwhelming majority" of mothers yearn for full-time motherhood and resent the economic and social pressures that compel them to work. She even castigates policy analyst William Galston, by her admission "a notable defender of the family," for asserting that a family policy for the 1990s "must accommodate the 'right' of women to participate in the workforce."[8]

The Working Mother: Victim, Villain, Heroine?

> Mothers today are having such a hard time balancing the demands of family and work that they are looking back wistfully to the traditional *Leave It to Beaver*–type family structure and doubting their own success in rearing their children, according to a survey.[9]

So opened a 1997 article in the *Baltimore Sun* reporting the results of a Pew Research Center poll released in time for Mother's Day, reprinted in other newspapers under the headlines "Motherhood Harder Today, Moms Yearn for '50s" and "Some Mothers Wistful for June Cleaver Era." Eighty-one percent of the women surveyed agreed that it was more difficult to be a mother than a generation ago; 56 percent felt today's mothers were doing a worse job than their own mothers did. Forty-one percent said the trend of more mothers with young children working was bad for society.[10]

But were these women yearning to trade places with June Cleaver? Not quite. Only one in four mothers with children under age eighteen said that given a choice, they wouldn't work outside the home; 29 percent would work full time and the rest part time. More mothers worked full time than would have chosen to do so, but full-time workers were only slightly less likely than full-time mothers (34 versus 39 percent) to report that their preference matched their status, and fewer than one in four would rather stay home. Among mothers employed part time, one in four preferred full-time work while only one in seven preferred full-time motherhood.

That working mothers often feel torn is no myth. In the 1990 Virginia Slims poll, about 60 percent said that their dual role at least sometimes put them under a lot of stress. But that doesn't mean they longed for domesticity: fewer than one in four women with full-time jobs said that being a homemaker was the "most interesting and satisfying" option (40 percent of homemakers preferred a marriage in which both spouses work and share household duties). More recently, asked to name two or three things that would make their lives better, just 7 percent of women picked "being able to stay home and take care of home and family."[11]

Yes, there are women who have always thought they would go back to work after a short maternity leave but find the pull of motherhood hard to resist. For others, the dream of going home may work best as a fantasy. I know a small business owner, a mother of three, who did go home and lasted less than a year; she certainly didn't need to work, with the money she had from the sale of her company, yet she accepted a position heading a business project that probably required *more* time away from home. I know a woman who, when she became pregnant with her first child, told people she was going to sell her court-reporting business and be a "milk and cookies mom" like her own mother; she now has two children and is still running the business. And I know women for whom the choices turn out to be more complex, such as the bank executive and mother of two who went home, back to work and home again in just over a year, finally settling for a lower-status, less demanding job that would eventually allow her to work her way back up the ladder.

Are women forced to work by economic necessity? Journalist Robert Samuelson has knocked holes in the familiar argument that due to falling wages, it now takes two earners to attain the living standards one income used to provide. Since the 1970s, inflation-adjusted wages have dropped for less educated, low-skilled male workers while men with college degrees have gained ground, yet it is their college-educated wives who are most likely to work. In 1993, 61 percent of all married women but 71 percent of the women married to the richest fifth of American men were in the labor force.[12]

Indeed, many working women may not give much thought to whether they "choose" to work. The vast majority of Americans agree that both spouses are responsible for contributing to family income; "having to work" may have become almost as uneventful for women as it has always been for men. In one study of working mothers, about 25 percent of professionals and managers, 40 percent of women in technical and clerical jobs, and 70 percent of blue-collar workers said they worked out of need. Yet the majority also enjoyed and took pride in their jobs. ("Before, they thought I couldn't do anything," said one low-level clerical worker.) Just over a third of working-class women, and fewer than one in five professionals, strongly wanted to spend more time at home. And most were cool to the view that "mothers shouldn't have to work outside the home."[13]

There is no doubt that many women find full-time motherhood deeply rewarding (though, interestingly, there is evidence that home-makers who would rather be working suffer far more distress than working women who would rather be at home). But even women who are employed primarily for financial reasons may often derive other satisfactions from work. In a 1995 survey, about half of women who had ever stopped working by choice said that they missed the feeling of self-sufficiency and self-confidence they had derived from their jobs. Proponents of domesticity often deride the idea of work as "fulfilling," and it's true that Betty Friedan and other champions of careers have often sounded as though every working woman were developing a cure for cancer. Still, a job, even if it's not very "meaningful," can be a source of psychic as well as financial independence: an identity separate from intimate relationships; a sense of accomplishment in a sphere in which you are supposed to be judged by objective standards.[14]

Are mothers in our culture still "demonized" for working, particularly if they can afford to stay home? This issue came up during the widely publicized 1997 trial of Louise Woodward, the British au pair accused of killing the baby in her care, when some people seemed eager to put the mother on trial for pursuing her medical career instead of caring for her two children.

But the anti–working mother backlash was greatly blown out of proportion. Yes, Dr. Deborah Eappen got a few letters chastising her for selfishness and greed, but she said they were outnumbered about 100 to 1 by sympathy mail. Some radio talk show callers voiced such opinions as well, but on the shows I heard, career woman haters were hardly "jamming the airwaves," as Margaret Carlson wrote in *Time*. (*Nation* columnist Katha Pollitt apparently went scraping the bottom of Internet chat rooms for people who thought the mother killed the baby.) And some criticism of the parents was directed at their child care choices—leaving a teenager with an infant and a toddler instead of paying more for a trained nanny—rather than at the mother's career.[15]

In fact, Americans are probably as conflicted about working mothers as are many mothers themselves. About 40 percent agree at least somewhat that "a preschool child is likely to suffer if the mother works" (though fewer than one-third of people under age thirty share this belief); yet more than two out of three think that mothers who work are good role models. Just one in six women and one in five men are willing to express disapproval of mothers' holding jobs while raising their children.[16]

Whether children actually suffer when both parents work

remains a subject of heated debate. When Pennsylvania State University researcher Jay Belsky reversed his pro–day care stance in the 1980s and concluded that infants in group day care were at risk for insecure attachment to parents and aggressive behavior later in life, fellow psychologist Sandra Scarr accused him of colluding in a "backlash against the women's movement." Belsky has charged that critics of his reports on the negative effects of maternal employment have engaged in methodological nitpicking to which no one would have subjected similar studies on the effects of poverty or maternal depression—or studies reporting that mothers' employment was *good* for children.[17]

In 1996–1997, a major study by the National Institute of Child Health and Human Development (NICHD) was trumpeted as giving day care a stamp of approval. "The Kids Are All Right," proclaimed *Time*. Skeptics warned that the rejoicing on the front pages was premature: infants who spent a lot of time in day care did have slightly less positive interactions with their mothers as toddlers—if the care was of poor quality, or if Mom wasn't warm and responsive in the first place. Still, a child's mental and emotional development was far more affected by the home environment than by day care. (It's worth noting that day care as defined in the study included fathers, who cared for one-fifth of the kids whose mothers worked.)[18]

Yes, the day care boosters in the mainstream media were much too sanguine about the NICHD study: too cavalier about evidence that nonmaternal care was likely to make things worse for children already at risk due to the mother's lack of warmth and sensitivity, too quick to dismiss other research showing a small but consistent increase in insecure attachment when the mother works full time in the first year (at least when the infant is in a day care center: children in family day care seem to fare no worse than those with mothers at home). But the other side has erred just as much on the side of alarmism.[19]

Ironically, to make their case, some conservatives cite two recent studies rating most day care in the United States as low quality. What they omit is that these studies gave the highest marks to the institutional, government-regulated day care that conservatives so dislike and the lowest marks to care by relatives (perhaps because the family caregivers in these studies were mostly poor and uneducated). The NICHD study, with a more representative sample, not only painted a more encouraging picture—up to 80 percent of children were getting good or excellent care—but found that care by relatives was better. Moreover, the care labeled bad or mediocre by the experts was rated as good by nine out of ten parents. And aren't conservatives the ones who usually insist that parents know best?[20]

In a *National Review* article on the woes of working mothers' children, Maggie Gallagher greatly overstates a weak link between full-time maternal employment and child misbehavior in a study by Jay Belsky—and never mentions that the mothers in the study were disproportionately young and poor (only 16 percent had attended college). Data from more representative samples suggest that, except at the bottom of the economic ladder, children whose mothers are continuously employed may have *fewer* behavioral problems.[21]

Some researchers suggest that children whose mothers have good occupational prospects have lower cognitive skills if the mother does little or no outside work in the early years—and that, when there are frequent shared mother-child activities, children of working mothers do better in school than children of homemakers.[22] There is other evidence that two careers need not spell the death of healthy family life:

• The Pew poll showed that families with working mothers ate dinner together only slightly less often than families with mothers at home and attended religious services together just as often. Nearly 40 percent of mothers employed full time were there when the kids got home from school.[23]

• The mother's employment does not reduce the time that school-age children spend interacting with parents, partly because working mothers' children interact more with their fathers; in one large study of ten- to thirteen-year-olds, parents in two-income households spent *more* time doing homework with their children.[24]

• Mothers who work, especially those who work part time, are more likely than homemakers to volunteer at school, attend Parent-Teacher Association meetings, and go to class plays and varsity games.[25]

Some critics of the dual-career lifestyle, like radio pop psychologist and best-selling author Dr. Laura Schlessinger, invoke the children as the final authority: if you were a child, would you choose to be in the hands of a nanny or a day care worker? But deferring to children is hardly a traditional value. Indeed, another psychologist who preaches a conservative message, tough-love parenting guru

John Rosemond, treats working-mother guilt as an aspect of the pernicious coddling of American children. But aside from the question of whether the child who clamors for Mommy to stay home is asserting a basic need or being a self-centered brat, do most kids feel deprived when their mothers work?[26]

Sure, some accounts of precocious tots who beg Mom to find something to do because they can't stand being her "project" sound like self-serving fictions by adults. Yet there really are children who say that having a working mother bothered them far less than the mothers feared. Despite reports that some daughters of professional women are discouraged by watching their mothers juggle career and family, it appears that the more years a college woman's mother has been in the labor force, the sooner she herself plans to resume work after having a child. And four out of five young adults believe that their mother made the right choice about working—or not working.[27]

People who allow their children to be shortchanged by their career ambitions *should* be censured. The problem is the either-or mentality that treats accommodations and compromises as irrelevant—when, for example, the formidable Dr. Laura snaps at a caller who plans to have a child and work out of her home, with a friend coming over to help with the baby, "Why don't you just get a pet?"[28]

No one can "have it all"; most employed mothers make plenty of trade-offs. Work *is* changing in response to the needs of working parents, and not just by government fiat. A year before the Family and Medical Leave Act was passed, nine out of ten workers surveyed said that some leave benefits were available to them, and 95 percent said their supervisors were accommodating when they had family problems. More people than ever are working at home, by arrangement with employers or as independent contractors or entrepreneurs.[29]

Still, while the juggling act that women perform is not a disaster, it's hardly an idyll. The 1989 book, *The Second Shift,* by sociologist Arlie Hochschild struck a chord with many working women and gave a name to their unequal domestic burden. Hochschild's survey of 120 couples is at odds with a large body of research: a number of time-use studies find that when paid work and housework are combined, employed women put in *one hour* a week more than men, not *fifteen hours* as she claimed. But women achieve this near parity by spending less time on the job, which tends to hold down their earnings and slow their advancement. Although many women don't mind, others resent making sacrifices their husbands aren't expected to confront.[30]

Some books on the work-family dilemma devote only a few pages to fathers, and many young women who ponder balancing kids and career seem to give relatively little thought to their future mate's role. Yet it is increasingly clear that even with the best support systems for mothers, equality in the workplace will remain a fantasy unless men share equally at home, as writer and legal scholar Rhona Mahony argues in a book titled *Kidding Ourselves.*[31] And mainstream America agrees. In the 1995 Virginia Slims poll, people were asked what needs to change "for working women to balance evenly their job, their marriage, and their children." Sixty percent of women (and 53 percent of men) said "men helping more with household and child care." Better day care trailed far behind, at 26 percent.

A Father's Place
When Republican congresswoman Susan Molinari gave up a promising political career in 1997 to take a job in television that would allow her more time with her young daughter, many saw this as another example of women sacrificing ambition to motherhood. It was a reminder that "it is different to be a mother [than] a father," asserted conservative pundit David Frum.[32]

Less than a year later, Molinari's husband, Bill Paxon—a rising star in the Republican party and a contender for the post of House majority leader—made the surprise announcement that he, too, was leaving Congress. Paxon said that after spending two days alone with his two-year-old daughter, he realized that he would have to be away from her too much if he stayed in politics. He felt that it wouldn't be fair to his wife to put the burden of domestic cares on her alone, but he was also "jealous every day" of the time she had at home and "all the hugs and kisses" she was getting from their child. "You can't do it all," Paxon said.[33]

The nurturing father has been celebrated in the popular culture since 1980, when *Kramer vs. Kramer,* in which an advertising executive discovers hands-on parenthood after his wife walks out, won the Oscar for Best Picture.[34]

But is the New Dad for real? Many feminists say that he is mostly a media fantasy, a distraction from the depressing reality of men's neglect of their children. Most traditionalists agree. Maggie Gallagher argues that what the media tout as the new equality or role reversal is a loss of ground for women, who are saddled with both breadwinning and homemaking responsibilities while the men have an easy time. (As an example, she cites an article about a non-traditional couple and rather egregiously downplays the husband's contribution to household chores.)[35]

Often, conservatives who deplore the view that fathers are irrelevant don't think much of the New Father. To neoconservative commentator Norman Podhoretz, the bottle-feeding, diaper-changing dads are "avoiding the responsibilities of fatherhood" ("providing food, shelter and moral authority") as surely as the men who abandon their children. David Blankenhorn, author of the 1995 book, *Fatherless America,* stresses emotional bonding and hands-on involvement and professes to "applaud much of the New Father vision"— but goes on to scoff at "genderless" fatherhood in terms that echo Podhoretz's jeremiad: "The New Father is a missing father." And some champions of family values seem befuddled. In *The Assault on Parenthood,* Dana Mack alternates between celebrating the emergence of stay-at-home dads and suggesting that a revival of family must be based on "distinct mothering and fathering roles."[36]

The conservative critique of New Fatherhood has several key themes: (1) Men can't and won't care for small children as women do, and if they are told that it's the only way to be a good father, many will just "bail out." (2) A man has few incentives to commit to the father role if there's nothing about it that makes him feel more like *a man.* (3) Gender-based roles provide children with two different, equally essential kinds of parenting: mother love is unconditional; father love must be earned.[37]

Intuitively, the view that women are better suited for child care rings true. Mothers not only have a unique physical link to babies but are uniquely equipped to nurse them. No amount of effort has succeeded in getting boys to play with dolls, though they are no less nurturing than girls when caring for a puppy.[38]

Yet biology offers no simple answers. Primate males' behavior toward the young runs the gamut from "primary caregiving" to indifference. Among humans, physiological response to recorded infant cries (such as changes in pulse rate) is generally found to be similar for both sexes. Observed with their baby brothers and sisters or with other infants, girls tend to be more affectionate and more interested, but these patterns vary by age and ethnicity, and there is vast individual variation. In one study, preschool girls spent about 40 percent more time than boys interacting with their baby brothers or sisters, with no extra encouragement from mothers (though they were also much more likely to be hostile to the infants). But of the two children in the sample who showed much higher interest in the baby than everyone else, one was a boy.[39]

It is true that media reports about "New Age dads" who demand "shorter workweeks, time off to mind sick youngsters and reductions in business travel" are often based on anecdotes rather than solid evidence. Full-time fathers may have their own newsletters and Internet sites, but they are still a rarity. And some fathers who are hailed as living proof that men too give up fast-track careers to devote themselves to their kids can be more properly described as making career adjustments. Jeffrey Steifler, who resigned as president of American Express but stayed on as manager of two venture capital portfolios, cut his hours away from home by about 40 percent.[40]

Still, despite feminist griping and conservative gloating, the nurturing father is much more than a media fad. My mother, a music professor, was talking to a recently married former student about his plans to start a family. The great thing, he told her, was that since his wife was a schoolteacher and he was teaching piano at his own studio, they didn't need day care: his wife was usually home by four o'clock, and he didn't start work until four, so one of them could always be around.

Young fathers I know handle the tiniest children with remarkable comfort, skill, and warmth. Looking at families in restaurants, I see dads who seem every bit as attentive and responsive as moms (on some occasions, *more* so), and couples who take turns picking up and comforting a crying or fretting child. I hear grandparents marvel at how different fathers are with their children than they were a generation ago.

Surveys of corporate employees show that, increasingly, men as well as women are turning down relocations and promotions for family reasons. And while a much-ballyhooed surge in the numbers of preschoolers in Dad's care while Mom works—from 15 percent of children with employed mothers in 1988 to 20 percent in 1991—turned out to be a blip, father care is hardly a fringe phenomenon.

Nearly 3 million American men spend some time taking care of the kids while their wives work, and 2 million are the principal child care providers.[41]

In a 1996 *Newsweek* poll, over half of fathers said that they shared child rearing equally, and a quarter claimed to do more than their wives; only 2 percent admitted doing "a lot less." Predictably, mothers had a different view: 30 percent felt that they did "a lot more" than their husbands, 3 percent said they did less, and only one in three reported equal sharing. This "Rashomon effect" shows up in other surveys. Overall, however, recent studies find that fathers with employed wives provide 30 to 45 percent of basic child care, with their share increasing as children get older.[42]

Work-family conflict is also an increasingly pressing issue for men, although Blankenhorn scoffs at the idea: real men, he says, see breadwinning as a "key component of their paternal responsibility." (Later, he grudgingly acknowledges that some of the fathers who exemplify the "good family man" were concerned that "the demands of their work meant less time at home.") Three out of four fathers in a 1990 *Los Angeles Times* poll felt that the job they did as parents suffered because of work pressures, 57 percent felt guilty about spending too little time with the children, and 39 percent said they would have liked to be home full time. In other studies, mothers are more likely than fathers to want shorter hours and flexible schedules, but the gap between actual and preferred work hours is somewhat *larger* for men. And while the number of men taking advantage of paternity leave is growing at a snail's pace, men *are* showing more interest in work-family programs: in 1997, when Texas Instruments announced a seminar on balancing work and home, 120 men tried to sign up for the 70 slots.[43]

Researcher Claudia Shuster found that new fathers in dual-income middle-class families complained about the lack of opportunities to work part time or on a flexible schedule ("I don't think people realize just how hard it is for me to get up and leave the house to go to work," said one man) and worried, almost as much as did working mothers, that they would miss "seeing the baby change and do new things."[44]

There's no need to be starry-eyed about the progress we have made toward equal parenting (much of it is offset, alas, by the rise in father absence). Today's college women, strong believers in "having it all," are still far more likely than men to anticipate limiting their careers to accommodate family needs, even though more men than ever say that they would like to cut back on work when their children are young. And while the New Dad is no myth, neither is the father who shirks child care duties and remains on the emotional periphery of his children's lives.[45]

But often we are too quick to assume that fathers are shirkers. After *Time* magazine profiled harried working mom Lori Lucas as a representative of the female vote in 1996, some female letter writers castigated Lori's live-in boyfriend Mike as a "sexual parasite" who "thinks parenting stops at conception." Actually, of the six references to Mike in the story, two had to do with his job and three with his participation in housework and child care.[46]

I am troubled, I admit, by the implications for women of the model offered by neotraditionalists like Blankenhorn and sociologist David Popenoe: mothers tend to children's physical and emotional needs; fathers raise them to the higher level of becoming self-reliant adults. (Many men are troubled by Blankenhorn's belief that a father must respect the primacy of the mother-child bond and accept second place in the child's emotional life.) Popenoe, who stresses his support for women's gains, notes that the need for role differentiation is limited mainly to the home and to early childhood. Yet, if both parents do work that requires self-assertion and competitiveness, is it realistic to expect only one of them to set these traits aside when it comes to child rearing?[47]

Even Blankenhorn concedes that differences between mother and father love are "tendencies," overlapping and "frequently subtle." The mother obsessed with her child's success is a familiar figure. Some of Blankenhorn's "good family men" delight in bottle feeding and sound like "androgynous" New Dads—except, supposedly, for their commitment to providing.[48]

As usual, the stereotypes are not baseless. Even some feminists acknowledge the role of paternal influence for achievement-oriented women. In a survey of middle-class parents in the 1980s, mothers and fathers mostly shared the same concerns about their teenage children, but fathers attached much more importance to self-reliance, *particularly* for girls.[49]

But there is also evidence that assertive and independent women are influenced by mothers who have these qualities; that working mothers and fathers are very similar in their expectations from preschoolers; that teenagers see few differences between their mothers and fathers in making them feel loved and encouraging autonomy. Aside from fathers' more vigorous physical play with young children, the sex-specific patterns are too elusive to sustain an argument for the indispensability of fathers.[50]

This is not to say that the father is just, in Blankenhorn's words, "an extra set of hands"—hands that don't have to belong to a father or even to a man. Whatever their division of labor, men and women bring an intangible but essential masculine or feminine quality to what they do. There is no need to worry about "genderless parenting" because gender is not going away. Even if "primary caretaker" fathers may, to Blankenhorn's horror, see their mothers as role models in domestic management, they don't seem to suffer from gender identity confusion any more than do career women who see their fathers as role models. One man who cut down on work to care for his child, because his wife had a more secure job, told an interviewer, "I'm doing things that are feminine but I realize that it is not feminine to change a baby [or] give baths."[51]

Blankenhorn is right that men who work hard so that their wives can devote themselves to nurturing their children deserve credit too; many traditional breadwinners are devoted and loving fathers. But it also makes no sense to knock the New Father, particularly when so many women claim equality in formerly male spheres. A large study of families confirms that young people have better relationships with fathers who shared in child care; grown children of "fifty-fifty fathers," particularly sons, also tend to be closer to other relatives, have more friends, and be more involved in the community. And, while Blankenhorn warns that the blurring of parental sex roles makes for less happy marriages, most studies find that the more the father is involved in child care, the less depressed and the more satisfied with the marriage both spouses are likely to be.[52]

How Much Equality Do Women Want?

> I work. So does he. So I suppose I should want him to share equally in everything involving the children. But I don't. Frankly, I'm fiercely possessive of my title as Mom. . . . My children love their father, and he loves them. . . . But deep down I do not want him to be as important as I am, even if that means more of the work falls on my shoulders.[53]

The "second shift" is almost invariably framed in terms of "faster-changing women and slower-changing men," as Arlie Hochschild put it. But a few feminist mavericks, such as legal scholar Rhona Mahony, author of *Kidding Ourselves,* argue that women are held back by their own attitudes and expectations just as much as they are by male recalcitrance.[54]

True, women generally hold more "progressive" views than men do about sex roles in the family; this is often a source of marital friction. Two-thirds of women and 56 percent of men say that men don't do their fair share of housework and child care. And yet two out of three men *and women* also agree that in this domain, "women still want to be in charge."[55]

It's not that mothers don't want *more* paternal involvement in child rearing, as some conservatives have claimed. In *The Motherhood Report,* three-quarters of the women wanted their husbands to be more involved, just not *too much* more. Only one in four strongly endorsed fifty-fifty parenting; two out of three "seemed threatened by the idea of equal participation."[56]

Some researchers, too, conclude that women's reluctance to "let men in"—either because they don't trust the father's competence or because they are unwilling to give up turf—is a major barrier to fathers' involvement. Yes, some fathers won't touch a diaper; and some mothers will demand the father's participation, only to sabotage it by criticizing the way he burps the baby or puts the toddler to bed. A woman who acknowledges that her husband has more patience with the kids may still look for reasons that he wouldn't make a good "primary caretaker" (he can't do the laundry right).[57]

Oh, come on, some will scoff. Ever heard a woman complain that her husband is *too* involved with the kids?

Actually, yes. In a 1995 *Redbook* article, "My Husband Is Too Good a Father," Beth Levine describes the feelings of a mother whose child cries for Daddy more often than for Mommy. Levine is no champion of traditional roles: before her son was born, she very much wanted her husband—like herself, a freelance writer working at home—to be a fifty-fifty father:

> There is an old saying: Be careful what you wish for because you might get it. In my case, I did get a husband who was involved, creative, energetic, instinctual in his parenting. . . .
> And you know what? I hate it. I'm ashamed, but I hate that I am not the center of my child's universe.

When I am honest with myself, what I really want is for Bill to be an eager but charmingly inept father, a soldier to my general.[58]

A few other women have confessed to this unseemly jealousy: to feeling secretly thrilled when a husband shows his parental incompetence and disappointed when he copes well in Mom's absence. Some men also talk about the difficulty their wives have had accepting the idea that the father could be better at handling the child: "To compensate," said an attorney who switched to part-time work to care for his daughter, "my wife read books about child care, sometimes criticizing me if I didn't follow the experts' recommendations."[59]

In the 1994 book *Peer Marriage,* sociologist Pepper Schwartz reports that many women committed to equal parenting in theory start "hogging" the baby when they become mothers, and often settle into traditional roles unless they make an effort to curb their possessiveness (often because the father rebels at being shut out).[60]

Yet only a few of the feminist writers who advocate a more equal sharing of child care responsibilities have started to acknowledge the dirty little secret of maternal chauvinism (none have confronted it as candidly as Anne Roiphe in her quirky, sweet, painfully honest book *Fruitful: A Real Mother in the Real World*). And some actively reinforce it: *Washington Post* columnist Judy Mann gloats that whether the mother works or not, she is likely to be the parent to whom children turn for emotional support or advice.[61]

One could argue that even though mothers want fathers to do less than half, the fathers still usually do less than the mothers would like them to, so one might as well forget about equal parenting. But could some men be discouraged by knowing that they will never be more than a soldier to Mom's general? As author Sam Osherson put it, "There's no great value in [Dad] running around in a Snugli if his wife is directing everything and making all the decisions." Could it be that by guarding their unique place in the children's lives, many mothers are subtly discouraging fathers' involvement and ending up with even less than they want?[62]

To achieve her just world in which women are no more likely than men to be primary parents, Rhona Mahony advocates massive social engineering, such as federal subsidies for stay-at-home dads but not moms. Without it, she admits, both tradition and the biological facts of childbearing and breast-feeding will pull more women toward primary parenthood.[63] The government, of course, has no business promoting nontraditional (or traditional) sex roles. But this hardly means that such arrangements are a bad choice for individuals.

Maternal chauvinism is not the only female attitude that gets in the way. Even ambitious women are unlikely to see less career-oriented men as suitable mates, preferring to marry a man at least as successful in his work. Some may want the option of leaving the workforce; many others feel that, as Katie Roiphe has written, a less successful, less ambitious man isn't masculine enough to play their "romantic lead." But even if, as many conservatives argue, the preference to "marry up" is part of women's evolutionary heritage, that doesn't mean some women can't find happiness by setting it aside.[64]

Marie, an accountant who told her tale in a magazine article titled "I Was Ashamed of My Husband's Job," had planned to hire a nanny when her maternity leave was up. But her husband Kip lost his management job and offered to care for the baby; he turned out to be a great father. Later, he turned down a demanding position in his field and began working evenings as a waiter. After an ugly scene in which Marie berated Kip for not having a "real job," and after a female coworker in the throes of a child care crisis told her how lucky she was not to have such worries, she had an epiphany and decided to accept her husband the way he was: "I realized you can't have it both ways."[65]

Even if Marie's discomfort with Kip's failure to be a "real man" was partly in her genes, her decision to put these feelings behind her was obviously good for her and her family. Nontraditional arrangements have also worked well for some female corporate pioneers who shattered the glass ceiling while their children were young, and while their husbands curtailed or gave up their careers.[66]

Given equal opportunity, most people will balance work and family like Blankenhorn's "good family men," adopting a "pragmatic, non-ideological approach" with a premium on flexibility. This attitude may be equally far removed from a conscious effort to revolutionize sex roles and from Blankenhorn's general fixation on preserving them.[67]

The semitraditional arrangements in which women have joined men in the workplace but perform much of their traditional role at home suit many people. For others, they may spell trouble. In an article on the conflict between motherhood and careers, corporate lawyer Jill Natwick Johnston describes her decision to turn down a dream job and follow her husband to a town where he has a new business, but where her career opportunities will be slim at best. She is aware that her situation is the fruit of her choices: to marry a man focused on his work, to be "the primary parent." Johnston proclaims herself "lucky" to have these options, but she also reflects that "we can choke on that very abundance of choices."[68]

I wonder how many women who make such a sacrifice end up feeling resentful, and how it may affect their kids. Maybe women who are committed to career success but resist equality at home *don't* know what's good for them; maybe they overestimate their ability to "do it all" and underestimate the costs, to themselves and their children. This doesn't mean that all women must give up the "primary parent" role—only that a feminist worth her salt would tell them that, as Marie realized, they can't have it both ways.

Feminism Meets Fathers

> Most American children suffer from too much mother and too little father.   —Gloria Steinem, "A New Egalitarian Life Style"[69]

> A Smother-Father believes that *he* is the "mother" or that he is a better "mother" than his wife is.
>   —Phyllis Chesler, *Mothers on Trial*[70]

One can abhor coercive schemes to push people into nontraditional roles and yet support a social movement to promote shared parenting. There was a time when it seemed that feminism could be such a movement. In the 1970s and 1980s, *Ms.* advocated "child-care leave for fathers" and published quite a few positive articles about father-child relationships. In her 1983 book, *Family Politics*, Letty Cottin Pogrebin, a founding editor of *Ms.*, was thrilled that men were "materializing in childbirth courses" and staying home with the kids.[71]

But something funny happened on the way to equal parenting. Feminism shifted its focus from the New Dad to the Bad Dad: the domineering patriarch, the disappearing deadbeat, the ogre who beats and rapes his children. A few years after her valentine to nurturing fathers, Pogrebin wrote that most women who love their fathers are merely conditioned to forgive their bad behavior and that "the multiple shortcomings of fathers . . . amount to a social calamity of major proportions."[72]

Gloria Steinem still pays lip service to the importance of fathering: "We need to know not only that women can do what men can do, but also that men can do what women can do," she said on TV on the twenty-fifth anniversary of *Ms.* But the magazine she founded has funny ideas about promoting fatherhood. Here's what it has published on the subject in recent years: A woman recalls her father's violence; a man recalls his father's violence; a woman recalls her father's and stepfather's violence; a writer discusses her novel about a black teenager molested by her father; a judge is blasted for giving custody of a child to the father.[73] Elsewhere, in an essay ostensibly supportive of male participation in "mothering," feminist theorist Sara Ruddick notes that she has only to look at the world around her—in which fathers are either "absent" or "controlling and abusive"—to start "fantasizing about a world without Fathers."[74]

Others openly defend maternal chauvinism. In a law review essay proposing that custody disputes be resolved by giving the final decision to mothers, University of Chicago law professor Mary Becker belittles men's love for their children and suggests that if most mothers don't want fathers to participate equally in child rearing, it's because they know that men are "too indifferent [and] too self-centered."[75]

The backlash against fathers who seek custody has been particularly vicious. In the 1986 book, *Mothers on Trial,* feminist psychologist Phyllis Chesler bemoans the fact that good mothers (a broad category that includes a busy serial adulteress who compared her children to "maggots" in her diary) were being robbed of their children by bad men. While Chesler sometimes suggested that men did not deserve custody because they weren't the caregivers, she was openly hostile to father involvement: "Absent and emotionally distant fathers already have a mesmerizing effect on their children. Present and emotionally intimate fathers probably have twice the mesmerizing effect."[76] *Mothers on Trial* was warmly praised by Gloria Steinem, Letty Cottin Pogrebin, and Lilian Kozak, chair of the Domestic Relations Task Force of the New York State NOW.

Increasingly, feminists began to champion solo motherhood, as both a matter of women's autonomy and a way to raise children without those nasty men around. American University law professor Nancy Polikoff, former counsel to the Women's Legal Defense Fund, states that "it is no tragedy, either on a national scale or in an individual family, for children to be raised without fathers." In *Backlash,* Susan Faludi gloats that as support for out-of-wedlock motherhood rose in the 1980s, "the biological father increasingly didn't have . . . much of a say at all" in women's decisions about childbearing.[77]

Amid all this talk of male evil and female empowerment, a paradox looms: the rhetoric of maternal supremacy perpetuates the old-fashioned idea of child rearing as woman's sphere.

Katha Pollitt, an outspoken proponent of the view that liberated women can have kids on their own ("Children are a joy; many men are not"), is also a sharp critic of "difference feminism." Yet, noting with approval that "the lives of the sexes are becoming less distinct," she fails to see that the rise of single motherhood makes them *radically* distinct.[78]

In the 1920s, feminist Crystal Eastman urged women to pursue careers and men to share housework. She also preached and practiced "marriage under two roofs"—wives and husbands living separately. Then, notes historian Rosalind Rosenberg, "Eastman was surprised when her children developed the view that fathers were visitors while mothers were people who worked all day and did housework in the evening."[79] For many of today's children, fathers may not exist even as visitors.

CHAPTER THREE

Oppression Stories

One of patriarchy's most effective devices for disabling girls and women is to entice us into believing the seductive lie that women and men are treated equally in this culture.

—Judy Mann, *The Difference*[1]

What does life have in store for a girl born into a middle-class American family in the late twentieth century? When *New York Times* columnist Anna Quindlen looks at her daughter, what she sees are not opportunities no women of past generations (and few men) could have imagined, but a grim and perilous future: the poor thing will be told that "girls aren't good at math" and will learn to keep quiet; college professors will treat her studies as a "hobby"; less capable men will be paid more and get promoted first. Quindlen muses that over the years, she has learned to focus on the gains and see "the glass half full"—until she had a daughter and her anger at the treatment of women was reignited.[2]

The title of the 1990 column, "The Glass Half Empty," sums up the drift of many reports on women's lot. Women's magazines run stories on "The Schoolgirl Scandal," "Unequal Justice," and "Why Doctors Mistreat Women." Much of the *New Yorker*'s special "women's issue" in 1996 was a catalog of women's wrongs, with artwork featuring such nuggets as, "The average salary of a black female college graduate is less than that of a white male high school dropout" (in fact, it's 80 percent higher). A 1994 *U.S. News and World Report* cover story, "The War Against Women," counts the ways in which women everywhere are victims of everything—even of "success" in the West, apparently because not all have made equal gains.[3] Indeed, in many ways, gender politics in the 1990s were shaped by a best-seller that warned that the glass for women was not just empty but getting emptier.

Losing Ground?

In an October 1991 Gallup poll, three out of four American women said that the social and economic status of their sex had improved in the past decade. But according to a book released the same month, *Backlash: The Undeclared War Against American Women* by Pulitzer Prize–winning reporter Susan Faludi, they were sadly deluded. "The monitors that serve to track slippage in women's status have been working overtime since the early '80s," wrote Faludi. This slippage, she asserted, was the result of a society-wide "backlash"—if not an organized plot, then something very much like it, a frightening thing compared to "watchtowers" that flash blinding "high-security floodlights."[4]

By luck or harmonic convergence, the publication of *Backlash* coincided with Anita Hill's charges of sexual harassment against Clarence Thomas. The tide of female "rage" supposedly unleashed by the Senate hearings became a big news event. In *Newsweek, Backlash* was invoked as a chronicle of a decade-long "assault on women, progress and common sense" underlying the anger.[5]

Certain things about the book ought to have set off alarm bells: Faludi's intolerance toward any critique of feminism; her glib dismissal of work-family conflicts; the gloating over male misery.[6] Yet except in the conservative press, there was universal praise, especially for the quantity and presumed quality of Faludi's research. The *New Yorker* commended her "thorough and conscientious" reporting. "She overwhelms the reader with facts and statistics," marveled Eleanor Clift in the *Washington Post.* The same newspapers and magazines Faludi accused of leading the charge against feminism led the applause.[7]

No one undertook to check the facts and statistics. Later, a few egregious errors were pointed out, such as the claim that women over age thirty-five are at lower risk of having Down's syndrome babies than younger mothers. Reports on economic data from the 1980s also challenged Faludi's assertion that women's progress in the workplace had stalled, showing that it was after 1980 that it really took off.[8] Still, since the publication of *Backlash,* the belief that there has been a sustained antifeminist backlash has become entrenched. In an intelligent, insightful *New Yorker* essay criticizing feminism's embrace of recovered memories of sexual abuse, including bizarre tales of ritual abuse in satanic cults, Joan Acocella writes, "The eighties was a period of vigorous backlash against feminism. In that tormented context, many feminists clearly felt that any woman alleging abuse, even by a devil with a tail, had to be believed."[9]

But was the backlash any more real than the devil with a tail? The inaccuracies in *Backlash* are not just a few errors in a factoid-filled book, as Faludi has dismissively asserted. Her figures on "working women's declining status" are either contrary to government figures (she writes that "the pay gap . . . in all full-time managerial jobs was growing worse," when the female-to-male earnings ratio in such jobs rose from fifty-nine cents to a dollar in 1980 to sixty-six cents in 1989) or taken out of context. Thus, she claims that "the proportion of women in some 'élite or glamorous fields'" such as professional sports, geology, economics, or biological and life sciences "shrank slightly in the last half of the '80s." In fact, the numbers were fluctuating, not shrinking. Women economists made up 38 percent of the profession in 1983 and 35 percent in 1988; but by 1989, the last year for which Faludi cites labor statistics, their proportion in the field was on the rise again, to more than 36 percent. (In 1990, it was a record 44 percent, though Faludi may not have had access to this data.) And during the same period, the proportion of women working in all the natural sciences had risen from 20 percent to 27 percent.[10]

In other areas, Faludi's arguments suffer from similar factual deficiencies. (Her sources for particular statements are sometimes impossible to examine, since they are cited in such a way that one cannot tell which source supports which specific claim.) Her claim that the 1980s were marked by skyrocketing violence against women as a sign of "rising male wrath" is contradicted by available crime statistics. She asserts that "reported rapes more than doubled from the early '70s—at nearly twice the rate of all other violent crimes and four times the overall crime rate in the United States." Reported rapes did more than double from 1970 to 1990, as did other violent crime rates, but most of that increase took place in the 1970s, which Faludi regards as a decade of progress. From 1980 to 1990, the rate of reported rapes rose by 15 percent, compared to 23 percent for all violent crime. As for rape rates growing four times as fast as overall crime rates, a 1993 article in the *Social Science Quarterly* concludes that this claim is unsupported by "any source of data, official or otherwise."[11]

Or take Faludi's grim picture of women's political realities: antifeminists in charge in Washington, declining numbers of women "in both elective posts and political appointments." She is right about the hostility to independent women behind the "pro-family" rhetoric of many social conservatives, but social issues were never high on the Reagan agenda (much to the dismay of New Right activists), and Reagan's tax reforms actually favored two-career marriages by reducing the "marriage penalty" on couples pushed into a higher tax bracket by a second income.[12]

The claim that "with Ronald Reagan's election, women began disappearing from federal office" is little more than hyperbole: 12 percent of Reagan's senior appointees were female, down from 14 percent under Carter. Omitted, too, is the fact that under Bush, the number went up to 20 percent. The drop in the number of women in senior White House posts, "from 123 in 1980 to 62 in 1981," was likewise followed by a steep increase, reaching 227 in 1988.[13]

In Faludi's scenario of the backlash in electoral politics, the alleged media mugging of vice presidential candidate Geraldine Ferraro in 1984 was so demoralizing that in 1988, the number of women running for office fell to a ten-year low. But the Ferraro effect apparently took a while to manifest itself. A year after the 1984 election, activists working to elect women were upbeat; former National Women's Political Caucus head Kathy Wilson said that Ferraro had "raise[d] the tolerance threshold for women candidates." There was no sign of dampened female spirits in 1986, when *Washington Post* columnist Judy Mann wrote that "recognition of the political staying power of women may be the most historically significant element to emerge from this election." Compared to 1984, there were slightly fewer women running for Congress, but more of them won; record numbers ran for governor and attorney general. Even in 1988, while the number of female congressional candidates dropped again, the number of winners was up.[14]

Faludi's chronicle of women's political travails stops at 1989, without a word about the 1990 elections (though the book mentions some events from early 1991). That year, the number of women running for office reached an all-time high, with seventy candidates for the House and eighty-five major party nominees for statewide offices. In fact, 1990 was supposed to be the original "Year of the Woman." Twenty-nine women won House seats, and Washington, D.C., elected its first female mayor. Said Women's Campaign Fund executive director Jane Danowitz, "We broke the glass ceiling."[15]

What gave *Backlash* a special edge was the startling claim that in the 1980s, not only conservatives but institutions rarely suspected of right-wing sympathies—the news media and the entertainment industry—were trying to turn back the clock for women. According to Faludi, Hollywood's brief love affair with women's lib in the 1970s in films like *An Unmarried Woman* was followed by an all-out assault on the independent woman, expressed most starkly in the 1987 hit *Fatal Attraction,* with its contrast between the good stay-at-home wife and the evil, crazy, single, career woman.

Fatal Attraction's anti–career woman bias may have been real enough (it was widely criticized when the film was released). With Faludi's other bête noire, *Baby Boom,* she is on shakier ground: its heroine, who discovers her maternal instincts and falls off the fast track, does not become a "country housewife" but is miserable at home until she starts a million-dollar business marketing gourmet baby food. And Faludi's handling of other films is even more creative.[16]

From *House of Games* (the man "slips the cold careerist woman back under his thumb"), she lops off the finale in which the woman gets even. Movies that have strong heroines or show women combining success and love get a thumbs down for various reasons: the astronaut in *Aliens* battles monsters, but only to protect an orphan "who calls her 'Mommy'"; Tess in *Working Girl,* whom critic Janet Maslin saw as "an unbeatable mixture of street smarts, business sense and sex appeal," gets ahead with help from powerful men. A backlash motif ("fears about strong women's powers") is even unearthed in *Sleeping with the Enemy,* in which a battered wife finds her freedom and kills the abuser when he goes after her. And films that just won't fit into the backlash mold, such as *Legal Eagles,* with Debra Winger as a spirited lawyer who wins the case *and* Robert Redford, are expediently ignored.[17]

On television, Faludi claims, the backlash "banished feminist issues" in the early 1980s and then "reconstructed a 'traditional' female hierarchy" that glorified suburban housewives and put down working women, especially unmarried ones.[18] Yet in 1984 alone, TV movies tackled equal pay *(A Matter of Sex),* date rape *(When She Says No),* and domestic violence *(The Burning Bed).* One study found that by the late 1980s, when women's issues came up in network series, the feminist side was clearly favored 70 percent of the time. In 1987, supposedly "the backlash's high watermark on TV," series with working women as lead characters were at an all-time high: 75 percent of female TV characters, compared to 56 percent of actual women, were employed. The main complaint of the National Commission on Working Women was that their jobs were too glamorous and did not present a realistic picture of working women.[19]

In Faludi's narrative, shows that feature powerful career women are omitted, or acknowledged in passing (*Murphy Brown* and *L.A. Law*), or brushed off as tainted with femininity: the heroines of *Designing Women* are "home-based interior decorators." Or else they are dismissed because they lasted a season or less. But that's more than one can say for the *All New Queen for a Day*, a planned revival of a 1950s game show that had women vying to top each other's woes, with which Faludi wraps up her chapter on "The Backlash on TV": it never aired at all.[20]

The news media's relationship with feminism followed, in Faludi's script, the same pattern as Hollywood's: having tried to co-opt the movement in the 1970s with glitzy images of Single Girls and corporate Superwomen, the press reversed itself and went on a "rampage" against liberated women. Women were assailed with warnings about "the wages of feminist sin" (spinsterhood, barrenness, working-mother burnout) or seduced with tales of reformed sinners giving up careers for "cocooning."[21]

Faludi's chief example is the coverage of the Harvard-Yale study of marriage patterns, dramatized on the cover of *Newsweek* with a graph of older women's plummeting chances of tying the knot—the source of the infamous pseudo-factoid that a single woman in her forties was more likely to be killed by a terrorist than to catch a husband.[22] Admittedly, it wasn't journalism at its finest, and the hype did have an element of gloating.

Yet even here, Faludi's account has trouble spots. For one, apparently eager to cast Yale sociologist Neil Bennett as the villain, she skirts the fact that he and coauthor David Bloom condemned any attempts to treat their study as a warning to uppity women and stressed that many women were content with their single state. Quoted in the *Chicago Tribune* magazine, Bennett assailed the "very sexist position implying women should be married."[23] Faludi must have known about that article: she wrote it herself.

Nor is it true that a Census Bureau study that found much better marriage odds for women was ignored by the media: Bennett and Bloom, at least, caviled that "feminists and nonfeminists alike quickly embraced the Census Bureau's figures."[24] Faludi says that the *New York Times* ran a front-page story on single women afflicted by the man shortage, "citing the Harvard-Yale study as proof" and "dismissing the entire critique as 'rabid reaction from feminists.'" In fact, the

Times story gave the Harvard-Yale study and the Census report equal space. And if "rabid reaction from feminists" doesn't sound like the *Times,* that's because the *Times* didn't say it: it spoke of "a *strong reaction from feminists* who argued that many women are single by choice" (italics added).[25]

And the marriage-study analysis is one of Faludi's better moments. Consider her treatment of a 1986 *Newsweek* cover story, "Making It Work: How Women Balance the Demands of Job and Children," whose real message, she claims, was that mothers could "go home or crack up."[26] As evidence, Faludi cites the opening "morality tale" about a stressed-out executive mom who quit her job. But she drops the second paragraph, about a mother who chose to stay home but felt "miserable" and went back to work—turning a pair of vignettes meant to show women torn between the seventies "Supermom" and the fifties "Perfect Mother" into an endorsement of the latter. A passage rendered as, "'A growing number' of mothers have reached 'the recognition that they can't have it all,'" actually reads, "But for a growing number of mothers the recognition that they can't have it all—at least not all at the same time—is tempered by encouraging evidence that there are ways to make it work." The article stressed women's desire to work and noted that "children of working mothers may actually have advantages." It ended with a comparison of working mothers to "candles in the night—inspiring women to keep the faith and forcing the workplace to see the light."[27]

Faludi also heaps scorn on *Newsweek*'s claim that fathers are doing more at home. The magazine, she scoffs, "made much of its one example, 'Superdad' R. Bruce Magee." In fact, Magee was the first of *seven* fathers profiled in "The Real 'Mr. Moms,'" a companion piece to the feature on working mothers.[28] Maybe Faludi was so disgusted she never got past the first paragraph.

In the case of a 1981 article identified as an early sign of the backlash—"'The women's movement is over,' began a cover story in the *New York Times Magazine"*—one may wonder if she got past the first five words, or noticed the quotation marks: "'The women's movement is over,' said my friend, a usually confident executive, who is also a wife and feminist."[29] Did Faludi go on to read the assertion that "the women's movement in some form will never be over," or the warning of "deadly danger" to women's rights from conservatives in Congress and the judiciary? Did she read the part where the author—none other than Betty Friedan—discusses ways to reinvigorate the movement? Friedan's proposed strategy of transcending feminism's antimale, antifamily sexual politics may not be to Faludi's liking. Still, her essay was hardly an obituary for feminism: it was titled "Feminism's Next Step."

These examples are all too typical of Faludi's treatment of her material. A mostly optimistic, decidedly pro-feminist *Time* article on the issues facing women in the 1990s is represented by a single quotation that expresses doubts about feminism; *Newsweek's* celebration of "womanpower" on prime-time television becomes an article "griping" that "independent women were 'seizing control of prime time.'"[30]

Her sins of omission are worse. Faludi never mentions that few of the "backlash" phenomena she assails—the New Right, the "spinster panic," *Good Housekeeping's* "New Traditionalist" ads—escaped scathing criticism in the media.[31] She never mentions the many items that contradict her portrayal of media in the grip of a backlash: the glowing cover story in the August 1984 *U.S. News and World Report* hailing women's new roles, or the magazine's equally glowing story on single women in 1987; the *New York Times Magazine* piece, "The Working Mother As Role Model"; the many sympathetic articles about the women's movement or about female accomplishments in traditionally male fields; the editorials urging support for mothers "in their dual roles of parent and worker."[32]

Of course, there was resistance to women's new roles in the 1980s, just as there had been in the 1970s (recall the success of Marabel Morgan's *The Total Woman*). But as polls show, the liberalization of attitudes on gender issues continued throughout the "backlash decade."[33] Many men and, as Faludi admits, many women felt threatened by the erosion of traditional roles. What they saw, however, was not a culture supportive of their fears but a culture that glorified career women while making homemakers invisible.[34]

"Once you've read this hair-raising but meticulously documented analysis," *Newsweek,* one of Faludi's favorite targets, wrote about *Backlash,* "you may never read a magazine or see a movie or walk through a department store the same way again."[35] Or, maybe, read a book.

Inequities and Fictions

Of course, just because there was no backsliding in the 1980s does not mean that women have achieved equality with men. We know that, at last report, women who work full-time make seventy-six cents for every dollar men make, and fewer than 10 percent of senior corporate executives are women.

Many people who believe that gender inequality is a serious problem nonetheless acknowledge that these disparities are not explained by discrimination alone. In part, they are the legacy of the traditional roles that were the expected life path for most women until recently. In 1968, fewer than a third of teenage girls expected to be in the workforce when they were thirty-five. Today, the earnings of younger women, who are more likely to have trained for a profession in anticipation of working for most of their adult lives, are much closer to those of their male peers: eighty-three cents to a dollar for women in their late twenties and early thirties, and ninety-four cents for women under twenty-five.[36]

Even women who have launched their careers in a liberated age tend to make somewhat different choices than men do. The American Bar Association's 1995 report on women in the legal profession, which treats the lower rates at which female attorneys achieve partnerships in law firms as solid evidence of discrimination, also acknowledges (without recognizing the contradiction) the role of personal priorities. Women, the authors note, "often base their choice of work environments on how their environment can accommodate their personal needs," including family life, and "are attracted to work in the public sector because the hours required are generally less onerous."[37]

In her book *Speaking of Sex,* which argues that American women are still victims of systematic injustice, Stanford law professor Deborah Rhode concedes that women's enduring role as "primary parent" is a major factor in workplace inequality. (This is underscored by a study that analyzed the salaries of men and women with MBA degrees: single women earned nearly the same as single men; women in childless dual-income marriages were behind by a 6 percent margin; those who had children made 12 percent less than fathers in two-earner families and 29 percent less than sole-breadwinner fathers.) Rhode treats this role as something imposed on women by society and men. But often it is at least in part a reflection of their personal preferences—even if Rhode insists on putting the words *choice* and *choose* in quotation marks.[38]

Not that sex discrimination is extinct. No doubt there are still men in power who don't think women belong in "men's" jobs; even without intentional bias, women may be shut out of the "old boys' network," or "mommy-tracked" against their will. A portion of the gender gap in pay cannot be explained by differences in education, occupational field, or years of experience. What is remarkable, however, is that some feminists still insist that the disparities are due *entirely* to discrimination—and that some journalists still listen.

"Somebody is pocketing 24 cents. Somebody benefits from women's cheap labor," NOW president Patricia Ireland said on a television panel in 1998, after the pay gap had shrunk from seventy-four to seventy-six cents to a dollar, suggesting that this is what women are paid *for the same work as men*. A story posted on the ABC News web site about the narrowing of the wage gap explicitly talked about women earning less "for the same work"—and quoted Ireland's ominous warning that companies and men were pocketing women's twenty-four cents.[39]

At a symposium on affirmative action in early 1997, one of the speakers mentioned a recent article in *Fortune* showing that the barriers of sexism in the corporate world remained so powerful that many successful women were bailing out. When I looked up the article, it turned out to be about something very different: successful corporate women who reassessed their priorities at midlife and left to start their own businesses, work for nonprofits, or pursue new careers as artists, psychologists, or even private detectives. (Male executives grappling with a "midlife crisis," the article noted, rarely feel free to make such leaps; some say their wives won't let them.) The *Fortune* story stressed that the "glass ceiling" was not the issue; many of the women had walked away from major promotions.[40]

Even the belief that girls are victims of gender bias in schools—which, unlike claims of discrimination in the workplace, is contradicted by strong evidence that on many indicators, females are doing *better*—remains alive, despite the best efforts of debunkers. When New York City opened an all-girl public school in Harlem in 1996, the project sparked a lively debate on single-sex education. But neither side questioned the school's stated raison d'être: the notion that "the present educational system shortchanges girls."[41]

In fact, girls get better grades and are more involved in academic clubs, student government, and every extracurricular activity except sports. On the latest National Assessment of Education Progress tests, high school girls are behind boys by five points in math and eight points in science, but boys lag behind by far larger margins—fifteen points and seventeen points—in reading and writing, respectively. Girls make up close to half of students in math and science magnet schools and are excelling in science fairs and competitions.[42]

In higher education, women now earn 55 percent of all bachelor's and master's degrees. Some of this disparity is due to older women going back to school, but among full-time college students under age twenty-five, 52 percent are women, even though they do not outnumber men in this age group. (Among African-Americans, the female edge has grown large enough to be a cause for concern: almost twice as many black women as black men now receive college degrees.) In 1993, freshman women were more likely than their male peers to plan to seek advanced degrees.[43]

The shortchanged-girls myth was popularized by two sensational reports by the American Association of University Women (AAUW): *Shortchanging Girls, Shortchanging America* (1990), which purported to show a dangerous drop in girls' self-esteem, and *How Schools Shortchange Girls* (1992), a review of research on gender bias in schools.[44] The bulk of this research came from the work of American University professors Myra and David Sadker—work that, as Christina Hoff Sommers showed in *Who Stole Feminism?* she has been unable to find in any peer-reviewed academic journals and contained at least one significant error. (The Sadkers had to issue a semiretraction of their widely reported claim that boys call out answers in the classroom eight times as often as girls, which Sommers traced to their misreading of their own data.)[45]

The Sadkers' principal charge is that boys get more attention from teachers (though they have been fuzzy on the magnitude of the gap). But the extra attention comes almost entirely in the form of scolding, even when boys aren't misbehaving more. Most studies show that boys are not called on more often than girls, and there is no support for the claims of gender-bias mavens that boys are given more time to answer before the teacher moves on or that boys get more feedback.[46]

Indeed, the poll of schoolchildren that the AAUW used as evidence of a self-esteem crisis among adolescent girls (another claim contradicted by virtually all available research) suggested that whatever problems girls may have, bias in school is not one of them. When asked, "Who do teachers think are smarter?" 81 percent of the girls and 69 percent of the boys said "girls." The majority also

believed that teachers paid more attention to girls. Girls were as likely as boys to say that teachers called on them often and listened to
them and that they often spoke in class. Somehow, the AAUW for-
got to publicize those particular findings.[47]

Despite some recognition that the sexism-in-schools story has
another side, critics like Sommers have barely made a dent in the
conventional wisdom. The hand wringing over girls' self-esteem,
spurred on by Mary Pipher's best-seller, *Reviving Ophelia,* with its
chilling portrait of a "girl-poisoning" culture, still gets a platform in
the press and a boost from government initiatives. Feminist legal
scholar Susan Estrich still speaks of the AAUW's shortchanged-girls
reports as "serious, thorough academic studies."[48]

Nor have the media been inoculated against credulity. In 1996,
the American Bar Association issued a report on women in law
schools based on testimony from students and faculty. The report,
Elusive Equality, dwelled on horror stories of sexist behavior while
briefly conceding that most female students viewed their law school
experience as positive. Ample space was given to vague grievances
("we feel we are not welcome") and complaints that should have
cheered a male chauvinist: that the "Socratic method" in which the
professor relentlessly challenges a student's answers "has a much
more traumatizing effect on women," or that the environment is too
competitive. All this bellyaching was widely publicized under such
headlines as "ABA Report Finds Bias Against Women."[49]

Bad Medicine: Anatomy of a Myth

The arrival of Viagra in 1998 quickly sparked a debate about gender
bias, after reports that many insurance companies that had agreed to
pay for the anti-impotence drug (in limited quantities) were not
paying for birth control pills. According to *Washington Post* columnist Judy Mann, the sexist double standard was "absolutely clear and
incontrovertible."Yet aside from whether a drug meant to fix a medical problem is really the same thing as contraception, the whole
controversy may have been about nothing: the *Washington Post*
reported that "more than half" of Viagra prescriptions and "slightly
more than half" of birth control prescriptions were covered by
health plans.[50]

All these passions were fueled in part by the perception that the
"double standard" was just one example of a more pervasive bias.
As one columnist wrote, "Traditionally, the health problems of

women haven't been taken very seriously—by men." It's a belief hardly limited to radical feminists. Around the same time, singer Carly Simon, battling breast cancer, was quoted as saying, "There's the feeling that if this were a man's disease it would have been licked already."[51]

This charge—likely to elicit more intense emotions than sexism on the job or in school—has been made by columnists and editorial writers, TV talk show hosts, women's magazines, politicians in Congress, and public officials including the Health and Human Services secretary, Donna Shalala, and President Clinton. A series on women's health broadcast by ABC in 1994 opened with the declaration that "America's health care system traditionally hasn't treated women equally or fairly," with breast cancer and heart disease cited as examples. According to former congresswoman Patricia Schroeder, "When you have a male-dominated group of researchers, they are more worried about prostate cancer than breast cancer."[52]

It's ironic that Schroeder would choose prostate cancer to make her point. In 1993, Congress appropriated $39 million for prostate cancer, which kills about 34,000 men annually, and over $400 million for breast cancer, which kills 42,000 women.[53]

And this wasn't just an attempt, spurred by rising female influence in politics, to correct past imbalances. Breast cancer activism did not become a political force until 1991; yet from 1981 to 1991, the National Cancer Institute had spent $658 million on breast cancer research and $113 million on prostate cancer. The Medline database has 17,951 English-language entries under "breast cancer" for 1966–1991, compared to 1,784 for prostate cancer (and 8,643 for lung cancer, the leading equal-opportunity killer).[54]

Some of the discrepancy reflects legitimate priorities: fewer years of life are lost to prostate cancer, which kills, on average, ten to fifteen years later than breast cancer. But the same logic justifies the greater attention to heart disease in men, who die of heart attacks three times as often as women before the age of sixty-five; between ages sixty-five and seventy-four, the ratio is two to one. Until the 1980s, writes Dr. Elizabeth Rosenthal, hardening of the arteries was viewed as a normal part of aging, and "large studies concentrated on 'premature' coronary artery disease—which really *is* a man's disease." This perception was changed less by gender politics than by an aging population in which women too were more vulnerable.[55]

"Half of all Americans who die of heart disease are women," an indignant Oprah Winfrey declared in October 1994, when Leslie Laurence and Beth Weinhouse were on her show promoting their book, *Outrageous Practices: The Alarming Truth About How Medicine Mistreats Women.* "But when doctors tested aspirin on heart patients, they tested 22,000 men and not a single woman."[56]

The study of the role of aspirin in heart attack prevention in male doctors (not patients) has become a symbol of male bias in medicine. Yet Dr. Lynn Rosenberg, a Boston University epidemiologist, told me that "in terms of getting an answer relatively fast, it made sense to do the trial the way it was done" and then to decide if a similar study needed to be done in women. Why? When studying heart attack prevention, it makes sense to look at a group in which one can expect a fairly high rate of heart attacks; an equally reliable study in women would require a much larger pool. For the same reason, when a trial testing the benefits of a low-fat diet was conducted as part of a *two-sex* study of cholesterol and heart disease, it was limited to males with high cholesterol in order to reduce the sample to "a feasible level."[57]

The claim that women have been left out of heart disease research is a gross exaggeration. The leading study of cardiovascular health, the Framingham Heart Study, has followed a sample that began with 2,336 men and 2,873 women in 1948. The Nurses' Health Study, launched in 1976 with 100,000 women, has yielded key findings on how women's hearts are affected by smoking, oral contraceptives, hormone therapy—and aspirin. When the early results of the infamous all-male aspirin study were released in 1988, a similar nurses' study (less rigorous, since the nurses recorded their own aspirin intake while the doctors were randomly assigned to a treatment or placebo group, but hardly negligible) had been underway for three years.[58]

Overall, one study found, women have made up about 20 percent of subjects in clinical trials of treatments for coronary heart disease. This number is not as low as it might seem, given the sex ratio among patients under age sixty-five. (Older people of *either* sex are rarely included in drug trials because of frailty and coexisting illnesses.) Nor was a "male model" mindlessly applied to women: sex differences in outcomes of surgery and drug therapy for heart patients were already being studied in the 1970s.[59]

Dr. Marcia Angell, executive editor of the *New England Journal of Medicine,* agrees that there was not enough of an effort to include more women in clinical research in cardiology (though she stresses that many factors other than sexism were responsible). But was the care of female patients compromised as a result?[60]

It is true that women receive aggressive, high-tech tests and treatments such as coronary bypass grafts and angioplasty (opening clogged arteries with a catheter) less often than men. But several studies have found that when women are similar to men in age and condition, they get similar care; if anything, doctors may *overestimate* the chances of a woman having severe heart disease. And some researchers conclude that the real problem is men at low risk being needlessly hospitalized or referred for surgery from which they are unlikely to benefit. Yet even articles acknowledging that "less care" for women doesn't necessarily mean worse care often run under such headlines as, "Studies Say Women Fail to Receive Equal Treatment for Heart Disease."[61]

Of course, doctors and patients should be educated about the fact that heart disease isn't just a man's problem. But this can be accomplished without cries that medical research has been done "largely to the benefit of men only." Vital statistics tell a different story. From 1970 to 1989, death rates from cardiovascular disease dropped by 29 percent for men and 26 percent for women—a slight difference probably due largely to the decreasing gender gaps in smoking and other risky behaviors.[62]

In the early 1990s, there was an outcry over a government report showing that women's health projects accounted for less than 14 percent of National Institutes of Health (NIH) spending in 1987. This figure was cited by congresswomen in the effort to pass legislation requiring more funds for women's medical needs and establishing a federal Office of Women's Health. What was rarely mentioned was that NIH funding for male-specific health projects accounted for just *under 7 percent* of its total expenditures; 80 percent of the money went to study diseases that afflict both sexes.[63]

These diseases have been studied in women as well as men. Nearly 90 percent of research on stroke (which affects men 20 percent more often) has included women, and sex differences have been extensively investigated. The first large trial of treatment for moderate hypertension in the 1960s, conducted in conjunction with the Veterans Administration, was all male. But in 1970, the National Heart, Lung and Blood Institute recommended a study that would "include both sexes [and] all races." Such a study, with 3,600 women and 4,400 men, was conducted between 1973 and 1978.[64]

Women were never left out of cancer research (for example, they outnumbered men by two thousand in a major national study of body iron levels and cancer risk in the early 1970s). One example of "bias" cited by journalists Leslie Laurence and Beth Weinhouse in their book *Outrageous Practices* is that in 1989, women made up 44 percent of subjects in National Cancer Institute studies of colorectal cancer, though "51 percent of colorectal cancers occur in women"; but would a six-point gap strike most people as an outrage?[65]

Even more bizarre is the claim Laurence and Weinhouse make that endometriosis, an inflammation of the uterine lining that can cause sterility, was not even considered real well into the 1980s, since "most doctors assumed women's excruciating pelvic pain was all in their heads." In fact, over four thousand articles on endometriosis appeared in medical journals from 1970 to 1990, and studies of hormonal treatments for this condition go back to the 1970s.[66]

Another women's health crusader, former NIH director Bernadine Healy, told the millions of women who read the *Ladies Home Journal* that "there may be no better example of gender bias in the annals of medicine than the neglect of STDs [sexually transmitted diseases] in women."[67] In fact, a search of the Medline database shows that of the articles on STDs in medical literature between 1966 and 1990, 12 percent dealt only with men and *20 percent* only with women.

Medline also shows that over two-thirds of all studies and trials in that period included both sexes—and of the rest, more than half involved only women. While the female edge is due partly to reproductive research, there have also been more all-female than all-male studies of diabetes, kidney disease, and chemotherapy.

This is not to say that medical research doesn't have blind spots where women are concerned, particularly in areas stereotyped as male. More than 30 percent of studies of alcoholism have been limited to men, while fewer than 6 percent have focused only on women. AIDS, which began as an overwhelmingly male disease and still afflicts many more men, is another area where female-specific problems did not get enough attention for a long time. By the mid-1990s, though, women were *overrepresented* in an NIH-funded AIDS clinical trial: they made up over 30 percent of the subjects, even though they accounted for about 12 percent of AIDS cases.[68]

What about the charge that nearly all drug testing has been done on men? From 1977 to 1993, Food and Drug Administration (FDA) guidelines barred fertile women from the early stages of drug trials, with an exception for life-threatening illnesses. This was actually done in response to women's health concerns, in the wake of publicity over vaginal cancer in women whose mothers had taken DES while pregnant. But women still participated in the later stages of trials: testing for efficacy and side effects and long-term monitoring in larger samples. Indeed, the guidelines required drugs to be studied in the groups that would use them; FDA surveys in 1983 and 1988 found that "both sexes had substantial representation . . . in proportions that usually reflected the prevalence of the disease in the sex and age groups included in the trials." In 1988, the FDA also recommended that results be analyzed by sex, age, and race, though a later review found that this was done in only about half of 1988–1991 trials.[69]

At a 1993 conference, pharmaceutical executive Dr. Janice Bush agreed that detection of sex differences in drug trials was sometimes important, but cautioned against assumptions that bad faith was the only obstacle: trials large enough to obtain valid comparisons would cause research costs to explode. What is needed, most experts agree, is a careful effort to identify the *uncommon* cases where sex differences are "clinically meaningful"—not an across-the-board quota, and surely not panic-mongering about women as "experimental subjects" taking drugs untested in people like themselves.[70]

The case against what feminist wits call "medical mal(e)-practice" includes other offenses, from patronizing treatment to unnecessary surgery. According to *Outrageous Practices,* "20 to 90 percent" of hysterectomies performed in this country are "medically unjustified." Yet as the vagueness of this estimate indicates, there is considerable debate on the issue. (Ironically but perhaps predictably, efforts by managed care health plans to curb hysterectomies have also been denounced as antifemale.) There are far more hysterectomies and cesarian sections in the United States than in Europe, but this difference in medical attitudes is just as stark when men are involved. In a 1993 survey, nearly 80 percent of American urologists but 4 percent of their British colleagues would recommend a radical prostatectomy (which poses far more risks than hysterectomy, including loss of sexual functioning and bladder control) for a man in his sixties with a tumor confined to the gland.[71]

In 1993, a Commonwealth Fund health study based on a survey of twenty-five hundred women and one thousand men emphasized that 25 percent of women and only 12 percent of men said that their doctors "talked down" to them or treated them like a child. But the Commonwealth Fund survey had not asked about patients' current doctors, as the "survey highlights" implied; what the survey asked was whether the respondent had ever been treated that way in her adult life. The highlights and the media coverage also left out an awkward fact: while close to 90 percent of men and women were happy with their regular physicians, *more* women rated their doctor as "excellent" on such items as "really care[s] about you and your health" and "make[s] sure you understand what you've been told about your medical problems."[72]

None of this means that there are no chauvinistic doctors. Yet three-quarters of the women in the Commonwealth Fund survey had *never* felt that a physician treated them with condescension, and only 10 percent thought a doctor had ever treated them differently because of their sex.

Of course, when people are told repeatedly that medicine is infected by gender bias, women's problems will be blamed on sexism. In 1997, a National Cancer Institute report challenging the recommendation of annual mammograms for all women in their forties and advising that women decide for themselves in consultation with their physicians caused an uproar and was the subject of a congressional hearing, partly due to perceptions that the medical uncertainty reflected neglect of women: "If this was a health problem unique to men, would more money have been spent trying to figure out how to detect it and what to do about it?" inquired Dee Dee Myers on CNBC's *Equal Time.* A month later, a parallel dilemma for men—the American College of Physicians' recommendation against routine prostate cancer screening for men over age forty—received no comparable attention.[73]

The notion of antifemale bias in medicine may have helped win more funding for women's health, sometimes at men's expense; but in the end, it may not be so good for women. The rhetoric about "male medicine" may drive some to avoid a politically incorrect but medically beneficial hysterectomy or "medicalized" childbirth.[74] The gender-bias myth may promote bad science. (In 1993, serious questions raised by a National Academy of Sciences committee about the design and costs of the Women's Health Initiative, a massive clinical trial launched by the NIH under Bernadine Healy, were ignored after Healy and Representative Patricia Schroeder accused the four-man, seven-woman panel of trying to "cut corners" on women.)[75] And inevitably, it promotes bad politics: gender antagonism implicit in the charge that men don't care about women's health, paternalism implicit in the notion that women's health problems deserve special attention.

"The Beleaguered Sex"

On many measures, women in America are at a disadvantage compared to men. Awareness of this situation has led to important efforts to promote equity, from corporate initiatives to link young women with mentors to school projects encouraging girls' interest in math and science. The problem is that male disadvantages (such as the problems boys have in schools) are ignored, and real or imagined biases women face are magnified into the general claim that American women remain, as politician-turned-talk-show-host Geraldine Ferraro put it, "the beleaguered sex."[76]

With this mindset, antifemale biases are seen everywhere. Let a journalist note that Hillary Clinton has alienated many people by not showing the humility expected of leaders, and immediately an irate letter writer makes the amazing claim that no one has ever reproached House Speaker Newt Gingrich for lack of humility. Let a TV comedy series, *Ally McBeal,* portray a heroine who is bright, spunky and successful but emotionally confused and prone to comical blunders, and it is blasted for sexism—even though the male characters on the show aren't any less neurotic or more mature.[77]

This may not be very helpful for individual women. (In a survey at Harvard Law School, women who shared radical feminist politics and were keenly sensitive to real or perceived sexism were far more likely than women with "individualistic" career goals to report a drop in self-confidence.) But in the view of some feminists, such attitudes help keep the movement alive. In *Speaking of Sex,* Stanford law professor Deborah Rhode frankly acknowledges the stake feminists have in persuading people that women in our culture still suffer inequities that "no just society could tolerate": the more people believe that the "woman problem" has been largely solved, the less they will support feminist political causes. Rhode even concludes that, "ironically enough, [women's] progress has created its own obstacles to further change."[78]

Radical feminists are known for melodramatic exaggerations. An author in the journal *Gender and Society* notes the role of the witch-hunts in seventeenth-century Europe in silencing and repressing women, then cites *Backlash* as evidence of "how women are confronting this today."[79] But only slightly less outrageous comparisons are made outside the academic fringe. *New York Times* columnist Frank Rich compared the lie told by bomber pilot Lieutenant Kelly Flinn to cover up her affair with an enlisted woman's husband to the lie told by Nora in *A Doll's House* (then playing on Broadway) to secure a loan she couldn't get without a male co-signer.[80]

The mainstream media do not typically liken the condition of modern women with that of accused witches or Victorian-era wives. Still, the penchant for painting a bleak picture of women's lot manifests itself in many ways, including lack of skepticism toward general claims of sexism as well as individual "oppression stories" like Kelly Flinn's (whose threatened court-martial was decried as an example of a double standard, despite evidence that women were court-martialed for adultery in numbers *below* their proportion of military personnel). Sometimes, even female miseries that ostensibly have nothing to do with politics are exaggerated. In 1998, when the *New York Times* reported that cancer cases and cancer deaths in the United States were dropping, the subtitle of the front-page story said that "minorities and women are still particularly at risk." But the article itself belied this assertion: while cancer rates had decreased for men more than for women, women's rates were still lower than men's.[81]

And yet charges of discrimination at work or in school, or even of bias in medicine, are not the heart of the modern-day feminist indictment of the patriarchy. These complex, often prosaic issues are displaced by far more inflammatory ones: physical and sexual violence inflicted on women by men. To show that, in the words of Andrea Dworkin, "we are in a situation of emergency," it is not enough to argue that women are second-class citizens. One must declare, as Dworkin does, that when one looks at the everyday lives of women and girls in our culture, "one is looking at atrocity"—that "the war against women is a real war."[82]

PART TWO

Innocent Women and Bad Men

CHAPTER FOUR

The Myth of Gender Violence

We live, I am trying to say, in an epidemic of male violence against
women.   —Katha Pollitt, "Violence in a Man's World."[1]

In April 1994, Wall Street executive Sarah Auerbach
was shot to death by her ex-boyfriend Rick Varela in a
dry cleaning store. The murder, followed by Varela's suicide, dominated the New York papers for days. There were moving tributes to the
young businesswoman and reports on the "all-too-common pattern"
of violent obsession. The police commissioner discussed strategies to
ensure protection for victims of domestic violence.[2]

A few months earlier in Queens, New York, supermarket deliv-
eryman Michael Gronenthal was ambushed outside his home and
shot dead by a former girlfriend, who then killed herself. A neighbor
said that she had been "bothering" Gronenthal ever since their
breakup. The event was covered in one brief story in the *New York
Post,* with no comments from the police commissioner.[3]

Partly, the class angle accounts for the difference. Yet the gender
factor also made the death of Sarah Auerbach a microcosm of female
victimization. Someone left flowers near the store where she died,
with a note: "Sarah—God bless you and all the other women who
have been murdered."[4] One can hardly imagine such a shrine to
Gronenthal.

In feminist usage, "violence against women" is not just any crime
whose victim happens to be female. The fatal shooting of two girls
by their mother—which merited a brief item in the *Boston Globe,*

on a page that prominently featured a report on a picket of an X-rated video store protesting "violence against women"—doesn't qualify. The phrase implies systematic terrorism "perpetrated by the gender class men on the gender class women," as Andrea Dworkin put it with her usual elegance.[5]

In *Speaking of Sex,* hailed by the *New York Times Book Review* as a "balanced, sobering and sober book," Stanford law professor Deborah Rhode writes: "We fail to see sexual abuse as a strategy of dominance, exclusion, control, and retaliation—as a way to keep women in their place and out of men's." Testifying before Congress, former NOW Legal Defense Fund director Helen Neuborne asserted that women and girls who are raped or battered are victims of "systematic crime of bias against women."[6] In 1994, Congress institutionalized this view in the Violence Against Women Act (VAWA), which contains a provision allowing victims of sexual and domestic violence to sue their alleged assailants in federal courts, not for personal injury but for violating their civil rights on the basis of gender.

Nor have the media been immune to this view. Newspapers and magazines, including the *Ladies Home Journal,* have run articles and columns about gender-based "hate crimes" and "terrorism" and about "the war against women." Even the 1998 tragedy in Jonesboro, Arkansas, in which two boys opened fire on their classmates, killing four girls and a female teacher, elicited some commentary about "boys who are being trained by their parents, other adults, and our culture and media to harass, assault, rape, and murder girls" (never mind that violence by male juveniles is directed primarily at other boys). When violence is not placed in an explicit political context, it is still often framed in terms of collective male brutality: "The greatest public health threat for many American women is the men they live with" (Anna Quindlen); "Beating up women in the friendly arena called home is a favorite sport of many men" (*New York Times* columnist Bob Herbert).[7]

In April 1996, *New York* magazine offered a sampling of recent tales of mayhem in a column titled, tongue only slightly in cheek, "The Beast: Is Manhood the Root of All Evil?"[8] Yet around that time, there were plenty of brutal acts by women in the news. Children were thrown out of windows and beaten to death. In the New York area, a college student tried to arrange a hit on her boyfriend's infant daughter, and a woman was held in the gruesome axe murder of her estranged husband. In Connecticut, Janet Griffin was convicted of savagely killing her female ex-lover's new girl-friend and the victim's nephew, who had the bad luck of being on the scene.[9]

The Invisible Victims

No one would dispute that while women are *capable* of horrific crimes, men commit such crimes more often. What is truly bizarre about the feminist concept of "violence against women" is the implication that women are the primary victims. Commenting on women and depression, *Washington Post* columnist Judy Mann reasoned that obviously, "a class of people . . . beaten up at home and raped almost routinely on college campuses are going to suffer much more from depression than people who aren't victimized."[10]

The authors of a book called *Femicide* pause to clarify that they "do not claim that women are murdered more frequently than men," and even cite numbers showing that they are murdered about three times less frequently—but wriggle out by reasoning that "men are rarely murdered simply because they are men."[11]

Leaving aside the question of whether motive matters to the one who is being murdered, what does it mean that women are killed "because they are women"? Killers who target women the way a racist targets blacks—like Marc Lepine, who shot fourteen female engineering students at the University of Montreal yelling curses at "feminists"—can be counted on the fingers of one hand. Some feminists see serial killers like Ted Bundy as "gynocidal" gender terrorists. But how, then, does one explain Jeffrey Dahmer, John Wayne Gacy, and other predators whose victims were male, or child killers who do not discriminate by sex?[12]

In fact, men are much more likely than women to be victims of every violent crime except rape. In some sense, of course, women are raped "because they are women." But does that make it a bias crime, as many feminists assert—the sexual equivalent of lynching? Rape may be a crime of violence more than lust, but the violence is channeled into what is indisputably a sexual act. When a man's sexual impulses are directed toward women, chances are that his sexual aggression will be too. Gay men are at least as likely to be raped by their dates as heterosexual women. Studies also show that 6 to 10 percent of sexual assaults involve male victims—not even counting assaults on boys or prison rape. One civil rights lawsuit filed under VAWA involved a woman alleging sexual abuse by a priest—acts that, an appellate court held, "may reasonably be inferred to be intended . . . to relegate another to an inferior status" and thus to be motivated by gender bias. Yet surely, if there is one type of sex crime that affects plenty of male victims, it's sexual abuse by clerics.[13]

Nor does research support the notion that rape is usually motivated by misogyny. Psychologists who study sex offenders identify several types, of which the woman-hating "anger rapist" is just one. Many are after sexual gratification; others are driven by anger at the whole world, and are also prone to violence against other men. Indeed, rapists as a group seem no more hostile to women than other criminals; as personality types, they are most similar to murderers, whose victims are mostly male.[14]

The paradox of crime and gender is that while men are much more likely to be victims of violent crime, women are more afraid. Fewer than one in four men but close to 60 percent of women say that they would be afraid to walk alone late at night in their neighborhood. This sense of vulnerability stems in part from women's lesser physical strength—something shared by the elderly, whose fear of crime also exceeds the actual risk. It also has to do with fear of rape (which hardly proves that rape is "gender terrorism"). But the lives of men and women are closely intertwined; men fear less for their personal safety but show more "altruistic fear" for others, primarily spouses and children.[15]

In the gender-war worldview, keeping women in fear is a collective male enterprise in which concerned husbands and dads have a stake: "The man who does not want his wife, sister, or daughter to go out alone because he fears for her safety may benefit from the limits on her activities"—presumably because she'll stay home and cook.[16] Actually, it's more likely that he will have to pick her up when she stays out late, and I doubt that his typical reaction is, "Good. Now I can make sure she doesn't meet any men!" The unwritten rule that men will serve as bodyguards for female family members and friends may be seen as fostering feminine dependence and masculine pride, but it can also be a serious burden to men, often requiring them to risk their own safety.

Of course, brutal crimes *are* committed daily against women and girls; they inspire such horror that when someone blames misogyny, it seems heartless to quibble. Yet the perpetrators often place little value on life regardless of sex. The teenagers involved in the rape and brutal beating of a Central Park jogger in 1989—characterized by women's groups, Anna Quindlen, and *Glamour* magazine as an antifemale hate crime—also attacked men on their "wilding" rampage. "Wilding," one boy told a detective, meant "going around, punching, hitting on people." *People,* not just women.[17]

The limitations of the focus on "gender-based" violence are evident in the response to the abuse of two of the first four female cadets at the Citadel by male upperclassmen. The incidents, in which the women reportedly had their shirts set on fire and were forced to drink tea until they became ill, were widely portrayed as sexist harassment and investigated as possible civil rights violations. A *New York Times* editorial conceded that "male freshmen were made to suffer many of the same humiliations" but vaguely asserted that the women had it worse, and upbraided the Citadel for its lack of commitment to gender integration. Eventually the school expelled one male cadet and punished nine others.[18]

Yet a 1992 *Sports Illustrated* story about hazing at the then all-male Citadel makes the women's ordeal sound like a picnic. One cadet was forced to hang from a closet shelf by his fingers with a saber pointed at his scrotum; others told of having their heads dunked in a sink until they passed out. All this went unpunished.[19]

Indeed, it is arguably violence against men that is often treated callously. In wars, atrocities against "women and children" are viewed with a special horror. Reports of the sexual abuse of women in prison by male guards have prompted more concern and calls for action than the far more widespread and more brutal sexual assaults on male prisoners. Consciously or not, both sexes tend to see a crime as worse when the victim is female.[20] In large part, such attitudes are rooted in old-fashioned chivalry. This double standard, however, has been reinforced rather than challenged by feminism—at least the kind that sees "gender violence" as central to female subordination.

It's not just feminists who downplay violence done to men. In 1993, the *New York Times* ran a story titled "High Murder Rate for Women on the Job," with the subtitle, "40% of Women Killed at Work Are Murdered, But Figure for Men Is Only 15%." But the Labor Department data cited in the article showed something else as well. Of 6,083 workplace fatalities in 1992, 93 percent were male; 848 men and 170 women were murdered. Indeed, there were almost *twice* as many men murdered at work as there were women who died *from all causes combined*.[21] Why not "High Death Rate for Men on the Job"?

When some male students in Professor Magda Lewis's feminist theory class at Queen's University in Ontario brought up "notions of violence as a *human* and not a gendered problem," the professor was so appalled by this heresy that in her essay on feminist teaching, she classified it as subtle violence against women.[22]

But is violence truly "gendered"? Although female crime has increased in the past two decades, women still account for no more than 15 percent of violent crime arrests, up from 10 percent in the 1970s. And yet with aggression, as with so much else, there is no clear line separating the sexes—as we should know in a century that has seen female concentration camp guards, terrorists, and guerrilla fighters.[23]

Women in the United States are more homicidal than men in Japan. According to federal statistics, more American women are attacked by other women than by husbands or ex-husbands. In New York City, black women are arrested for assault and robbery at higher rates than white men, and for homicide at rates nearly as high. (I mention this not to generalize about racial characteristics, but to point out that gender must be considered in the context of socioeconomic status and cultural environment.) Many feminists prefer to see female criminals as victims of abusive men, but there is ample evidence that women resort to violence for the same reasons as men, including economic gain, adventure seeking, and injured pride. Aside from sensationalism about "girls in the gang," the kind of violence once considered the province of young males has become more common among females. In the fall of 1997, New York was jolted by a rash of gang-related slashings and stabbings by teenage girls quarreling over boys, over turf, over perceived insults.[24]

The sexes may be even more similar when it comes to violence that rarely makes the crime statistics. In one large survey, 15 percent of men admitted resorting to violence the last time they were angry with a man, while 3 percent reported assaulting a woman; 7 percent of the women had been violent toward a man and 5 percent toward a woman.[25]

Inasmuch as one can speak of "male violence," it is hardly in the male-versus-female sense imagined by Professor Lewis: its targets are mostly male, particularly when victim and offender are strangers or nonintimate acquaintances. Consequently, feminist theories of "gender violence" tend to focus on violence in the family and in close relationships, which is indeed far more likely to involve women as victims—but also to involve women as aggressors.

Maybe, suggests Israeli criminologist Sarah Ben-David, women's identity is still more tied to the domestic sphere, and so are the passions that lead to violence. But the nature of public and private violence may play a role too. Some research suggests that women may be as aggressive as men when there are no witnesses and responsibility for the violence is diffused, which rather accurately describes the conditions of violence in the home.[26]

Woman Battering . . . or Domestic Violence?

We have heard the appalling statistics. Every fifteen (or twelve or nine) seconds, a woman in the United States is beaten by her husband or boyfriend; two (or four, or six) million are battered every year; one in three (or one in two) will be assaulted by a partner in her lifetime. If women were attacking men in such numbers, NOW president Patricia Ireland told the faithful at the organization's 1993 convention, there would be a national alarm: "Church groups would mobilize . . . reports would come out, asking 'What do these women want?'"[27]

And yet the first major study of domestic violence, the 1975 National Family Violence Survey, concluded that by both men's and women's reports, women hit their mates as often as did men. Half of the violence was reciprocal, with the rest almost evenly split between male-only and female-only violence. Similar surveys in 1985 and 1992, the same ones that have given us the figures of two million women battered every year, found just as many men assaulted by wives and girlfriends.[28]

Confronted with these figures, women's advocates typically cry "backlash." The numbers, they say, come from a few discredited studies that lump self-defense together with aggression: in reality, 95 percent of the victims are women.[29]

True, the 1975 survey asked only who hit whom, not who hit first or why. The researchers, Murray Straus and Richard Gelles, were themselves inclined to think that female violence was mostly defensive, which still couldn't account for wives who attacked nonviolent husbands. But in 1985, mutually violent partners were asked who initiated the physical conflict in the latest fight. (Contrary to charges that the survey equates "starting an argument with throwing the first punch," the interviewers were given special instructions to avoid this misunderstanding.) By both spouses' reports, it was the woman about half the time.[30]

Far from being "discredited," these findings have been replicated by a growing volume of research on marital and dating violence. In 1997, California State University psychologist Martin Fiebert compiled a bibliography of seventy such studies.[31]

The "it's always the man's fault" school counters that female-initiated violence can still be in self-defense. Maybe, having been battered before, the woman sees the warning signs and hits first, to deter the abuser or just to end the tension of waiting. One study classifies a violent woman as a victim if her partner was the first ever to use violence in the relationship, even if she was usually the aggressor later on—*or if she was the initial aggressor but he used violence more often.* (Heads she wins, tails he loses.) Some say that even if she reports being the *sole* aggressor, it may be because she succeeded in keeping the man from assaulting her.[32]

Applying a "gender-sensitive assessment" to couples in marital therapy, State University of New York psychologist Dina Vivian concluded that while low-level violence such as pushing and slapping was mostly mutual, men were the primary aggressors in 75 percent of couples involved in more severe abuse. Assuming that "gender sensitive" doesn't mean "female biased," this still means that one in four battered spouses are men. (Some of Vivian's other research shows more parity in spousal violence. In her 1995 study of couples in marital counseling, wives reported using serious force almost twice as often as husbands, and just 20 percent said that it was in self-defense.) A major recent survey cosponsored by the Centers for Disease Control, in which questions about domestic assault were framed in terms of concerns for personal safety, also found a three-to-one ratio of female to male victims. This is not "symmetry," but it's very different from the picture we usually get.[33]

Then what about the statistic that 95 percent of domestic violence is male-on-female? This figure comes from the Justice Department's 1972–1992 National Crime Victimization Surveys (NCVS), in which people were not specifically asked about domestic violence but about being attacked by anyone. These surveys also found relatively few domestic assaults on women (about half a million a year), and women's advocates charged that much domestic abuse was being missed because women didn't think of it as a crime. Of course, that goes doubly for male victims.[34]

In response to these complaints, the NCVS was redesigned to

include direct questions about assaults by intimates. While this boosted women's reports of victimization by 70 percent, men's reports *tripled:* in the new survey, men were the victims in 15 percent of all assaults by current or former partners and *25 percent* of aggravated assaults. Twenty percent of assaults on women but 40 percent of those on men qualified as aggravated—probably not because women use so much more extreme violence when they attack men but because even with prodding, men are less likely to disclose minor violence in the context of an interview about crime.[35]

The new Justice Department figures still show a far smaller proportion of male victims of abuse than the Straus-Gelles family violence surveys, which focus on specific acts (being punched, kicked, hit with an object). But they also still show far fewer male assaults on women than four or even two million a year. Battered women's advocacy groups nimbly switch back and forth between different sets of data: one to show that abuse is epidemic, another to show that nearly all the victims are women. Feminist sociologist Mildred Pagelow, a rigorous skeptic about "husband-beating" statistics, cites studies claiming that 21 to 35 percent of wives suffer "repeated beatings" and calls these numbers a "conservative estimate"![36]

Feminists who dismiss battering by women as a figment of the antifeminist imagination point out that there has been no study of an actual sample of male victims. Actually, that's no longer true. Canadian researcher Lesley Gregorash interviewed battered husbands for her 1993 master's thesis, and in the United States, journalist Philip Cook spoke to about a hundred subjects for his 1997 book, *Abused Men.* California psychologist Janet Johnston's studies of violence during divorce and separation included unilaterally abusive wives as well as mutually combative couples.[37]

The work of sociologists Anson Shupe and William Stacey and counselor Lonnie Hazlewood, coauthors of three books on domestic violence, who discovered violent women while studying violent men, also includes extensive material on violence by women, based on police records and observations in counseling programs. Much of the abuse was mutual, but women were the sole perpetrators in as many as one in three cases. The victims ranged from a meek professor whose wife monitored all his movements and once went after him with a spiked-heel shoe to an unemployed man whose companion knocked him around for "not trying hard enough to find a job."[38]

If there haven't been more studies of the "other side" of domestic violence, it may be because such research has its perils. "You end up being accused of supporting men's violence just because you talk about women's violence or take it seriously," says Lonnie Hazlewood. In the 1980s, when he headed the Austin, Texas, Family Violence Diversion Network (FVDN), which directs men arrested for domestic assault into counseling, Hazlewood wanted to present a paper on the men's reports of violence by their partners at the conference of the Texas Council on Family Violence. Hazlewood (who later resigned from the FVDN and now runs the Austin Stress Clinic) says that it was rejected and that he was ostracized by the advocacy community.[39]

His story is hardly the worst. The first scholars to raise the issue of female violence in the late 1970s—sociologists Murray Straus of the University of New Hampshire and Suzanne Steinmetz, now at Indiana University/Purdue University—became targets of vicious harassment, including nasty rumors, heckling, and at least one bomb threat. Ten years later, the tactics had become more civilized. R. L. McNeely, a professor of social welfare at the University of Wisconsin who published an article challenging the one-sided view of domestic abuse received letters by members of local advocacy groups threatening only to have his (nonexistent) federal research grants blocked.[40]

Intimidation aside, scholarship on family violence is often influenced by ideological commitments. University of Pittsburgh psychologist Irene Frieze, a prominent feminist expert on violence against women, suppressed her findings on dating violence for years because they indicated that women were the aggressors more often. (When the university finally publicized the data, NOW quickly denounced it as fraudulent.) When I called psychologist Janet Johnston to clarify some points about female aggression in her study of divorcing couples, she snapped nervously, "I don't wish to be quoted in any context of saying that women are violent in the family. It's divisive, it would be pitting me against the women's movement and I don't want that."[41]

"We cannot be co-opted into believing that women use violence the way men use violence, to control and dominate," writes Lynda Carson, program director of the New Jersey Coalition for Battered Women (who also admits that when she first heard talk of female batterers, she "didn't want to deal with the issue at all"). Yet several studies in which men and women were specifically asked about their reasons for violence toward their partners found that the motives were quite similar—primarily anger and coercion.[42]

Although the motives are similar, the outcomes may not be. "Women are physically weaker, so they can't do much harm," feminist author Wendy Kaminer told me, adding, "To say that women physically abuse men anywhere near as much as men abuse women is like saying the moon is made out of green cheese."[43]

Just how much greater is the danger to women in domestic warfare? In the 1985 National Family Violence Survey, women were six times more likely than men to seek medical care due to a marital fight; in other studies, the ratio is between four to one and two to one. According to a 1997 Justice Department report, about 200,000 women and nearly 40,000 men a year are treated at hospital emergency rooms for injuries at the hands of current or former partners. Men thus account for at least 16 percent of domestic violence victims seen in emergency rooms—or more, since a third of men with violence-related injuries (compared to one in five women) did not identify their assailants. Considering how embarrassing and even freakish it seems to be a battered man, male victims may also be more likely to blame the injury on a mugging or an accident.[44]

Clearly men's general physical advantage hardly makes them invulnerable. (Feminist literature on lesbian battering cautions against assuming that the abuser is the larger woman.) Reena Sommer, a Canadian psychologist who wrote a doctoral thesis on spousal abuse, points out that "women compensate by using weapons or sneaking up on a man when he least expects it." In Janet Johnston's study of violence in divorcing couples, more wives reported bruises, but more husbands had sustained cuts. Boiling water and other scalding liquids, often aimed at the face or genitals, seem to be another female weapon of choice in domestic quarrels.[45]

Men may also be disabled by the deeply ingrained belief that a man should never hit a woman, not even if she is violent. As a teacher reports telling his students when some of them argued that O. J. Simpson wasn't wrong to hit Nicole if she hit him first, "If a woman hits a man, he should at the most gently restrain her."[46]

And if gentle restraint is not enough? In 1996 in Philadelphia, Sherry Barker went on a drug-induced rampage with a paring knife, repeatedly stabbing her boyfriend, Fred Hill, killing their infant son, and then wounding herself. Hill, a large man who worked as a prison guard, never struck back—not when Barker woke him by pummeling him with her fists, and not when she cut him on the neck. "I tried to push her off, that's all," he told reporters. "I kept saying, 'Sherry, stop, stop.'" Bleeding profusely, he was able to stumble out of the house and hide.[47]

It is also worth noting that some studies looking at the psychological harm of spousal violence, such as stress and depression, find that men are affected almost as badly as women. Even the claim that "women live in fear of men and men do not live in fear of women," plausible at first glance, doesn't hold up. The one study to back this view was based on a sample in which *all* the husbands were violent but half of the wives were not—and variation within each sex was so high that over 40 percent of spouses with elevated levels of fear were men. Janet Johnston, on the other hand, found that wives in mutually abusive couples were "assertive, feisty, and quick to respond to a perceived confrontation with a counterattack," while nonviolent abused husbands were often quite terrified of their wives' rages—and with good reason: several of the women had threatened their spouses with guns or rammed their cars.[48]

Some men may find it funny when the "little woman" lashes out. Many deny or downplay their fear. "She can't hurt me—I'm six foot four," said one man when I asked if he had been afraid of his ex-girlfriend, who not only slapped him around but once walked behind him poking him in the back with a big knife. It's not manly to be scared of a woman. And yet in a 1992 survey, 14 percent of men in violent marriages, compared to 30 percent of the women—a smaller difference than one might expect—said that they had felt in danger in a marital fight in the past year.[49] (Of course, when it comes to male violence toward women, feminists never pause to say that it isn't really battering if the woman isn't afraid of the man.)

Fear is not instilled by physical force alone. Mildred Pagelow, the sociologist who specializes in belittling the issue of female violence toward men, admits that a weaker person can terrorize a stronger one—when the weaker person is an infirm *man:* "The psychological abuse," she writes, "apparently made [women] so fearful . . . that they failed to see the relative physical weakness of their abusers."[50]

But surely women too engage in psychological terrorism—sometimes using the courts as a weapon. That's what happened to Dan, a California computer engineer whose glamorous girlfriend turned vicious when he refused to co-sign an application for a loan she couldn't get because of bad credit. She scratched his face and kept him awake at night, yelling and berating him. The woman was no match for him physically, but when he pushed her away, scraping her elbow, he ended up in jail. When he came back, she greeted him with the words, "See what you get when you fuck with me?" and threatened to have him arrested again. "I just broke down and cried," says Don, who had to ask his mother to stay with him for protection. He was finally able to get the woman out of his life after she was jailed for passing bad checks—and after he overcame his embarrassment and got a restraining order.[51]

Indeed, one paradox of the feminist orthodoxy on domestic violence is that for female victims, its definition of battering does not require physical assault. This is true not only of tracts like Lenore Walker's *The Battered Woman* ("A battered woman is a woman who is repeatedly subjected to any forceful physical or psychological behavior by a man in order to coerce her to do something") but of publications by shelters and agencies serving battered women. These pamphlets often stress that "you do not have to be hit to be abused" and lists such forms of abuse as "humiliating you with sexual taunts," "criticizing you for small things," "making you feel bad about yourself," "threatening to leave you," even "denying you sex." Government agencies, too, seem increasingly willing to accept these definitions. "Verbal degradation" as a category of abuse is included in official domestic violence intervention protocols and materials for victims. A poster I saw on the New York subway in 1998 urged women suffering "emotional abuse"—illustrated by remarks like "You're fat," "Why weren't you home last night?" or "Stupid"—to call the city's domestic violence hot line. Yet surely all these are ways in which women can torment their mates at least as effectively as men can.[52]

Some feminists claim that only male batterers erupt in extreme violence if their victim tries to walk away. Tell that to Brian Lee McCue, the Pittsburgh man whose allegedly abusive wife JoAnn was arrested on charges that she slit his throat with a kitchen knife— luckily missing the major arteries—when he went to sleep after telling her he wanted out of the marriage.[53]

Domestic violence rarely culminates in murder. About thirteen hundred women a year—6 percent of all homicide victims in this country—are killed by their husbands or boyfriends (though battered women's advocates sometimes arbitrarily inflate the figure to four thousand). About six hundred men are killed by their wives or girlfriends, excluding homicides ruled negligent or justified.[54]

In feminist lingo, "women who kill" has only one meaning: women who lash out after years of abuse, fearing for their lives. No doubt this is true of some women. But blanket statements like feminist psychologist Lenore Walker's assertion that "women don't kill men unless they've been pushed to a point of desperation" make little sense. Criminologist Coramae Richey Mann, for one, has concluded that most female perpetrators of domestic homicide are not victims but "the victors in a domestic fight."[55]

Sometimes the man's death is clearly the climax of escalating violence by the woman. Such was the case with Tommy Overstreet, a Long Island, New York, delicatessen clerk whose life ended in 1997 at the age of twenty-two. Tommy and his wife, Yliana, who had married and had a child as teenagers, had a stormy relationship; she was always accusing him of staying out late (he worked twelve-hour days) and running around. They had separated but then reconciled, and Tommy dropped the restraining order he had obtained after she slashed his arm. Their final argument ended with her plunging a knife in his chest and blocking his escape. Tommy managed to run for the door when Yliana grabbed another knife and stabbed him in the back.[56]

The best evidence against the cliché that "women who kill" are primarily victims comes from some poster children of the movement for clemency for battered women convicted of killing their husbands or boyfriends. After Ohio governor Richard Celeste commuted the sentences of twenty-five such women in December 1990, an investigation by the *Columbus Dispatch* found that fifteen had not mentioned any abuse at the time of arrest or trial, and several had explicitly said that they weren't battered. After shooting her lover, Troy Wattleton, Linda Cooper (who had an earlier assault conviction for stabbing her first husband) told the police, "Troy never hits me. Troy will walk away from me." Even some women who *had* been beaten struck out when the man was leaving them (not quite the same as killing an abuser because you see no other way out). Indeed, quite a few of the Ohio Twenty-Five seem to have been driven by the "masculine" motives of jealousy and sexual possessiveness. Marilyn Frederick, who was separated from her husband, Harry, went to his girlfriend's home and attacked them both. As Harry escorted her out, she drew a gun and shot him. Asya Cole, who claimed that her boyfriend was killed in a struggle over a gun he had held to her head, had been publicly threatening to shoot him because of his womanizing ways. Having made good on her promise, she called his latest paramour and said, "You're next."[57]

In the media, the topic of female violence in the home crops up once in a while, in an opinion column or on a TV talk show. But serious coverage of domestic violence focuses almost exclusively on men assaulting women—with a lot of credence given to such dubious claims as, "Domestic violence is the leading cause of injury to women, exceeding car accidents, rapes and muggings combined."[58]

Male victims, when acknowledged at all, are dispatched in one line saying that "95 percent of abuse victims are women." As Phil Cook points out in his book *Abused Men,* coverage of female violence toward men is often not placed in the context of "domestic violence"—except when it is alleged that the man abused the woman.[59]

In June 1994, after O. J. Simpson was arrested on charges of murdering his ex-wife and her friend, the Portland *Oregonian* ran a long story about crimes of passion. Much of it focused on a man who shot and wounded his wife, while the case of a woman who shot her husband was accorded two short paragraphs—and the rather striking disparity in their sentences—nine years for him and two for her—was left without comment. Four years later, when Phil Hartman, the popular comedian, was fatally shot in his sleep by his wife Brynn (who then committed suicide), news stories talked about her "emotional demons," particularly her battles with drugs and alcohol. Friends were quoted as saying that "she had trouble controlling her anger" and that Hartman had to "restrain her at times." But the words "domestic violence" or "battering" never appeared. Had the roles been reversed, feminists would have cited this as one more example of how the media ignore and trivialize the abuse of women by reducing it to domestic "turmoil."[60]

Even articles about the rise in the numbers of women arrested for domestic violence due to tougher laws (women now account for 15 to 20 percent of such arrests in some jurisdictions, up from 5 to 10 percent in the 1970s) often emphasize women as victims: abused women jailed for striking back, wicked men concocting false charges to torment their wives or gain advantage in a divorce.[61]

To some extent, this reflects not only political ideology but more visceral attitudes. "Leave the studies aside for a second," *Crossfire* co-host Michael Kinsley archly implored columnist John Leo, who argued that the public was getting a distorted view of domestic violence. "Just from looking around you . . . what you know about your friends . . . doesn't it seem inherently implausible to you that women are as violent as men?"[62]

Of course, from looking around him, Kinsley probably doesn't know many women who are beaten by men. He might also know more than he thinks about men who are beaten by women. He may well have heard about the hijinks of *Beverly Hills 90210* vixen Shannen Doherty, whose ex-boyfriend sought an order of protection after she allegedly threatened him with a gun and tried to run him down with her car. He just never thought of it as "domestic violence"—much as a policeman, shocked to learn that a violent woman was charged with killing her husband hours later, explained that he had never thought women were capable of real violence, having never seen anything more serious than his mother breaking an ashtray over his father's head.[63]

Once you became aware of the issue, it's like the feminist "click." You notice when, in a *Ladies Home Journal* "Can This Marriage Be Saved" feature titled "He Hit Me," the wife admits that there has been "pushing and slapping—on both sides." You notice when, in a TV program on domestic violence, the background report shows a policeman saying that it is not unusual for the woman to be the aggressor, but the panel discussion is only about men abusing women. You notice that Maria Montalvo, the nurse who drove to her in-laws' house where her husband had gone after a fight and torched her car with their two children inside, had a history of assaulting her husband—though the issue of spousal abuse was, once again, ignored in the coverage of her trial.[64]

Some people who have no political predisposition to the idea of men as victims of battering have discovered it almost in spite of themselves. Lisa LeBelle, a health education teacher in New Jersey who has thoroughly assimilated the feminist jargon of "gender violence," concedes that the "other side" has been brought up by her seventh- and eighth-grade students in class discussions:

> They say, "How come everything says 'He against her, he against her?'" I've had students tell me that they had witnessed their mothers physically and verbally abusing their fathers. There was one girl whose mother had slammed a car door on her dad's hand.[65]

For Pat, a social worker and a battered women's advocate since the late 1980s, the discovery was much more personal. Pat freely admits that she once scoffed at the notion of men being battered by women: "I was one to say, Come on now, this is ridiculous, they're just trying to manipulate the system." And then, she says, "it happened to my brother." She had known that her brother was in a bad marriage, but had no idea how bad until he was going through a messy divorce and she offered him her assistance. "I reviewed his case files, and I sat back and said, 'Wow.' It was a clearcut domestic violence case. She had hit him with a car. She had stabbed him with a fork five times. She had attacked him in the shower. When it hits close to home and you know the person's character, you understand."[66]

Excuses and Double Standards

> Women have reached a dangerous crossroads. On the one hand, we are discovering our capacity for explicit masculine-style aggression. On the other hand, even as we commit traditionally male acts of violence, a chorus of voices rises to proclaim our innocence.
>
> —Patricia Pearson, *When She Was Bad*[67]

The physical differences between the sexes are a good reason for making some distinction between a man slapping a woman and a woman slapping a man. But when the damage is equal, a double standard persists. In *Four Weddings and a Funeral,* the hero's jilted bride knocks him out and gives him a black eye—and it's supposed to be funny. In real life, when a softball umpire wrote to Dear Abby that he was being teased as a wimp after a female player hit him and broke his nose, Abby complimented him for not hitting back and added that the "Amazon" should be "traded to the Giants," without a word of condemnation.[68]

This is one double standard most feminists are happy to perpetuate. Interestingly, they often downplay differences in physical strength, instead emphasizing "unequal power relationships" (though surely the balance of power in any male-female relationship, at least in modern Western societies, is a complicated matter). Since women have less power than men, "it does not make sense to view their use of violence as abuse of power," assert authors Kevin Hamberger and Theresa Potente.[69]

If female powerlessness is a given, even unprovoked female violence becomes less reprehensible. So if "there is no excuse for domestic violence" for men, just about any excuse will do for women. Some advocates, including Lenore Walker, whose book *The Battered Woman* is a bible of the battered women's movement, suggest that some female assaults on men may be justified by men's verbal abuse or emotional neglect—echoing the batterer's classic "she provoked me" excuse.[70]

In New Jersey in 1994, two staffers of the Jersey Battered Women's Service wrote to the divorce attorney of a woman who had been arrested for assaulting her husband, to confirm that she had been abused by him. Aside from alleging that he had grabbed and pushed her three years earlier, the letter stressed "emotional abuse." For example, when the wife wanted to hire a babysitter, the brute insisted on having his parents watch the kids. The circumstances of the wife's arrest were described quite accurately: during an argument, "Mrs. C. grabbed Mr. C. by his necktie [and] he pushed her away. Mrs. C. then punched his face and her nail cut his neck." This was listed as "physical abuse" *by the husband.*[71]

Women "provoked" into more extreme violence can be seen as victims too. Betty Broderick, the California housewife who killed her wealthy ex-husband and his new wife—and claimed that the divorce and her alimony payments of *$16,000 a month* amounted to "white-collar domestic violence"—was the subject of sympathetic articles in *Ladies Home Journal* and *Mirabella;* an essay about Broderick in a feminist anthology on women and violence lamented that support for battered women who fight back had not extended to "'fighting back' against an *emotionally* abusive husband."[72]

Perhaps the one instance in which female violence is abhorred as much as male violence is when children are the victims. As an anti–death penalty activist noted, "When a woman kills a husband or boyfriend, there is some part of the jury's mind that wants to believe the victim may have done something that brought death on himself. But when a woman has killed her own children . . . the heart of a jury turns ice-cold." Yet, as the gradual shift in the image of Susan Smith suggests, even child killers can get sympathy if they can claim victimization by a male.[73]

Child killing is also the one category of homicide where female offenders predominate: 55 percent of parents who kill their children are mothers. Women are also responsible for most nonfatal child abuse cases (the perpetrators are disproportionately single mothers, while men and women in two-parent families are equally likely to be the abusers).[74]

Many advocates are reluctant to admit this. "If you can protect the mothers, then you can protect the children, because mothers are the first line of defense," I was told by Kristian Miccio, an attorney with Battered Women's Services in New York. Like Maria Montalvo, the New Jersey woman who burned her small son and daughter alive to punish their father for leaving? Or Ywilda Lopez, whose daughter, Elisa Izquierdo, had lived with her father until he died and she was turned over to her mother, to be tortured to death at the age of six?[75]

In a 1988 article, researchers Evan Stark and Anne Flitcraft claim that "men are primarily responsible for child abuse, *not women,*" on the basis of a retrospective review of suspected abuse cases; but from their muddled presentation, one cannot tell if the data support the conclusion. Stark and Flitcraft make no effort to hide their biases: even if Mom is beating the kids, it's out of anger at her "political subordination." But the false claim that violence toward children is mostly a male crime crops up in more reputable places. A *New York Times* story about identifying child abuse describes the typical abuser as "a boyfriend or stepfather." Even the U.S. Advisory Board on Child Abuse and Neglect has asserted that most child abuse fatalities "are caused by enraged or extremely stressed fathers or other male caretakers."[76]

A 1995 *Atlanta Journal-Constitution* story on multiple murders of family members ("familocide") focused *exclusively* on "killer dads" and threw in some boilerplate rhetoric about how abusive men "view their wives and children as property"—though the accompanying graph showed that about a third of such murderers are mothers. An earlier article on killer moms by the same reporter, Beth Frerking, portrayed the women as abused and dominated by men. An Associated Press report said that mothers "kill out of a twisted sense of love." After a horrific tragedy in St. Paul, Minnesota, in which Hmong immigrant Khoua Her was charged with strangling her six children, a *Minneapolis Star-Tribune* article titled "Why Do Mothers Kill Their Children?" used even more compassionate terms: "very, very depleted women," "totally abandoned." Meanwhile, battered women's advocates rallied to Her's defense, citing the occasional (and apparently mutual) violence between Her and her estranged husband, who had been barred from their home for about a month. "When a woman [is] so alone that she wants to kill herself and her children, it's not her fault," said one activist.[77]

Even when mothers who kill are held fully accountable, there are some things that are never said about their crimes. No one says that, far from being an aberration, these acts are representative of female evil. Indeed, feminist theorist Sara Ruddick has made the rather extraordinary argument that the fact that women *so rarely* commit violence against children, given how socially powerless women are and how often these helpless children provoke them, is a shining testament to maternal virtue.[78]

Some feminists warn that to label the man who murders a woman or a child a monster is to detach him from "the male half of humanity," letting ordinary men off the hook. At times we are also urged not to demonize mothers who kill. *New York Times* columnist Frank Rich opines that we are appalled by Susan Smith's crime because it reminds us of our own impulses to hurt loved ones, and of "the thin line that separates the unhinged few who act on such impulses from those of us who do not."[79] But the implications are different: the killer mom is connected to *all* humanity in a plea not to judge her too harshly; the killer male is connected to the *male* half of humanity to project his guilt onto all men.

A Human Issue

> Men who assault their wives are actually living up to cultural prescriptions that are cherished in Western society.
> —R. Emerson Dobash and Russell P. Dobash, *Violence Against Wives: A Case Against the Patriarchy*[80]

The notion of male violence against women as an instrument of patriarchal oppression has infiltrated mainstream discourse to a remarkable degree. A federally funded pamphlet says that our society "has accepted the use of violence by men to control women's behavior." A 1991 front-page story on domestic violence in the *Seattle Times* proclaimed that the problem "is not with individual abusers but with a violent, patriarchal culture that for millennia has said that women belong to men" (and quoted an "expert" as saying that the batterer is "like any man, but more so").[81]

Certainly one can find historical evidence of such attitudes— though, along with laws and customs that sanctioned a husband's use of physical "discipline," one also finds, as early as the 1600s, evidence of "cultural prescriptions" condemning a man who raises his hand to a woman. In *Othello,* the Venetian ambassadors are appalled when Othello strikes Desdemona. In the American colonies, Cotton Mather pronounced wife beating "as bad as any sacrilege"; the Victorians considered it abhorrent.[82]

In 1968, well before feminists began to raise consciousness about battering, 25 percent of American men and 17 percent of women said that under some circumstances they would approve of a husband slapping his wife. This hardly suggests a cherished norm: *three out of four men* felt that a fairly minor act of violence toward one's wife was *never* acceptable, presumably even with extreme provocation. One researcher who largely endorses the feminist view of family violence, psychologist Neil Jacobson, writes that "if our culture did not in some sense sanction wife abuse, it would occur much less frequently." In fact, it occurs repeatedly in no more than 3 percent of families.[83] By that logic, one can argue that infidelity was culturally sanctioned for wives in the 1950s or even the 1850s.

Perhaps the need to portray battering as a product of "normal" patriarchal socialization, more than the desire to malign men, explains many feminists' penchant for distorted or fictitious statistics. But there is no "war against women." It is not true that one in four pregnant women are beaten; counting minor scuffles, it's closer to one in twenty. It is not true that 25 to 35 percent of women in emergency rooms are there due to battering, or that domestic violence is the leading cause of injury to women. According to emergency room data gathered by the Justice Department and the Centers for Disease Control, about 1 percent of women's injuries are inflicted by their male partners. Even if we assume that four out of five such cases are missed, domestic violence would still rank far behind falls (27 percent of injuries) and automobile accidents (13 percent).[84]

Some social trends that feminists welcome, such as the new visibility of same-sex relationships, raise further doubts about the "battering as sexism" model, as feminist legal scholar Elizabeth Schneider concedes. Violence among gay men could be blamed on men's patriarchally bred lust for power, which will seek another outlet when there's no woman to kick around. But why on earth, if battering is a product of male dominance, do lesbians in some studies have the highest violence rates of all? Why did a survey of bisexual women find that more had been physically and sexually abused in relationships with women than with men? However one may strain for a politically correct explanation—lesbians batter because they are "socialized" into a violent male culture, or because of internalized homophobia and misogyny—it just makes no sense.[85]

Some men in some subcultures undoubtedly feel that it's their right to maintain male authority by force. Yet much literature on abuse, including feminist research, suggests that the batterer often emerges from the violent incident not dominant but contrite.[86] Without condoning his behavior, is it heretical to suggest that the victim sometimes has the upper hand because the man who hits a woman stands convicted, in her eyes and his own, as morally inferior?

One formerly battered woman, comedienne Brett Butler, mentioned this dynamic in an interview when she was asked about a scene from her show *Grace Under Fire*. Grace's penitent ex-husband says, "I only hit you because I didn't know no other way to win an argument." She replies, "That's funny. I thought the only way I could win an argument was to get you to hit me." The man who uses violence, Butler explained, "lose[s] the fight" morally, while the victim is empowered as "the recipient of pity, of making up, of apologies." Butler, who described the violence in her marriage as a "pathetic dance of power," added wryly, "I was battered, so I'm allowed to say it."[87]

Of course, this is not true of every abusive relationship. Some victims are utterly terrorized; some sociopathic batterers do not feel a twinge of remorse. Some men, and some women, use violence to impose their will; many others hit because they lose control, no matter how much advocates may resent this idea. Reality can't be reduced to the mantra of "power and control."[88]

What causes family violence, then? There is probably no single answer. For all the pieties about how battering cuts across class and socioeconomic lines, it is disproportionately common among the poor and unemployed. Although poverty is no excuse for assaultive behavior, it is clearly a major factor. So is drug and alcohol abuse (also downplayed by feminist theorists). University of British Columbia psychologist Donald Dutton and other researchers find "borderline personality"—a psychological disorder marked by proclivity for intense relationships, fear of abandonment, and proneness to rage—to be strongly associated with male battering of women, far more than patriarchal attitudes. Violent women probably share these traits. Shupe, Stacey, and Hazlewood describe an abusive girlfriend who felt that "the relationship was alive" only when "they argued intensely enough to arouse violence."[89]

Dutton notes that "intimacy itself . . . seems to be the crucial factor" in domestic violence. Elizabeth Schneider, the feminist scholar, who has no intention of giving up the rhetoric of "male domination," nonetheless concedes that the understanding of abuse should include "the ways in which power and control operate in all intimate relationships."[90] To "power and control," add insecurity, dependency, jealousy, and frustration.

I have heard it said that we can see many situations in a new light given "what we now know about domestic violence." But this new "knowledge" seems to narrow rather than broaden our understanding of violent relationships, reducing everything to a woman-as-victim formula.

Some feminists would like to make the formula still cruder. Ann Jones, author of the acclaimed book, *Next Time, She'll Be Dead,* bristles at the use of terms like "crime of passion" and "love triangle." She would expunge all references to feeling and substitute straight-up gender politics: "What happens is simple: A man wants 'his' woman to do what he wants. She won't. He uses force to get his way." (Jones also believes that research on psychological disorders in batterers is "crap": "Nobody wants to admit that men do this because they like to.") But is it "simple"? If the man who murders a woman after a breakup acts as an enforcer for "a police state where every man is deputized," in Andrea Dworkin's words, what about the man who takes his own life? Do gender politics alone explain how passion turns into rage, in men or women?[91]

Insofar as violence driven by "love" may be viewed with some sympathy, women probably get the benefit of it more than men. Consider the tale of beauty queen Tracy Lippard, who drove to the home of her pregnant rival, Melissa Weikle, attacked the woman's father with a hammer before she was subdued, and allegedly bragged to cellmates that she had planned to rip Melissa's belly open. At the trial, Lippard painted herself as a victim of love: "Any woman who's been two-timed . . . knows the feeling." The jury found her guilty only of misdemeanors, rejecting the more serious charges that involved premeditation—even though in addition to the hammer, she was carrying a gun, a knife, and lighter fluid when she showed up at the Weikle home. A news report described her as "an articulate, striking woman who had never found a man who cared enough to put her photo in his wallet."[92]

In July 1997, eighteen-year-old Stacy Hanna was found dead on a deserted road near Richmond, Virginia. She had been slashed, kicked, beaten, bashed on the head with a cinder block. After four teenagers, all female and all gay, were arrested for her murder—with jealousy the apparent motive—gay activists voiced concern that the focus on the story's lesbian angle would fan the flames of homophobia. "It's not an issue of gender violence," said Wendy Northup, president of the Richmond Organization for Sexual Minority Youth. "It's really an issue of youth violence."[93]

Yet the idea that violence between men and women is not an issue of "gender violence" but of human violence is anathema to most battered women's advocates and feminists. One might wonder why. If you want to stress the urgency of a problem, wouldn't you try to show that it affects *more* people? If, like attorney Gloria Allred, you wanted to stress similarities between the sexes, wouldn't you welcome evidence that women can be as mean and as lethal as men? A more inclusive view of family violence, advocates warn, poses multiple dangers: attention and resources diverted from abused women to men, battered women blamed for their victimization. So far, however, abused men have not gotten a penny from the government or major charities, and one can read pages of congressional speeches deploring the abuse of women (or children) and not find one reference to male victims.[94]

Lurking behind the feminists' practical concerns is a philosophical one. As Hamberger and Potente note, "The terms 'batterer' and 'abuser' are highly connotative, evoking . . . revulsion and disgust at the idea that someone could harm, maim, or kill his partner for no other reason than to dominate. . . . More neutral terminology seems justified in women's violence."[95] What's at stake, then, is women's claim to the moral high ground.

There is no reason that domestic violence should be seen as less worthy of concern if it is viewed as an issue for both sexes or a product of something other than male dominance. Battering is still horrible even if it is no longer political. But that will never do for those whose real agenda is the struggle against "male power."

CHAPTER FIVE

Legislating the Gender War:
The Politics of Domestic Abuse

A year after Susan Finkelstein's live-in boyfriend was charged with assaulting her, Susan, a freelance editor in her thirties who lives in a small midwestern town, felt abused by the system. "I had no rights," she says. "Nobody listened to me, nobody wanted to hear my story." What angered Susan was not that her alleged batterer was treated too leniently but that he was prosecuted at all.

It started when Susan and John, a fortysomething college administrator, got into a heated argument while driving home. John decided to pull over and step out of the car; Susan tried to stop him, and they got into a scuffle. "I may have scratched him, he may have pushed me," she says. "It got physical, but there certainly wasn't any beating."

Finally they cooled down and got back on the road—only to be stopped by a police car. Susan recalls thinking that John may have looked like a drunk driver if he drove erratically during the argument. In fact, a passing motorist had seen the altercation, written down their license plate number, and called the police. Despite Susan's assurances that John hadn't hurt her, he was taken away in handcuffs. It was department policy, an officer told her, to make an arrest in a domestic dispute.

After a night in jail, John was arraigned on a domestic assault charge and barred from contact with Susan, who had to stay with a friend. Her efforts to convince the judge and the prosecutor that nothing had happened were futile. On a lawyer's advice, John pleaded no contest. He had to attend ten weekly counseling sessions for batterers, a three-hour drive away, at the cost of $400.[1]

What happened to John and Susan is no aberration. It's one of many stories from the trenches of the War on Domestic Violence.

The campaign against family violence is, without question, a noble cause. Launched by feminists in the 1970s, it was partly a reaction to the tendency to treat most violence between intimates as mere family discord—not a legitimate exercise of male authority, but a mainly lower-class vice in which legal intervention was best avoided. Battered women's advocates deserve credit for creating support systems that have helped millions of women leave abusive relationships and convincing the public and the courts to take abuse seriously. Even those who believe the pendulum has swung too far generally agree that change was necessary.

Unfortunately, the baby comes with a lot of toxic bathwater. A combination of the gender politics of the battered women's movement and the zeal common to many crusades against social evils has led to a new extreme: a situation in which all too often, any relationship conflict is treated as a crime.

Enforcing the Party Line

"There's nothing like working in the battered women's movement to feel truly abused," says Renée Ward, who served as director of a Minneapolis shelter for battered women from 1982 to 1984. A movement outsider with a background in sociology and public health, Ward had no idea what lay in store when she took the job at the shelter. She found it to be "a very unhealthy environment," partly because of animosities among staff. Ward attributes this to the fact that "having been a battered woman was the primary qualification for staff members," and the women often continued to enact the "victim-victimizer roles" of abusive relationships in their interactions with coworkers and supervisors. But above all, she recalled ten years later, "it was a terrible, terrible experience because of the pressure of ideology":

> Racism, patriarchy, homophobia, oppression of the masses were talked about endlessly, as part of the indoctrination that had to go on for everyone at the shelter, including the clients. It seemed like expressing any other ideas or raising any questions was not really

tolerated. There was a lot of hostility to men. I didn't think that was very successful in working with the women, because most of them wanted to be in a relationship with a man.[2]

Reflecting on the gains of the battered women's movement two decades after its birth, Charlotte Watson, a shelter director in Westchester, New York, told a journalist that her sisters-in-arms had to fight an uphill battle: "We were called antifamily, man-hating, castrating, ball-busting lesbians." Yet public support was not slow in coming. To "win legal and social service reforms . . . and capture the imagination of a nation in approximately eight years are extraordinary achievements," veteran activist Susan Schechter noted in 1983. (Did it occur to her that these successes undercut her own claim that the battering of women was "socially approved"?)[3]

Many activists saw mainstream support as a mixed blessing, fearing that the lure of government or foundation money would compromise their politics. "I can't be as angry at men as I want to be," a shelter worker complained. Schechter herself warned about the peril of losing sight of the movement's revolutionary goals: "When we see ourselves only as providers of service rather than as agents of social change and organizers of women, our shelters become an end in itself." Even seeking to end violence was not enough, unless accompanied by a feminist analysis of male domination. Still, Schechter suggested, using moderate language was all right as long as it was a cover: "Since we do operate in several different worlds at once, we at least need to be clear about our own political vision."[4]

The idea of camouflage as a strategy to win mainstream backing has been expressed with striking candor by other advocates. Pamela Johnston, coordinator of Women's Transitional Care Services in Lawrence, Kansas, in 1979–1980, explains that the shelter's policy of barring male participation (in the spirit of "womyn helping womyn") was "challenged by community supporters and funding sources" and matter-of-factly adds: "To pacify and secure that essential support, WTCS has instituted an advisory board of womyn and men" which "sets no policy, makes no decisions for the group, and has no veto power."[5]

Johnston's article, an angry account of an "Attack from the Right" that jeopardized the funding of WTCS and led her to resign, offers clues that the "antifamily" and "man-hating" clichés had more than a grain of truth. Johnston denies that the shelter imposed feminist dogma, yet says that its work was based on the assumption that "the nuclear family, as the primary unit of patriarchy, is inherently oppressive to womyn." She scoffs at charges of lesbian recruitment yet makes no secret of her view that lesbians make the best battered women's advocates ("Many heterosexual womyn, wishing to remain open to men, are unwilling to fully name men as the violators").[6]

The situation at WTCS was not unique, as tales from defectors like Renée Ward suggest. Dyan Kirkland, a social worker once active in Minnesota community groups dealing with domestic abuse, paints a similar picture. Kirkland ran afoul of the members of the advocacy community when she organized a seminar on domestic violence for divorce mediators. The party line rejected mediation as a danger to battered wives; Kirkland shared their concerns but felt that it was all the more crucial to teach mediators to spot abuse and help victims. Part of her crime, she suspects, was to arrange the event without consulting the advocacy groups, though activists opposed to mediation were invited to speak. "I got phone calls that were very hostile and angry; we were picketed," recalls Kirkland, who has since broken her ties to the movement. "It was horrible."[7]

Another survivor of the movement's politics—Barbara Raye, former director of the battered women's program in the Minnesota Department of Corrections—caught some grief for supporting Kirkland's seminar ("Buttons were thrown at my staff as they came in to do the training"). Unlike Ward and Kirkland, Raye had an extensive background as an activist and was personally comfortable with much of the movement's feminist philosophy. Her heresy was to allow that there could be other legitimate views.[8]

According to Raye, many of those at the forefront of the movement were determined to ensure that state funding for domestic violence programs went only to organizations that embraced a feminist analysis of battering as a "conspiracy of men to oppress women." This litmus test was especially problematic in working with minority activists, who were inclined to see men as fellow victims of racism and poverty. Programs also had to distribute abortion literature to qualify for funding. One casualty of this requirement was a center opened by a pro-life black woman minister, which, Raye felt, could have helped many women whom more orthodox programs failed to reach. When Raye began to question the movement's orthodoxy and its monopoly on programs for battered women—and other things, such as many shelters' resistance to accountability for the state funds they spent—she too was branded a traitor.

"Many women in the movement became fierce abusers of other

women who tried to work in the movement," says Ward. This startling analogy, which may reflect the advocates' own penchant for
broad definitions of "abuse," is echoed by Kirkland and others, such
as Trenna Perkins, the head of an abusers' treatment program in
Raleigh, North Carolina, who tried to get the North Carolina
Coalition Against Domestic Violence to amend its mission statement to include serving whole families, not just "women and their
children," and says she found herself ostracized by members who
opposed her viewpoint. Eve Lipchik, a Milwaukee family therapist
who favors joint counseling for some couples in abusive relationships (strongly opposed by battered women's advocates), has been
shaken by the hostility she has encountered when discussing her
work at conferences. "The advocates say men are violent and cruel
and mean," observes Lipchik, a self-proclaimed feminist, "and that's
exactly what these women are to women who disagree with
them."[9]

As these comments show, the situation in Minnesota is hardly
unique, though perhaps more extreme than in many other states. Jan
Dimmit, director of the Emergency Support Shelter in Kelso,
Washington, since 1992, recalls that when she took the post, the
shelter had a strict no-men-allowed policy: "The first week, my husband came to fix some leaky faucets. The staff was so indoctrinated
in the idea that all men are bad and no man will cross the door that
I felt as if I'd committed a major sin." (All but one of the original
staffers eventually left.) Today, Dimmit says, she is "kind of shunned"
at state gatherings because of her willingness to "advocate for victims regardless of sex." In North Carolina in 1998, a small rural victim services organization was denied a federal grant, apparently
because the advocate-stacked review panel didn't like its stated goal
of "strengthening family unity" and its insufficiently high estimates
of abuse cases in the county. In Hawaii, an investigation of the
Family Crisis Shelter system in 1994 turned up a host of familiar
complaints, from feminism as the main job qualification to relentless
obsession with racism.[10]

Not all domestic violence programs are politicized, though a
majority probably are. A nationwide survey of shelters in 1988
found that about half stressed feminist activism over assisting
women—and that's a conservative estimate; 40 percent of the survey
forms were not returned, and the more radical organizations, wary
of cooperating with researchers, may well have been overrepresented
among the nonrespondents.[11] In 1996, my research assistant sent a

questionnaire to a sample of shelters. Of the ten directors who replied, only three believed that there was *any* room in the domestic violence movement for a view of abuse as a matter of individual or family pathology rather than gender oppression.

Moreover, the organizations that act as the "official" voice on the issue—the National Coalition Against Domestic Violence (NCADV) and its member organizations in all fifty states, the National Resource Center on Domestic Violence, the Family Violence Prevention Fund—are thoroughly ideological. The NCADV's mission statement connects "violence against women and children" to "sexism, racism, classism, anti-semitism, able-bodyism, ageism, and other oppressions." Literature from national and local programs, often funded by the government or by major charities, assert that "men batter because our culture says that they can and should control women" and "battering is the extreme expression of the belief in male dominance over women."[12]

The battered women's movement has won a remarkable degree of mainstream acceptance. Its leaders, including Susan Schechter, sit on the federal Advisory Council on Violence Against Women set up by Attorney General Janet Reno and Health and Human Services Secretary Donna Shalala in 1995. Advocacy groups have received hundreds of millions of dollars in federal and state funding; their members frequently testify before legislatures and help produce government literature on domestic violence. They lobbied successfully for the passage of the Violence Against Women Act (VAWA), which not only ensures them a steady flow of public funds but gives a congressional seal of approval to their view of domestic violence as antifemale terrorism. At a 1998 symposium at the New York Bar Association, Andrea Williams, staff attorney with the NOW Legal Defense and Education Fund, proudly declared that "VAWA is the advocates' bill, because the advocates are the ones who drafted it."

But the zealots could rest easy: respectability did not dilute the movement's "political vision." Nine years after Schechter spoke at the Second Annual Conference of the Texas Council of Family Violence and issued her warnings about focusing solely on helping abused women rather than overthrowing the patriarchy she saw as the cause of abuse, the keynote speaker at the council's 1992 conference was Andrea Dworkin, the writer whose feverish antimale, antisex diatribes have made her name synonymous with feminism's lunatic fringe.

Women Betrayed

The orthodoxy of the battered women's movement, with its us-versus-them view of male violence and its denial of female aggression, clearly has troubling implications for men. But Virginia Goldner, a senior faculty member at the Ackerman Institute for Family Therapy in New York and enough of a feminist to speak of "dominant patriarchal social norms," cautions that "conceiving of women as the guardians of goodness and men as the purveyors of badness" is not good for women, either—if only because no one knows what to do with "violent, angry and irresponsible women."[13]

Women abused by their female partners have been the most obvious casualties of the advocates' fixation on the men-versus-women message. Lesbian battering was a taboo issue for years. Even now, sociologist Claire Renzetti of St. Joseph's University in Philadelphia (a bona-fide feminist) reports that abused lesbians remain second-class citizens in battered women's programs. Although nearly all the service providers she surveyed in 1991–1992 claimed to welcome lesbians as clients, more than two-thirds had no brochures or materials on lesbian battering, and very few made efforts to reach out to lesbian victims. In Renzetti's earlier study of battered lesbians, some women worked at domestic violence shelters or agencies but didn't think they could get help there, and a few could not go to the local shelter because that was where their abuser worked.[14]

The politics that dominate domestic violence advocacy may end up hurting women in abusive heterosexual relationships as well. "The militants encourage women to get angry and never let go," says one former activist in the movement who had been an abused wife herself. "In some ways it keeps the movement alive, but it's not good for the individual. You can be angry about women, or men, being victims. But to take your anger about being wronged and nurse it for the rest of your life, that's not healthy. You have to move on. They don't allow women to stop hating."

Virginia Goldner, the family therapist at the Ackerman Institute, tells the story of a client whose husband's violence toward her had stopped after they completed a couples therapy program, and who joined a support group at a battered women's shelter for "insurance" and companionship: "Some months later, she came back . . . saying she'd been feeling worse about herself since joining the group, because 'everyone was supposed to hate the men, and want to leave them.' She was ashamed and confused about not feeling that way."[15]

To make things worse, the group also condemned couples therapy (making the woman feel that she had a shameful secret), another movement dogma that surely harms many women as well as men, shutting them off from what studies show to be an often effective way to end violence in relationships. Such is the power of orthodoxy that while the editors of the 1993 volume *Current Controversies in Family Violence* found quite a few scholars who favored joint counseling, *not one* would contribute an essay in its defense.[16]

The ostensible reason for the ban on joint counseling is that it's not safe for a woman to disclose violence in front of the batterer. Mental health professionals who support joint counseling believe that this issue can be addressed with some simple precautions: interviewing each partner separately at first and terminating joint counseling if there is any sign of danger. But safety is not the only issue. What rankles the advocates is the implication that both partners have to change their behavior.[17]

Virginia Goldner may well be right when she suggests, despite her misgivings, that for women in thrall to a violent, domineering man, "the ideological purity and righteous indignation of the battered women's movement is all that protects them from being pulled back in the swamp of abuse."[18] For many, involvement with militant activists is just a phase. But a woman who remains stuck in that phase cannot, in human rather than political terms, be seen as a success story. And while any woman or man can make the choice to join a militant movement, it's not the same when an abused woman who desperately needs help can't get it without the politics.

Advocacy Power

Even people who have never sought out the battered women's movement may find their lives affected by its growing clout.

It's impossible to tell how many veterans of the movement are working within the criminal justice system as prosecutors, like Sarah Buel, an abused-wife-turned-activist with a penchant for extreme rhetoric and striking but sometimes erroneous factoids, who was an assistant district attorney in Massachusetts from 1988 to 1996.[19] Others have found niches in victim services. Pamela Johnston, whose account of her battles with the right in Kansas in 1980 was mentioned earlier, turned up in the 1990s as executive director of the Victim Information Bureau of Suffolk County in New York.

Even without official jobs, activists can have a great deal of power in the system; sometimes, says Massachusetts lawyer and state legislator James Fagan, they wield "more authority than the district attorneys."[20] As part of domestic violence task forces, they help write domestic violence intervention protocols used by police, prosecutors, and courts. These protocols happen to give the advocates a prominent role at every step in the legal process: police officers on a domestic violence call are instructed to encourage the victim to contact the local battered women's group. There's nothing wrong with giving a role to advocates who can ensure that victims of crime (domestic or not) are treated well—except when these advocates are more committed to the cause than to helping the victims, or when their perception of every situation is colored by gender politics.

There are other ways in which advocacy groups influence the system. They conduct officially sponsored training seminars for police, prosecutors, and judges. In the training materials, familiar pseudo-statistics abound ("physical abuse is the number one cause of medical injury to women," "one out of every seven married women is raped by her husband"), while politically incorrect facts and theories ("Battering is about couples getting into a brawl [and] beating each other up") are listed as "myths."[21]

In Ohio in 1997, the principal speakers at five training conferences for judges, prosecutors, and police were University of Cincinnati psychologists Dee Graham and Edna Rawlings, coauthors of the 1994 book *Loving to Survive,* which asserts that "all male-female relationships [are] more or less abusive" and that "women's bonding to men, as well as women's femininity and heterosexuality, are paradoxical responses to men's violence against women"—a mass Stockholm syndrome in which the victims bond with their captors. Graham and Rawlings have received a $120,000 federal grant from the National Institute for Justice, and an additional $75,000 from the state of Ohio for research on boosting the rate of convictions in domestic violence cases.[22]

In many jurisdictions, women who make a domestic violence call are routinely referred for counseling to battered women's groups. Some police departments have established programs under which volunteers from these groups accompany officers to domestic disturbances. A New Jersey policeman told me that some members of these "crisis intervention teams" were very helpful and open-minded, but others had "an ideological agenda" and automatically took the woman's side. A glowing newspaper profile of Kate Roberts, an advocate working with such a program in Florida, suggests that concerns about bias are not misplaced.

In one episode, the team responds to a fight between habitual brawlers; the man is "cut above the eye with an ashtray." Roberts advises *the woman* to get a restraining order and contact a shelter. (The man is advised to end the relationship and go stay with a friend.) Another woman wants her live-in boyfriend out and claims that he threw her baby at her, dropping the child on the floor. The man denies it; the woman's older daughter confirms his story; and the baby is unhurt. Yet Roberts treats the woman as the victim, telling her to "get Mike evicted and get a restraining order."[23]

Then there are the batterer treatment programs into which men charged with domestic abuse are often ordered by the courts. These programs are not uniform. In the Austin Family Violence Diversion Network, the focus is on anger management, conflict resolution, and communication, though sex roles are discussed as well. But groups like EMERGE in Massachusetts, the Oakland Men's Project in California, the Domestic Abuse Intervention Project in Duluth, Minnesota, and RAVEN (Rape and Violence End Now) in St. Louis are essentially gentlemen's auxiliaries of the battered women's movement, stressing political reeducation about "male privilege."[24] Glenna Auxier, a Florida divorce mediator and crisis center counselor who took a training course based on the Duluth batterer treatment model, describes it as "male-bashing by people who had not worked out their personal issues."

Whether anyone, even a lawbreaker, can be forced to enter a program that promotes a particular ideology is an interesting constitutional question. (Some drunk-driving defendants have challenged court-ordered Alcoholics Anonymous attendance on the grounds that AA's religious outlook violates their freedom of conscience, and have been granted permission to substitute nonreligious recovery groups.) One might say that if anybody deserves to be brainwashed by radical feminists, it's batterers. But some men may be guilty of nothing more than a mutual scuffle, or having a tantrum and smashing a glass, or grabbing a woman's arm.[25]

In "treatment," they must confess to such forms of "abuse" as "criticizing her friends," "sulking," and "not giving support, validation, attention, compliments or respect for her feelings, opinions and rights." Any complaints about women's behavior, including "she assaulted me," are dismissed as "excuses." Some of the activist counselors even seem to think that a little abuse by a woman may not be a bad thing for a man: "Learning to sit and 'take it' non-violently might be just what he needs," sneered RAVEN volunteer Jeff Sutter in an Internet exchange about men assaulted by their wives.[26]

Cops, Courts, and Domestic Violence: Crackdown or Witch-hunt?

Suppose, suggested *Time* columnist Margaret Carlson in the wake of O. J. Simpson's acquittal on murder charges, that it was not his wife, Nicole, but his pal Robert Kardashian that the ex-football star had repeatedly roughed up. Surely, she wrote, these assaults would not have gone unpunished: "Smashing in Kardashian's face would have gotten Simpson arrested and given him pause; beating up Nicole got him phone therapy."[27]

That the law has traditionally condoned men's violence against their female partners has become conventional wisdom. A booklet published by one battered women's program states that wife beating was not outlawed in the United States until 1892; Kristian Miccio, an attorney with Battered Women's Services in New York, told me it was legal until the 1960s, because women were "sexual property." "Welcome to the U.S. of A., where life is cheap and women's lives are always at discount," writes *New York Daily News* columnist Linda Stasi about a case in which a man was acquitted in the severe assault of an ex-girlfriend.[28]

Certainly the legal treatment of domestic violence in the past left much to be desired. What is *not* true is that anything short of killing or maiming one's wife was legally sanctioned. The first laws established by the Massachusetts colonists in 1642 prohibited "bodilie correction" by husbands. Feminist historian Elizabeth Pleck found that nineteenth-century municipal courts "invariably accepted a woman's claim of physical abuse and took some action"—from a reprimand to jail or a "peace bond" which he forfeited by repeating the assault.[29]

True, a few rulings by southern appellate courts in the nineteenth century sanctioned moderate use of force toward wives. Yet as the judges themselves recognized, these decisions were outside the mainstream of judicial opinion. By the mid-1870s, these courts also agreed that "the husband has no right to chastise his wife" (though adding a plea for noninterference where "no permanent injury has been inflicted, nor malice, cruelty nor dangerous violence shown by the husband"). Prosecutors and judges were often reluctant to jail a family breadwinner, but he didn't always go unpunished: "Whenever a drunken man beat up his wife, I beat the man up myself and gave him a taste of his own medicine," wrote a police captain who served in New York in the 1880s.[30]

Treating domestic violence as a family problem rather than a crime was considered the progressive approach in the 1960s, when coercive law enforcement tactics in general were not too popular and many offenses against the public order were being decriminalized. A 1967 police training manual said that "in dealing with family disputes, the power of arrest should be exercised as a last resort"; in a 1973 publication, the American Bar Association endorsed this view, urging conflict resolution instead.[31]

Obviously, these policies were often improper. In an episode observed by researchers in the 1970s and described by criminologist Lawrence Sherman in his book *Policing Domestic Violence,* the woman, with a bruised face and bleeding lip, wanted her companion arrested. The officers did threaten to arrest him when he started mouthing off. Mostly, though, they focused on getting to the bottom of the conflict—the woman thought she was married to the man, but he was actually in the process of divorcing his wife—and departed once the man reassured them that he was going to his mother's house and that everything would be fine.[32]

It's easy to see this as appalling disregard for women. But Sherman cautions that the perception of sexism rests partly on the false premise that the laws are strictly enforced in other cases. Surveys of urban crime data in the 1970s showed that the police were reluctant to interfere in any violent personal dispute. In one study, arrests were made in fewer than a third of assaults when the perpetrator was present, with little difference between domestic and nondomestic cases. Consider another incident recounted by Sherman: a policeman responding to a disturbance outside a bar found a man with blood on his face, who claimed that another man had attacked him and demanded that charges be filed; the other man protested his innocence; the patrolman ignored them both and left after resolving a parking dispute.[33]

Are men who attack wives and girlfriends treated more leniently than nonfamily assailants after arrest? That's what Kathleen Ferraro, a women's studies and criminology professor who identifies herself as "scholar/activist/survivor of male violence," expected to find when she analyzed the handling of violent offenses in 1987 and 1988 in Maricopa County, Arizona. In fact, she discovered that most assaults of *any* kind were either not prosecuted or were prosecuted as misdemeanors. Among felony cases, domestic assaults were *less* likely to be dismissed than nondomestic ones. Only 11 percent of defendants got any prison time, but the victim-offender relationship had no effect on the severity of the sentence.[34]

So what would have happened to O.J. if he had beaten up Bob Kardashian and not Nicole? If the facts had been otherwise similar—if Kardashian had suffered only some bruises and a split lip and didn't want to press charges—it is likely that there would have been no case and no sentence, not even phone therapy.

In the late 1970s, due partly to the influence of the battered women's movement, prevailing views on the efficacy of arrest in domestic fights started to turn around. By 1982, most states had empowered police officers to make arrests in misdemeanor domestic assaults they had not witnessed, even if the victim didn't sign a complaint, a reform applauded by most law enforcement personnel and family violence experts. But as the rate of arrests remained low, many jurisdictions began to *require* arrest, taking discretion away from the police. This trend, on the benefits of which there is far less agreement, has been boosted by the post–O. J. Simpson attention to domestic abuse and by incentives for pro-arrest policies in the federal Violence Against Women Act of 1994.

In the 1980s, such policies got a boost from a Minneapolis study suggesting that arrest reduced the risk of further battering, though the authors of the study, Lawrence Sherman and Richard Berk, advised against mandatory arrest. Later research found that in some communities, particularly those with many unemployed minority men, arrests could cause violence to *escalate*. When, citing this evidence, Sherman urged the Wisconsin legislature to repeal the mandatory arrest law, an assemblywoman accused him of seeking to "embolden abusers." By 1992, fifteen states and the District of Columbia, and many municipalities elsewhere, had introduced mandatory arrest; in 1994, Congress decided to encourage it through federal grants under the Violence Against Women Act.[35]

Christopher Pagan, an attorney who was a prosecutor in Hamilton County, Ohio, until 1997, estimates that after the passage of a 1994 state law requiring police on a domestic call to make an arrest or file a report explaining why no arrest was made, "domestics" went from 10 percent to 40 percent of his docket. Not that more real battering was coming to his attention: "We started getting a lot of push-and-shoves, or even yelling matches. In the past, police officers would intervene and separate the parties to let them cool off. Now those cases end up in criminal courts. It's exacerbating tensions between the parties, and it's turning law-abiding middle-class citizens into criminals."[36]

Many police officers agree. "We need domestic violence law but we need common sense, too," says Pete S., a veteran small-town policeman in New Jersey who stresses that he doesn't miss the days when a woman could be bruised or bloodied and the police couldn't arrest the man unless she signed a complaint. Now, he says, it's the opposite extreme: "Sometimes the wife's begging, 'Don't arrest him, the kids are here,' and you *have to* arrest."[37]

It isn't just police*men* who chafe at having their hands tied. If you hit your neighbor and bruise his arm, Los Angeles policewoman Susan Yocum wrote in 1989, the cops "may try to get you and your neighbor to resolve the situation without legal intervention." But "if a man hits his wife and a similar bruise appears on her, the police officer . . . has no option. Regardless of the wife's desires or the husband's explanations, he will be taken to jail immediately and booked on a felony charge of spousal abuse."[38]

Sally Gilmore (not her real name), a policewoman in a working-class New Jersey town, believes that mandatory arrest rules often force cops to act against their better judgment. Once, she recalls, a woman who was told that her ex-boyfriend couldn't be arrested for screaming at her suddenly "remembered" that he had also hit her, and showed what was clearly an old bruise. "I asked, 'When did this happen?' and she said, 'Just now,'" says Gilmore. "I knew she was lying, but I had no choice," says Gilmore.[39]

Increasingly, no offense is too trivial not only for arrest but for prosecution. In 1996, Seattle city councilman John Manning, who came home and was shocked to find his wife loading her belongings into a truck, was charged with assault for grabbing her shoulders and sitting her down on the tailgate (Juana Manning was not injured but had some pain in her lower back when the police arrived). He pleaded guilty, received a deferred prison sentence, and agreed to complete a batterer treatment program. The *Seattle Times* editorialized that the case gave "a public face" to the tragedy of domestic violence.[40]

The same year, Michigan judge Joel Gehrke made headlines when he gave convicted spouse abuser Stewart Marshall a literal slap on the wrist, citing the wife's adultery with her husband's brother as a mitigating factor. This episode, which provoked cries about judges who condone wife beating, should have raised questions instead about frivolous prosecutions. Aside from the fact that many of the jurors believed Chris Marshall had set up the incident as a divorce tactic, Stewart's assault consisted of grabbing her by the sweatshirt and shoving her against the wall; she didn't suffer a single scrape. A woman juror who backed Judge Gehrke's decision explained that the jury "had to say guilty" because "if you touch, it's battery."[41]

Claims are still made that the justice system denies women equal protection by treating spousal abuse less seriously than other assaults (it was certainly not true by the 1980s). Now, however, some crusaders want it to be taken *more* seriously. In 1996, the sponsor of a New York bill toughening penalties for misdemeanor assault on spouses, ex-spouses, and partners vowed to oppose a version that would cover all assaults: "The whole purpose of my bill is to single out domestic violence," assemblyman Joseph Lentol told the *New York Times*. "I don't want the world to think we're treating stranger assaults the same way as domestic assaults."[42]

That year, California abolished a provision allowing a defendant in a misdemeanor domestic assault to have the incident expunged from his record if he compensated the victim and underwent counseling, an option still available to the accused in other assaults (and meant, said the bill's author, state senator John Burton, for "a spat in a bar between equals"). And a new federal law made domestic violence the *only* misdemeanor for which a person lost the right to own a gun.[43]

Saving Women from Themselves

Increasingly, women who do not want to press charges—like Susan Finkelstein, whom we met at the beginning of this chapter—are labeled victims against their will, as mandatory arrest policies are compounded by no-drop prosecutions.

Uncooperative victims are a major problem for prosecutors in spousal abuse cases (reminding us that it's not *quite* a crime like any other). In Kathleen Ferraro's study in Arizona, almost 40 percent of victims in domestic assault cases, compared to about 6 percent in non-domestic ones, wanted to drop the charges; the request was usually denied. Judicial conferences feature panels on how to deal with a "reluctant or hostile victim." This issue was brought into the spotlight by the 1996 trial of football star Warren Moon, whose wife, Felicia, was forced to take the stand against him and testified that she started the fight by lobbing a candlestick at her husband. Moon was acquitted.[44]

It is often assumed that when women recant or refuse to press charges, it's out of fear or psychological dependency on the men. But reality is far more complex. Some battered women pride themselves on being able to take care of their problems (though they may be tragically wrong). Sometimes, as with Susan and John, the incident is genuinely trivial. Or else the accusation may have been false, made in anger, and later regretted.

Deborah Beck (not her real name), a counselor in an abusers' program in Florida, who generally *supports* no-drop policies, saw this happen with her daughter Angie, a troubled young woman with a drinking problem, and her live-in boyfriend:

> She was drunk and her boyfriend wouldn't give her money to buy more booze. So she goes out and calls the police saying he has locked her out—which he probably had because he didn't want trouble—and fills out a report saying he threatened her, she's afraid of him, and so on.

The police took Angie home and arrested the young man. When she sobered up, she was horrified and tried to back out, to no avail. With her mother's help, she hired a lawyer, and her boyfriend was eventually allowed to plead no contest.

Sometimes the "reluctant victim" insists that *she* was the aggressor—and she may be telling the truth. The strangest case of this kind unfolded in St. Paul, Minnesota, in 1994. It started when Jeanne Chacon, an attorney in her thirties, called the police and accused her fiancé, law professor Peter Erlinder, of assaulting her. A few days later, she told authorities a very different story: prone to violent outbursts due to childhood abuse, she had lashed out at Erlinder, and he had tried to restrain her with a "basket-hold" technique her own therapists had suggested. The therapists confirmed this, and Chacon tried not only to get the charges dropped but to represent Erlinder, in court. Nevertheless, the case went ahead. (Before the trial, Chacon attacked Erlinder so violently that he had to seek medical aid. She was not charged.) Erlinder was acquitted after the jury heard from Chacon and her therapists.[45]

A few years ago, James Dolan, first justice of Dorchester District Court in Massachusetts, warned that "the system itself may be engaged in a subtle form of abuse by denying women the right to continue a relationship without submitting to the authority of the court." Some victims may be so clearly in danger and so obviously irrational in their desire to continue the relationship that they must be saved from themselves. But except for extreme cases, wrote Judge Dolan, their decisions should be respected.[46]

Interestingly, some battered women's advocates also oppose no-drop prosecutions, which, they argue, disempower battered women and undermine their sense of control. Their position is bolstered by at least one study that found that when women are able to dismiss charges, recidivism among batterers is significantly reduced (presumably because it gives the woman leverage).[47] But other activists, more willing to work with the system and to see battered women as victims mired in "learned helplessness," usually prevail. With his "benign abuse" metaphor, Judge Dolan may have used the term *abuse* as loosely as the advocates do. Yet quite a few women might agree with his assessment: "I felt battered by the prosecution," Jeanne Chacon told a reporter after the trial.[48]

"I told a prosecutor that I didn't appreciate being told what was best for me by someone who didn't know me," recalled Susan Finkelstein. "She said, 'It strikes me as odd that you don't appreciate the fact that we're trying to protect you.' What I said didn't matter. It seems so ironic that in trying to give women a voice, they are taking away their voices."

Presumed Guilty

> Your job is not to become concerned about the constitutional rights of the man that you're violating as you grant a restraining order. Throw him out on the street, give him the clothes on his back and tell him, see ya around. . . . The woman needs this protection because the statute granted her that protection. . . . They have declared domestic violence to be an evil in our society. So we don't have to worry about the rights.[49]

The speaker was Ocean City, New Jersey, municipal court judge Richard Russell, dispensing advice at a training seminar for fellow judges in 1994.

These comments, captured on tape and printed in the *New Jersey Law Journal,* raised a few eyebrows but earned the judge only a mild chiding from the Administrative Office of the Courts. Two years later in Maine, Judge Alexander MacNichol was denied reappointment by Governor Angus King (a fate suffered by only three other judges in the state in thirty years) because battered women's advocates were complaining about his "lack of sensitivity" to women applying for restraining orders, which, the judge's many defenders said, meant simply that he listened to both parties.[50]

Restraining orders or orders of protection, which prohibit not only molesting the plaintiff but approaching or contacting her—by mail, by telephone, through a third party—have become a popular weapon against domestic violence. Laws making such orders easily available against current or former spouses or cohabitants date back to the 1970s. More recently, many states have streamlined the process of getting an order, extended eligibility to people who had dated but not lived together, and introduced harsh measures against violators: warrantless arrest, pretrial detention, stiff sentences.

In Massachusetts, which boasts some of the toughest policies in the country, nearly sixty thousand restraining orders are issued every year. Remarkably, an official analysis found, fewer than half involve even an *allegation* of physical abuse.[51]

Under the Abuse Prevention Law, a temporary restraining order can be issued *ex parte*—without the defendant being present or even notified, much less informed of the specific allegations against him, which may be surprisingly trivial. Elaine Epstein, past president of the Massachusetts Bar Association, recalls "affidavits which just said someone was in fear, or there had been an argument or yelling, but not even a threat."[52] Epstein stresses that in the "old days," it could be hard for truly abused women to get protection. (In 1986, Judge Paul King was blasted by the *Boston Globe* for refusing to order a man out of the house, despite a police report that he had beaten his wife, because he didn't "see any bruises" on the woman, who wore a coat in court.) Yet she is equally convinced that the pendulum has swung too far, as she wrote in the Massachusetts Bar Association newsletter in a column titled "Speaking the Unspeakable":

> The recent media frenzy surrounding domestic violence has paralyzed us all. Police, prosecutors, judges and attorneys alike all seek to protect themselves from potential criticism. . . . The facts have become irrelevant. Everyone knows that restraining orders and orders to vacate are granted to virtually all who apply, lest anyone be blamed for an unfortunate result. . . . In many [divorce] cases, allegations of abuse are now used for tactical advantage.[53]

Once a temporary order is granted, a hearing must be held within ten days to determine if it should be extended for a year. That's when the defendant can tell his side—in theory. In fact, writes Boston attorney Miriam Altman, the deck is stacked against him: normally inadmissible evidence such as hearsay is allowed; cross-examination may be limited; "the mere allegation of domestic abuse . . . may shift the burden of proof to the defendant." And, lawyers say, it's very unlikely that the judge will give serious weight to exculpatory evidence. "I don't need a full-scale hearing," one judge told attorney James Fagan (who is also a state legislator) when he tried to call witnesses to dispute a woman's claim of harassment by his client. The only issue, the judge declared, was whether he felt that the woman was fearful—"it isn't even who's telling the truth."[54]

In 1990, the Massachusetts Supreme Judicial Court ruled that a claim of "fear" was not enough to support a restraining order; there had to be some evidence that the plaintiff was "in fear of imminent serious physical harm" and that the fear was "reasonable." However, most judges don't like taking chances and are satisfied with the plaintiff's positive response to the question, "Are you afraid of bodily harm by the defendant?"[55]

Once the order is in effect, any contact becomes a criminal act punishable by up to two and half years in jail or a fine or both. A defendant can be convicted despite evidence that the "victim" agreed to meet him or even *initiated* contact.

The pressure on prosecutors and judges to go after violators aggressively comes not only from women's groups but from the media. In a 1994 article followed by an irate editorial, the *Boston Globe* revealed that many courts dismissed 33 to 75 percent of the violations. Whether the charges had merit never came up: courts with low rates of dismissals and high rates of incarceration were "the best"; those at the other end, "the worst."[56] Meanwhile, the *Globe* shows no interest in cases of men jailed for accidental "contact" at the courthouse or a divorce-related document sent by mail. One man asked a telephone operator to tell his ex-wife that his dying mother wanted to see her grandchildren, and spent over a hundred days in jail. Another was arrested for violating a restraining order (based on uncorroborated allegations of abuse) by stepping out of his car to pet his dogs when he came to pick up his son, and again for returning his son's call.[57]

Robert Byers, a Georgia contractor, found himself in the middle of a particularly twisted saga. In 1993, his wife, Lori Anderson, left with their eight-year-old daughter. He soon learned that they were with her relatives in Massachusetts and that the police were trying to serve him with a restraining order. He drove to Massachusetts for a hearing; his request for a continuance so that he could get a lawyer was denied and the order extended for a year, barring him from all contact with his wife or child. He was not even supposed to know where they lived.

Byers went home and filed for divorce. When the Georgia court had trouble locating Anderson to notify her of the custody hearing, he returned to Massachusetts, tracked her down, and went to serve her with the papers. He was arrested for violating the restraining order and, unable to make bail, was locked up for three months. Finally, he pleaded guilty to the violation in exchange for time served and a suspended sentence.

In October 1994, Byers won custody in Georgia and petitioned a Massachusetts court for the return of his daughter. The next day, Anderson filed a complaint that he had loitered in her driveway and made threatening calls to her sister. Byers was arrested and denied bail. In February 1995, he was found not guilty by a five-woman, one-man jury; the judge also threw out his earlier suspended sentence after reviewing the evidence.

Two hours after his release, Anderson got a new temporary restraining order. A probate judge finally ended this farce by ruling that Massachusetts was bound to respect the Georgia custody decree. Byers was able to take his child home—after a total of nearly two hundred days behind bars.[58]

Most feminist activists are offended by the very idea that women could lie about abuse to gain advantage (they are dismayed, for instance, by the suggestion that domestic violence training for judges and prosecutors might include guidelines on how to detect impostors). Yet even these advocates are willing to allow that restraining orders can be misused—by men. When it turned out that a man who broke into his ex-girlfriend's apartment and shot her and two other people had earlier obtained a temporary restraining order against her, advocates noted that "batterers often use restraining orders as a coercive tool, regardless of the facts" and that a temporary order was very easy to get.[59]

Critics such as Patrick Flynn, a fathers' rights activist who calls the abuse prevention law a "civil liberties holocaust for middle-class men," claim that most restraining orders are based on false accusations, made to gain leverage in a divorce. Reliable numbers are hard to come by. Many of the defendants are clearly not choir boys: in one study, 54 percent had been charged with drug and alcohol offenses, and one in four had been in jail or on probation prior to the restraining order's being issued—figures Massachusetts authorities have used to pooh-pooh claims that restraining orders are routinely misused. Yet 23 percent of the men had never been charged with a crime, and the records of some others consisted of complaints (*not* convictions) of abuse or of violating a prior restraining order.[60]

Even if, as supporters of the law maintain, only 4 to 5 percent of the charges are false, that amounts to about two thousand a year *in Massachusetts alone*. It's hardly a trifling figure when people are kicked out of their homes, cut off from their children, sometimes jailed, and severely disadvantaged in divorce and child custody litigation—and acquire the equivalent of a criminal record (their names are entered in the domestic violence registry) without the safeguards of a criminal trial.[61]

Interestingly, critics and defenders of the law seem to agree on how it works: "I think judges grant the restraining orders without even asking too many questions," said state legislator Barbara Gray, a sponsor of the original abuse prevention statute (now retired). Rather nonchalantly, she allowed that misuse of restraining orders was "always a possibility." Could anything be done about it? "Not really," Gray replied, "because then you're saying to a judge: On an emergency basis, you have to look at this woman and see whether you think she's telling the truth."[62]

The policies in Massachusetts are hardly unique. In Connecticut, writes Arnold Rutkin, editor of the legal journal *Family Advocate,* many judges treat protection orders as "a rubberstamping exercise," and the due process hearings held later "are usually a sham."[63]

In New Jersey, a woman whose estranged husband called her to threaten "drastic measures" if she didn't pay the household bills, and then had her phone disconnected, received a permanent restraining order on the grounds of "harassment." Another man was barred from the house (and ordered to continue making the mortgage payments) because he had abused his wife by repeatedly telling her that he no longer loved her and was going to seek a divorce. When state appellate courts moved to curb these excesses, resulting in fewer restraining orders, an outcry from advocates was quick to follow.[64]

In Missouri (where, in a one-year period in one county, nearly 40 percent of petitions for orders of protection did not allege any physical force and only 14 percent contained charges that warranted prosecution for assault), a survey of attorneys and judges for the Task Force on Gender and Justice in the early 1990s found numerous complaints that the "adult abuse" law was resulting in blatant disregard for due process and misuse for "litigation strategy" and "harassment." The task force agreed, "reluctantly," according to one panel member, to include these claims in the final report, but with the disclaimer that the manipulation of the system by women wasn't a real problem.[65]

In the post-O.J. frenzy of 1994, the Michigan legislature decided to allow restraining orders to take effect as soon as they're issued, before the defendant has been served—which means that he can face criminal charges for something he didn't know was a crime, creating obvious opportunities for entrapment. Kay Schwarzberg, a Michigan attorney, believes this almost happened to a client of hers who, at the tail end of a bitter divorce, was to pick up his belongings at the marital home on a mutually agreed-on date. Just in case, Schwarzberg asked a police officer to check the registry on protection orders. Sure enough, one had been filed the very day the wife's attorney had confirmed the date. Had the husband gone to the house, he could have landed in jail for three months.[66]

Stalking legislation, first enacted in California in 1990 and now on the books throughout the country, is another remedy that seeks to prevent violence before it occurs. The impetus for these laws has come from shocking crimes that, in retrospect, seemed predictable, such as the 1992 slaying of twenty-six-year-old Connie Chaney in Illinois by her estranged husband, who had repeatedly attacked her and was out on bail after allegedly raping her at gunpoint.[67]

It may well be that for the most part, stalking laws are used against truly dangerous people—often to cap off other serious charges. The first man sentenced under the Illinois law had repeatedly threatened his ex-girlfriend before following her to a college class, where he beat and choked her.[68]

But the statutes are often worded broadly enough to cover more ambiguous behavior. The Illinois law requires two or more instances of "following" or "surveillance" combined with an overt or "implied" threat; other statutes cover conduct causing "emotional distress." When there is no sign of violence, where does one draw the line between persistent or eccentric advances and stalking, between annoying and threatening behavior? Is it a crime when a middle-aged city councilman, distraught by a woman's decision to end their relationship, pesters her with late-night phone calls, parks outside her store, and leaves notes on her windshield begging her to take him back? Yes, said the authorities in Georgia.[69]

Cases stemming from dissolved marriages or relationships can be especially difficult. Ted Herbert, a forty-seven-year-old Illinois policeman, was charged with stalking his estranged wife, Eileen, over incidents that included writing to her in violation of a protection order and dropping off groceries for his stepchildren when she was out. The charge was reduced to a misdemeanor after revelations that while she was being supposedly terrorized by Ted, Eileen had written to him many times, called him (once to give him her new work number), and gone to his home.[70]

Some argue that even if the law is vague, prosecutors know better than to file frivolous charges. But in a climate where women's safety concerns are sacrosanct, prosecutors and judges may prefer to err on the side of caution. For the innocent defendant, this may mean months in jail because of the no-bond provisions of many such laws. In the first stalking case in Illinois to be heard by a jury, Giovanni Incandela spent four months in jail on a charge made in the middle of a divorce, only to be found not guilty after less than an hour of deliberations. Another alleged stalker was locked up for over a year before being acquitted. "On the word of one person, without a trial, we effectively put people away," public defender Greg O'Reilly told the *Chicago Tribune*.[71]

Stalking laws operate on something disturbingly akin to a presumption of guilt. Louis Chatroop, a Des Plaines, Illinois, computer consultant, went to civil court to collect a $3,800 debt from an exgirlfriend; by curious coincidence, she called the police that very day to report him loitering near her building. Two weeks later, she sought a restraining order, this time adding that he had brandished a gun (a detail that she had omitted when she first spoke to the police). Then she claimed that he had followed her in his car. Chatroop's new girlfriend swore that he was with her at the time; he had no criminal record and no history of violence; his own ex-wife had only good things to say about him. His accuser, on the other hand, had previously made and withdrawn a stalking charge against another ex-boyfriend. Nonetheless, Chatroop was charged and held without bond. After languishing in jail for eleven months, he agreed to plead guilty to a minor charge of intimidation by phone to secure his release.[72]

Justice for All or Gender Justice?

Does the zero-tolerance approach to domestic violence apply to everyone—or are women presumed innocent not only before but sometimes *after* they have been proved guilty?

Undoubtedly the crusade against abuse has swept up some women in its wide net. A New Jersey woman had a restraining order issued against her because she vocally disapproved of her estranged husband's cohabitation with another woman; she violated the order by berating him for bringing "that slut" to a birthday party for one of their kids and got six months probation with community service. Two months after Wisconsin's mandatory arrest law took effect, a Milwaukee mother was arrested for slapping her backtalking teenage son. In many states, "dual arrests" and arrests of women as sole perpetrators have risen sharply.[73]

The activists' reaction, however, leaves no doubt that the War on Domestic Violence was meant to be a war against men. "If women are violent, we'll deal with it . . . because we want women to stay out of jail and to get the best, most helpful, the most comprehensive advocacy," a New Jersey Coalition for Battered Women official wrote with admirable frankness. Lonnie Hazlewood, the former director of the Family Violence Diversion Network in Austin, Texas, says that "an item showed up on the agenda of the domestic violence task force, 'Why Are Battered Women Getting Arrested?'" Due to feminist lobbying, some states amended their laws to specify that the "primary aggressor" must be arrested (which, in an incident witnessed by Lawrence Sherman, the criminologist, meant that a husband whose wife hit him after he had yelled at her was the one to get locked up). An anti–dual arrest clause was also inserted in the pro-arrest provisions of the Violence Against Women Act.[74]

As VAWA headed for a vote, Sally Goldfarb, an attorney with the NOW Legal Defense Fund, told me that dual arrests were a "discriminatory" way to punish battered women for bothering the police. But according to Deborah Beck, the domestic violence counselor in Florida, it's often the other way around: "Only one person gets arrested where they both should be." That person is usually male, even when the woman started it and when the man suffers more damage—for example, when he holds her down after she hits him over the head with a bottle, which happened to a man in Beck's program. Susan Finkelstein was told by the arresting officer that the policy was to arrest the "larger" person (a creative way to get around gender neutrality). Reports in the media occasionally reveal this bias, such as a Michigan story that made a humorous headline or two: an inebriated woman slugged her husband in the face with a cucumber hard enough to cause a welt; they scuffled, the police arrived, and he was arrested for hitting her.[75]

The paternalistic tendency not to take female violence very seriously is often reinforced by politically correct training. A Massachusetts manual notes that "injury alone doesn't determine who is the abuser" and warns against falling for such "excuses" as, "She hit me first."[76]

If violent women are presumed to be abused, then the campaign against abuse means greater leniency for them, even when their violence turns deadly. Self-defense is, of course, a basic right. Whatever the advocates may say, this right was recognized for battered women before the modern wave of feminism. Some legal theorists argue that traditional concepts of self-defense focus on "encounters between men of roughly equal size and strength" and view violent acts outside their context. Yet in 1902, a Texas woman's murder conviction was reversed because her husband's past brutality had been excluded at her trial. A defendant, the court ruled, could present proof that "the deceased was a person of ferocity [and] excessive strength" to show that he or she was in danger. In the 1940s and 1950s, several appellate courts ruled that prior asaults and disparities in physical strength had to be considered to determine if the person acted reasonably in response to a threat.[77] No doubt, some abused women defending themselves have been wrongly convicted (as have some men). But the advocates' concerns go beyond rectifying such injustices. The battered woman syndrome, a theory formulated by feminist psychologist Lenore Walker and widely challenged on scientific grounds, was a way to extend the notion of self-defense to women who strike when they are in no immediate danger, maybe when the man is asleep or unconscious, supposedly because the battering leaves them so psychologically paralyzed that they see no way of escape except to kill.[78]

Yes, in *some* extreme cases, a woman who kills a sleeping batterer may be compared to a kidnap victim who kills the sleeping abductor. Robin Elson, a California woman who fatally shot her husband as he lay in a drunken stupor, may have been such a hostage. Jack Elson had thwarted her two earlier escape attempts and threatened to kill her and the children. (Robin, who said she was trying to get out and fired the gun when she saw Jack move, was acquitted.) But many women who claim to "fight back" are neither financially dependent nor socially isolated.[79]

Expert testimony on the battered woman syndrome is now admissible in all fifty states and is often used in outrageous ways. (Lenore Walker once tried to explain how the syndrome could make a woman take out a lucrative insurance policy on her husband and target-practice before shooting him in his sleep, then stage a burglary and go to a disco.) To say that it has become a license to kill is quite an exaggeration: only a quarter to a third of the women who use this defense are acquitted. But does this mean that gender politics have not influenced the treatment of women who kill their husbands or boyfriends?[80]

The advocates insist that such women are still treated quite harshly and cite shocking numbers: the average sentence for a woman who kills her mate is fifteen to twenty years; for a man, two to six. This factoid, picked up by *Time* magazine and other media, is attributed to findings by Michael Dowd of the Battered Women's Justice Center at Pace University.[81]

Time doesn't say exactly where Dowd "found" this. A Justice Department study of the disposition of domestic homicides in the seventy-five largest urban counties in 1988 paints a very different picture: 87 percent of men charged with killing their spouses pleaded guilty or were convicted, compared to 70 percent of the women. Of these, 94 percent of the husbands and 81 percent of the wives received prison sentences—on average, 16.5 years for husbands and 6.0 years for wives. While some of the disparity was due to the fact that more women had been "provoked"—assaulted or threatened—before the slaying, the authors noted that "the average prison sentence for unprovoked wife defendants was 7 years, or 10 years shorter than the average 17 years for the unprovoked husband defendants."[82]

Still, the questionable numbers are cited to advocate clemency for women convicted of killing their partners. Investigative reports on some of the women released in mass pardons by Ohio governor Richard Celeste and Maryland governor Donald Schaeffer in late 1990 and early 1991 turned up details that seriously undermined their claims of self-defense. In Massachusetts, one of the seven women who won early release after being profiled in the Academy Award–winning documentary *Defending Our Lives* later went back to jail for assault with a deadly weapon (and another for theft). In New Hampshire, June's Briand, who put four bullets in her sleeping husband's head, was pardoned by Governor Stephen Merrill five years short of the fifteen-year minimum to which she had agreed in a plea bargain—even though not only Jim Briand's relatives but a coworker and friend of June's asserted that he never physically abused her, and Jim's daughter, who was seven years old when her father died, testified that June, a heavy drinker and drug user, used to beat her.[83]

Other cases never go to trial. In Brooklyn, New York, in 1987, Marlene Wagshall shot her sleeping husband, Joshua, in the stomach after finding a photo of him with a scantily clad young woman. He was crippled for life; she was charged with attempted murder. Yet on the basis of her uncorroborated claims that Joshua had beaten her in the past, district attorney Elizabeth Holtzman, a champion of women's rights, allowed Wagshall to plead guilty to assault with a sentence of *one day in jail* and five years probation.[84]

And juries, as well as prosecutors and judges, can be swayed by gender politics. In a 1998 column, writer/professor Elayne Clift describes persuading her fellow jurors to convict a man of stalking on ambiguous evidence because she thought of "the Clothesline Project" commemorating women who died at the hands of men. Around the same time, the trial of Virginia politician and developer Ruthann Aron on charges of plotting to kill her husband and another man ended in a hung jury, despite damning evidence, because a female juror insisted on seeing Aron as a victim of mistreatment by men.[85]

Casualties of War

Even in the midst of the War on Domestic Violence, we hear about women being killed by men whom the courts did little to stop, such as twenty-one-year-old Kristin Lardner, shot in Boston in 1992 by an ex-boyfriend who then killed himself. Michael Cartier had a lengthy rap sheet that included the attempted stabbing of another woman; yet he never spent much time in jail, no one checked his record when Kristin sought a restraining order after he beat her up, and the assault charge was processed at a sluggish pace. While Kristin may have been reckless—she failed to report two instances of Cartier's stalking—the system clearly failed her, though I doubt that it was due to indifference to "the evil done to women," as Kristin's father, *Washington Post* reporter George Lardner, wrote with understandable bitterness.[86]

Does this evident apathy contradict the stories of excessive zeal? Actually, the two can coexist quite well, just as horror stories of children yanked from parental homes on flimsy suspicions of abuse coexist with horror stories of abused children who are returned to their tormentors. Some child welfare experts say that overzealous probes of frivolous accusations lead to *underenforcement* where action is needed most, since the system gets too bogged down in trivial pursuit to single out the serious cases.[87]

It's probably the same with domestic violence. Law enforcement and the courts, says sociologist Richard Gelles, fail to differentiate between minor claims of abuse and cases rife with danger signs (though with the best preventive strategies, intimate homicide is not always predictable: research by Lawrence Sherman, the University of Maryland criminologist, challenges the popular notion that it is usually the culmination of a history of violence). David Gremillion, a physician who has seen serious harm done by both domestic violence and false accusations, adds that the system may work better for manipulators than it does for real victims too scared or too unsophisticated to navigate its channels.[88]

Balancing the rights of the accused against the safety of victims is hard. Most of us do not consider a police state a proper price to pay for absolute security. Yet when someone objects to overbroad domestic violence laws or raises concerns about unscrupulous pseudo-victims' taking advantage of the system, the typical response is that in view of "the devastating statistics" on domestic violence, one must give priority to protecting women.[89]

Yet even if one decides that it's better for ten innocent men to be jailed than for one woman to be killed, there is no evidence that the crackdown saves lives. A man who is going to kill a woman and is ready to take his own life or face a murder rap won't be deterred by a charge of violating a court order, as too many news stories show. Several studies cast doubt on whether restraining orders have any protective effect, except perhaps for women who were never severely victimized. If so, peddling them to people in real danger is like giving cancer patients a drug that cures the common cold.[90]

Meanwhile, the laws can make it easy for spousal assault charges to be used as a weapon. The image of manipulative women crying abuse may seem offensive. But if some men use their physical advantage against women, should we be shocked if some women use their legal advantage against men? Such tactics were openly advocated by two women who toured the country in the late 1980s giving women-only seminars on "playing to win" in a divorce. (New federal legislation proposed in Congress in 1998 as an expansion of VAWA would create further incentives for false charges by creating a host of benefits for abused women, based on the alleged victim's statement alone—from priority in public housing and social services to expanded employment rights.)[91]

Ethics aside, we should ask—without creating a new "abuse excuse"—whether being on the receiving end of these maneuvers may not push some nonviolent people over the edge. Says James Fagan, the Massachusetts attorney and state legislator, "People with nothing to lose are dangerous people."

The problem is not that there is too much concern with domestic violence. Although severe abuse affects a fairly small portion of the population, family violence in its milder forms can still have harmful consequences, especially to children. But we have seen this issue almost entirely through the distorting lens of the battered women's movement. The result is a one-size-fits-all approach that lumps together battering and marital discord, ignores the two-way dynamics of troubled relationships, effectively denies some couples the opportunity to reconcile, and discourages solutions based on mutual responsibility and learning to get along—solutions that in many cases could work.

"There were many awful men, to be sure, and many awful situations," says Renée Ward, looking back on her days as a shelter director. "But I think that for the advocates, their personal agenda got in the way of asking how—*if*—men and women could live together." Such an agenda should never have been allowed to dictate public policy.

CHAPTER SIX

Sex Crimes, Political Crimes

Today, any man can be accused of rape, at any time, for any
reason. . . . All that is needed to send a man to prison is the accusation.
— James Anderson, "Confessions of a Mad Dog Rapist in Prison"[1]

When the crime is acquaintance rape, the usual positions of complainant and defendant are often reversed: Inside and outside the
courtroom, the man charged with a crime of violence is the object
of sympathy, while his alleged victim finds herself on trial.
— Katha Pollitt, "Men, Women and the Question of Consent"[2]

The discussion of how the system treats rape usually
boils down to these two extremes. Feminists point to
high-profile acquittals: William Kennedy Smith, the men at St. John's
University accused of sexually assaulting a woman student.[3] But
Mark Bravo, a former nurse in Los Angeles, might well agree that an
accusation is enough to send a man away. In 1990, a mental patient
at the hospital where he worked said that a "Tony Bravo" raped her.
Despite an alibi corroborated by several coworkers, Bravo was convicted. Luckily for him, the woman later named someone else as the
rapist, and new DNA tests showed that Bravo could not have been
involved (whether the woman was actually raped is unclear). Bravo
was freed after three years in prison.[4]

Even if things don't go that far, a mere accusation can have severe
consequences. In 1996, Los Angeles sheriff's deputy Harris Mintz
was accused of raping a woman in the neighborhood he patrolled.
Then there were shocking new charges: Mintz's wife of four years

claimed that he had sexually assaulted her on several occasions. A few months later, Mrs. Mintz admitted that she made up the story to punish her husband for getting in trouble. Prosecutors still insisted that the first accuser (who had collected a $100,000 settlement from the county) was "very credible"—until evidence turned up that she had falsely accused another man of rape two years earlier and had told an ex-roommate she had concocted the charge against Mintz. By the time the case collapsed, he had spent five months in jail.[5]

When feminists began to agitate for changes in the treatment of rape, they had a good case. Earlier in this century, many eminent jurists saw rape complainants as vengeful, spurned women or sex-crazed neurotics. Just twenty years ago, jurors in rape cases were given a special warning, based on the dictum of seventeenth-century British jurist Lord Matthew Hale, that the testimony of the woman should be treated with caution since a charge of rape was "easily made and difficult to defend against, even if the accused is innocent." Often juries were told to consider evidence of "unchaste character" (going to bars alone, extramarital liaisons, or use of birth control) as detracting from an accuser's credibility or suggesting that she was more likely to have consented.[6]

The belief that a woman had to resist "to the utmost" also lingered for a long time. In 1977, a New York appellate panel overturned a rape conviction because the woman, who gave in after the man hit her, had not resisted enough. The ruling, later reversed, caused such an uproar that the legislature changed the statute.[7]

Still, the treatment of victims, particularly in stranger rape cases, wasn't wholly barbaric. "Unchaste character" testimony was sometimes barred, and even feminists conceded that such tactics were rarely used in cases of brutal rape, since they might backfire. By the 1960s, most courts recognized that submission to threats was not consent.[8]

In the following decade, feminists waged a highly successful effort, supported by both civil libertarians and law-and-order groups, to eliminate the resistance requirement and bar the use of "unchastity" to impeach the complainant. Yet even then, some commentators sympathetic to these goals cautioned against "sacrificing legitimate rights of the accused person on the altar of Women's Liberation." And by the 1990s, even some former sex crimes prosecutors were expressing concerns that the pendulum had swung too far.[9]

Calling It Rape: "No Means No" and Beyond

> Politically, I call it rape whenever a woman has sex and feels violated.
> —Catharine MacKinnon, *Feminism: Unmodified*[10]

The debate about rape and the law is complicated by the fact that there doesn't seem to be much agreement anymore on what rape is. We can all agree (I hope) that a person always has the right to say no, no matter how far things have gone, and no one has the right to force sex on another. But what does that mean? Take this scenario from a college pamphlet:

> A couple have been going out for a while and have had sex before. After a dinner date, they return to his place where he begins to take off her clothes. She pushes him back, saying "no" . . . he pulls her firmly against him, says "yes" and continues to undress her. They have intercourse.[11]

Is this rape? I have no idea. Does she try to get out of his embrace? Does he restrain her? Does she push him away again and tell him, "I said, no"? Or does she eagerly await his caresses?

What if a woman is in bed with her lover and says that she just wants to talk, but her lover keeps touching and caressing her, and she finally gives in and fakes an orgasm? Such a story ran in 1992 in the Massachusetts Institute of Technology paper, the *Thistle,* under the title, "When She Says No, It's *Always* Rape." (The "rapist," by the way, was another woman.) When I showed the article to Virginia MacKay-Smith, an assistant dean at Harvard and a leader of the university's Date Rape Task Force, she was positive that if a student came to her with such a complaint, she would "feel no hesitation to report it to the police" or bring administrative charges.

What if the woman says no and the man threatens to dump her or "make[s] fun of her for being a prude"? According to a 1997 article in a popular magazine for teenage girls, he's a date rapist using "psychological intimidation."[12]

And what about drunken sex? Clearly, if a man takes advantage of a woman who has passed out, that's rape. But there are also situations like the one described in a letter to Ann Landers by a woman who met a man in a bar and ended up in bed with him after two drinks, only to feel disgusted with herself the next morning: "I phoned my girlfriend and told her what happened. She said, 'You were raped.' I told her I didn't see it that way." Amazingly, Ann replies: "Yes, your friend is right." (Are people commonly absolved of responsibility for their actions because they've had a couple of drinks?)[13]

In a 1991 essay rebuking "apologists for date rape," writer Susan Jacoby recalled an episode from her youth. Involved in a troubled relationship, depressed and confused, she invited an ex-boyfriend over for a sexual interlude—and changed her mind on the way to the bedroom. That he didn't force himself on her but simply left in a huff, she wrote, was no more than should be expected of a civilized human being. Readily conceding that some women enjoy being coy and some men enjoy coaxing a woman further than she meant to go, Jacoby stressed that these games have nothing to do with rape: one can easily tell the difference "between a half-hearted 'no, we shouldn't' and tears or screams; between a woman who is physically free to leave a room and one who is being physically restrained."[14]

Jacoby is right, but she wrongly credits the anti–date rape activists with the same common sense. To them, "no means no" makes no allowances for tone of voice. MacKay-Smith, the Harvard dean, told me that a distinction between a half-hearted "no" and tears and screams "opens the door to a lot of interpretation and a lot of harm." Kathryn Geller Myers of the Pennsylvania Coalition Against Rape said that "after the first 'no,' there should be no progression of seduction or whatever"; anything that follows is rape. Does this mean that once you say no, your partner has no right to try to change your mind? "That's exactly what I'm saying," replied Myers.[15]

Imagine what would happen if we were to apply these principles to other areas of life. If a friend nagged you into lending him your car, we would call it acquaintance carjacking. If someone talked you into going on an unwanted trip by making you feel guilty about refusing, that would be kidnapping. If a relative from out of town wanted to stay at your place and did not take repeated hints that this wasn't such a good time, that would be no different from thugs forcing their way in at gunpoint.

Robin Warshaw, whose 1988 book *I Never Called It Rape* is a bible of date rape activism, insists in the foreword to the 1994 edition that date rape is nothing less than forced sex, involving physical coercion, threats, or incapacitation (even if the victim doesn't consider it rape). Dismissing concerns about overbroad definitions of rape as "backlash" and "rape-denial," Warshaw admits that she has seen "occasional materials" using such definitions. She forgets to mention that among those materials is a text to which she contributed, and which she lists among the resources at the end of her book. The 1991 volume *Acquaintance Rape: The Hidden Crime* includes, under the heading "Types of Acquaintance Rape," an essay on "Nonviolent Sexual Coercion," defined as "verbal arguments not including verbal threats of force," such as "everyone's doing it."[16]

Nor does Warshaw acknowledge that some widely publicized studies of date rape use the term loosely. A campus survey by Stanford University's Rape Education Project generated such headlines as, "Date Rape Common, Stanford Study Says; 33% of Women, 12% of Men Tell of Forced Sex." These findings were understandably characterized as "shocking." Yet aside from the fact that a mere 10 percent of the "victims" believed they were raped, 75 percent of this "forced sex" involved "continual arguments and pressure," and another 10 percent involved alcohol.[17]

I wonder if Warshaw, whose own experience of acquaintance rape was a brutal assault by a knife-wielding ex-lover, is troubled when someone like Katie Koestner emerges as a spokeswoman for the anti–date rape movement. A graduate of the College of William and Mary who now lectures on sexual violence, Koestner became a media darling when she went public as a victim of date rape. Yet she acknowledges that the young man she accused did nothing more than keep pressing for sex despite her repeated refusals, and even that she didn't say "no" immediately prior to intercourse.[18]

The activists routinely blur the lines between actual violence and "emotional coercion." "No one has the right to verbally pressure or physically force you to have sex," states a leaflet of the Bergen County Rape Crisis Center in New Jersey. Of the respondents to a survey my research assistant sent to rape crisis centers, two-thirds said it was rape if a man got a woman into bed by using emotional pressure but no force or threats of bodily harm. Some elaborated: "Yes, such as threatening to leave her." Even if the woman never said "no" because she didn't want to hurt his feelings, many would treat her as a rape victim. One of the few people in the field to have publicly criticized these views—Gillian Greensite, director of the rape prevention program at the University of California at Santa Cruz—says that she has encountered "real hostility and narrow-mindedness" from her colleagues.[19]

For many activists, the strictest interpretation of "no means no" is not enough: nothing less than an explicit "yes" will do. The notorious Antioch College sexual offense code, which mandates verbal consent every step of the way, from undoing a button to penetration, may be unique, but many colleges and universities have instituted less extreme versions of such policies. In 1994, a senior at Pomona College in California was nearly prevented from graduating because of a rape complaint brought with a two-year delay. The woman admitted that she willingly went to his room after a party, let him undress her, and never said no—but claimed that she never gave her consent, defined by the school as "clear, explicit agreement to engage in a specific activity."[20]

Katha Pollitt's vitriolic review of *The Morning After*, Katie Roiphe's critique of "rape-crisis feminism," was titled "Not Just Bad Sex." But some feminist theorists are candid about their view that the date rape crusade *is* about bad sex. Philosopher Lois Pineau, who believes that good sex is "communicative sex," would require the accused man to prove that he took steps not only to ensure the woman's explicit consent but to find out "what she liked," since "it is not reasonable for women to consent" otherwise. (Columnist Ellen Goodman thinks it's a brilliantly provocative idea.) Others suggest that requiring women to give verbal consent to sex is a good way to subvert the convention of female passivity, though they still assume that it's the man who will do the asking, while the woman is relieved even from the responsibility of fending off unwanted advances.[21]

Of course, there is always communication in sex; it just doesn't have to involve words. A physical overture is a nonverbal request for permission to proceed; the response is a nonverbal "yes" or "no." Most people, women or men, have a visceral aversion to communicating sexual intent directly; even code-abiding Antioch students reportedly resort to the wry euphemism, "Want to activate the policy?" Partly it's because we want to camouflage the vulnerability that comes from expressing sexual need; partly because, as women's magazines often point out when warning about the baneful effects of self-consciousness about one's body, good sex is about letting go. This does not mean that, as Katha Pollitt caricatures the position of verbal consent critics, talk in intimate encounters kills eroticism; but lucid, clear-headed negotiations certainly do.[22]

"No means no" absolutism is just as far removed from real life. In a 1988 study by feminist researcher Charlene Muehlenhard, 60 percent of sexually active college women admitted that they had on occasion said "no" while fully intending to have sex; nearly all had said "no" when they weren't sure. (A woman could also say no and mean it, and then change her mind.) Psychologists Lucia O'Sullivan and Elizabeth Allgeier have found that not only young women but young men use "token resistance" in sexual situations—to avoid being seen as interested just in sex, to slow things down out of concern for the relationship, to add spice and challenge to the mating dance. Three-quarters of men and women alike regarded these interactions as enjoyable.[23]

Both Muehlenhard and some feminist commentators who acknowledge her inconvenient findings insist that even if many women say "no" when they don't really mean it, men should still be punished for ignoring a woman's "no" when she does mean it. (This argument speaks volumes about their belief that only men should be held responsible for sexual miscommunication.) But does the belief that "no" doesn't always mean no put women in danger of rape, as these scholars suggest? These fears are not supported by a poll in which 60 percent of young men said they would *not* stop immediately "in the heat of passion" if the woman said "no"; the vast majority said they would stop if she sounded upset or said "no" more than once, and virtually all the rest said they would stop if she resisted physically.[24]

Feminists are free to advocate "communicative" sex with no ambiguity and no loss of control. They certainly have every right to say that it's wrong to pressure a reluctant partner into unwanted sex; most people would agree. The problem is that the debate about proper sexual norms has been framed as a debate about rape. As critics have pointed out, this trivializes real rape: one can't keep saying that "rape is a life-threatening situation" and using the word for situations in which no threat to life exists. (One paradox most feminists sidestep is that when "nonviolent sexual coercion" is redefined as rape, many men qualify as victims of rape by women.)[25]

But "calling it rape," to borrow the title of a play widely performed on college campuses in the 1990s, has its advantages for the advocates: it chills the debate about sexual norms. When a sexual assault counselor warns that "the blind give-and-take of sexual negotiations" can lead to "game playing, deception, and confusion," one can say, "That's life." But when he asks, "Isn't rape prevention important enough for us to . . . modify our behavior?" one can't easily say "no."[26]

The rape label also places what many feminists consider nonconsensual sex within the scope of the law (or sanctions by college panels). The advocates' power rests on intimidation, not persuasion. In a list of "Ten Reasons to Obtain Verbal Consent to Sex," Bernice Sandler, head of the National Association of Women in Education, quickly goes from the dubious assertion that "many partners find it sexy to be asked, as sex progresses, if it's okay" to "you won't go to jail or be expelled."[27]

Force and Consent: The Legal Debate

> The criminal law ought to say clearly that women who actually say no must be respected as meaning it; that nonconsent means saying no; that men who proceed nonetheless . . . have acted unreasonably and unlawfully. —Susan Estrich, "Rape"[28]

The strict construction of "no means no" has made significant inroads into the justice system in the last two decades. Curiously, the *Yale Law Journal* article titled "Rape" by then–Harvard Law School professor Susan Estrich, and her subsequent book, *Real Rape,* which played a seminal role in the development of legal thinking on the issue, never addressed situations in which the man proceeds with nonforcible advances after the woman says "no." Estrich's examples were of women who were clearly in fear. In *State v. Rusk,* a Maryland case from the late 1970s, the woman gave the man a ride home from a bar and reluctantly followed him into the house after he took her car keys. She testified that she tearfully begged him to let her go, but he "kept saying 'no.'" Finally, she asked, "If I do what you want, will you let me go without killing me?" and gave in after he said yes.[29]

The man's conviction was upheld, but three of the seven appellate judges dissented because the woman did such a poor job of defending her virtue. The victim's submission, they wrote, had to "stem from fear generated by something of substance." Yet surely what is wrong here is not the argument itself but the view that being in a strange neighborhood at night, with a man who won't let you leave, is not a substantial cause for fear.

In 1986, when Estrich's essay appeared, the California Supreme Court ruled in *People v. Barnes,* another case in which the woman gave in without a fight. The defendant's methods of persuasion after she rebuffed him included grabbing her by the collar, bragging that he could "pick her up with one hand and throw her out," and warn-

ing her not to upset him. The court affirmed that even without
resistance, sexual intercourse "by means of force or fear of immediate and unlawful bodily injury" was rape. This position wasn't very
different from the *Rusk* dissent; it simply showed a better understanding of reasonable fear.[30]

It's interesting to compare this to a controversial Pennsylvania
case a few years later. Robert Berkowitz, a junior at East Stroudsburg
University, was accused of raping a nineteen-year-old sophomore.
The young woman, who was dating another student but had previously engaged Berkowitz in rather explicit sexual banter, had come
to his dorm room looking for his roommate, who was out. They sat
on the floor and talked about her man troubles; then Berkowitz
leaned over and started kissing her and fondling her breasts, despite
her protestations that she had to go and meet her boyfriend.
According to the young woman, she said "no" in a "scolding" tone
but never tried to push him away or get up (by her own account,
she was not pinned down). Berkowitz admitted that he heard her
whisper "no" but claimed that she returned his kisses, moaning
"amorously." She made no attempt to leave when he went to lock
the door, which, as she knew, could still be opened from the inside
with a simple turn of the knob.

By her account, Berkowitz then "put [her] down on the bed" and
removed her pants while she was "kind of laying there"; after he
entered her, she softly moaned "no." Again, he confirmed the "no"
but also claimed that the young woman moaned "passionately" and
helped him undress her; after they started having sex, he noticed a
"blank look on her face" and asked what was wrong. (They both
agreed that he withdrew and ejaculated in about thirty seconds.)
The girl told her boyfriend what happened, and he called the
police.[31]

Berkowitz was found guilty. However, an appellate court reversed
his conviction, concluding that there was no evidence of "forcible
compulsion." When the Pennsylvania State Supreme Court upheld
this ruling in 1994, women's groups were up in arms. The media
hewed the party line, often condensing the facts in a way that made
them seem less ambiguous. Activists blasted the court for telling victims that they had to "physically resist and risk serious bodily
injury." Yet the ruling specifically noted that the victim "need not
resist" when there is force or threats to induce submission.[32]

"I did . . . what everyone taught us to do in college," Berkowitz's
"victim" told a local paper. "If we were being raped, say 'no' and

don't fight, because you could wind up dead." Although studies suggest that fighting back may improve women's chances of avoiding
rape without raising the risk of injury, a rape victim (like a robbery
victim) certainly should not be *required* by law to resist a violent
assault. But was there a violent assault in *Berkowitz*—or was the
young woman the victim of a date rape education that never
explained the difference between rape and persistent, nonviolent
sexual advances? She herself had admitted that she was not threatened. There was, as the court stressed, no evidence that she "could
not have walked out . . . without any risk of harm or danger to herself." Susan Estrich herself found the case troubling: "Is a man guilty
of rape if a woman says no but just doesn't bother to leave?"[33]

Yet in response to the outcry from feminists, Pennsylvania politicians were quick to pass a bill making sexual assault without force or
threat, based solely on a "no," a second-degree felony punishable by
up to ten years in prison. In other states, too, the law has been inch-
ing closer to the hard-line interpretation of "no means no."

In 1994, three weeks after the *Berkowitz* ruling, the Colorado
Court of Appeals explicitly rejected the reasoning of the
Pennsylvania court and affirmed a conviction in such a case by a
two-to-one vote.[34] The woman had claimed that the defendant not
only ignored her "no" but overpowered her in a violent struggle.
The jury rejected this story, which was contradicted by physical evidence, and acquitted Gregory Schmidt of first-degree sexual assault,
which requires the use or threat of force, but they convicted him of
second-degree sexual assault: penetration by any other means "reasonably calculated to cause submission against the victim's will." This
verdict, the court of appeals said, was supported by Schmidt's own
story that after "messing around," the woman said no to sex (mainly
for fear of being found out by his wife) and that he still pulled off
her panties and had sex with her, assuming that everything was fine
since she didn't protest again. What did he do to cause her unwilling
submission? The court resolved this question simply: once permission is denied, *anything* the defendant does to obtain sex fits the bill.

Most rape statutes still require force or threat, but that hardly settles the issue. In a 1992 ruling, the New Jersey State Supreme Court
managed to turn a law defining sexual assault as penetration by
"physical force or coercion" into an Antioch-style explicit consent
requirement.

Fifteen-year-old C.G. claimed that she woke up at night to find
herself being assaulted by M.T.S., a seventeen-year-old boy lodging

at her mother's house. According to M.T.S., she had invited him to bed and willingly engaged in kissing and fondling, but became very upset when he "stuck it in." By both accounts, he stopped and left immediately after she slapped his face and verbally rebuked him. C.G.'s mother took her to the police the next day, after the girl said that M.T.S. had raped her and she wanted him out of the house. At the trial, the judge concluded that the girl's story of sleeping soundly while being stripped of her shorts and underpants was implausible, and that the boy probably told the truth—but that he was guilty anyway, since she had consented to "heavy petting," not to sex. (As a juvenile, M.T.S. was sentenced to probation and a small fine.)

The conviction was set aside on appeal, on the grounds that the element of force was missing—and then reinstated by the New Jersey State Supreme Court, which held unanimously that without "affirmative and freely-given permission," penetration itself constituted force. The court did vaguely suggest that permission could be granted through "physical actions." But it repeatedly stressed that the victim "need not have said or done anything" to deny consent, and no questions can be asked about why she didn't protest.[35]

Proof and Credibility

Broadly or narrowly defined, rape can still be difficult to prove or disprove. In the past, the accuser's testimony had to be corroborated by other evidence—a rule that, feminists not unreasonably argued, was discriminatory, since no corroboration was required for robbery or assault. Yet only a minority of jurisdictions ever strictly enforced this requirement—often a "prompt outcry" was considered sufficient to meet it—and by 1980, it was virtually extinct.[36]

Just because corroboration is not legally necessary does not mean that it's unimportant; without it, a conviction is far less likely for any crime. Interestingly, in her 1986 article, Estrich rejected the claim that rape was treated differently from other serious crimes: "The downgrading of cases involving prior relationships, less force, and no corroboration is characteristic of the criminal justice system." But in rape cases, Estrich wrote, "corroboration may be uniquely absent": there are usually no eyewitnesses, no material evidence—such as a weapon in a felony assault or the loot in a robbery—and no injury if the victim is too frightened to resist. Therefore, she concluded, giving "equal weight" to corroboration for rape, robbery, and assault was not "neutral" but actually unfair to rape victims.[37]

But then it follows that, to be "fair," *we should convict defendants in rape cases on less evidence and give the complainant's word more weight than in other crimes.* And that makes all those old misogynistic warnings about how difficult it is for an innocent man to defend himself against a charge of rape seem uncomfortably close to the truth.

Yet the notion of the special credibility of rape complainants is gaining a foothold in the criminal justice system. Sometimes it is even codified in law.

In California since the 1900s, juries were told that a rape defendant could be convicted on the accuser's word alone, balancing the warning to treat her testimony with caution. Although the cautionary instruction was eliminated in 1975, the other one survived. In 1992, attorneys appealing a conviction in a her-word-against-his case argued that this gave the prosecution an unfair edge: since jurors were also admonished to review carefully any claim based on the word of a single witness, to stress that the complainant's testimony was sufficient could suggest that she was entitled to more credit than other witnesses, including the defendant. The California Supreme Court disagreed, opining that the instruction was still needed to counteract prejudice against rape victims. By then, rape cases tried in California had a 92 percent conviction rate, just behind homicide.[38]

For some modern juries, it seems to take a great deal to override the credibility of a woman who says she was raped. In 1996, Michael Ivers, a junior at Michigan State University, was tried on charges of sexually assaulting a first-year student he had met at an off-campus party. Ivers testified that they went back to his apartment and had consensual sex; the young woman claimed that she had an alcoholic blackout and remembered nothing from the moment they left the party together to the moment she found herself in bed with him. One might say her word against his left plenty of reasonable doubt: an intoxicated person can forget a block of time without losing consciousness. But in this case, it was her word against his and two others': Ivers's roommates testified that they came into the room and turned on the lights three different times while the young woman was there, and that she was fully conscious—once even asking that the lights be turned off—and did not ask for help. Nonetheless, Ivers was convicted.[39]

To some, the very idea that a woman who says she was raped may be lying is akin to heresy. ("Feminism," Catharine MacKinnon has written, "is built on believing women's accounts of sexual use and abuse by men.") In 1988, a University of Michigan student who had posted a message in an electronic forum about false allegations of date rape received a letter from a school administrator warning that his comments reflected "an insensitive and dangerous attitude" and could lead to a charge of "discriminatory harassment."[40]

Activists may even refuse to believe a "victim" if she says she lied. In 1991, when a Davis, California, woman admitted making up a story of gang rape that had plunged the town into a three-week frenzy, a few zealots suggested that women recant out of fear or "denial." Many bristle when the media publicize stories of falsely accused men: "Why such a big article on a wrongful accusation when we know that more than 99 percent of the time, victims don't lie?" gripes a letter to the editor.[41]

The media, for the most part, uncritically repeat the "advocacy statistic" that false complaints account for no more than 1 or 2 percent of rape reports, the same as for other crimes. Actually, FBI statistics show that about 9 percent of rape reports are "unfounded"—dismissed at the earliest stage of investigation, without charges being filed. The feminist party line is that many, if not most, of these are valid complaints, nixed because they lack sufficient proof or because the authorities distrust acquaintance rape claims. But dismissals due to insufficient evidence usually occur further down the pipeline, and those complaints, which may or may not be false, are *not* included in the "unfounded" category. Generally a complaint is unfounded only when the alleged victim recants, or when her story is not just unsupported but *contradicted* by evidence.[42]

Measuring false allegations is all the more difficult since policies on unfounded criminal complaints differ from one jurisdiction to another, resulting in very different numbers. A *Washington Post* investigation showed that in seven counties in Virginia and Maryland, almost one in four rape reports in 1990–1991 were unfounded; when contacted by the newspaper, many "victims" admitted that they lied. More shocking figures come from a study by now-retired Purdue University sociologist Eugene Kanin, who reviewed the police records of an Indiana town and found that 45 of 109 reports of rape filed from 1978 to 1987—41 percent—were false *by the complainant's own admission.*[43]

Could some real victims have recanted under pressure from sexist

cops? The town's police did use the controversial practice of subjecting complainants to lie detector tests, which has been criticized on
scientific as well as political grounds (the polygraph rarely misses
liars but may have a high error rate with truthful subjects) and is
now banned in many jurisdictions. But Kanin also analyzed police
files from two state universities—where lie detectors were not used
and all sexual assault victims were interviewed by a female police
officer—and came up with similar results. Kanin also points out that
when a specific man was accused, the details of the recantation
always matched his story.[44]

Nor can Kanin be dismissed as a backlasher. His pioneering
research on "male sexual aggression in courtship" goes back to the
1950s and is still cited in feminist literature on date rape. He is also
careful not to lend credibility to once-prevalent notions that "crying
rape" is a product of some innate defect in the female psyche or of a
secret rape wish. Some false complainants, of course, are emotionally
disturbed. But for most women in the study, the fabrication served a
practical purpose, like many other crimes committed by men or
women: an "alibi" for a possible pregnancy (used by girls with strict
parents or wives whose husbands cannot, for whatever reason, be
credited with the conception), or an attempt to cover up an illicit
encounter that may become known in some other way, or revenge
for rejection or betrayal. Kanin notes that although a false accusation
of rape may seem to be an extreme response to such situations, people *do* commit extreme acts, even murder, over "petty and commonplace transgressions."[45]

Kanin cautions against generalizing from his data. Still, he says,
they warrant the conclusion that "false rape accusations are not
uncommon." Other estimates from prosecutors and law enforcement
officers (some of whom say that they believed the phenomenon was
extremely rare until they learned from experience) suggest that
between one in eight and one in five rape complaints are
fabricated.[46]

To recognize that some women wrongly accuse men of rape for
revenge is no more antifemale than it is antimale to recognize that
some men rape women for revenge. Is it so unreasonable to think
that a uniquely damaging and stigmatizing charge will be used by
some people as a weapon, just as others will use their muscle as a
weapon? Indeed, feminists could have argued that false allegations
often reflect the lingering double standard that may make a girl
think it's better to be a rape victim than a slut.

Feminists often decry our culture's alleged eagerness to believe "the old myths of the lying woman." In fact, it's the "victims don't lie" myth that is deeply entrenched today, in the academy and the media alike. There is virtually no research on false allegations. Kanin, who says that a female colleague openly told him he should give up his project, believes that the topic "is not considered appropriate." His study, it should be noted, received no press coverage. The TV series *Law and Order* has tackled many controversial issues in a balanced way but has never done an episode in which a man accused of rape proved to be innocent.[47]

In 1997, after the much-publicized rape charges against two Dallas Cowboys players were revealed to be false, Geraldo Rivera devoted an hour on his newly respectable daytime talk show to "rape hoaxes." But the program repeatedly stressed that accusations of rape are overwhelmingly true. A woman whose alleged assailant had been acquitted was treated as a bona-fide victim, and one guest, a psychologist, said that just because a woman recanted didn't mean she had not been raped. Less than ten minutes of the show dealt with a clearly innocent man. Imagine a program on rape that focused primarily on false accusations.[48]

"Thank goodness," writes New York prosecutor Linda Fairstein in her book *Sexual Violence,* "[the victim's] testimony—when it is credible— is all that is needed to convict a rapist, as it is any other criminal."[49]

But what does "credible" mean? Fairstein herself describes an incident case in which a woman who gave a highly convincing account of being raped by her boss while working late and whose behavior was "consistent with [that] of a rape survivor," turned out to be that classic character from the treatises of the chauvinistic jurists of yore: the woman scorned. She admitted the lie after the boss, a married man who had ended their affair, produced proof that she had accompanied him on trips, including people who had seen her in his hotel room in a negligee. A man of more discretion might have had worse luck.[50]

There are objective ways of gauging credibility: whether the person's story is consistent or keeps changing, whether verifiable details check out. But too often it has much to do with subjective impressions. Feminists complain that a rapist may go free because the woman is not a "good victim": too calm, too angry, too flashy. But juries may also convict because they like the victim or dislike the defendant. After interviewing jurors from thirty-eight rape trials in the late 1970s, criminologist Gary LaFree concluded that if the man's defense was consent, unfavorable perception of his character was the best predictor of a vote to convict.[51]

Of course, character and demeanor matter in almost any kind of trial, but they may assume a disproportionate importance when believing one party or the other becomes the central issue. Ironically, this creates a strong incentive for character assassination. Estrich recognized this in a 1991 speech: as more "hard cases" of coerced sex with little force and no corroboration go to court, and a woman can no longer be blamed for putting herself in harm's way, the only option for the defense is to attack women's credibility, portraying them as "nuts and sluts" and thus perhaps reviving "skepticism and distrust of women complainants." This, in turn, gives feminist crusaders a strong incentive to push for laws that would keep damaging information about the alleged victim out of the courtroom—no matter how relevant such evidence may be to the case.[52]

Shielding the Accuser

The same year that Estrich voiced her alarm about the "nuts and sluts" defense, many advocates were outraged by such a strategy in the case of Gary Hart (not the politician but a Maryland realtor). His accuser, a thirty-four-year-old waitress, claimed that they had been dating platonically and that she was staying at his house overnight because of plumbing problems at her apartment when he brutally attacked her, though there was no physical evidence of the struggle she described. According to Hart, they had been sexually involved and the woman got angry when he said he wasn't taking her on a trip. The defense stressed the complainant's emotional instability, her tendency to react to rejection with sometimes violent rage, and her history of making fantastic claims of sexual assault to psychiatrists and police.[53]

Whatever really happened, it seems clear that excluding the compromising information about the woman would have been terribly unfair; yet many reacted as if this were a gratuitous character attack. A woman wrote to the *Baltimore Sun* that even if the alleged victim was not raped, she suffered "a brutal form of abuse . . . inside the courtroom."[54] Yet if Hart was innocent, he was abused far worse. The negative publicity even forced him to sell his business.

Some courts have barred such "abusive" inquiries. In Oregon, James Anderson was accused of raping Donna R. while both were patients at the White Oaks substance abuse clinic in 1985. Anderson insisted that the sex was consensual and that Donna made up the charges as a ploy to sue White Oaks, which discharged her the morning after the alleged rape because she wouldn't sign up for long-term treatment. Unlike Hart, Anderson was barred from using evidence of his accuser's troubled past—and was convicted.[55]

There were other differences. Hart was a polished businessman who testified in his defense. Anderson, an alcoholic with prior arrests for disorderly conduct and assault, was kept off the stand by his attorney, who also presented a somewhat contradictory defense suggesting either that the sex was consensual or that Donna misidentified her rapist. But the verdict was clearly based on the jury's perception of the accuser's credibility, despite serious contradictions in her testimony. At first, Donna said that she repeatedly tried to tell clinic staffers she had been raped, but "they said, 'We don't wanna listen to it,'" and that her request to talk to "a lady" was rudely denied. (In fact, a female volunteer had helped process her discharge.) On cross-examination, when asked about specific staff members who had been on duty, Donna acknowledged that she had not spoken to any of them about the attack.

Donna then suggested that she was too embarrassed to talk about it. The prosecutor picked up this point in his summation, scoffing that the defense expected a rape victim to "just walk up to one of the staff" and discuss "those most intimate details." But there was something the jury didn't know: the day before, she had discussed equally "intimate details"—an alleged earlier rape and childhood sexual abuse by a brother—with one of the counselors. The jurors never heard him testify about this and never saw his notes ("Client ... has a lot of other issues around incest/rape"), because all information about Donna's sexual history had been excluded under the rape shield law. This prevented the defense not only from challenging her veracity on this issue but from pointing out that Donna had given several contradictory accounts of her prior sexual abuse.

Perhaps Donna was raped. But the case seemed to leave ample room for reasonable doubt, *particularly* if one had access to the facts that undercut Donna's credibility as a witness. For Anderson, who was supposed to be innocent until proved guilty, this knowledge could have made all the difference.

◎

The 1997 trial of sportscaster Marv Albert, accused by his longtime friend and sex partner Vanessa Perhach of oral sodomy and assault, was notable mostly for its tawdry details of transvestitism and kinky sex. But it also raised the issue of the use and abuse of laws intended to prevent sexual assault victims from being revictimized in court.

Albert's attorneys wanted to introduce Perhach's alleged conduct with other men, particularly men who left her—as Albert, who was getting married, was about to do. According to the defense attorneys, she had harassed and threatened an ex-boyfriend's family; her methods of revenge may have included false accusations of crimes. A former lover also asserted that biting, on which the assault charge against Albert was based, was part of her sexual repertoire. All this was barred by Arlington, Virginia, circuit court judge Benjamin Kendrick, yet a woman who claimed that Albert had sexually assaulted her several years earlier was allowed to testify. With the defense's hands tied, Albert pleaded guilty to misdemeanor assault. All this struck many observers, even those most sympathetic to victims' rights such as Geraldo Rivera, as flagrantly unfair.[56]

Several months later in the notorious "cybersex" case in New York, a judge's controversial rape shield ruling had far more serious consequences. Oliver Jovanovic, a graduate student in microbiology at Columbia University, was convicted and sentenced to a minimum of fifteen years in prison for the kidnapping and sexual abuse of a Barnard College student whom he met after corresponding by e-mail. At his place, by the young woman's own account, she let Jovanovic undress her and tie her up; she claimed that he then kept her against her will for twenty hours and sexually tortured her. The defense argued that there was no torture—indeed, the woman's claim that Jovanovic painfully rammed a baton into her rectum was disputed by medical evidence, and the jury acquitted him on the counts pertaining to this act—and that the bondage was consensual. This argument was crippled by Judge William Wetzel's decision to exclude portions of the e-mail in which the Barnard student discussed sadomasochism (referring to herself as a "pushy bottom," an S&M slang term for a submissive who likes to goad the dominant partner into going further than the dominant wants) and her sadomasochistic relationship with another man ("now i'm his slave and its painful, but the fun of telling my friends 'hey i'm a sadomasochist' more than outweighs the torment"). The law may have ended up shielding perjury. On the stand, the woman testified that she never gave Jovanovic any indication of interest in S&M, which the e-mail would have—to put it mildly—called into doubt.[57]

Rape shield laws, which existed in forty-six states by 1980 and are virtually universal today, are one of the more popular aspects of rape law reform. In 1991, 73 percent of Americans agreed that the woman's past sexual life should not be an issue in a rape case (which is not only compassionate but sensible: just because she slept with two or twenty men doesn't prove she agreed to sex with *this* man). But what they had in mind was probably very different from the circumstances in the Albert or the Jovanovic case.[58]

The accuser's past sexual conduct is not automatically excluded, just as, before shield laws, it wasn't automatically allowed. Her prior relations with the accused are generally admissible; so is evidence that the pregnancy or disease alleged to have resulted from the rape may have been caused by sex with someone else. In some states, other evidence may be admitted at the judge's discretion "in the interests of justice." Most of the time, however, the burden is on the defendant to show that the value of this evidence to his case outweighs its "prejudicial effect" on the complainant. In several states (including Alabama, Iowa, Pennsylvania, and Washington), courts have held that excluding evidence of an earlier false or dubious rape complaint by the accuser does not deny the accused a fair trial—even, perhaps, if the evidence is relevant to the question of his innocence.[59]

Prior sexual conduct can become an especially thorny issue when the charge is based on the contention that the victim could not give valid consent due to mental impairment. This was the focus of a heated controversy in 1993, when several high school athletes in Glen Ridge, New Jersey, were tried for sexually assaulting a teenage girl with the mental capacity of an eight-year-old. The girl testified that she complied with their sexual demands so as not to "hurt their feelings." To dispute the claim that she was incapable of consenting to sex, the defense produced evidence of her sexually provocative behavior at school and even blamed the girl's mother for not protecting the poor boys from this oversexed temptress. These tactics didn't work (three of the four defendants were convicted) and were widely viewed as despicable. Perhaps better guidelines were needed on the use of sexual history in rape cases hinging on mental competence. Instead, in a knee-jerk response to pressure from NOW, state legislators passed a bill barring all use of such evidence.[60]

The dangers of such a blanket ban are illustrated by a 1990 Wisconsin case in which a woman diagnosed with multiple personality disorder (the reality of which is now in doubt) accused a man of seducing one of her "alters" without the consent of the main personality.[61] Mark Peterson, who maintained that he had no idea she was mentally ill, was found guilty of rape. The verdict was set aside because of the judge's refusal to allow a defense psychiatrist to examine the complainant; the district attorney later announced that he would not retry the case to spare her further anguish. His decision may have been influenced by the discovery that a key prosecution witness, who testified that he had told Peterson of the woman's condition, had been sleeping with her himself.[62]

If the "victim" could have consensual sex with one man, it seems logical that she could consent to sex with another. Yet if this information had surfaced before or during the trial, the shield law might have prevented the jury from ever hearing about it.

Thus, in a double whammy, feminist-initiated reforms have made it easier to bring credibility-contest rape cases to trial *and* more difficult to raise legitimate questions about the credibility of the accuser. The 1993 trial of Charles Steadman in Wisconsin on charges of raping his foster sister Jessica P. exemplifies both trends.

Twenty-two-year-old Jessica, who had previously had sexual relations with eighteen-year-old Charles, claimed that after a playful chase to retrieve a cigarette she had snatched from him, he cornered her in a bedroom and raped her, then forced his way into the bathroom while she was washing up and raped her again. Charles said that the sex in the bedroom was consensual and that nothing happened in the bathroom. There were no signs of force; Jessica did not try to get out of the house or seek help after the alleged first assault; her undamaged clothing did not match her story of being forcibly undressed in a struggle. The jurors had enough doubts about her story to clear Steadman on the first count of sexual assault, pertaining to the sex in the bedroom. Yet they convicted him on the second count.

In this case, what the jury never knew was that when Jessica filed the complaint, she herself was facing charges of sex with minors. (She eventually got probation with mandatory psychiatric treatment and orders to have no unsupervised contact with boys under age sixteen.)[63] Clearly, this could have given her a motive to lie, particularly since she had been having sex with Charles when *he* was a minor. If she did fabricate the story, she might have done so because she thought that being a victim would improve her legal situation as a defendant; she might have worried that if her encounter with Charles became known, she would get in more trouble with the law and with her family. None of these possible motives could be introduced at Steadman's trial: Jessica's legal problems were related to her past sexual activities and hence inadmissible.

Upholding not only Steadman's conviction but the eight-year sentence (just below the maximum, despite his clean record), the court of appeals reasoned that his "rehabilitative prospects" were reduced by "refusal to acknowledge guilt, in the face of strong evidence of culpability." That evidence was the word of a woman whose serious credibility problems were never disclosed to the jury.[64]

The Benefit of the Doubt

No one knows how often men are sent to prison on the basis of false allegations of rape. We know only about the lucky ones who are eventually exonerated. In Maryland in the 1980s, Mark Bowles served thirteen months of his sentence for raping his ex-girlfriend Kathryn Tucci before she confessed that she lied, out of distress over some unrelated "traumatic events." James Liggett of Everett, Washington, was convicted in 1991 of raping a woman he had met through a dating service, and spent a year in prison before her story fell apart—not only because she reported an eerily similar rape by another man from the same dating service (a navy serviceman who was investigated by military authorities and cleared after he passed a lie detector test) but because a private detective Liggett hired found out that she had a history of unstable behavior, including dubious claims of rape.[65]

When men's rights activists claim that all it takes to put an innocent man behind bars is the cry, "He raped me," they obviously exaggerate. An analysis of rape cases in ten states in 1990 found that on average, 43 percent of the suspects were convicted or pleaded guilty. Few were acquitted at trial; in nearly half of the cases, the charges were dismissed—an outcome equally likely in conservative North Carolina and liberal Vermont.[66]

Many feminists and their supporters view the high rate of dismissals as an obvious injustice, though official statistics indicate that charges of robbery are about as likely, and felony assault charges *less* likely, to end in conviction. The 1993 Senate Judiciary Committee report, *The Response to Rape: Detours on the Road to Equal Justice,* issued to support the Violence Against Women Act, adds up statistics on how many rape complaints lead to arrest, conviction, and incarceration and concludes that 88 percent of victims "will never see their attacker . . . behind bars." The assumption that every report was truthful and every accused man was an "attacker" was never questioned.[67]

It is true that district attorneys sometimes dismiss valid but difficult cases. Alice Vachss, a former sex crimes prosecutor in Queens, New York, decries such dismissals as "the soft underbelly of collaboration in sex-crimes prosecution," blasting colleagues who turn away "cases without incontrovertible proof." But Vachss's own attitude veers toward the opposite extreme. She mentions a case she took to trial despite "a disturbing sense of doubt." The teenage accuser, who claimed she had been fondled by a man for whom she babysat, got caught in lie after lie and had reason to make up the story: the alleged abuse greatly improved her rocky relationship with her mother. Yet after losing the case, Vachss is "haunted" by the thought that she let the girl down—*not* that she put an innocent man through a legal nightmare.[68]

Traditional attitudes at their worst may, as feminists have charged, result in a Teflon system to which few rape complaints stick, but prosecutorial zeal on behalf of women (whether driven by principle or public relations) may result in a Velcro system that clings to the most dubious charges. "The police pass the buck to the prosecutors, the prosecutors pass the buck to the jury; the idea is not to exercise any discretion at all," says Court TV commentator Rikki Klieman, who has been both a defense attorney and a sex crimes prosecutor in Massachusetts.

In New York, Desmond Robinson, a black ex-cop who had earlier gained fame when he was shot by a white officer while working undercover, was accused of sexually assaulting a policewoman during a night of bar hopping. In one of the bars, witnesses had not only seen the two of them fondling each other but heard them having sex in the women's room. The woman first denied it, then admitted it—though she still insisted that later that night, Robinson forced her to perform oral sex. Still, assistant district attorney Lisa Friel forged ahead, eager to make the point that consensual sex does not entitle a man to further sexual access and willing to blame the inconsistencies on the shame and "denial" typical of rape victims. For five more months, she interviewed witnesses and spent hundreds of hours with the "victim." When the woman changed her story again and insisted that there was never any consensual sex between them, Friel finally dropped the sexual assault charges and let Robinson plead guilty to misdemeanor assault for a drunken brawl he had with the woman in a parking lot outside a bar.[69]

In an even more implausible case in Maine, the state attorney's office proved more tenacious. Robert O'Malley, a middle-aged jail guard, was prosecuted for sexually assaulting an inmate, Jeanine Magryta—despite records showing that he was not on duty the day of the alleged attack, a doctor's conclusion that his medical condition rendered him incapable of having a full erection and performing the acts she described, and Magryta's history of dishonesty coupled with an obvious motive to fabricate: a $1 million lawsuit. A jury took two hours to acquit O'Malley after a two-year ordeal that cost him over $70,000 in lost wages and legal fees.[70]

With rape as with domestic violence, stories of excessive zeal in pursuing alleged culprits can always be countered with other stories. The judicial system is not a monolith; the outcome of a case depends on the attitudes of the local police, prosecutors, and judges, even on the idiosyncrasies of jurors.

In a 1993 article, *Washington Post* writer Phyllis Richman described her experience of serving on a jury, which convinced her that "it remains nearly impossible to win a conviction in a date rape case." The defendant, Jawad Elamri, had met the alleged victim in a bar and invited her to a restaurant across the street, which he managed and which was closed at the time. She claimed that he locked the door and made her submit to his advances by showing her a gun. Elamri had given several versions of what happened; the woman's story was consistent, and some of its details—including the gun under Elamri's jacket—were corroborated by other people at the bar. Yet some jurors, especially the men, felt that if the woman had been unwilling, she would not have given in so easily; the fact that a friend who was at the bar with Elamri had let the alleged victim feel his gun through his jacket was seen as proof that she wasn't scared of guns. For the second time, the case ended in a hung jury.[71]

Assuming that Richman's account leaves out no facts favoring

Elamri, one case with a number of unique circumstances (including the defendant's Moroccan background, which led to multicultural speculations about his perceptions in dealing with women) says only so much about the big picture. It's not hard to find cases of men convicted of rape with far less evidence. Think of Robert Berkowitz, who was not even *alleged* to have done anything to threaten his "victim" or stop her from leaving.

Moreover, some much-publicized tales of judicial outrages against rape victims are not as simple as they are made out to be. Thus, the tale of a Florida jury that acquitted a rapist because the victim wore a lace miniskirt and no panties is almost entirely a myth, as an investigation by Elinor Brecher of the *Miami Herald* showed.[72]

The furor over the 1989 verdict was sparked by the jury foreman's comment that "she was asking for it, the way she was dressed"—though he tried to explain that "'it' meant sex, not rape." The real issue, jurors said, was that Blandina Chiapponi had told too many lies for them to believe anything.

Her story of abduction and rape at knifepoint had some circumstantial support; besides, Stephen Lord was charged with similar crimes against two women in Georgia, one of whom testified at the Florida trial. Several jurors told reporters that they hoped he would "hang" for the Georgia rape, for which he eventually received a life sentence.[73]

And yet Lord's claim that Chiapponi offered him sex for $100 and cocaine—and cried rape after they got into a car accident, for fear of being found with the drugs and arrested—wasn't entirely absurd, if only because there was some support for his claim that she was a prostitute. (Yes, her outfit, and the fact that she was wearing it at a truck stop at 3 A.M., was part of the picture, as was her previous employment—"innocent," she claimed—at at least one massage parlor.) In an effort to conceal this, she was evasive about everything from her job to her activities that evening, and played an innocent who couldn't say "vagina" before a jury that later heard her obscenity-laced statement to the police.[74]

Brecher's exposé, coming two months after the uproar, could not burst the myth—not even at the *Miami Herald* itself. A 1990 editorial applauding a bill that banned the use of the woman's clothes as evidence of consent in rape trials noted that "a rapist was acquitted in Fort Lauderdale after the defense attorney showed the jury the victim's lacy miniskirt and claimed that she was a prostitute."[75]

Genuine outrages do happen. In the 1992 "condom rape" case in

Austin, Texas, a grand jury refused to indict because it saw "consent" in the woman's plea that the man who was about to rape her at knifepoint put on a condom. The local and national outcry caused a new grand jury to be convened, and the man was indicted and later convicted.[76]

But when an injustice goes the other way, there is no outcry—at most, an occasional diatribe from a newspaper columnist. Liberals normally sensitive to defendants' rights were remarkably indifferent to strong evidence that Mike Tyson was denied a fair trial; the only concerns were voiced by black activists and perceived (correctly) as motivated by racial solidarity.

Yet after Tyson's conviction, legal commentator Stuart Taylor wrote that the appeal "should be like shooting fish in a barrel." The judge had barred testimony by three women who came forward claiming to have seen Tyson and Desirée Washington necking in his limousine (which did not prove that she consented to sex but confirmed Tyson's story and contradicted hers). She also had refused to instruct the jury that the prosecution had to prove not only that Washington did not consent, but that Tyson "did not reasonably believe that she had consented." And there was the issue of Indiana's unique system in which the prosecutor was allowed to select the trial judge.[77]

Nevertheless, the Indiana Court of Appeals upheld Tyson's conviction in a ruling characterized by Columbia University law professor George Fletcher as a "mélange of contrived reasoning and bad law." (Could the judges have been reluctant to undo what had been hailed as a great victory for women?) Although the court agreed that having prosecutors handpick judges was "totally inappropriate," it concluded that this did not affect the fairness of Tyson's trial, even though many thought Judge Patricia Gifford, a former sex crimes prosecutor and a date rape hardliner, had clearly favored the prosecution. As for the testimony about Tyson and Washington necking in the limousine, the majority nonchalantly suggested that it was not vital; yet opposing the admission of this evidence at the trial, the prosecution had stated that its effect would be damaging "beyond words."[78]

In fact, the information about the witnesses barred from testifying—and the disclosure that during the trial, Washington already had an agreement with a lawyer to handle a civil suit, which she denied on the stand—was enough for five of the twelve jurors to say that they would have changed their vote to convict.[79] None of this means that Tyson was innocent. It simply means *reasonable doubt.*

Feminists often complain that the victim in a rape trial has to "prove her innocence," and that the man still gets the benefit of the doubt when it's her word against his. But perhaps that is only a different way of stating a basic principle of our legal system: the defendant is presumed innocent until proven guilty. If there is any reasonable doubt, he must be acquitted.

Some feminists don't believe there should be a presumption of innocence when a woman accuses a man of violating her. After the Marv Albert trial, defending the judge's decision to admit compromising information about Albert's past but not about the woman's, attorney Gloria Allred decried "the notion that there's some sort of moral equivalency between the defendant and the victim."[80] Yet as long as the defendant has not been convicted, he and the victim *are* moral equals in the eyes of the law.

Yes, the presumption of innocence means that a case involving a prior relationship and no physical evidence of force will be very difficult for the prosecution to win if the defendant can offer a plausible scenario of consent. And so it should be. The maxim that it's better to let ten guilty people go free than to convict one innocent person has been used to justify sleazy legal tricks that have nothing to do with guilt or innocence; but it's our best guiding principle where genuine uncertainty exists.

This does not mean that nothing can be done about such cases. Civil suits, in which the burden of proof is less stringent, are one alternative. In criminal cases, it would not be unfair to defendants to admit previous charges of sexual assault as corroboration, even if they were not prosecuted—as long as these are accusations that were reported and found credible but lacking sufficient proof. Jurors should be able to weigh the probability that several women would falsely accuse the same man, especially if their accounts suggest a similar pattern (at least if the complainant in the new case did not know about the earlier charges). The defense, too, should be allowed to explore any elements of the accuser's background that are relevant to the case.

I doubt that many people want a return to the days when a woman was expected to defend her virtue almost to the death to prove rape, and stood little chance of proving it if she had no virtue. But is it better, for women as well as men, to hold men guilty until proven innocent? Every man wrongly convicted or needlessly dragged through a legal ordeal is some woman's son, brother, husband, father, or friend.

The politicization of sex crimes has backfired on women in other ways. When the "victims don't lie" axiom expanded to include children, the wave of child abuse witch-hunts destroyed the lives of many women as well as men, without a peep of protest from a single prominent feminist. Indeed, many feminists, including Gloria Steinem, have championed the cult of "recovered memories of sexual abuse," which has caused many mothers to be falsely accused and many daughters to be truly victimized, by "therapy" that led them to believe that they had been subjected to unspeakable acts (and often turned women who had sought help for mild depression or anxiety into real basket cases). When scholars and commentators began to question these recollections, many feminists were quick to cry backlash. "Violence against women and children . . . is a privilege that men do not relinquish easily,"[81] wrote Harvard psychiatrist Judith Herman.

Twenty years after rape law reform began, we should be able to avoid the extremes in defining force or measuring credibility. A woman shouldn't have to resist a violent attack; but as the California Supreme Court noted in *Barnes,* her actions "must be measured against the degree of force manifested or in light of whether her fears were genuine and reasonably grounded." Women who report rape do not deserve to be presumed liars, but neither are they entitled to what feminist sociologist Margaret Gordon quaintly calls "the benefit of belief." In the words of George Fletcher, "It is important to defend the interests of women as victims, but not to go so far as to accord women complaining of rape a presumption of honesty and objectivity."[82]

CHAPTER SEVEN

Sexual McCarthyism

In the fall of 1998, the fiasco stemming from President Clinton's affair with White House intern Monica Lewinsky popularized a new term: *sexual McCarthyism*. Clinton supporters hurled this charge at Independent Counsel Kenneth Starr, whose investigation had uncovered the affair and the ensuing lies under oath, and at the Congressional Republicans who were pushing for impeachment hearings on the basis of these offenses. The president's critics responded by hurling the same accusation back at the pro-Clinton forces who were busy outing the ancient sexual lapses of some Republicans.[1]

Sexual McCarthyism is real. But it hardly started with Ken Starr or Bill Clinton. As a national epidemic, it began seven years earlier when Anita Hill's allegations of sexual harassment nearly torpedoed the Supreme Court nomination of Clarence Thomas. It led to such practices as secret files in which uncorroborated claims of harassment could be kept without the knowledge of the accused, in order to show a "pattern" in the event of future complaints. It invaded private lives: in some workplaces, colleagues who become sexually involved were required to report the relationship and sign a consent form; in sexual harassment suits, defendants were interrogated about irrelevant consensual affairs, as Clinton was interrogated about Lewinsky in a deposition for the lawsuit filed against him by Paula Jones. And before sexual McCarthyism reached the President of the United States, it shattered many other careers and lives.[2]

Like many other causes gone wrong, the crusade against sexual harassment is based on a real issue. In the 1950s, the term *sexual harassment* did not exist, but advice columnist Ann Landers responded sympathetically to office workers complaining of unwelcome familiarities. A hundred years ago, the plight of factory girls preyed on by lecherous bosses aroused much public indignation. In an Arthur Conan Doyle story, when the employer of a governess accused of murder admits that he tried to seduce the young woman, Sherlock Holmes rebukes him: "I don't know that anything she is accused of is really worse than what you have yourself admitted." (Even radical feminists might not place harassment on a par with murder, though some do describe it as "violence against women.")[3]

Today, the leaders of this crusade have often framed the issue as one of a patriarchal plot rather than individual bad acts, discouraging personal resolution of male-female conflicts and imposing a virtual taboo on discussions of female responsibility. Worse, the definition of harassment has grown like the Blob, swallowing up trivial or ambiguous acts—sexual jokes, compliments, "leers," requests for dates—and spreading over an ever-wider range of interactions between men and women who work or study together. In 1994, a column in a New Jersey newspaper titled "Sexual Harassment Policy May Be Overdue" quoted a county employee who gave examples of the offenses that such a policy should combat: an official stopped by her desk and joked, "Is it my time to go out this week or did I blow it?"; another, an older man, would "hug and kiss you" in a "grandfatherly" way. Four years later, a headline in the Princeton student paper the *Daily Princetonian* announced, "Princeton Student Dining Hall Workers Experience Sexual Harassment." Some young women, it turns out, were "uncomfortable" because their male coworkers were "too friendly" and ogled pretty women in the dining hall; one reported that a male cook had struck up chats with her and once asked—horrors!—if she had a boyfriend.[4]

In recent years, expanding definitions of sexual harassment have been the object of some derision. Nonetheless, over half of Americans, both women and men, agree that telling dirty jokes in front of a coworker of the opposite sex is "definitely" or "probably" sexual harassment, and about a quarter frown on saying, "You look very attractive today."[5]

Whether these interactions amount to harassment seems to be determined solely by how the "victim" feels. At a high school seminar I attended, the trainer displayed on the overhead projector a picture of a giant eye, to illustrate the idea that sexual harassment is "in the eye of the beholder." Of course, it could also have stood for "Big Sister Is Watching You."[6]

Harassment, Harassment Everywhere

The concept of sexual harassment made its debut in the 1970s and quickly gained political and legal recognition. But it remained a peripheral issue, barely mentioned in most articles about the women's movement and its agenda, until the 1991 battle over Clarence Thomas's Supreme Court nomination and Anita Hill's claim that Thomas sexually harassed her when she worked for him at the Equal Employment Opportunity Commission (EEOC) in the 1980s.

Hill's story, told to the Senate Judiciary Committee before a national television audience, was that Thomas had asked her out a few times, with no hint of retaliation (her civil service status guaranteed her a job in any case), and engaged her in graphic sex talk to which, by her own account, she never objected. The partisan debate focused not on whether these charges amounted to much, but on whether they were true—and to many, even that didn't matter. One editorial calling for a "national consciousness-raising" on sexual harassment opined:

> Anita Hill may or not be telling the truth. . . . But her story makes women remember off-color jokes they may have rolled their eyes at [or] that time, perhaps when they were young, that a boss or colleague got a little too cozy and they didn't say a word about it.
>
> In this sense, Anita Hill is every woman trying to make it in a man's world.[7]

Both men and women were inclined to believe Thomas. But the consciousness raising went ahead anyway. Women in offices across America "shared their experiences and their anger," wrote *Time*. "Sexual harassment—like rape, like abuse, like pornography—unites women," wrote Ellen Goodman, oblivious to the possibility that not all women were united.[8]

There was some legitimate anger. One ex-stewardess wrote in *USA Today* about how, back in the 1960s, tipsy male passengers would snap at her girdle and comment on her "knockers." Other tales were far more ambiguous. A *Washington Post* reporter recalled a ten-year-old episode in which she was pursued by an official at (of all places) the EEOC. He was "good-natured" about being rebuffed and continued to give her good leads; she felt "flattered" and got "favored treatment" over other reporters. Yet, looking back, she felt certain that she was harassed.[9]

Some commentators acknowledged that the issue was fraught with innocent missteps, but only to admonish males to learn to "get it." Deborah Tannen explained that "men find [sexual banter] titillating and women find it intimidating," but men may be confused because women "hide their negative reactions" to avoid conflict. That some women might find sexual banter titillating was not a subject that often came up. The few female voices warning that the harassment crusade could put women back on "the Victorian pedestal" drowned in the storm of female "rage."[10]

Looking back on the Hill-Thomas hearings six years later, commentator Christopher Hitchens suggested that "everyone was slightly out of their skull that week."[11] But after the dust had settled, the new awareness of sexual harassment remained a permanent part of the cultural landscape. The NEXIS news database shows over 8,000 references to sexual harassment in the press in 1992 (compared to fewer than 1,500 in 1990), 9,430 references in 1993, 14,908 in 1994, and 11,620 in 1995.

In this climate, the most trivial misdemeanors could become big news. In 1992, fifty-six-year-old New York Transit Authority executive Ron Contino made headlines because, talking to his staff on the speakerphone while recovering after heart surgery, he joked about having sex with two female colleagues to prove his recuperative vigor. Although Contino was quick to apologize and the "victims" were ready to forgive and forget, he was still demoted and had his pay cut.[12]

The next year, New York State assemblywoman Earlene Hill caused a furor by revealing that several years earlier, a male legislator had failed to move to let her get to her seat and jocularly invited her to climb over his legs, while another had said "sex" instead of "six" while reeling off numbers in a speech and, to cover his embarrassment, joked, "Whenever I think of Earlene, I think of sex." (Governor Mario Cuomo lauded Hill for helping "increase sensitivity," and *New York Newsday* urged her to lodge a formal complaint.) And a disgruntled employee's charge that the director of the Massachusetts Commission Against Discrimination had "stared" at women at the office and told mildly risqué stories—for instance, about his niece wanting to mark her first menstrual period in a family calendar of important events—merited several articles in the *Boston*

Globe and an investigation by the EEOC (by which he was ultimately exonerated).[13]

One might say that the legacy of Anita Hill was not so much awareness of sexual harassment as the blurring of distinctions between the serious and the petty. In 1995, after Senator Bob Packwood resigned under the weight of accusations from more than twenty women he had groped and otherwise molested, Hill wrote a peevish essay complaining that the Senate still didn't get it ("What if the alleged conduct had only been verbal, and could be dismissed as mere flirtation?") and called for a "national effort" to connect Packwood-style sexual aggression with "run-of-the-mill sexual-misconduct charges."[14]

By blurring the distinctions, the crusaders are able to depict the problem as epidemic. A typical technique is to describe some appalling incidents—a man masturbating in front of a female coworker, a woman being handcuffed to a toilet and having her head dunked, a boss raping an employee—and then assert that these are not "isolated examples," since research shows that "over half of all women experience harassment during their academic or working lives." Never mind that the "harassment" overwhelmingly consists of sexual remarks, jokes, or looks. An article in a journal for government administrators admonishes readers to "remember that none of it is really 'harmless.'"[15]

On one occasion, many feminists did come out for a narrower definition of harassment: when former Arkansas state worker Paula Jones alleged that then-governor Bill Clinton had her brought to his hotel room, fondled her and exposed himself, asking for oral sex. Katha Pollitt noted that "it doesn't seem to be sexual harassment," since Jones lost no pay or promotions; law professor Susan Estrich took the same view. Eleanor Smeal of the Feminist Majority Foundation said it was "a marginal sexual harassment case at best": "There either must be a quid pro quo [or] a pervasive and severe atmosphere of sexual harassment, and indeed it must be shown that it was unwelcome."[16]

What would happen to Anita Hill under this standard? Asked this question on a talk show in 1997, Estrich replied that the real issue was whether Clarence Thomas belonged on the Supreme Court: "I don't think she would have had a suit in a court of law." Estrich somehow omitted this point when, in 1991, she described Anita Hill as a classic victim of the sexual harassment plaguing so many working women.[17]

In fact, actions described as sexual harassment in the media often fall short of the legal standard: surveys in which every woman exposed to "unwelcome" sexual humor is counted as a victim never ask if it was "pervasive or severe."[18] Worse yet, even laws and public policies have dangerously blurred the lines between egregious abuse and minor incivility or mere miscommunication.

The Law and Its Shadow

In 1974, a Yale University graduate student active in left-wing causes heard about Carmita Wood, a clerical worker who left her job after complaints about her sexually abusive boss were ignored, and was denied unemployment benefits because she had quit for "personal" reasons. Incensed because the law provided no recourse in such situations, the student drafted a brief arguing that sexual harassment systematically deprived women as a class of equal opportunity, and was thus a violation of Title VII of the 1964 Civil Rights Act barring sex discrimination in employment.[19]

The graduate student was Catharine MacKinnon, the future star of feminist jurisprudence. Her brief became the foundation for the entire structure of sexual harassment law.

In 1976, champions of the harassment-as-discrimination theory scored their first court victory in a classic case of a woman fired because she wouldn't sleep with the boss. Four years later, the EEOC amended its sex discrimination guidelines to include "unwelcome sexual advances, requests for sexual favors, and other verbal or physical conduct of a sexual nature" which either involved pressure to trade sex for job-related benefits or had "the purpose or effect of unreasonably interfering with an individual's work performance or creating an intimidating, hostile, or offensive working environment."[20]

In 1986, sexual harassment law reached the Supreme Court in *Meritor Savings Bank v. Vinson,* a case pursued by a strong team of feminist litigators, including MacKinnon, with support from women's groups and members of Congress. Bank teller Mechelle Vinson claimed that her boss, Sidney Taylor, repeatedly forced her into sex, threatening to fire her and even have her killed if she didn't submit. For nearly three years, Vinson got promotions and kept silent, until she quit—or, according to the bank, was fired for taking too much time off. With contradictory accounts by other employees, the truth in this bizarre tale remained elusive. (The high court did not address the facts; the case was later settled, reportedly for a modest sum.) *Washington Post* reporter Mary Battiata noted that as one delved into it, concerns about lawsuits by "jilted lovers" and "pink-collar Machiavellis" began to make sense.[21]

If true, Vinson's charges arguably belonged in the criminal courts as rape. But the issue before the Supreme Court was whether she had a valid claim of sexual harassment: unlike an employee penalized for refusing the boss's demands, she had suffered no economic damage. It still could have been a quid pro quo if Vinson had avoided harm only by submitting to Taylor's advances. But the activists wanted a test for "environmental" harassment. The Reagan Justice Department too urged the Court to uphold the EEOC guidelines. Unanimously, the Rehnquist court did just that: sexual misconduct "sufficiently severe or pervasive" to "create an abusive working environment," even without actual or threatened reprisals, was a civil rights violation.[22]

And so a case involving allegations of rape paved the road for policies that cover off-color jokes. MacKinnon summed it up: "We made this law up from the beginning, and now we've won."[23]

Although the doctrine of sexual harassment as sex discrimination has become well established, it remains, as political scientist Ellen Frankel Paul has written, "a defective paradigm."[24]

Take the following examples of discrimination from a pamphlet distributed by a large city's human rights agency in 1996:

- the 55 year old male who was fired by the newly hired manager saying, "you're too old for this job."
- the secretary who was frequently told sexual jokes by her coworkers and supervisor.
- the wheelchair user who had to pay a higher cab fare to carry his wheelchair.[25]

It is obvious that the second example doesn't belong here. Unlike the other victims, the secretary suffers no economic damage, nor is there any evidence that she is treated differently from men. Surely not only the legislators who passed the 1964 Civil Rights Act but the feminists who fought to have it extended to women never dreamed of establishing a constitutional right for Americans to (as one sexual harassment prevention trainer put it) "do their job and go home without having to hear jokes, stories or comments of a sexual nature."[26]

Even in the worst-case "sleep with me or you're fired" scenario, surely the fact that only one sex is subjected to this indignity is not the worst thing about it. A bisexual boss could do this to both sexes; a male supervisor could do it to women and a female or gay supervisor in the same office, to men.

Justice Ruth Bader Ginsburg has stressed equal treatment— "whether members of one sex are exposed to disadvantageous terms or conditions of employment"—as the cornerstone of harassment law. But hostile environment claims often rest on the assumption that women are hurt by behavior (such as sexual jokes) that doesn't bother men. The activists themselves seem confused: "A good test [is] whether the defendant would have said the same things to his or her daughter, mother or wife. Or did the employee have to put up with something men did not have to put up with?" says Helen Norton of the Women's Legal Defense Fund, leaping from a standard based on female modesty to one based on equality. A male attorney talks about "the road to workplace equality" and then proposes a flagrantly paternalistic "kid sister test": how would you feel if your kid sister or "anyone with whom you've traditionally had a protective relationship" were exposed to such goings-on at your office as "banter about Viagra"?[27]

There is also the issue of same-sex harassment—not just homosexual overtures but sexualized hazing—which reached the Supreme Court in 1998. The sexual taunts and assaults the male plaintiff allegedly suffered at the hands of three other heterosexual men on an all-male oil rig were clearly outrageous, but, just as clearly, he wasn't singled out due to his sex. The Court's tortured attempts to grapple with these questions laid bare the fact that, as legal commentator Jeff Rosen put it, "the expanding edifice of sexual-harassment law is built on quicksand."[28] The catch-22 is that what's fair— equal protection from abuse—is not logical if harassment is defined in terms of gender bias.

These logical flaws in the harassment-as-discrimination doctrine were pointed out by the unenlightened courts that initially rejected this interpretation of Title VII. And, as Ellen Frankel Paul has argued, such problems could have been avoided if sexual abuse in the workplace had been treated as a tort (a willful or negligent injury) rather than as sex discrimination. Indeed, a few such suits were successfully filed in the mid-1970s. But the gender warriors explicitly rejected this approach because it would have treated incidents of sexual harassment as (in Catharine MacKinnon's words) "outrages particular to an individual woman rather than integral to her social status as a woman worker."[29]

The current law of sexual harassment poses other dilemmas that the courts have so far evaded. It inevitably abridges freedom of speech—which, unlike the "right" to be free from sexual jokes on the job, is actually mentioned in the Constitution. True, speech in the workplace has always been subject to policing by employers; but as UCLA law professor Eugene Volokh and other commentators have pointed out, it's a very different matter when the government forces employers to impose such restrictions.[30]

The problems are compounded by the notorious subjectivity of the "hostile environment" concept, despite attempts to introduce the objective test of what a "reasonable person" would find offensive. According to a U.S. Department of Labor pamphlet, if someone at work "made sexual jokes or said sexual things that you didn't like," or displayed a picture you consider "pornographic," and if it's "making it hard for you to work," it's illegal. But does this mean that you dread going to work every morning—or that you're occasionally distracted? Or that you're the sort of person who has a fit over a copy of *Esquire* with a G-rated cover photo of an actress buttoning up her bra? (Yes, this really happened, prompting a full investigation and eventually costing the culprit his job at a wastewater treatment plant in Olympia, Washington.)[31]

"If I run a stop sign, I have broken the law even if I did not intend to," a male EEOC official has said, defending the emphasis on the victim's response rather than the offender's intent. But while one may fail to see a stop sign, its reality is hardly "in the eye of the beholder."[32] If traffic laws were modeled on harassment policies, there would be no stop signs or speed limits; you could be fined for failing to stop when someone expected you to, or going at a speed that made another driver uncomfortable.

Such a focus obviously makes it quite difficult for the accused to defend himself. When Arizona state legislator Richard Kyle threatened to sue for defamation after two aides accused him of harassment, *Arizona Republic* columnist Keven Willey suggested that any attempt to fight back could only hurt Kyle by raising questions of his conduct. Even if his actions such as putting his arm around a woman's shoulder were innocent, Willey wrote, sexual harassment is about "shades of gray" and "it's the perceptions of the person alleging harassment that matter most," so Kyle could only lose.[33]

Moreover, the legality of an act may depend not just on who it's done to but on who does it. As far back as 1983, humorist Art Buchwald had a woman define the difference between "harassment and old-fashioned flirting": "If you like the guy and think he's cute, he's flirting. . . . If you don't like him, he's harassing you."[34] The Buchwald hypothesis is confirmed by an experiment. College women read a scenario in which a woman is asked out for a drink by a male coworker to whom she has previously said no. In different versions, the man was either married or single, and an attached photo showed him as good looking or plain. Two percent of the women who got the script with the handsome bachelor thought they would feel extremely harassed in the woman's place, compared to 11 percent when the man was attractive but married, 14 percent when he was single but homely, and 24 percent when he had the misfortune of being neither single nor sexy.[35]

Maybe the married man deserves the harsh judgment. But what about the lonely guy who isn't blessed with sex appeal? Life isn't fair, but must the law be unfair as well, allowing the women who reject him to make his attempts at courtship illegal?

The Supreme Court revisited sexual harassment in 1993 in *Harris v. Forklift*. In this case, there were no allegations of physical assaults or sexual demands (the boss's infamous remark, "Let's go to the Holiday Inn to negotiate your raise," was clearly understood to be a joke), only of demeaning humor, and the issue was whether the plaintiff could have a valid claim of harassment even if she had suffered no psychological harm. In a laconic unanimous decision, the Court said that she could.

Although the ruling stressed "a middle path between making actionable any conduct that is merely offensive and requiring . . . a tangible psychological injury," it gave few clues as to where the line should be drawn. In a concurring opinion, Justice Antonin Scalia left little doubt that he thought the Court was making bad law, but basically threw up his hands: "I know of no test more faithful to the inherently vague statutory language than the one the Court today adopts."[36]

The outcome after the case was remanded to the lower courts shows how arbitrary the line between more offensiveness and sexual harassment remains. In 1994, a U.S. district judge found Forklift liable and awarded Teresa Harris, a former rental manager, over $150,000. (The case was settled after further appeals.) But the decision was *not* based on the notorious misdeeds of her boss Chuck Hardy, who had called Harris a "dumb ass woman," teased her about the size of her behind, and asked women to fish for change in his pants pockets. For two years, the judge found, none of it rose to the level of illegal harassment because Harris never let on that she was upset. After she did, and threatened to quit, Hardy apologized profusely—but a month later, when Harris announced that she had landed a big contract, he joked that she must have promised the customer sexual favors. This one remark, made *after* Harris had informed Hardy that his antics were "unwelcome," transformed his vulgarity into sexual harassment.[37]

One could argue that just because a woman suffers in silence doesn't mean that it's not harassment. One could also argue that if a woman goes along with a man's bawdy humor for two years and then tells him to cut it out, he may slip into his old habits with no malicious intent. Either way, the Court's reasoning makes little sense.

Harris also shows the pitfalls of legal solutions to complex human problems. In the harsh glare of the courts and the media, it was easy to paint Hardy as a sexist pig and Harris as an ill-used woman, pelted with taunts like, "We need a man as the rental manager." But this can be seen instead as silly but hardly malevolent teasing if we know that Hardy himself had hired Harris and talked her out of quitting, that she and her husband were friends with the Hardys, or that she often stayed at the office to drink beer and trade sexual banter with coworkers.[38]

Curiously, Harris did not start objecting to Hardy's behavior until after his business relationship with her husband soured. This doesn't necessarily mean that she was out for revenge. Perhaps, when Hardy was no longer a friend, things she had once found innocuous (as did other women at the office) began to seem irritating and degrading—and Hardy just didn't get it. But is the legal system equipped to "get" such subtleties?[39]

"Conduct considered harmless by many today may be considered discriminatory in the future," warned the Ninth Circuit Court in a 1991 ruling on sexual harassment.[40]

Lately, however, some appellate courts have moved in the other direction. In 1995, the Seventh Circuit reversed an award to a woman whose boss had made a few sexual comments (including a remark about masturbation as a cure for his loneliness) and stressed that the law was not meant to "purge the workplace of vulgarity." More recently in *Oncale,* Justice Scalia stressed that "male-on-male horseplay or intersexual flirtation" should not be confused with harassment, and urged "careful consideration of the social context in which particular behavior occurs."[41]

But these admonitions are no substitute for specific standards, which remain vague and inconsistent. Additionally, as commentator Walter Olson has pointed out, victories for defendants "are hard to turn into reliable precedent," since current legal doctrine "encourages lower courts to look at the 'totality of the circumstances' in each case anew, rather than developing definite rules."[42]

Party-line feminists pooh-pooh the notion that the courts are flooded with frivolous claims of sexual harassment. The complaints women file, they say, are about abuse no one should have to tolerate, from sexual extortion to sexual assault.

Indisputably, many cases involve egregious behavior. Few would deny legal redress to plaintiffs like the three women in *Hall v. Gus Construction Co.,* who were hired as "flag persons" with an all-male road crew and quit after a three-month reign of terror in which the men forcibly groped them and urinated in their lunch boxes and water bottles.[43] But the courts also see remarkably trivial claims, some of which go a long way. Debra Black, former land acquisition manager for the Cincinnati developer Zaring Homes, won a $250,000 judgment in 1995 on the basis of six incidents:

- At a breakfast meeting, a male manager picked up a pastry and said, "Nothing I like more in the morning than sticky buns."
- Discussing a property next to a Hooters restaurant, two managers suggested such nicknames as Hooterville and Twin Peaks.
- At a company party, the chairman invited Black and another woman to sit by him, saying, "I love to be surrounded by beautiful women." Black said she was offended not by the remark but by the nasty looks from some unidentified female employees.

- At a meeting, someone "snickered" at the name of a property owner named Dr. Busam.
- Talking about a property near a bar, an executive (who was supportive of Black) supposedly teased her about "dancing on the tables" there. None of those present, including a manager who had left Zaring after failing to get a promotion, corroborated this.
- Black heard her boss refer to a female county official who was giving him a hard time as a "broad."

Black never complained and never considered suing until after she was fired from the company (for supposedly attaching a sheet with the president's signature to a document he hadn't seen). While she claimed the ribald talk left her an emotional wreck, she had merrily discussed X-rated movies and her own sex life with male and female colleagues. The trial judge barred some of this evidence but allowed testimony about a sexually hostile environment at Zaring, involving mostly *women's* behavior: a female sales rep had brought a penis-shaped eraser to a staff party; a woman executive had joked about male genitals and menstrual periods.[44]

The same year in Missouri, former Wal-Mart clerk Peggy Kimzey was awarded a record $50 million in punitive damages (later reduced to $5 million). She had complained that her supervisor, Bud Brewer, was yelling at her and calling her "dummy," and that she smelled liquor on his breath. After the management investigated but found no cause to discipline Brewer, Kimzey turned down an offer of another position where she would not have to work with him, quit her job, and sued for sexual harassment.

The behavior Kimzey complained about had no sexual elements. Other workers testified that Brewer, who had developed a bad temper after his wife died, was mean to women and men alike. (There have been other attempts to use sexual harassment charges as a weapon against rude and obnoxious bosses, from whom workers have no other legal protection.) But she also claimed that three years earlier, he had made a couple of vulgar jokes about her body—jokes that Kimzey conceded she didn't regard as harassment back then. Indeed, she had indicated on employee questionnaires that she enjoyed the informal atmosphere and had asked to return to the same department after taking time off to care for a sick relative.[45]

The award to Debra Black was later overturned, and Wal-Mart

may yet win on appeal. But even victories cost employers time and money, so generally they prefer to settle—or, better yet, not get sued. Since companies can avoid liability by showing that they do not tolerate sexual harassment, the incentive is to err on the side of regulating any behavior that might be actionable. Business magazines advise that "sexual bantering," "compliments with sexual overtones," and "suggestive remarks" should be "nip[ped] in the bud." The 1997 jury award of $26 million to the Miller Brewing Co. executive fired for discussing a racy episode of the TV comedy show *Seinfeld* may have been, as one commentator put it, a "wake-up call to corporate management" that overreacting to a harassment charge could be costly as well; but rather than being able to relax, companies are likely to be caught in a damned-if-you-do, damned-if-you-don't predicament. And two Supreme Court rulings in 1998 actually increased the pressure on employers to scrutinize workplace behavior, extending liability to cases in which the victim did not take advantage of existing procedures for bringing a complaint.[46]

Most of the suppressed activities and materials—such as a post-Bobbitt *New Yorker* cartoon of a man saying, "What's the big deal? I lopped off my own damn penis years ago"—probably would not be grounds for a lawsuit. But one never knows. "A Dog Named Sex," a piece of humor whose posting on interoffice e-mail has led to stern warnings, might seem utterly innocuous enough to have appeared in Dear Abby's column ("I told the clerk I wanted a license for Sex. He said, 'I'd like one, too!' . . . I said, 'You don't understand. I've had Sex since I was nine years old.' He winked at me and said, 'You must have been quite a kid.'"). Yet this story figured in at least one court case that the plaintiff won.[47]

Thus, regardless of cases that are tried or complaints that are filed, countless lives are affected by what happens in the shadow of the law, under rules that the law indirectly shapes. Numerous government agencies have enacted policies of "zero tolerance" of "sexual humor and innuendo." Many corporations have followed their example. Honeywell's handbook lists "staring" as an offense; Boeing outlaws "blond" jokes.[48]

Consultants and lawyers who toil in the booming sexual harassment industry have an obvious motive, ideology aside, to encourage or at least not to discourage overreaction. A striking example of their thinking can be found in the Sexual Harassment Prevention Game™, designed by Seattle consultant Chuck Hatten for corporate workshops. You move ahead or back on the board and win or lose play money depending on the answers you pick in case cards based mostly on true stories. Here are some scenarios:

• A female janitor complains that she feels sexually harassed by posters of scantily clad women being kept in the locker room. The posters, it turns out, depict female bodybuilders and belong to another female janitor, who explains that she is into body building and uses the posters for inspiration. Correct answer: the offending posters must be removed.

• A man occasionally passes by a woman's desk, looks at her, and runs his tongue over his lips, though he never says anything more than "Hello." Harassment or not? A "maybe" is not enough; you must agree that "a reasonable woman would determine his behavior to be harassment."

• Some men at the office get together for weekly lunches; women aren't invited because the guys trade raunchy jokes. The only correct answer: invite the women and cut out the jokes. (That women might join in the joking is not even an option.)

• A man is turned down for a date and brings the woman flowers a few days later; she accepts but tells him she wants to keep the relationship professional. That's *not* harassment—as long as he never brings flowers again.

No, this is not a parody or a humorous novelty item. Hatten's product has been bought for use in employee training programs by U.S. West, Boeing, McDonald's, the San Francisco division of AT&T, and the city governments of Philadelphia and Cincinnati. More than 90 percent of Fortune 500 companies now have harassment prevention training, up from 58 percent in 1988.[49]

Stanford law professor Deborah Rhode concedes that there are "occasional examples of overreaction," as when a graduate student working in a university office was told to remove from his desk a small photo of his bikini-clad wife after two young women complained. But these, she says, are "aberrant" cases that never result in punishment and are vastly outnumbered by cases in which real and serious complaints are ignored, by employers and even by the courts.[50]

But just because some real offenders may get off the hook doesn't mean that other people are not crucified for trivial or fictitious transgressions.

Some of the worst stories come from college campuses, where bureaucratic fear of liability meets feminist zealotry. Notorious cases like that of Donald Silva, the University of New Hampshire creative writing instructor fined and suspended for using a couple of sexual metaphors in his lectures, are the tip of the iceberg. Professors have been disciplined for being too friendly with female students, or assigning essays on sex-related topics to which one student happened to object. In 1997, University of South Florida art professor Charles Lyman was suspended for three weeks over one remark—possibly in poor taste, but occasioned by the offended student's involvement in an equally tasteless display: a photo (made by the young woman's boyfriend and shown in a campus exhibition) of several items hanging from a clothesline, including a picture of the "victim" and a picture of a penis. The professor's crime was to quip, "I saw you hanging next to a penis yesterday."[51] But victims of the sexual harassment crusade, some of them women, can be found outside the academy as well, in the public and private sectors:

• In Seattle in 1996, county ombudsman David Krull asked soon-to-be-wed assistant ombudsman Amy Calderwood if she wanted to see a funny item from the Internet, warning that she might find it offensive. He got a green light. But after reading the mildly off-color piece, "Instruction and Advice for the Young Bride"—which purports to be a Victorian text on how to avoid sex—Calderwood made a complaint. Later she revealed another shocking detail: in the nine months she had worked for Krull, he had made several comments about her "great hair days." Krull's apology was not enough: the county council voted ten to three to fire him.[52]

• Tom Pierce, a manager at Commonwealth Life Insurance Co., exchanged humorous sexually suggestive cards (such as "Sex is a misdemeanor. De more I miss, de meanor I get") with office administrator Debbie Kennedy. After being denied a merit increase, Kennedy, who had engaged in other risqué behavior with Pierce and other male coworkers, complained of sexual harassment. Pierce was demoted with a significant pay cut and transferred to another office; he wasn't even allowed to come back for his personal belongings, which were dropped off at a fast food restaurant.[53]

• In 1994, several female tellers and managers at United Jersey Bank shared some laughs over cutouts of male nudes from *Playgirl* (half an hour before closing, with no customers in the bank). A male teller took offense and complained. The women were ordered to apologize to him and were suspended without pay for as long as two weeks; some were demoted.[54]

• Sometimes action is taken even when the "victim" doesn't complain. In one case, a corporate manager was reported for hugging a secretary in her cubicle. As it turned out, he was comforting her after she had learned of her mother's death, and the complainant had a grudge against the boss for denying her a promotion. Nevertheless, the review concluded that the manager may have violated company policy prohibiting "sexual touching," and he was placed on probation for a year.[55]

The Children's Crusade

The 1996 story of Johnathan Prevette, the six-year-old suspended from school for a day for smooching a girl on the cheek, drew national attention to the crusade to stamp out kiddie sexual harassment.[56]

The U.S. Department of Education had encouraged school districts to treat sexual teasing as a violation of Title IX (which forbids discrimination in education) since 1988, when a California mother brought a complaint about her daughter's verbal abuse. But after Anita Hill, and especially after the Supreme Court ruled in 1992 that schools could be held liable if they didn't stop such behavior, sexual harassment became the educational issue *du jour*. Jittery schools began to ban "leering" and "sexual gossip." California passed a law requiring public schools to have harassment policies starting in fourth grade. Minnesota Department of Education gender equity specialist Sue Sattel accused California of making it "OK for little kids to sexually harass each other."[57]

As in the workplace, the crusade against harassment in schools focuses on some horrific acts, from sexual assault to taunts directed at a seven-year-old on the school bus about having oral sex with her dad. That's what happened to Cheltzie Hentz, who became the youngest plaintiff to win a federal sexual harassment suit when the U.S. Department of Education found that the school's response to complaints from Cheltzie's mother was not "timely" enough.[58]

No one thinks such behavior is all right. But should it be handled like any other disciplinary problem, or singled out as a civil rights matter? In the school context, the discrimination model is especially absurd, since the harassment often involves same-sex bullying (this contradiction is evaded in sexual harassment prevention materials, which simply assert that girls can harass girls and boys can harass boys). A *Los Angeles Times* reporter who investigated a feminist cause célèbre in Petaluma, California—an eighth grader whose life was made unbearable by her schoolmates' teasing about her alleged proclivity for self-gratification with a hot dog—found that although the girl's suit against the school focused on boys' behavior, her worst tormentors were girls.[59]

As always, the horrific acts are blended with trifles. A much publicized American Association of University Women report on sexual harassment in schools got the victimization rates up to 85 percent for girls and 76 percent for boys by counting sexual jokes, comments, and the like as sexual harassment. In an ABC News report on the AAUW sexual harassment survey, the story of an eleven-year-old terrorized by a boy who threatened her and exposed himself was followed by footage of a boy mussing a girl's hair or making as if to kiss her on the cheek.[60]

Nor is it clear that the putative victims want to be rescued. At seminars for teachers, the need to "educate" girls that "the boys aren't just joking around, that it's sexual harassment" is a frequent topic. "Many girls consider this behavior acceptable and they laugh and joke about it," lamented a high school social worker at a 1993 conference at Douglass College in New Jersey.[61]

To help these benighted creatures, sexual harassment prevention programs are proliferating. In especially progressive states such as Minnesota, children as young as seven are educated about sexual harassment, which includes "someone touching you when you don't want them to" (even when horsing around in the playground?) or "swear words about your penis, vulva, breasts or buttocks." The appropriate response, the tots are told, is to say "Stop it! That's sexual harassment, and sexual harassment is against the law."[62]

Some young people learn the lessons well. In 1998 at Walt Whitman High School in Montgomery County, Maryland, popular track coach Christopher Flynn was fired after two girls unhappy about failing to make the all-county cross-country team accused him of sexual harassment. His crimes consisted of "immature" quips, talking about his personal life, and using Marine Corps-style yelling and derision to motivate the runners—methods that, one of the plaintiffs told a reporter, were fine for boys but not for girls, because "they'll cry."[63]

Is Sex Sexist?

Many crusades have unintended consequences. But are the extremes of the drive to stamp out sexual harassment an accidental by-product of too much zeal, or do they have something to do with the agenda behind the crusade?

Whenever the harassment warriors are accused of an antisex animus, they invoke the standard mantra: *Sexual harassment is not about sex; it's about power.* No one ever explains how this jibes with the shibboleth that male behavior intended as harmless fun is often perceived by women as sexual harassment.

But while Catharine MacKinnon originally defined harassment as "the unwanted imposition of sexual requirements in the context of a relationship of unequal power," the lines between unwelcome advances by superiors and by peers are increasingly blurred. In a 1994 survey of federal workers showing that 44 percent of the women had been "sexually harassed," only about a quarter of the offenders were of higher rank. There's even talk of "contrapower harassment" by lower-status men. A much-publicized 1993 study on the harassment of women physicians by male patients (which, apart from a few reports of sexual touching, consisted of suggestive looks or comments, "inappropriate" gifts such as a tape of love songs, and requests for dates) noted that "the vulnerability inherent in their sex appears to override their power as doctors."[64]

Many personal accounts of "harassment" clearly have much less to do with power than with sexual attraction. One journalist opens her story with an episode that "haunts" her two years later: a man who had been a regular source told her over drinks that he had always wanted to sleep with her. She said no, and he made no further advances. "Whether or not it constituted harassment may be up for grabs," the author adds grimly, "though I certainly know where I stand on the matter." Ironically, she then repeats the sexual-harassment-is-not-about-sex-it's-about-power cliché.[65]

In fact, the formula is disingenuous because, to the ideologues, *sex* is not about sex but about power. According to Catharine MacKinnon, whose work was so instrumental in crafting sexual harassment law, feminist theory "treats sexuality as a social construct of male power: defined by men, forced on women."[66]

MacKinnon's is not an isolated voice. "Because of the inequality and coercion with which it is so frequently associated in the minds of women, the appearance of sexuality in an unexpected context or a setting of ostensible equality can be an anguishing experience," writes Boston University law professor Kathryn Abrams, who can barely bring herself to concede that women like sex.[67] Abrams asserts that "pornography" at work creates a hostile environment not just because it offends women but because it encourages men to view women in a sexual way (not that it ever would occur to them otherwise!), which is "strikingly at odds with the way women wish to be viewed in the workplace." This argument was cited in a 1991 court ruling ordering a Florida shipyard to ban not only *Playboy*-style pinups but mere possession of "sexually suggestive" materials, including locker-room calendars or a *Penthouse* a worker might read on a lunch break.[68]

Some feminist legal scholars suggest that "apparently consensual relationships" between coworkers, or at least between bosses and subordinates, should be banned because they create "a sexualized workplace that encourages sexual harassment." Even the often sensible Susan Estrich has come close to endorsing this view (except, apparently, when one of the coworkers is a Democratic president of the United States); she has even asserted, on the basis of a survey showing that most women would be offended by a sexual proposition at work, that most women aren't interested in workplace romance. That would no doubt be news to the editors of *Cosmopolitan,* which publishes office flirting tips about looking playfully at a man's crotch or "accidentally" showing off sexy underthings.[69]

Feminists with less capacity for wishful thinking admit that many women "experience some sexual behaviors in the workplace as pleasurable"—only to conclude that women just don't get it.[70]

Shortly after the Hill-Thomas hearings, feminist sociologists Patti Guiffre and Christine Williams interviewed waitresses working in "sexualized" environments rife with banter and physical horseplay, from hugs to pats on the behind. Generally the women enjoyed these antics. These were not meek creatures resigned to being mistreated. They readily condemned sexual exploitation by bosses as well as occasional advances that turned abusive, such as a man's grabbing and shoving a woman who wouldn't go out with him. Giuffre and Williams see this as deplorable tolerance for "sexual domination" at work. Sexual harassment, they explain, "is hard to identify, and thus difficult to eradicate . . . in part because our hegemonic definition of sexuality defines certain contexts of sexual interaction as legitimate."[71]

One might dismiss this as academic gibberish. Unfortunately, yesterday's academic gibberish becomes today's legal precedent. Kathryn Abrams's ruminations on the perils of sexuality for women were quoted in at least two landmark rulings. In another case, *Cardin v. VIA Tropical Fruits,* a federal court in Florida upheld a claim of a sexually hostile environment based primarily on racy cartoons and written jokes. Some of this material was circulated by women, and much of it made fun of male anatomy: one cartoon showed a woman peering under the sheets at her mate, captioned, "Where's the beef?" The court conceded that the humor "depicted both men and women" but explained, in pure MacKinnonite terms, that "verbal and visual sexual humor" in the workplace "may tend to demean women . . . because such joking defines women as women by their sexuality, and consequently may create practical obstacles to effective performance."[72]

The assumption that "sexualization" demeans women has trickled down into popular discourse. Ellen Goodman asserts that male sexual attention makes women fearful: "The wolf whistles and the pinups . . . carry the threat of verbal and physical assault." Common tips on avoiding sexual harassment include not saying anything to a woman that you wouldn't say to a colleague of the same sex ("Would you tell another guy you like the way he does his hair?") and steering clear of "anything . . . you wouldn't do to Mom"—which implies that female coworkers are to be seen as asexual. Even *Cosmopolitan's* 1994 "Life After College" supplement warns, "Sexual bantering is one way to say, 'You're a woman. You don't belong here.'"[73]

Sexual conduct at work can be a way of treating women as male playthings, or a way to humiliate women and even force them off the job. Sometimes it may create fear. Kerry Ellison of *Ellison v. Brady,* in which a federal appellate court first endorsed a "reasonable woman" standard, had good reason to be scared by the obsessive attention of a disturbed coworker (which hardly justifies the court's conclusion that *normally,* "women who are victims of mild sexual harassment may understandably worry whether [it] is merely a prelude to violent sexual assault").[74]

But sexual humor can also be a form of bonding, a way of saying, "You're one of us," as it is in single-sex settings. Some women who have succeeded in traditionally male fields say that the biggest mistake women make is to interpret the teasing as gender-based hostility.

Sexual banter can indeed affirm our sexual identity. But why the leap from "You're a woman" to "You don't belong here"? (And, if a man thinks that way, is getting him to stop seeing his female colleagues as women the answer?) Sometimes the woman may read, "You don't belong," into it. And maybe one can't blame her.

Feminists didn't invent the notion that women could be sexual *or* respected, sexy *or* smart; such attitudes were a legitimate feminist grievance. Even in the 1980s, many career women interviewed by psychologist Beth Milwid were less upset about being treated as "sex objects" than about having to choose between being sexual and being taken seriously, about the perception that they couldn't "have a good time the way the guys do" and still get ahead.[75]

A female newcomer on "masculine" turf can understandably feel threatened when attention is drawn to her sexuality. One may sympathize with Bernadine Healy (later the director of the National Institutes of Health) when, as a professor at the Johns Hopkins Medical School in 1982, she was upset by being lampooned in a bawdy skit in a campus club show, though male faculty members were satirized as well. But to complain, as she did, inevitably sends the message that women are too frail to take it on the chin.[76] To protect women's vulnerabilities is to institutionalize them, making female powerlessness a self-fulfilling prophecy.

The good news is that if the "demeaning" effect of much sexual expression at work is in the woman's mind, it's in her power not to let it get to her—*not* to grin and bear it when she is abused, but to reevaluate her response to sexual expression that *is* about sex (or humor), not power. One manager told Beth Milwid that she used to see a man's sexual interest as a signal that she wasn't taken seriously as a professional:

> Now, I just think it means I'm attractive. . . . If I'm not interested in them, I'm not interested. But being a sexually alive person doesn't mean you're not powerful, and it certainly doesn't mean you're not capable.[77]

Indeed, there is increasingly no contradiction for men, as a male law professor put it, "in viewing one's colleague simultaneously as an attractive sexual being and a competent co-worker." (Sexual harassment "expert" Susan Webb gripes that "men will compliment a woman on what she's wearing, rather than the report she wrote," as if they can't compliment both.) Feminists might be expected to cheer the demise of the false dichotomy between female sexuality and competence—the modern Madonna-whore syndrome. Instead, they reinforce it: "Treatment that sexualizes women workers," writes Kathryn Abrams, "prevents them from feeling, and prevents others from perceiving them, as equals in the workplace."[78]

Inevitably, the campaign against "sexualization" extends beyond work to streets, parks, shopping malls, movie theaters, and other public places. Carol Brooks Gardner, women's studies professor at Indiana University, opens her book, *Passing By: Gender and Public Harassment,* with an account of an innocuous flirtation by a gas station attendant, and carps that she wants to be seen "more as a citizen than a source for gender games." Primly disapproving of women who enjoy these "games," Gardner makes it clear that her target is the "heterosexualist romanticism of public places." A 1993 *Harvard Law Review* article proposed a "street harassment" law formulated so broadly that an "unwelcome" pickup line in a bar might have qualified.[79]

Actually, an unwelcome pickup line in a bar ("Baby, you are one hot mama") *was* classified as harassment in a 1994 study widely reported under such headlines as "Sexual Harassment Is Treated Lightly on TV, Study Says." One of the authors, University of Dayton professor Thomas Skill, conceded that nearly all this behavior took place outside work or school and thus wasn't *legally* sexual harassment; however, he said, it was important because TV instills wrong ideas about sexual interaction that can be acted out at the office. Perhaps, to achieve the harassment-free work environment, freedom of speech—for which the MacKinnonites have as much regard as they do for heterosexual romance—would have to be suppressed not only in the workplace but in the world at large.[80]

The Befuddled Male

What bothers men about the sexual harassment campaign, Ellen Goodman opines, is less the ambiguity than the power shift. Once, "men made the rules" while women worried about how their demeanor would be perceived by men; now, "men are worrying about how they should behave and how they are perceived—by women."[81]

In fact, while women in the past bore the brunt of the consequences of sexual misbehavior, the division of power was never *that* one-sided. (Can a grown-up seriously think that before feminism, men didn't worry about how they were perceived by women?) The slap in the face was a symbol of women's cultural authority to keep male behavior in check; albeit in a context of economic and social subordination, women in Western societies have played a key role in enforcing decorum.

But the old rules were fairly simple, and the obligations they imposed on men and women were mutual if unequal (men could relax in the company of other men and "loose" women): Gentlemen didn't use bad language, make ribald jokes, or talk about sex in front of ladies; ladies didn't do that, period. These norms have crumbled, partly due to feminist efforts to get women off the pedestal.

In some ways, it has been noted, the new feminist standards of "respect for women" bear an uncanny resemblance to those prefeminist norms. But contrary to some conservatives' wishful thinking, the sexual harassment crusade is not a back-to-the-pedestal movement. It demands for women the privilege of being treated like a lady (when they feel like it) without having to act like one.[82]

A few years ago, I caught a cable TV comedy club special in the middle of a routine that would have made the proverbial sailor blush. In the 1950s, no respectable woman could have attended such a performance. In the 1990s, women made up at least half of the live audience and were having a great time. A man at that show might reasonably conclude that many women enjoy raunchy humor. But could he repeat the tamest of these jokes to a female coworker? Even if she enjoys watching such shows, he can't be sure that she wouldn't be offended. He can't even be sure that a woman who tells dirty jokes herself won't take offense at a joke he may tell.

And some courts would back her. In 1987, an appellate panel ruled that a woman's use of "foul language with sexual innuendo" did not bar her from seeking redress against similar behavior, as long as she had not "welcomed the particular conduct in question." The plaintiff, flight attendant Betsy Swentek, was described by former coworkers as "a foul-mouthed individual" who, on various occasions, put a dildo in her supervisor's mailbox, gave a cup of her urine to another employee as a drink, and grabbed a pilot's crotch "with a frank invitation to a sexual encounter." While Swentek disputed this testimony, the court held that it had no bearing on the case even if true. Her own complaint, it should be added, involved claims of fairly mild sexual antics, such as a pilot reciting dirty limericks or dropping on his knees and pretending to sniff at her crotch.[83]

Small wonder men are confused. "You have to be a fool to buy into any kind of suggestive banter at the office," a federal employee told me. "Since the woman is generally the sole judge of what crosses the line, maybe as far as she's concerned her last comment didn't cross the line but your comment did." Some women in his office, he said, had openly taunted men about this double standard: "One woman said something like, 'Well, I can say things that you can't, can't I?'"[84]

As those New Jersey bank tellers who thought they were having innocent fun with male nudes from *Playgirl* found out, women aren't entirely safe. More men are getting touchy about women's behavior—some catch the sensitivity bug, others enjoy the idea of turning the tables on women—and women can be touchy about it as well. In 1993, two nurses filed a suit (later settled by the hospital) charging that their female supervisor's penchant for ribald jokes and bawdy birthday cards created "an environment tainted with sexual harassment."[85]

More often, though, women can get away with it. One man who had lost his job over a trivial charge kept a "harassment diary" at his next workplace, a West Coast cellular phone company. His entries included loud conversations about a bawdy bachelorette party, a female manager making jokes about hiring men to be her sex slaves, and a woman teasing male coworkers by waving a picture of a topless woman in their faces.

In the media, too, behavior now off-limits to men is largely condoned for women. A 1993 *New York Times* article on a White House briefing for radio talk show hosts humorously noted that one female host "flustered the White House communications director, Mark Gearan, by asking if he would care to continue their interview in her hot tub." The same year, addressing a civic group, freshman congresswoman Marjorie Margolies-Mezvinsky was asked how Washington compared to her expectations and responded with a joke: A medical student is asked what organ can grow to eight times its normal size; she stammers and blushes, and the professor tells her that not only does she not know the answer—the iris of the eye—but she will have to "realign her expectations." A *Newsweek* story treated this as an expression of feistiness. Two years later, for telling a few jokes of that caliber at a banquet, U.S. Coast Guard spokesman Captain Ernie Blanchard was subject to a criminal probe that drove him to suicide.[86]

After graduating from college, a friend of mine worked for a small magazine. One day, a female coworker twice his age who wore garish makeup and dressed like a teenager called him into her office and offered to fix his posture. He stood uncomfortably while she stroked his back. When her hands wandered to the other side, he excused himself and bolted. A few days later, meeting him in the hallway, she shrieked, "Is that a banana in your pocket or are you just glad to see me?" He desperately wanted to be invisible. Such stories were not a part of the Anita Hill "teach-in": that unwanted sexual attention at work could cut both ways was at best an afterthought.

Although sexual harassment complaints by men have grown faster than women's complaints, they still comprise only about 10 percent of the total. (Close to half of men's claims, and just 15 percent of women's, are of quid pro quo pressures.) On the other hand, in a 1994 survey of federal employees, nearly a third of those who had experienced unwanted sexual attention at work were men. And in the 1993 AAUW survey, not only 85 percent of the girls but three out of four boys reported being "sexually harassed" in school, by the study's rather expansive definition.[87]

The AAUW stressed that the effects on girls were worse: they were much more likely to say that "sexual harassment" made them less confident and caused them to do worse in school. But maybe boys are simply less willing to admit that they let it get to them; complaining of sexual abuse, particularly by a female, is not a culturally sanctioned form of expression for males. And maybe girls, for whom it *is* culturally sanctioned, are a bit *too* willing to blame a bad grade on harassment.

Some studies suggest that the gender gap in perceptions of harassment has been vastly overstated. Still, there is no doubt that women and men often view sexual behavior differently. A woman is expected to feel demeaned if she is treated as "easy." A man is expected to feel flattered by sexual attention from a woman, since she presumably wouldn't approach just any man—and since there is still a belief that sex is a favor a man gets from a woman. Journalist Robert Wright, a proponent of evolutionary psychology, argues that these differences are in our genes and should be acknowledged as a basis for special laws to protect women.[88]

Whether sex differences are seen as natural or cultural, the assumption is always that they are in the direction of men seeing no harm in behavior that disturbs women. But a *Washington Post* story about high school boys' responses to "sexual harassment" by women included a complaint that suggests otherwise: "Where I do my community lab, it's this lady . . . she's always flirting with me . . . she starts rubbing on my thigh . . . but when I try to respond to her, she retracts. It's like a respect thing with her that I can't do that, but that she can do that with me."[89]

While women are more likely to complain of sexual pressure, sexual teasing may be a more male-specific gripe. It doesn't have to involve active provocation; many men, writes British author David Thomas, feel that "the overt sexuality of some women's clothes" can be a form of "passive harassment."[90] (Wright's description of male "wiring"—responsiveness to visual stimuli and a tendency to see provocative female body language as a come-on—would seem to support such an idea; but he apparently feels that only women's natural vulnerabilities merit protection.)

This argument infuriates many feminists, not only because it smacks of "she was asking for it"—though surely one can say that a woman invites sexual attention without implying that she invites sexual assault—but because it raises the issue of female "sexual power." This notion, once invoked to deny women equal rights, understandably makes women nervous: the siren enslaving besotted men is a favorite figure of the misogynist imagination.

Still, the stereotype has a kernel of truth. Despite the sexual revolution, sex is still, to a degree, seen as something men want from women. Whether or not men need sex more, female sexual signals often physically affect men in a way that has no easy role-reversed equivalent. It's an effect some women exploit: "At my office, I have half the guys walking around with hard-ons because of my long legs, short skirts and swishy walk," one young woman bragged to a researcher.[91] Some men might resent this. If sexual harassment includes so intangible an assault as a leer, why not a miniskirt?

In the same way, we rightly see the imbalance of economic and social power when a middle-aged boss makes a pass at a secretary; but any mention of the personal power an attractive young woman may wield in such a situation is taboo. Consider the case of Sandra Zowayyed, a receptionist at a silk screen manufacturing firm who claimed that she was sexually harassed by Mike Lowen, the middle-aged company president. Once he gave her a note that read, "You have very playful eyes. Do you play?" Zowayyed also charged that Lowen repeatedly brushed against her and made "goo goo eyes," causing her anguish and embarrassment. Yet according to her supervisor, Elaine Blevins, Zowayyed would laugh about Lowen's infatuation with her, boasting that she had him "wrapped around [her] little finger." Blevins reported this to a senior manager (also female); Zowayyed refused to apologize, was fired, and filed a lawsuit.[92]

Perhaps, as she claimed, her joking was a way to relieve the strain caused by Lowen's advances. But is it inconceivable that she was indulging in a fantasy of a powerful older man in thrall to her charms? Can such psychological intricacies be untangled in a court of law? Much depends on personalities: the older man may be needy and vulnerable, or dominant and willing to exploit his status; the younger woman may be insecure and pliant, or self-assured and willing to exploit her sexuality.

"Men use power one way, women another, but both tend to deny their power," writes film critic Molly Haskell in a thoughtful essay about sexual dynamics at the office, only to conclude that men have the upper hand: "In many of the stories I've heard, women somehow end up with the burden of having to *intuit* which way the wind is blowing."[93] Could this be because the stories were told by women? Men might counter that *they* bear the burden of making the first move, of having to "intuit" how the woman will respond, of facing rejection. But when the affronts women suffer are politicized, the other half of the equation is omitted, and we are left with men as wolves and women as lambs.

A Cure Worse Than the Disease

The sexual harassment crusade has undoubtedly redressed some real wrongs but in the process has created more problems than it has solved. Consultants, lawyers, and feminist theorists often talk about the high costs of sexual harassment, not only in litigation but in psychological injuries, stress-related ailments, and damage to productivity and morale on the job. But what about the costs of the war on harassment? Being raked over the coals for sending "A Dog Named Sex" over office e-mail, or ordered to take down a cartoon about the Bobbitts, is hardly a morale booster.

I once listened to NOW Legal Defense Fund executive director Kathryn Rodgers—whom I couldn't even get to sympathize with the female bank tellers penalized for giggling over nude male pictures—argue that cracking down on sexual harassment was good business: why let employees waste time on tomfoolery when they're being paid to work? (So much for humanizing the workplace!) Yet studies show that humor, including sexual banter, may have important psychological benefits for workers.[94]

The human cost of this crusade also includes the incalculable: relationships that never got a chance to bloom in the chilly climate of the new workplace. The story of TV journalist Sam Donaldson's courtship of his wife, Jan Smith, twenty years ago—he was considerably higher in status, and pursued her despite her repeated objections—could be a classic story of sexual harassment. One article on electronic romance at work tells the story of a woman who began receiving anonymous messages on her office computer: "Eventually she confronted her suspect . . . who immediately confessed. They were still dating at last report."[95] This tale could have ended as easily with, "He was in sensitivity training at last report," a thought likely to discourage more cautious suitors, particularly since even a relationship that starts out as consensual can be reimagined as sexual harassment later on.

"Every time a man and a woman meet at the water cooler now, Anita Hill [is] right there between them," Andrea Sankar, an anthropologist at Wayne State University, told *Newsweek* a year after the Hill-Thomas hearings. (This was apparently supposed to be a *good* thing.) In many offices, the ghost of Anita Hill is raised only as a joke. But some companies now require two employees entering a "social and/or amorous relationship" to sign a legal agreement attesting that the relationship is "welcome, voluntary and consensual" and does not violate the company's harassment policy. Big Sister is watching.[96]

Just how oppressed many people have felt by what one journalist called "the pressure-cooker politesse" of the post–Anita Hill era was evident from the audible sigh of relief when the story of President Clinton's affair with Monica Lewinsky suddenly made it okay to talk about sex and tell salacious jokes at the office. Whether this thaw will last is another matter. Karen Mathis, director of the American Bar Association's Committee on Women in the Profession, sniffed that such behavior "will slink back into its hole."[97]

Personal relationships aside, some women worry that harassment hysteria is damaging them professionally: men are wary of asking a female colleague to join them for a drink or of mentoring a woman ("unusual interest" in a woman's career can be cited as evidence of wrongdoing). Nor are women helped by the perception that harassment charges are used as a weapon in office politics.[98]

The indiscriminate use of the "sexual harassment" label may even hurt true victims of sexually abusive behavior at work: the concept stretching, meant to stigmatize trivial offenses, also trivializes serious ones. In 1992, when CBS ran a promo for a *60 Minutes* segment about claims of harassment at the Bureau of Alcohol, Tobacco, and Firearms (which involved stalking and attempted rape), I surely wasn't the only one whose first thought was, "Another story about dirty jokes and pin-ups." Much of the responsibility lies with the people who insist on equating these women's complaints with Anita Hill's.

Behavior that shouldn't be illegal can still create problems. Individuals differ in their tolerance for sexual innuendo, and coworkers can irritate each other in a lot of ways, sexual or not. But today's climate discourages them from resolving such conflicts on a personal level. (In Chuck Hatten's "Sexual Harassment Prevention Game," the answer *always* involves formal action: the supervisor who receives a complaint cannot just talk to the offender, let alone suggest that the complainant talk to him first.) Besides, it's ludicrous to demand the same standards of propriety in every workplace; whatever happened to "diversity"? A person who finds his or her work environment too "sexualized" or too buttoned down should be expected to adjust or get another job.

Those who see the attention to sexual harassment in the 1990s as a positive development sometimes suggest that after early excesses, things will settle down.[99] But it is likely that the crusade will roll on until it runs into some real resistance. The charges of sexual misconduct against President Clinton in 1998 may prove to be a turning point. The public's apparent willingness to shrug off the sex scandals was, at least in part, a rebellion against the post–Anita Hill régime with its policing of sexuality and its gross invasions of privacy—and the pro-Clinton feminists' evasions and excuses made the culture safe for such a rebellion, stripping feminists of their authority to speak out on the issue. Unfortunately, critics of "sexual correctness" were not sufficiently organized to pick up the momentum the way the gender warriors capitalized on the momentum of the Hill-Thomas hearings. (That many conservatives were suddenly converted to the cause of sexual harassment in their zeal to get Clinton didn't help.)

To restore common sense, it's not enough to acknowledge that the war on harassment has its follies and excesses. What's needed is a new "teach-in" to challenge the premises of this war: to expose the absurdity of such shibboleths as "the only thing that matters is how the victim perceived it" and of catalogues of harassing acts that run the gamut from winking to rape; to emphasize both sexes' responsibility for sexual miscommunication; to remind us of the option of civility without adversarial terms like *sexual harassment*.

PART THREE

Toward a New Paradigm

CHAPTER EIGHT

Men and Their Children

"**A** Chilling Message to Working Moms." "Working Moms: Guilty." So cried the headlines when, during the O. J. Simpson trial in 1995, the estranged husband of prosecutor Marcia Clark asked for temporary custody of their three- and five-year-old sons, claiming that she was "never home." In two notorious cases the previous year, University of Michigan student Jennifer Ireland had lost custody of her three-year-old daughter in part because she used day care, and a Washington, D.C., judge had cited the heavy work schedule of Senate staffer Sharon Prost, a mother of two, in awarding custody to the father, Ken Greene.[1]

A few champions of embattled mothers, such as publishing hot-shot Judith Regan (herself embroiled in a custody fight), openly advocated discrimination against fathers: "Women are simply better equipped biologically for parenting young children." Others said that *women* were victims of discrimination: "I mean . . . the number of men who have been working in court and no one has ever talked about taking their children away!" fumed Cokie Roberts on ABC's *This Week*—as if taking men's children away were not the typical outcome of divorce.[2]

Were mothers really getting a raw deal? Even *New York Times* reporter Susan Chira, who treats Marcia Clark and Sharon Prost as victims of anti–working mom bias, acknowledges that the fathers were not only actively involved in child rearing but more available to the kids. When Gordon Clark filed for temporary custody (which he didn't get), Marcia Clark was putting in sixteen-hour days and working weekends; yet she wouldn't allow Gordon more time with the boys and instead wanted him to pay for babysitters, out of his

$36,000 a year to her $96,000. In *Prost v. Greene,* the judge herself was a working mother but nonetheless was rather sarcastic about Prost's assumption that "a grant of custody to her was a foregone conclusion."[3]

The Michigan "day care" case, which eventually ended in a shared-custody agreement, was more complicated. The teenage dad, Steven Smith, didn't see his child until her first birthday and sought custody after the mother had sued for child support. But in the first year, Jennifer Ireland wasn't much of a parent either: she juggled high school, work, and cheerleading while her mother and sister cared for baby Maranda. According to Steve, he was asked to stay away because Jennifer was still considering adoption. It is a fact that once he had met his daughter, he began to see her regularly and to help with child care. When he filed for custody, things had turned sour between him and Jennifer, and the Irelands were trying to limit his contact with Maranda. (The request for child support, when Steve was earning twenty dollars a week, may have been part of that effort: Ireland told a magazine that she wanted him to pay for "the frills of having a child.")[4] Nor was Judge Raymond Cashen's decision based solely on the day care factor. He felt that the Smiths would give the girl a stable primary residence, as opposed to being shuttled between campus housing and the Ireland home; the same concern about residential stability had earlier led him to *reduce* Steve's time with Maranda.[5]

The careers-and-custody debate was revisited in 1998 when a Florida court ruled against Alice Hector, a partner in a major Miami law firm, and awarded custody of her two daughters to the father, Robert Young, who had given up his work as an architect and devoted much of his time to caring for the children and volunteering at their school. But in fact, it's not only mothers who are penalized for having demanding careers. In 1988, a New York court gave sole custody of a seven-year-old boy to a mother who was a compulsive liar (she made up a string of fictitious accomplishments for the child when enrolling him in kindergarten, followed by fictitious calamities to explain his problems to teachers), who called her son a "fucking little brat" when he wouldn't back up her lies, and who had made dramatic suicide threats when her husband found out she had squandered the family savings. An appellate court upheld the custody award, pointing out that the husband was a partner in a law firm while the wife's part-time job "rendered her better able to devote the time and attention necessary to care for the child."[6]

Kay Schwarzberg, a Michigan attorney and a divorced mother, scoffs at the notion that fathers get "extra points" for child care. One of her clients, she says, took nearly full responsibility for his four children once they were past infancy: he usually picked them up from day care, bathed them, and put them to bed. His wife, a medical researcher at a top university, never took more than six weeks' maternity leave despite opportunities to be at home longer. Shortly before the custody trial, the mother took a one-year leave from the university and got a part-time job—and received primary custody because she was "more available."

Overall, fathers' groups point out, mothers are granted custody 90 percent of the time. Feminists retort that when men ask for custody, they have the edge. "Contrary to public belief, *70 percent of all litigated custody trials rule in favor of the fathers,*" shouts the jacket of the 1996 book *Divorced from Justice: The Abuse of Women and Children by Lawyers and Judges* by Karen Winner. The "NOW Action Alert on 'Fathers' Rights'" adopted at NOW's 1996 national conference also asserts that "many judges and attorneys are still biased against women and fathers are granted custody 70% of the time when they seek it."[7]

This widely cited figure first appeared in *Mothers on Trial:* Phyllis Chesler reported that 70 percent of "custodially challenged" mothers in her sample lost.[8]

While even sympathetic reviewers noted the sloppiness of Chesler's use of statistics and her penchant for hyperbole (such as likening custody hearings to medieval witch trials), her "finding" was often presented as fact. There were other sources. According to sociologist Lenore Weitzman, author of the acclaimed book *The Divorce Revolution,* two-thirds of fathers asking for custody in the late 1970s in California succeeded. The Massachusetts Gender Bias Study reported that fathers who sought custody won sole or joint legal/primary physical custody 70 percent of the time.[9]

Even if true, this could mean that fathers seek custody only when they know they have a chance because there's something wrong with the mother. Indeed, explaining why few noncustodial mothers pay child support, the Gender Bias Study says that "women who lose custody often do so because of mental, physical, or emotional handicaps," which impair their earning capacity.[10] That aside, the high success rate of men in custody battles is another contender for the Phony Statistics Hall of Fame.

Weitzman never claimed to have found that men won two-thirds of *contested* cases: on the contrary, she stressed that when fathers got sole custody, it was typically by mutual agreement, and mothers won most cases that went to trial. The work from which the Massachusetts Gender Bias Study got its data did not separate contested and uncontested custody requests. It did show that mothers filing for sole custody got it 75 percent of the time (the rest usually received joint legal/primary physical custody) while the "success rate" for fathers was 44 percent.[11]

Other research shows little evidence of a male advantage:

• In Arizona, a recent study found, two-thirds of divorced mothers but only one in six fathers ended up with the custodial arrangements they wanted; women generally had a higher sense of control over the divorce process and were more satisfied with the outcome. Three-quarters of the men and a quarter of the women thought the legal system was slanted in favor of mothers; one in ten women and none of the men believed it was slanted in favor of fathers.[12]

• In an Ohio study, four out of forty-five contested custody cases resulted in an award of custody to the father.[13]

• A Stanford University study of one thousand California couples divorced in the mid-1980s found that if both parents requested sole custody when filing for divorce, the mother got custody 45 percent of the time, the father 11 percent of the time; the rest got joint physical custody. When she wanted sole custody and he wanted joint custody, the odds were more than two to one in her favor. Most of these disputes were negotiated. Five couples vying for sole custody fought it out to the bitter end of a trial; only one of these cases resulted in the father's victory, with joint custody ordered in another case.[14]

The one-sided campaign against domestic violence is likely to exacerbate this slant. (According to a Legal Aid attorney, not only physical but "emotional . . . violence on women" is a good reason to "cut [fathers] off from their children altogether.")[15] Of course, parental violence is not irrelevant. But aside from the use of false charges, the degree to which these provisions selectively target men can be seen from the case of David Nevers, an Illinois man whose wife had assaulted him several times and finally pleaded guilty to battery (with a suspended sentence) after pushing him down the stairs and causing him severe injuries.

Although a psychologist initially recommended joint custody with primary physical custody to the father, the judge decided that Jeanine Nevers would have sole custody of their three daughters, mainly because she worked part time and had been the "primary nurturer" (even though David had taken a much more active role in the two years before the divorce). The judge got around the domestic violence factor by proclaiming that the abuse had been mutual: "The conduct of Mr. Nevers has been . . . equally violent in a psychological way as Mrs. [Nevers's] was in a physical way." Yet in addition to her physical violence, Jeanine had, by her own admission, called David vile names, spit in his face, and belittled him in front of the children. He was guilty of such crimes as writing "Jeanine—act crazy" on a note board where family members' chores were written down.[16]

The vast majority of men never seek custody. But that does not necessarily mean they don't want it, as is often assumed. In the Stanford study, when fathers were asked about their preferences, 35 percent wanted sole custody; a third, joint physical custody. Yet more than a third of these men didn't even try.[17]

Some fathers, speculate authors Eleanor Maccoby and Robert Mnookin, may decide that the arrangement they prefer is impractical because they spend too much time at work and lack parenting skills; others may think that regardless of what *they* want, the kids are better off with Mom. Or they feel that their chances of success are "too remote to justify the necessary effort and family stress." The American Bar Association journal *Family Advocate* admonishes family lawyers to "warn fathers seeking custody that they face great personal pain and expense [and that] the price is often emotional damage to father, mother, and the children."[18]

The man can be "crippled," as one father told me, by the self-imposed chivalrous obligation to move out even if he doesn't want the divorce—giving the mother the advantage of an "established custodial environment." (If he insists on staying, the restraining order can be a powerful weapon.) And despite claims that women are handicapped by the inability to afford lawyers and experts, the fact is that *fathers* are more likely to have no attorney representing them in a divorce; the husband is usually ordered to pay at least part of the wife's legal fees, and women have far more access to free legal services.[19]

Feminists who believe the real bias in custody determination is against working mothers point to a survey in which 46 percent of family court judges in the late 1980s agreed that a preschool child is likely to suffer if the mother works outside the home (a view shared by roughly the same portion of the public at the time). According to Deborah Rhode, "many judges were prepared to shift custody to the father" if he had a new wife who stayed home. How many? *Fewer than 10 percent*—and over three-quarters of lawyers said that judges rarely or never transferred custody to fathers in such circumstances.[20]

Most family attorneys, and most divorcing parents, believe that a mother must be only a "good-enough mother" (in Chesler's words) to get custody but a father must prove that he is a *better* parent, preferably much better. Whatever prejudice some judges may harbor against career-oriented mothers hardly outweighs the bias against fathers, gender-neutral custody laws notwithstanding. Even being a "primary caretaker" doesn't always help: the at-home dad may be told that he should "get a regular job" and be more of a man. In 1985, New York family court judge Richard Huttner used words like *repulsive* and *pathological* to express his disgust for the "involved father" who wants to spend every minute he can with his kids.[21]

More often, a man's request for custody is seen as a tactical move to scare the mother into settling for less child support. Many feminists and traditionalists alike claim that such despicable bartering is common, an inevitable outcome of gender-neutral laws that ignore the mother's excruciating fear of losing her child. But although "custody blackmail" has been often decried and analyzed in theory, it has been rarely investigated.[22]

In the Stanford study, Eleanor Maccoby and Robert Mnookin were surprised to find no evidence of women bargaining away support. About 10 percent of fathers (and 7 percent of mothers) did ask for more custodial time than they had told the researchers they'd like to have. But if this was a ploy, it didn't work: men who filed for custody, and later settled, did not end up paying less child support. The authors concluded that "strategic use of custody claims may actually be quite infrequent"—not only because few men would stoop to that level but because "it may be very difficult for a father who does not really want custody to threaten effectively."[23]

University of California law professor Scott Altman argues that Maccoby and Mnookin may have missed cases in which fathers don't file for custody but terrorize mothers by *threatening* to do so. Family lawyers in his survey estimated that on average, 13 percent of their clients received such threats and another 8 percent offered to make financial concessions to avoid a custody challenge without being threatened. The study did not indicate how successful these threats were; other research finds no evidence that mothers who are very satisfied with the custody decree have had to "bargain" by settling for worse financial terms.[24]

Insofar as "custody blackmail" exists, the Stanford study suggests that "some mothers might be playing this game as well"; some fathers certainly suspect such tactics by ex-wives who assure them at the time of separation that they want to share custody fifty-fifty, then turn around and sue for sole custody.[25]

Rhode asserts, citing Altman's survey, that it is "almost always the mother" who is pressured to make financial trade-offs to prevent custody battles. Most of the attorneys did agree that women were more often on the receiving end of such tactics. Yet 16 percent said that all or most of their clients who had gotten such threats were men, and 29 percent said that it happened equally to both sexes. Half of those whose clients had given up money to secure custody without being threatened said that men did this at least as often as women.[26]

Even a father who has joint custody may still be treated as the "secondary parent." A Massachusetts doctor found that although his children spent a third of their time with him, the division of property and the payments he had to make to his ex-wife (herself a well-paid professional) were based on the assumption that she alone was caring for the kids: "It's almost as if when they're with me, it doesn't count; their real life is somewhere else and the court has to make sure that nest is feathered." In Georgia, a father who had to pay child support to his estranged wife (despite his lower salary) explained at a court hearing that his son lived with him almost half the time—only to be told by the judge that while he was to be commended for "spending time" with the boy, the mother was still responsible for parenting and he, the father, was responsible for providing child support.[27]

Indeed, as environmental consultant Alex Sagady of East Lansing,

Michigan, learned, a formal decree of joint physical custody may not even mean equal time. When Sagady and his wife, Lauren Preston (not her real name), separated, they agreed to share custody of four-year-old Andrea. A few months later, Preston asked for sole physical custody; Sagady got a temporary order mandating equal "parenting time" and sought to continue that arrangement when they went to trial in 1991. An "established custodial environment" clearly existed with both parents, as the mother acknowledged, and seemed to be working well for the girl. But Preston said that she had received a job offer elsewhere and wanted to be able to move. (In fact, she lived a few blocks from Sagady for the next three years.) Judge Thomas Brown's Solomonic solution was a "joint physical custody arrangement" under which Andrea would spend eight weeks in the summer with the father and the school year with the mother, with standard visitation.

"He took a sole physical custody decree and called it joint custody," says Sagady. Yet in a study of custody outcomes, this would count as a "victory" for the father.[28] Issuing his decree, Judge Brown conceded that it would not "provide Mr. Sagady with as much visitation as he has been enjoying." No matter how involved he may be, it seems, Dad is still a visitor.

Absentee Fathers or "Throwaway Dads"?

> Father's Vanishing Act Called Common Drama
> —*New York Times,* 1990[29]

In a society sensitive to stereotypes, few other groups have as bad an image as the divorced dad. He walks out on his kids and leaves them destitute so he can vacation in Hawaii with a blonde half his age. He is "Daddy Meanest," exemplified by Jeffrey Nichols, the investment banker who reportedly lived in luxury with his new wife while owing $600,000 to his three children.[30]

Some stories do try to add nuance to this picture. But mostly, the fathers who, in President Clinton's words, "have chosen to abandon their children" get the spotlight. An *Atlanta Journal-Constitution* editorial titled "Fathers Are Parents, Too" actually recognizes one form of parenthood: child support, which many men won't pay if they can "get away with it."[31]

There is nothing wrong with demanding that divorced parents

live up to their responsibilities. But reality is more complex than the movie-of-the-week tale of the innocent woman "Abandoned and Deceived" (the title of an actual movie of the week) by the male cad.

For one, most absent fathers don't walk out: two out of three divorces are initiated by mothers. This statistic runs so counter to our expectations that some suspect it reflects legal formalities: the wife files for divorce, but only because the husband has already left or because he pressures her into filing. But surveys of divorcing couples show that by a two-to-one ratio, the wife is the one who wants to end the marriage. Sometimes it's because the husband drinks or is abusive or unfaithful; most often, though, wives cite such nebulous reasons as "not feeling loved and appreciated."[32]

The cliché that divorced men make out like bandits, leaving women and children in the dust, owes much to Lenore Weitzman's 1985 book, *The Divorce Revolution* (based on a study of 228 men and women divorced in Los Angeles in 1977). Reading the book ten years later, I was struck by its crude juxtaposition of saintly wives and selfish, greedy husbands whom Weitzman wouldn't even credit with paternal feelings: she claimed that no father in her study wanted to see his children more often and 70 percent would prefer to see *less* of them, a finding so at odds with other research as to defy credibility. Nevertheless, with her sound-bite conclusion that the standard of living drops 73 percent for women after divorce and rises 42 percent for men, Weitzman became one of America's most quoted.[33]

Some scholars questioned these numbers from the start. In 1996, when Richard Peterson of the Social Science Research Council in New York reanalyzed Weitzman's data and found a huge error in her computations, and Weitzman admitted the mistake (blaming a computer foul-up), the media finally noticed.[34] The revised data yielded a 10 percent increase for men and a 27 percent decline for women in Weitzman's sample. But two years before the "73–42" percentage was laid to rest, a largely unnoticed study pointed to an income reduction for *both* spouses after divorce in the 1980s: 30 percent for women, 10 percent for men.[35]

There is also the issue of taxes, which few studies consider. A noncustodial parent usually cannot claim his children as dependents or deduct child support payments from his taxes, while the custodial parent does not have to report them as taxable income. When Arizona State University researcher Sanford Braver analyzed, with the help of a tax specialist, the effects of tax code provisions for a typical divorced couple with two children, he found that both parents suffered a slight decline in their living standards.[36]

Men may fare worse when other factors are taken into account: the cost of moving and setting up a new home; the children's medical expenses and insurance; the money the father spends on them during visitation. And while formulas that try to measure the economic status of divorced mothers and fathers are often based on per capita income, many expenditures—housing, utilities, car insurance, perhaps even food—are not proportional to family size. In Braver's sample of eighty-nine Arizona couples, wives had a 3 percent *increase* in their standard of living after divorce and husbands suffered a 4 percent *decline*.[37]

The clichés of *The Divorce Revolution* have driven our policies toward noncustodial fathers since the mid-1980s. Yet the deadbeat dad story has another side: "I prosecuted one deadbeat dad who had been hospitalized for malnutrition and another who lived in the bed of a pick-up truck," wrote Bruce Walker, who works at the district attorney's office in Oklahoma City. "Many times I prosecuted impoverished men on behalf of ex-wives who had remarried successful men."[38]

As with many other issues, the discussion of child support is awash in dubious statistics: for instance, that fathers underpay $34 billion a year. This is based on estimates of what would be owed if all single mothers had a support award *and* every nonresident father earned the median salary.[39] Yet in 1990, 42 percent of single mothers had no award, often because they didn't seek one. Usually these are never-married mothers, whose boyfriends are mostly poor, often incarcerated, and sometimes dead.[40]

Census Bureau statistics on payments to mothers who are owed support also paint an unflattering picture of fathers: only half pay the full amount and a quarter pay nothing (the remaining 25 percent pay, on average, about 70 percent of what is owed). One problem with these numbers is that they are based solely on mothers' reports. Yet noncustodial parents typically report paying about 30 percent more than custodial parents report getting. Obviously, each side has incentives to bend the truth—particularly if the noncustodial parent is behind on court-ordered payments or if the custodial parent is on public assistance. It's hardly a revelation that divorced spouses' reports diverge on many issues, each biased, as one research group put it, "in a self-serving (and 'ex-spouse-bashing') direction." The truth almost certainly lies somewhere in the middle.[41]

And there are complexities that census data omit. More than two-thirds of fathers make contributions on top of court-ordered support—in cash or other benefits: taking the kids on vacation, buying toys, paying for medical care or music lessons. As many as one in four divorced couples informally agree to reduce payments because the mother's income goes up, or the father's earnings drop, or the children are spending more time in his home. (A man may find himself in arrears on support for a period when the child was living with him.)[42]

When all this is considered, there are still many men who are not meeting their obligations. What is interesting is that the mothers who are not getting the money, and have good reason to engage in "ex-spouse-bashing," often acknowledge that the father *can't* pay. That's what two-thirds of these women said in a 1992 government survey.[43]

Every researcher except Lenore Weitzman has also found that poverty is a major factor. In one sample, among fathers with no employment problems in the past year, 5 percent paid nothing and 81 percent paid in full; among those who worked in seasonal jobs or had been unemployed, 45 percent paid in full and over a third paid nothing. A Wisconsin study found that only 12 percent of nonpaying fathers had annual incomes over $18,464, while over half made less than $6,155. Jeffrey Nichols aside, the men on the deadbeat dads most-wanted lists are not businessmen or brain surgeons; most are unskilled laborers.[44]

Men who father children they can't support are irresponsible. So are the women who have those children. But for all the laments about the "demonization" of poor mothers in the debate over welfare, no conservative has ever bashed welfare moms as viciously as conservatives *and* liberals bash "deadbeat dads." Most welfare opponents stress, sincerely or not, that women on public assistance want to be self-sufficient but are trapped by a system that promotes dependency; the deadbeat dad rhetoric nearly always assumes that the men willfully refuse to support their children. And while everyone recognizes that women who fall on hard times need help, a man who owes child support may not find much sympathy when he loses a job. According to Urban Institute scholar Elaine Sorensen, there is "a reluctance to reduce child support orders on the assumption that incomes will eventually improve": just *4 percent* of fathers are able to get a reduction when their earnings drop by more than 15 percent.[45] Even if a reduction is granted, it takes as long as six months—while arrearages mount. (If the custodial parent wants an *increase* because the noncustodial parent is making more money, the child welfare agency will file the motion, and the decision is likely to be expedited.)

Unemployed or underemployed divorced fathers are often suspected of being shirkers who choose to live off their parents and report little or no income rather than make payments to their ex-wives. There are undoubtedly such cases. But often men who lose well-paying jobs and are denied child support reductions—like a Pennsylvania father of five who went from making $25.00 an hour as an engineer to driving a delivery truck for $7.50 an hour—suffer considerable hardship trying to meet their obligations, going deeply into debt and cashing in their retirement accounts.[46]

There is also a noneconomic factor related to payment of child support: the role fathers are allowed to play in the children's lives. Census data show that payment rates are highest for fathers with joint legal custody (90 percent) and lowest for those who don't even have visitation rights (over half pay nothing). This is partly due to socioeconomic differences: men who have joint custody tend to be more affluent. But Sanford Braver has found that regardless of income, a father who feels that he has no control over the children's upbringing is far more likely to default on child support. "Control," stresses Sanford Braver, does not imply something dark and patriarchal—merely having a voice in important decisions. As one man put it, "I don't mean power, I mean the opportunity to impart respect, knowledge, and a sense of closeness."[47] According to Braver, many fathers

> feel disenfranchised, [feel] that they have no input into how their children are raised . . . that they become in effect parents without children. When this happens, withdrawal from the obligations of parenthood, financial support, and an emotional relationship with the child appears likely to follow.[48]

Formal visitation rights do not necessarily bring about a sense of empowerment. The nonresident parent can be denied access to school or medical records, or forced to pay tuition without being consulted about sending the child to a private school. Many find the very word *visitation* demeaning: "You're made into what is termed a *visitor,* like some distant relative."[49] Visiting fatherhood, with its trips to restaurants and amusement parks, almost inevitably has an artificial flavor.

Nearly three out of four divorced fathers interviewed by Virginia Polytechnic Institute psychologist Joyce Arditti complained about having too little time with the children, and most saw them at least once a week. Half also mentioned the mother's interference with visitation; one in five saw it as a serious problem.[50]

A man with a "liberal" arrangement allowing for extended stays says that when he went in the house to help his son pack, "my ex-wife would just stand there glowering at me, saying I didn't belong there. She didn't want me in the house, but she didn't want to help him pack either—so something he needed always got left behind."[51]

That wouldn't seem so bad to a father who comes at the scheduled time and finds no one home; or is told, over and over, that the child isn't feeling well or has a lot of homework; or is informed by his ex-wife that she is terminating his visitation for one reason or another, and has to go to court to get it reinstated.[52]

One of the biggest gripes of fathers' groups is that the legal system's zeal for child support enforcement evaporates when it comes to visitation. A parent who violates a visitation order can be jailed or fined for contempt of court. But civil orders are rarely enforced by the police, and it is a lengthy and costly process to bring a case before a judge, who may not be sympathetic. Recently, several states have made "visitation interference" a misdemeanor offense, but many prosecutors frankly regard such cases as a waste of time and money.[53]

Women's advocates such as child support enforcement activist Geraldine Jensen dismiss claims of visitation denial as a ploy by fathers to cover up their neglect of children, including the failure to exercise visitation rights. (Ironically, in 1981, an Ohio court found that "Mrs. Jensen severely limited [her former husband's] opportunities to maintain a relationship with his children.") But the men in Joyce Arditti's study were not "deadbeats" and had no need for excuses. And although up to 40 percent of custodial mothers do complain that the father stands up his kids, as many as three-quarters of fathers say that their ex-wives block visitation, don't let them make up for visits missed for legitimate reasons, or arbitrarily change visitation schedules. The fathers' stories are corroborated not only by children (in one survey of adult "children of divorce," 42 percent said that the mother tried to keep them from seeing the father) but by mothers: 25 to 40 percent admit denying visits to punish their ex-husbands.[54]

If a man is willing to impoverish his kids because he can't be with them, it doesn't say much for his fatherly love (even if he says the money isn't going to the kids anyway). But it isn't out of defiance alone that disenfranchised fathers pay less. Some, embroiled in legal battles, end up "supporting their attorneys rather than their children," as one activist put it. In a 1987 survey, fathers who went to court to enforce visitation spent over $4,000 a year in legal fees; they were ten times more likely than others to default on child support, by an average of $3,780. Ken Gruber, whose three kids were abruptly taken from Pennsylvania to Illinois, says that he fell behind on child support because the trips to Chicago cost him money and forced him to take time off work. He was jailed twice. His ex-wife suffered no consequences, despite a custody evaluator's conclusion that "the mother unilaterally decides any modifications of the court order and effectively sabotages the father's access to the children."[55]

"I've met guys who have vanished from their kids' lives," says Dean Hughson, an Arizona businessman and divorced father of three. "When I was married and I heard about someone like that, I used to think, 'What an asshole.' Now I understand how tough it can be when you need an okay from the court to see your kids."

Some studies found that among fathers divorced in the 1970s, between one-third and one-half lost virtually all contact with the children a few years later. More recent research suggests that the figure is closer to one in six.[56] Whatever the numbers, it would be wrong to conclude that these men have "walked away" by choice and without pain. Some withdraw because they feel that having to fight for access can only hurt them and the children. In one survey of fathers who had little or no contact with their kids, 86 percent wanted to be more involved. Even among the other 14 percent, many claimed that they weren't happy about the estrangement but had given up on trying to maintain a connection—though some seemed genuinely indifferent.[57]

In *Mothers on Trial,* Phyllis Chesler scoffs that only "fathers who became pregnant [and] gave birth" could be as devastated by losing their children as mothers are. Biology aside, she suggests, men just aren't "socialized" to see parenthood as central to their self-concept.

Yet even a traditional breadwinner's identity is rooted in his family role, and its loss can make work meaningless. Psychologically, divorce seems to hit men harder, which may have less to do with loss of marital companionship than with what fathers' advocates call "parentectomy."[58]

Studies by researchers who got the radical idea of listening to divorced fathers convey heartbreaking anguish and loss. One man said he would get drunk every time after seeing his children off, "because I'm depressed . . . it's hard to see 'em go." Some found it hard to be around kids: "I can't even look at a little girl about the same age as my little girl without thinking about her. . . . Not a day goes by that you don't, two or three times during the day, go in and suppress those feelings."[59]

I am not suggesting that in reexamining assumptions about father absence, we simply pass the black hat from men to women. Even the mother who subverts the father-child relationship is not always acting out of spite. She may sincerely feel that the father or his "significant other" is not good for the kids. She may want to make a "clean break" and may want the children to see the new man in her life as a father figure. (When fathers have sole custody, the pattern of the noncustodial parent's complaints about visitation denial and the custodial parent's counter-complaints repeats itself.)[60] Nor am I saying that there are no disappearing dads. Some would rather spend their time chasing women and their money on a new car. Others "disengage" for the same reason some mothers try to keep fathers away: to minimize contact with the "ex" and get on with their lives.

Unfortunately, while we deplore the "vanishing act" of divorced dads, we often do little to recognize those who are there for the children. In 1995, the New Jersey State Supreme Court ruled that a father who has the kids Friday afternoon through Saturday night, and who picks them up from school two weekdays and feeds them dinner, is essentially no different from one whose fatherhood consists of monthly trips to Pizza Hut: he must pay child support as if the mother were single-handedly raising the children.[61]

Joan Entmacher of the Women's Legal Defense Fund told me that while she applauded the father, township administrator Jim Pascale, for his involvement with the children, it didn't mean that "the children's standard of living should be reduced." As Pascale saw it, his motive was not to take money from his eleven-year-old son and twin nine-year-old daughters but to spend more of it directly on them rather than write checks to the mother (a manager earning

$52,000 a year to his $72,000)—for instance, when they shopped together for clothes and other things toward which he was paying support. His ex-wife usually agreed to deduct these expenses from his payments; but Pascale thought he shouldn't have to ask, just as she didn't have to ask him how to spend her money.[62]

The supreme court disagreed, finding that as "primary caretaker" Debra Pascale was responsible for the children day to day and should have full control over the funds allocated for their needs. A father who helped his children with their homework and took time off work when they were sick still couldn't be trusted to decide how to spend money taking care of them.

The Politics of Divorce

They call themselves "Beat-Dead Dads."

Parodying "Wanted" posters with mugs of "deadbeat dads," they print fliers that shout "NEEDED By Their Children!" with photos stamped "Throwaway Dad." They gather in support groups and communicate on the Internet, lobby state legislatures and testify before Congress. There are anywhere from ten thousand to fifty thousand people involved in fathers' rights groups nationwide. While they support men in high-profile cases such as the battle over Maranda Smith-Ireland, most activist fathers insist that their goal is presumptive joint custody. Many are involved with the Children's Rights Council (CRC), a national organization that emphasizes postdivorce coparenting and whose slogan is "The Best Parent Is Both Parents." "No court in the land has the right to take the kids away from one parent without a good reason," says Phil Gagliano, a New York salesman-turned-activist.[63]

On the way to this promised land, the movement lobbies for short-term goals: Increase "parenting time" and punish access denial (*visitation* is a dirty word). Reduce support payments if the father spends money on the children when they are with him. Allow non-custodial parents to provide child care themselves or through other arrangements, instead of paying the other parent's day care costs (so-called "Mrs. Doubtfire" legislation, named for the Robin Williams movie in which the father, disguised as a woman, gets his ex-wife to hire him as a nanny). Encourage mediation and parenting classes for divorcing parents.

These activists have had some success in getting their views heard in the media and in legislatures.[64] Nevertheless, they are still often viewed with suspicion—as child support evaders, angry men who can't get over a messy divorce, even woman haters.

Some of these men *are* angry—with good reason, they say. Some are consumed with rage at the "ex." And there are the bona-fide misogynists like Rich Zubaty, author of *Surviving the Feminization of America: How to Keep Women from Ruining Your Life,* or John Knight, coordinator of a fathers' group on the Internet, who advocates taking the vote away from women. Yet a surprising number of men in fathers' rights groups have achieved, sometimes at great cost, an arrangement that allows them equal or near-equal time. A few report getting primary or joint physical custody in a relatively bloodless divorce and say that they joined the movement to help other men and fight negative perceptions of divorced fathers. Many are remarried or in steady relationships. Some of their new partners become active in the fathers' cause; one article described second wives as "the most vociferous foot soldiers" in the movement.[65]

"When my future husband told me the story of his divorce, I was beyond shocked," says Robin Welch, a California woman with a teenage stepson and a young child of her own. "I had considered myself a feminist; my views changed completely." Welch, a public utility inspector, was inspired to go to law school and now heads a chapter of the Fathers' Rights and Equality Exchange (FREE). The second wives aren't just anxious to keep their husbands' money: often the husband is fighting to have the children spend more time with him or even move in, as Welch's stepson eventually did.[66]

There are also women working with the fathers' movement who have no personal ties to divorced men: mothers without custody who feel that all noncustodial parents share a common cause; feminists like FREE founder Anne Mitchell, a lawyer and single mother, who believe that current policies perpetuate female dependency; social workers and family counselors who believe the system is unfair to fathers. Kindergarten teacher Margaret Wuwert, president of the Ohio chapter of the CRC, is a former child support enforcement activist who jumped ship after talking to fathers' advocates at public meetings. (Forty percent of CRC state chapters are headed by women.)[67]

Feminists often charge that fathers' rights activists are out to preserve male power and control, yet much of their own rhetoric is a blatant assertion of female dominance. According to two feminist legal advocates, "Forced joint custody, like forced sterilization and forced pregnancy, is a denial of women's right to control their lives"—a right that obviously overrides the right of fathers and children to a relationship. University of Chicago law professor Mary Becker suggests a "maternal deference" standard: "when the parents cannot agree on a custody outcome, the judge should defer to the mother's decision on custody provided that she is fit."[68]

Despite formal disclaimers that her argument is not based on biology, Becker assails the gender-neutral "primary caretaker" standard for failing to credit "the reproductive labor only women can do." Becker is no traditionalist; on the contrary, she worries that the emphasis on hands-on care is bad for mothers who use paid caregivers (though she is outraged that a father who was "often aided by a babysitter" when alone with the kids was given custody). And so vigorous is her opposition to sex discrimination in other spheres that she advocates ending tax exemptions for churches in which women are denied equal roles. The feelings of conservative Christians who want their clergy to be male apparently don't deserve the same deference as the feelings of mothers who want the kids all to themselves.[69]

The frankly sexist reasoning of Mary Becker or Phyllis Chesler would probably make most feminists squirm. (After all, it was the attack on sex-specific laws by women's rights activists in the 1970s that led to the fall of the formal presumption of maternal custody.) But often, when it comes to these issues, mainstream feminists are no less sexist, just less candid.

At its 1996 national conference, NOW issued an "Action Alert on 'Fathers' Rights,'" accusing men who seek a role in their children's lives of "using the abuse of power in order to control in the same fashion as do batterers," and established a clearinghouse to combat such sinister proposals as joint custody, penalties for false charges of abuse, and mediation instead of litigation. (In a debate on television earlier that year, NOW president Patricia Ireland deplored fatherlessness and asserted that "men need to take equal responsibility for the family.") Assailing California's ultimately defeated "Mrs. Doubtfire" bill, women's groups complained that it would "allow non-custodial Dads to control child care decisions made by Moms"—and paid for by dads—and conjured visions of men leaving kids with "a 13-year-old neighbor [or] a 92-year-old grandmother."[70]

"Most of the time men don't want custody of their children, and even if they say they do early on, they're using that as an economic ploy," says law professor Nancy Polikoff, a former staff attorney at the NOW Legal Defense Fund. According to another feminist legal expert, if fathers want payments lowered when they have the children over a hundred nights a year, it just means that "all the men demand 101 nights" to get off cheap. To former NOW official Tammy Bruce, they are not even fathers—just "vindictive estranged spouses." According to battered women's advocate Sarah Buel, "over half of [fathers who win custody] are batterers."[71]

The charge of violence adds the final touch to the portrait of the divorced father as selfish and spiteful. Battered women's advocates have vehemently opposed joint custody proposals on the grounds that abusive men will merely use their access to the kids to terrorize their ex-wives, even when the proposals contain an explicit domestic violence exemption.[72]

Reading the Massachusetts Gender Bias Study, I came across an eye-opening comment by one attorney: she described herself as an "advocate for a woman and her children *against the wealthy father*" (emphasis added). Some champions of "women and their children," I realized, actually view fathers as their children's enemies.[73]

The Equality Presumption

Despite our affection for the nurturing divorced dad in movies like *Mrs. Doubtfire,* the assumption that mothers have a superior claim remains pervasive. It is reflected in the very language we use: she "loses her children"; he "takes her children." And if divorced fathers are treated as second-rate parents, unwed fathers are much lower on the totem pole. Their situation has improved since the early 1970s, when a single father's children could be given up for adoption without his consent even if he had raised them. But to this day, the unmarried father's rights can be easily thwarted.[74]

Michael Landy, a high school senior in St. Louis, opposed his girlfriend's plans for adoption as soon as he learned that she was having a baby. With her parents' help, she concealed the birth from Landy and skipped town; the adoption was completed in another state. Landy wrote to more than two hundred judges before he tracked down his daughter; he spent seven years trying to get her back. Eventually he decided that he did not want to disrupt the child's life and dropped the suit in exchange for being allowed limited contact with her.[75]

In recent years, some legal disputes of this kind—the "Baby

Jessica" case in Iowa, the "Baby Richard" case in Illinois—have ended in controversial victories for the birth fathers. These are heartwrenching cases; I am most sympathetic to concerns about taking a child from the only parents he or she knows. But where is the sympathy for fathers estranged from their children through no fault of their own?

Baby Richard's much-maligned dad, Otakar Kirchner, was away in his native Czechoslovakia when his pregnant live-in girlfriend, Daniela Janikova, heard a false rumor that he had married another woman. Determined to keep him from ever seeing his child, she made up a tale of abuse to move into a battered women's shelter, gave the baby away, and later told Kirchner the boy was dead. Although Kirchner has been portrayed as feckless, the fact is that he immediately began a search to find out what happened to his son. Yet the adoptive parents' supporters vilified him far more than they did the deceitful Janikova. "Our society . . . bombards us with tales about how much better off children would be if more fathers took interest in parenting," one father wrote bitterly to the *Chicago Tribune*. "Otakar Kirchner sifted through dumpsters looking for a sign that his baby was alive, and we somehow want to make him out to be the bad guy."[76]

Imagine the reaction if instead a father had taken a newborn baby from the hospital, arranged an adoption, and told the mother the baby was dead.

There are no easy solutions to custody disputes, whether between adoptive parents and biological fathers or between former spouses. The "primary caretaker" presumption rarely offers clear guidance. Mary Becker has a point when she says that less direct participation in physical caretaking may not equal less emotional involvement; of course, she means for this to apply only to mothers who delegate child care, but the same is true of many male breadwinners. Indeed, fathers' advocates argue that the "primary caretaker" standard unfairly excludes the provider role from its definition of "care": the woman who cooks for the children gets credit; the man who works to put the food on the table gets none.[77]

Besides, even if Dad spends half as much time with the kids as Mom, is it fair—or good for the children—that after divorce, he should become a weekend visitor?

Joint custody, the Holy Grail of fathers' rights groups, remains controversial. People are troubled by the idea of "yo-yo" children shuttled from place to place. When a 1989 study found that frequent contact with both parents may be psychologically harmful to children of divorced couples embroiled in ongoing bitter disputes, joint custody opponents (among them, naturally, the head of a NOW task force) were quick to use it as ammunition. Yet the author of the study stressed that her findings did not discourage joint custody except in the fairly small number of divorces accompanied by such high conflict—about one in ten.[78]

Comparing joint custody to sole custody is no easy task. Some researchers conflate joint *physical* and joint *legal* custody (in which the parents have equal authority over the children's education, medical care, and religious training). Joint physical custody arrangements are not only fairly rare but often voluntarily chosen by parents who are less hostile and more affluent than most divorced couples.[79]

Still, there is evidence that with joint *legal* custody, even when one parent opposed it, children not only see their fathers more but are better adjusted. Joint physical custody—again, without initial mutual agreement—appears to work no worse and perhaps slightly better for children than maternal custody, when measured by such symptoms as depression, anxiety, and aggressiveness. It is also clearly associated with higher satisfaction for fathers and perhaps even for mothers, while the dire warnings about less child support and more postdivorce litigation have failed to come true.[80]

And maybe, says Michigan attorney Kay Schwarzberg, if people know they won't be able to get their ex-spouse out of their hair as long as a child binds them together, they'll make more of an effort to stay married. A recent study seems to bear this out: from 1980 to 1995, divorce rates have declined most steeply in states with a high percentage of joint custody awards.[81]

Mary Becker's assertion that mothers are more passionately attached to children surely rings true to many people. In this regard, we may not have come very far since 1916, when a court wrote in a child custody ruling, "Mother love is a dominant trait in even the weakest of women, and as a rule far surpasses the paternal affection for the common offspring." Back then, of course, it was also thought that women's maternal qualities disqualified them from public life. All of these clichés may have *some* basis in reality. But today, those who believe that women in general are more likely to put family first generally agree that this should not affect the way individuals are treated. We start from the premise that women are equal in the public sphere; we should start from the premise that men are equal as parents.[82]

What would happen if the idea that "fathers are parents too" was taken seriously? It would be considered as contemptible for a woman to shut out her children's father (unless he is dangerous) as it is for a man to abandon his child. People who worry about having to tell their daughters that they might lose their kids after a divorce if they pursue a consuming career would also think about what to tell their sons. It would be inconceivable for the American Civil Liberties Union to defend a custodial mother's right to move while remaining silent about the disenfranchisement of fathers: if a court order forbidding the mother to relocate unless she relinquishes custody limits her freedom, a father who wants to be near his children is just as restricted by a sole maternal custody decree.[83]

There would still be conflicts and problems, but we would seek solutions based on the presumption of equality. In 1998, "Heartbroken in Oregon" wrote to Dear Abby that his estranged wife was planning to move 3,000 miles away to try to establish her business in Florida, and had rejected his suggestion that she leave their six-year-old daughter with him for the first six months. (He was not averse to relocating if his soon-to-be-ex-wife did settle there.) Abby advised him not to start a fight, since the girl "needs her mother." But if we started with the presumption that the girl needs her father as much, "Heartbroken" and the mother of his child would have to work things out. This doesn't mean that the father would have the unilateral power to block the mother's move, only that they would have to compromise—perhaps along the lines he suggested.[84]

At present, we keep fathers away and then point to their absence as proof that they don't care: "We have a nation of fatherless—not motherless—children. And it is not the women who have walked out," jeers Judith Regan in her screed against fathers who seek custody. Of course, some men *do* walk away, but even more are driven away.[85]

The biological fragility of a man's connection to his offspring has prompted some to argue that society must "coax" or force men into fatherhood. In David Blankenhorn's striking metaphor, "Men do not volunteer for fatherhood as much as they are conscripted into it by the surrounding culture."[86] Yet there certainly are men who volunteer, not due to social pressure but sometimes *in spite of it*—like the unwed fathers who fight for their children.

Biologically, men and women can never have quite the same connection to their children. That doesn't mean the father-child bond is weaker or more artificial; it is simply more vulnerable and may need more safeguards from disruption. Most men do not need to be conscripted into fatherhood. All they need is a real opportunity to volunteer.

CHAPTER NINE

Are Men Victims Too?

Masculism: The belief that men have been systematically discrimi-
nated against, and that that discrimination should be eliminated.
— The Oxford Companion to Philosophy[1]

At a 1996 diversity conference of the Social Security
Administration, deputy commissioner Ruth Pierce
decided to liven up a discussion with a joke: A mermaid caught in a
net offers to grant the fisherman a wish, so he asks to be made five
times smarter and, presto, she turns him into a woman. After two
men complained, Pierce apologized to them in writing; but
Commissioner Shirley Chater refused to reprimand her or require
an apology to all conference participants. On CNN's *Capital Gang*,
journalist Margaret Carlson advised the men to "get a life."[2]

This is just one example, says a small but passionate group of
activists, of how antimale sexism escapes censure in our politically
correct age. The issue, they argue, is not just male-bashing: it's that
disadvantages affecting men are not recognized as sexist because we
equate sexism with injustice toward *women*.

When American teenager Michael Fay was sentenced to be
caned for spray-painting cars in Singapore, the public debate focused
on whether harsh penalties were too high a price to pay for public
order. The fact that caning is imposed only on men was barely
noticed. What if a teenage girl were to be whipped for a petty
offense in a country where this penalty was reserved for females?
Wouldn't women's groups, politicians, and the media have treated
this as an outrage against women? Or suppose that American

women killed themselves four times as often as men, suffered ten times as many job-related fatalities, died seven years earlier, and were punished more harshly for the same crimes. Wouldn't we have had congressional hearings on these issues?

Only the 1998 execution of pick-ax murderer Karla Faye Tucker (the first woman put to death in Texas since the Civil War) finally focused attention on gender disparities in the use of capital punishment; before that, death row bias was discussed only in the context of race.[3]

A 1996 report on elderly suicides notes only in passing that men account for 81 percent of these deaths and never mentions that women's numerical edge in that age group makes the disparity even greater: a white man age seventy-five to eighty-four is nearly ten times more likely than a woman to take his own life.[4]

When the issue of gender disadvantage in these areas comes up, it's always *female* disadvantage, real or imagined. Evidence of bias against males, such as the fact that teachers yell at boys more, is transformed into bias against females (boys get more attention). Girls' higher rate of suicide attempts overshadows the fact that boys kill themselves nearly five times more often. Despite the well-documented fact that female defendants are treated more leniently, some feminists assert that women receive "more severe sentences" for stereotypically male crimes, or complain that women often serve longer portions of their sentences since more men are paroled early due to overcrowding. The most blatant example of legalized sex discrimination in our society—only men can be drafted and sent into combat—is usually discussed only in terms of opportunities denied to women in the military.[5]

Most feminists are loath to admit that there can be biases against men, or too preoccupied with women's injuries to notice. Katha Pollitt has cited the arrest of a Danish woman who left her baby in a stroller outside a New York restaurant as an example of harsh attitudes toward mothers, barely mentioning that the child's American father was arrested too, and omitting the fact that charges against the mother, but not the father, were quickly dropped (partly because the Danish government had interceded on her behalf). No feminist spoke up when a Virginia woman got an eighteen-month sentence for torturing her live-in boyfriend's small son and the boy's father got eight years for failing to intervene.[6]

A few men—some use the term *masculist;* others speak of "men's rights" or "men's liberation"—have challenged the deep-seated assumption that gender inequity is synonymous with female disadvantage. A few of them call for the restoration of "patriarchy," but most deny any hostility toward the women's movement. Their cause, they say, is simply the neglected other half of gender role transition.

Is There a Men's Movement?

In 1992, nearly half of Americans professed to agree that "the time has come for a men's movement to help men get in touch with their feelings and advance men's causes."[7] Still, there hasn't been a stampede to sign up. Men generally don't think of themselves as "we," nor do they want to.

Yet, to the extent that men have absorbed the message that the sexes should be treated equally and gender stereotypes are wrong, they may be more willing to respond with anger when these principles are violated—when men are stereotyped or when the effort to achieve equality goes only in one direction.

It's difficult to talk about men feeling adrift in an era of changing definitions of masculinity without lapsing into academic jargon or pop psychology. Nonetheless, there is some truth to it—not just because of changing roles, but because of the bad rap manhood has been getting in our culture. Says Mike Arst, a Seattle photographer and typesetter in his forties, "What was in the air was that masculinity was a problem; it could only be discussed in terms of what's wrong with it."

In the early 1980s, these feelings led Arst to the "mythopoetic" men's movement associated with Robert Bly. This movement, which sought to explore and affirm male identity through the archetypes of myths and folktales, became infamous for its "Wild Man" retreats in the woods as reporters came back with stories of middle-class white guys beating drums or running on all fours and growling to get in touch with their animal side. The ridicule was well deserved (though there was more truth than most feminists care to admit in what Bly had to say about the predicament of men looking only to women for guidance about what they should be). The movement still has its followers, but its moment has passed.[8]

More recently, the search for a male identity has led hundreds of thousands to Promise Keepers, the Christian men's movement that offers a mix of old-style religious revivalism, ultratraditional rhetoric about men taking back their role as leaders in the family, and talk of personal healing with quasi-feminist overtones: men are exhorted to show their emotions and not to be afraid of seeming weak. In another ironic intersection with radical feminism, Promise Keepers insist on blaming men for everything that's wrong with the world and are especially preoccupied with male sins against women.[9]

But there is also another men's movement—one that is trying to be to men what feminism has been to women: open their eyes to the injustices and biases they face because of their sex, and mobilize for social change to right these wrongs. It's hard to say how many men are involved in this political men's movement today; it has dozens of organizations, with membership ranging from the single digits to a few hundred. Groups like the National Coalition of Free Men and the National Congress for Men and Children and Men's Rights, and publications like *Transitions* and *Liberator* tackle issues like the "other side" of domestic violence, false accusations of sex crimes, stereotypes that burden men, men's health, and fatherhood. The Internet has helped them reach a wider audience. Rod Van Mechelen, the Seattle-based founder of the *Backlash!* and the *Egalitarian,* estimates that his World Wide Web page has about eleven thousand readers a month.[10]

What does it take to change men's reluctance to see themselves as a group with collective interests? Usually a personal run-in with a perceived injustice: a sexual harassment witch-hunt; reverse discrimination at work; most often, a messy divorce and custody battle (fathers' rights activists are the core of the movement). For a few young men, gender politics on campus have served as the catalyst for interest in men's issues. When Sean Gralton entered Boston Law School in 1993, he was supportive of feminist goals but increasingly irked by the rhetoric about date rape and domestic violence with its presumed-guilty attitudes toward men. When he learned that the Women's Law Association was planning to form a men's forum on gender issues—"to appoint the men who will speak for us"—he decided to act and announced the creation of the Men's Law Association. Although the group caused quite a stir and had some impact on campus debates, it attracted fewer than a dozen members, most of them women. Some men who were clearly interested, says Gralton, were afraid of being seen as antifeminist.[11]

For Mike Arst, the Seattle man who came to feel that society was treating masculinity as a problem, the breakup of his marriage in 1982 was less an education in gender bias than an experience that crystallized a general discontent. His involvement in the "mythopoetic" movement was brief, but he retained an interest in men's issues and later became coordinator of a men's issues forum on the Internet. Arst, who lives with a female companion, is no "angry man." In cyberspace, he has had heated arguments with masculist extremists who claim that "feminism is perfectly analogous to what the Nazis were doing in the 1930s." What has kept him involved in men's issues is concern about the "Big Sister" feminism that he sees as part of a larger trend toward state intrusion in private life. And he is still troubled by cultural attitudes toward men—from images that sanction female violence toward men to the tendency to vilify men *as a sex* in discussions of domestic abuse or sexual harassment.[12]

Other men have a background that makes them unusually willing to question stereotypes of male power and female oppression. "My mother was abusive to everybody in the family, especially my father," says Alan Rubinstein (a pseudonym), a computer professional and a married father of two. "Although she weighed barely 100 pounds to my father's 160 or so and was much shorter, she kicked and punched him with impunity. The most he would do was walk out for half an hour or so until things cooled off." Ironically, Rubinstein's mother also held to rigid notions of conventional masculinity:

> When my mother wasn't attacking my father physically, she was doing it verbally; one of her favorite lines was, "You're not a man!" This meant that he wasn't making enough money. I learned to hate the thought of having to "be a man." In my adolescence, when I worried about being sent to Vietnam, she railed that perhaps the army would "make a man" out of me. I was told that I'd have to kill people and that I might have to die. And my mother could demand that I face these things which she, simply because she was female, had been privileged not to have demanded of her.

Rubinstein entered college in the late 1960s as "a liberal primed to hate traditional sex roles" and welcomed the women's movement. When feminists began to address domestic violence, he was chagrined because they defined it solely as an issue of men abusing women. Still, he says, "I considered feminism a good thing because it was supposed to be for equality." A "men's consciousness" evening class he took in the early 1980s increased his misgivings. When Rubinstein tried to bring up his mother's violence, the women in the class "had the party line on how it was to be interpreted, and they wouldn't allow any other view. I felt like I was in some North Vietnamese reeducation camp."

After his sister's suicide, Rubinstein began to think more about their childhood and about the lack of resources a man in his father's situation would face if he tried to leave an abusive wife and take the children away. He became involved in men's groups on the Internet and started writing to journalists trying to raise the issue of domestic violence against men. "What I'd like most is to forget my past," he says. "But that's impossible—partly because, every time I open the newspaper and see a story about abused women, I get my nose rubbed in it."[13]

It's Always the Man's Fault

"If you start attacking men as a group," says a male friend of mine who attended feminist collective meetings in college but has since grown warier of feminism, "they will start acting like a group." Or at least speaking up for their sex.

Historically, as feminists have often pointed out, men were regarded as the human norm and women as "the Other." Feminism has not only displaced men from that traditional ground but has often depicted them as *less* than human. Forty years ago, notes writer Jeffrey Seeman, men were considered more rational and assertive; women, more compassionate and sensitive. Today, stereotypes of male superiority are taboo, while stereotypes of female superiority are very much alive—and negative male stereotypes are more popular than ever.[14]

The overt misandry of a Marilyn French or an Andrea Dworkin is a fringe phenomenon. But less extreme slurs are common, and not just in the form of sweeping statements about male brutality. Former *New Yorker* editor Tina Brown speaks of women and men in the media: "Men talk about what happened; women talk about what really happened. Men talk about what they are supposed to talk about; women talk about what really concerns them." In the *New York Times Book Review,* former book review editor Rebecca Sinkler quotes feminist literary critic Carolyn Heilbrun's observation that men don't regard their favorite writers as "friends" the way women do, and throws in an aside: "Ms. Heilbrun, like many of us, is quite fond of the particular men who share her life, but mistrusts the genotype." The movie *In the Company of Men,* in which two male managers seek revenge on womankind by wooing and then abruptly dumping a lovely deaf secretary, is hailed as "an exposé of sexism and a brave bit of truth-telling." An article on the film opens with the words, "Chad and Howard are similarly afflicted—they're men." (This is not a uniquely American phenomenon: a look at the British press, for example, reveals such self-explanatory titles as "New Man Shown to Be a Dirty Rat" and "Honestly, I Don't Hate Them, but Why Are Men Like That?")[15]

There is also the endless sniping that pervades popular culture: greeting cards that say "There are easier things than meeting a good man: nailing Jell-O to a tree, for instance"; "All Men Are Bastards" and "Men We Love to Hate" calendars; books with titles like *Why Dogs Are Better Than Men*. All this fare can be found in respectable stores, while male put-downs of women are relegated to the vulgar realm of Andrew Dice Clay. (Meanwhile, *Psychology Today* writes that "women's humor" is "positive" and "lets everyone feel good," while "men's humor" is "negative" and "makes some people feel good at the expense of others.") Continuing on the canine theme, some relationship books are based on the explicit premise that men are dogs in need of obedience training. A get-even book trashing the author's ex-boyfriend can find a main-stream publisher; one can hardly imagine the reverse. Even in a story on visiting a medium who claims to communicate with the dead, *New York Times* reporter Alex Witchel takes a gratuitous swipe: mentioning that she took a male friend along, she adds, "Most men find it hard to listen when a living person speaks to them, much less a dead one."[16]

Antimale humor also shows up at the office, from "If you want the job done right, get a woman to do it" mugs to an unfunny "Seminars for Men" catalogue ("Combating Stupidity," "How Not to Act Like an Asshole When You're Obviously Wrong," "Changing Your Underwear—It Really Works") circulated on office e-mail.[17]

These barbs may be trivial, though they wouldn't be so easily dismissed if directed at women. When four Cornell freshmen e-mailed a list of "Top 75 Reasons Why Women (Bitches) Should Not Have Freedom of Speech" to some friends and it got out on the Internet, professors and student activists demanded retribution, despite the culprits' protestations that they were trying to satirize chauvinistic attitudes ("She doesn't need to talk to get me a beer," "Big breasts should speak for themselves"). While Cornell's administration decided that there were no grounds for sanctions, its statement emphasized the boys' public contrition and voluntary penance: community service and a date-rape education class. Meanwhile, the women at the University of Maryland who put up fliers with male names randomly picked from the student directory under the heading "Potential Rapists" never even expressed regret.[18]

Most men say that they find male-bashing—in which, in one survey, half of women under age twenty-five unapologetically admitted engaging—at worst a minor irritant. But however seriously it's intended or taken, the men-are-scum talk contributes to an unspoken assumption that in any conflict between the sexes, "It's Always the Man's Fault" (as the title of one book proclaims).[19]

Even Karen Lehrman, who challenges "anti–men" feminism in *The Lipstick Proviso,* appears to regard mistreatment in personal relationships as a one-way street. She considers it a failure of feminism that many women "stay with abusive or even emotionally challenged lovers" and notes that "the primary problem for most American women today isn't how 'society' deals with women, it's how individual men do." Unlike orthodox feminists, Lehrman holds women accountable for putting up with it; but it does not occur to her that men may have just as many valid complaints about how individual women deal with them.[20]

The always-his-fault attitude is pervasive in women's magazines, despite the occasional column from the man's point of view. It's not just stereotypical male behavior that invites such abuse; men can also be assailed for acting in stereotypically female ways (being too clingy) or not being good sports when women behave badly in stereotypically male ways. In a column on "Shopping for a Boyfriend," a *Glamour* writer advises against going for the exotic and tells a warning tale from her college days: she dated a member of the Guardian Angels crime patrol, which was fun until he wanted "more of an emotional investment than I was willing to make"—and he wouldn't even fade away graciously but kept calling and writing for two months.[21]

The presumption of male guilt is evident in cultural perceptions of divorce: if the man leaves, he's the bad guy; if the woman leaves, he's still the bad guy who made her leave by behaving badly. There is no story of the "First Husbands Club," though there are plenty of first husbands who believe that they fulfilled their end of the marital bargain and were unceremoniously dumped. Our culture has also developed, as Katie Roiphe observes, a new double standard for adultery: the man who strays is a pig, the woman a victim or a liberated heroine. Prince Charles's treatment of Princess Diana has been widely deplored. But suppose that a *princess* had been forced by her family to wed a man who was bored by her intellectual interests and prone to outbursts that could be described as abusive. Would we have seen it differently if she resumed a relationship with her one true love, while her husband had a series of affairs and made harassing phone calls to a female acquaintance?[22]

The double standard applies to other relationship troubles. In 1997, a society groom who didn't show up at the wedding became Public Enemy Number One ("Did you consider castration as an option?" *Today* host Katie Couric asked the jilted bride, whose eagerness to turn adversity to media stardom made some people wonder if the groom made the right decision). A few years earlier, when a Long Island woman ran off to Canada days before her wedding without telling her fiancé or family, who spent several frantic days, *New York Times* columnist Frank Rich hailed her as a symbol of independent womanhood.[23]

The tendency to cast male behavior and motives in the worst possible light is common in pop psychology. Dr. Joyce Brothers tells a reader whose brother is heartbroken after being dumped by the woman he loved that "it takes men much longer to recover from the demise of a relationship than it does women," because "men are usually not in touch with their feelings, so they don't anticipate the breakup" and because rejection "shatters the male ego." Whether or not the generalization is correct, one suspects that if women took longer to recover, it would have been because they are *more* in touch with their feelings and more invested in relationships.[24]

Male-bashing is sometimes brushed off as unimportant since it poses no threat of real harm, while woman-bashing is linked to discrimination or actual violence against women. But is it irrational to suggest that the acceptance of antimale insults helps foster a social and political climate in which men are quickly presumed guilty of sexual harassment or domestic violence, welfare reform debates treat the male partners of single mothers as mere obstacles to the women's self-sufficiency, and the legitimate grievances of divorced fathers are ignored?[25]

The Unliberated Man

The one-sided approach to male-female relationships results in another double standard that provides the basis for the most serious "masculist" argument: women today have much more choice than men do between traditional and nontraditional roles. In his 1993 book *The Myth of Male Power,* something of a men's movement bible, Warren Farrell observes that when a couple marries,

> *she almost invariably considers three options:*
> *Option #1: Work full time*
> *Option #2: Mother full time*
> *Option #3: Some combination of working and mothering*
> *He considers three "slightly different" options:*
> *Option #1: Work full time*
> *Option #2: Work full time*
> *Option #3: Work full time*[26]

While many women may feel they *don't* have the option to stay home full time, the view that women should be able to have that choice is uncontroversial. Such a choice for men, who obviously have to work harder if the woman stays home, is rarely mentioned.

Some might scoff that this is a nonissue, since men are about as interested in staying home as they are in wearing high heels. Yet a 1995 survey found that only one-third of men eighteen to fifty-five said that they would work full time even if money was not an issue (compared to 15 percent of all women and 22 percent of women under twenty-five); 31 percent of women and 21 percent of men wanted to stay home full time, while the rest preferred part-time or volunteer work.[27]

Yet the disrespect of which women at home sometimes complain is nothing compared to the stigma attached to a man who lives off a woman. When the MSNBC cable network had a call-in show on the topic "What if she earns more?" the assumption, naturally, was that no enlightened male would object; but an e-mail that said, "Great. Maybe I can take more time off," elicited groans and a rebuke from host John Gibson: "You're a lout! Get out there and take care of your family!"[28]

Even women who take full advantage of their new opportunities often resent it when a man fails to carry his weight financially (a doctor in a study of divorced couples was bitter because her income had enabled her husband to take an important unpaid position in the synagogue). And some still believe they are entitled to be supported by a man.[29]

In 1994, a forty-year-old woman who signed herself "Growing Uneasy in L.A." wrote to Ann Landers about her relationship with her fiancé, who was handsome, loving, great in bed, willing to do housework—but barely employed and unambitious. "Uneasy," who made $65,000 a year, was wondering if he was "a lazy parasite": "Should I give him the boot and look for someone who can support me if I choose not to work?" Neither "Uneasy" nor Ann Landers noticed the irony in her desire to be able to exercise a choice that made a man a "parasite" in her eyes—though some male readers did.[30]

Traditionalists may argue that a woman has a right to expect to be provided for while she fulfills her child-rearing role (and it's inconceivable, of course, that a man could want the same). But "Uneasy" specifically mentioned that neither she nor her fiancé wanted children. She wanted to be able to quit her job for the same selfish reason that everyone suspects in men: to enjoy a life of leisure.

The "Power and Control Wheel," a diagram of abusers' tactics designed by battered women's advocates, lists "Being the one to define men's and women's roles" as a form of "Using Male Privilege." But today this is to some extent a "female privilege." The man will be condemned if he pushes his wife to go to work or to stay home. (This pattern begins in dating: if the woman expects the man to pick up the check and he balks, he's cheap; if she wants to be liberated and he insists on paying, he's a chauvinist.)

Women's options extend to far more than merely being able to return to woman's traditional place. Some women say that a stay at home reenergized them for their careers or enabled them to go in new directions. Regina Rochford, a computer systems manager, almost accidentally took up teaching English to immigrants while she was on maternity leave—and liked it so much that instead of going back to her job, she went for a degree in teaching English as a Second Language. "Many friends and family members thought I was insane, for I already had a master's degree and plenty of potential for a lucrative career. But I had found something I loved doing," writes Rochford, reflecting that many women have rushed into the newly open doors of "male" careers instead of choosing what suited them best.[31]

While expressing the hope that her daughter would not "feel limited by tradition or pushed by liberation," Rochford did not pause to ask if men could feel equally unbound. Surely there are men in systems management who would be happier as teachers. But would a man have felt as free to trade a more lucrative career for a lower-paying one, particularly with a baby at home—no matter how much his wife earned?

In a *New Woman* article about the thorny issue of who pays on dates, one woman mused that some men were being stingy out of resentment against women's liberation. Since she wasn't the sub-servient "Ultimate Woman," her boyfriend refused to be the "Ultimate Man." It didn't occur to her that there was anything illog-ical about her complaint. Nor does it occur to many feminists that the male "backlash" is less against equality than against the percep-tion that women want to have it both ways.[32]

Of course, some men feel all the more threatened when a woman won't let them play the ego-boosting Ultimate Man role. And some men too want it both ways: they want a woman who is their professional equal but lets her man be the boss, who earns half the money but does all the housework. Stereotypical expectations of male behavior cannot be blamed on women alone, as some "mas-culists" are wont to do: men are more likely than women to say that men should pay on dates, and somewhat less supportive of paternity leave—though, curiously, more in favor of women asking men out.[33]

But few feminists, even moderates like Karen Lehrman, are will-ing to admit that women's attitudes are a problem at all—except for women's failure to demand more equality and more sharing of housework and child care from men. Meanwhile, men's frustration with women's conflicting demands is seen as amusing at best and misogynistic at worst.

Equal Oppression?

The men's advocates have legitimate issues, but they don't have much recognition. Male claims of injustice are met with contempt from the same quarters where referring to female complaints as "whining" would be a no-no. One critic noted that the men fea-tured in Ellis Cose's *A Man's World* (the first book by a mainstream journalist to examine "masculist" arguments seriously) "respond to commonplace life challenges in proper victim fashion" and suggest-ed that the proper answer was, "Hey, buddy, go get a life."[34]

This attitude, men's advocates say, is itself a manifestation of sex-ism: complaining is considered unmanly. But it's much more compli-cated than that. Men who complain about "downsizing" or high taxes are not ridiculed; male crime victims or black men who com-plain of racism are not told to get a life. What provokes derision is men complaining of their lot *as men:* after all, everyone knows that men are the privileged sex.[35]

In their eagerness to counter this view, some "masculists" not only challenge the notion that women are oppressed *today* but argue that women were never oppressed any more than men (or even that they were *less* oppressed).[36]

The strongest attack on the assumption of historical male dominance comes from an unlikely source: Warren Farrell, in his previous incarnation a male feminist and (as his publicity materials always point out) the only man elected three times to the board of the New York chapter of NOW. Farrell's *The Myth of Male Power,* largely ignored by the media, stands conventional ideas about gender inequity on their head. Why do we hear about the clustering of women in low-paying jobs but not about the clustering of men in hazardous jobs? Why do we notice that the male-as-protector norm infantilizes women but overlook the burden on men? Why do we denounce the chauvinism of the old-fashioned husband who didn't want his wife to have a job but ignore the fact that he condemned himself to work harder to support the family?

Both sexes, Farrell argues, were equally enslaved by their historical roles: men provided and protected so that women could bear and nurse children. Since the survival of the species required more females, males were more "disposable"—the ones to risk their lives if necessary. But when technological progress eliminated most of the need for the old division of labor and enabled individuals to seek personal fulfillment, the reexamination of sex roles focused on the oppression of women because men were seen as the ones in power. As a result, male burdens—such as the male-only draft—remained largely intact.[37]

This is surely more accurate than, say, the worldview of Marilyn French's *The War Against Women,* which treats human history as one long chronicle of women's abuse by men.[38] Farrell is on to something feminists commonly ignore: traditional sexual arrangements have always had major elements of mutual sacrifice, not just subjugation. And sometimes his observations can be like the feminist "click," revealing familiar things in a new light.

When a corporate executive and his stay-at-home wife get divorced, we may think that she deserves an equal share of his money; but we don't look at the rewards she may have derived from her role—a closer bond with the children, more time for cultural interests—in which no court can give him a share. When a woman who went to law school in the 1950s recalls a male student saying, "I'm doing this because I have to, but why are you here?" we see this only as an example of the sexism women faced—not as a reminder that for some men, a career was no privilege but an unpleasant necessity.

But despite these insights, "masculist" analysis is seriously flawed. (Nor is it entirely original: "It is a commonplace to say that in modern families, and especially in the United States, woman has reduced man to slavery," noted Simone de Beauvoir in the late 1940s.) Take Farrell's claim that while governments in the past were run by men, "the family was female dominated."[39] Is it that simple? Surely earning power often confers power in the home. Nor can one discount the fact that before this century, a husband had considerable legal authority over his wife, including the power to have her committed to an insane asylum—even if the exercise of these powers was limited not only by affectional ties but by social disapproval.

Some wives in the 1950s or the 1850s undoubtedly ruled their households and their husbands with a firm hand. Others lived under a husband's thumb; most were probably somewhere in between. This balance of power always had a lot to do with individual temperament. But arguably, the henpecked husband in the past had outlets outside the home that the downtrodden wife lacked.

Or take the theme of the "sexual power" that men's sexual needs give women—the argument of Norman Mailer's 1971 polemic, *The Prisoner of Sex*. This notion certainly resonates with most men, and some women too. But this power has a downside. For sex to be a bargaining chip, the woman must deny her own pleasure. Lysistrata, the heroine of the ancient Greek comedy in which women forswear love until men end war, can barely keep her sex-starved troops from running off to the men. Besides, in the traditional scheme, men's sexual dependency on women has a parallel in women's emotional neediness. In this game, both players may feel powerless. He sees her as holding the cards because she makes him "earn" sex; she sees herself as walking a razor's edge between losing his interest by holding off and losing his respect by giving in, while fighting her own desire. (Of course, traditional relationships can also be based on affection and sensuality, which "masculists" obsessed with female manipulation of men are as prone to forget as are feminists obsessed with male domination of women.) In sexual and emotional realms, men and women may indeed have borne equal burdens, though each sex tends to dwell on its vulnerabilities.

Another "masculist" cliché is that women were always considered men's moral superiors. Roy Schenk, a Wisconsin writer and crusader against such evils as ladies' night specials in bars, even maintains that men's political and economic dominance was a mere attempt to compensate for their perceived spiritual inferiority.[40] In fact, female moral superiority is a fairly recent Western invention. The world's major religions blame woman for man's fall from grace and regard her as impure. Before the nineteenth century, women were commonly seen as devious, fickle creatures in need of male moral guidance.

This is only one way in which, not unlike radical feminists, "masculists" project modern assumptions onto other cultures. "A man who was addicted to a woman's beauty, youth, and sex would . . . make the irrational decision to support her for the rest of his life," Farrell says of the marital bargain, ignoring the role of female labor in preindustrial economies and the fact that a girl without a dowry used to be nearly unmarriageable. On women in Islam, he says, "If women had to promise to provide for a man for a lifetime before he removed his veil and showed her his smile, would we think of this as a system of female privilege?" We might—if she thereby gained the right to lock him up and to kill him for adultery. (Besides, Islamic men could traditionally divorce their wives at will.)[41]

"If we can make meaningful comparisons," says Ferrel Christensen, a self-described "liberal masculist/feminist" and former philosophy professor at the University of Alberta in Canada, "I'd say that in this culture in this century, men and women have been pretty equal. I would not say that this is true historically and at all times." It's more accurate to say, Christensen argues, that women received some compensation for their subordinate state—such as protection from various perils—and men's dominant role carried a high price, such as having to risk their lives to provide that protection.[42]

Would we call it "female privilege" if women did the hard work but were treated as adults? That's the case with China's Mosuo minority, where women run businesses, head households, inherit family wealth, and may bear a heavier burden than do men in patriarchal societies, since they are mostly responsible for traditional women's work as well (while men have more leisure time). A 1995 *Wall Street Journal* article portrayed the Mosuo as a "matriarchy" and applauded the independence of their women.[43] Maybe "privilege" is not an easier or safer life but a more active, productive, and responsible one.

The argument that gender oppression was always a two-way street misses another fact: *Traditionally, the "male sex role" was identified with the cultural concept of what it meant to be human.* The invisibility of male disadvantage is the flip side of historical male privilege: hardships peculiar to men are seen as a part of the human condition because masculinity blends into universal humanity.

There is no hint in Farrell's writings that to some extent, a man's work was always seen as a way not only to support his family but to leave his mark on the world, that the male "performer role" had a meaning beyond providing for women and children and included the highest reaches of the human spirit: artistic creation, the quest for liberty, the search for knowledge and truth.

Women's exclusion from this human enterprise was the issue that animated feminists from Mary Wollstonecraft to Betty Friedan. What Friedan saw missing from the feminine role was the "unique human capacity . . . to live not at the mercy of the world, but as builder and designer of that world." And while she suggested that "men may live longer . . . when women carry more of the burden of the battle with the world" (anticipating "masculist" concerns with the longevity gap), Friedan clearly felt that women were worse off for being left out of the battle.[44]

The vision of *The Myth of Male Power* is very different: being expected to strive is a dismal fate; admiring a man for his achievements is as sexist as admiring a woman for her breasts; the aphorism "Woman is, man does," once seen as relegating women to a demeaning passivity, becomes a male lament: "Men are not human beings, they are human doings."[45] If classical feminism challenged woman's place because it was at odds with Western values, masculism challenges those values themselves.

In this, it resembles nothing so much as radical feminism. In women's studies programs today, Friedan's words would be seen as reactionary. "Battle with the world" reeks of militarism; to celebrate the capacity for building and designing one's world is to glorify white male rape of the earth; the search for knowledge is a patriarchal idea of knowledge as possession.

The irony is that if "male" civilization and its accomplishments are dethroned, the notion of male privilege is much harder to sustain. If all those masculine pursuits are so worthless, was it so bad to be excluded from them? If the qualities traditionally prized in men are not virtues but flaws, why shouldn't men see themselves as victims? If liberty is a (white) male fiction, what difference is there between the burden of oppression and the burden of the risks accepted as the price of freedom? Thus, feminists unwittingly undermine their own critique of "patriarchy," paving the way for "masculists."

Masculist complaints about men's lot also bear an uncanny resemblance to feminist stereotypes of men: disconnected from feelings, obsessively competitive, incapable of friendship. Only the judgments differ: in one version, men are bastards; in the other, victims of their socialization. As *Playboy* "Men" columnist Asa Baber noted at a 1994 men's conference, "The men of this culture have been told by *both* the men's and the women's movement that they are not okay."

The most popular of these masculist-feminist clichés is that masculinity in Western culture is synonymous with denial of emotion. "From the first admonition of 'Boys don't cry' to the movie images of thick-skinned cowboys, my son will be taught that to reveal what he truly feels is a dangerous and provocative act," rues columnist Neil Chethik.[46]

Actually, in a 1978 poll, most Americans considered keeping one's feelings under control an important quality for both sexes. As a believer in the unfashionable virtue of reticence, I think the last thing we need is a movement leading us further down the path of emotional exhibitionism and conspicuous sharing of feelings. In fact, some psychologists are coming to the heretical conclusion that suppressing negative emotions may be good for us.[47]

That aside, a male friend of mine thinks that the notion of men being forbidden to have feelings in our culture is one of those ideas that become so pervasive that people repeat them without asking whether they bear any relation to real life. Forget the cowboys and consider Humphrey Bogart's characters in *Casablanca* or *The African Queen,* or the characters played by Jimmy Stewart, Cary Grant, or Clark Gable. These are not emotionally stunted men. Think of the finale of *It's a Wonderful Life.* Watch the scene in the 1947 film *Gentleman's Agreement* where the hero, a writer posing as a Jew to expose anti-Semitism, comforts his crying son who has been taunted by neighborhood boys.

Even in a much rougher age, "being a man" had a complex range of meanings. In *Macbeth,* when Macduff learns that his family has been butchered, Malcolm tells him (but only after consoling him and urging him to "give sorrow words") to "dispute it like a man." "I shall do so," Macduff replies, "But I must also feel it as a man." Nor is Western culture bereft of images of warm male friendship, from the Bible's David and Jonathan to Shakespeare's Hamlet and Horatio. In prefeminist days, as Carol Tavris recalls, "the stereotype was that men had all the great and true friendships . . . based on male bonding, true and faithful camaraderie, and sturdy affection." As manly a man as Theodore Roosevelt was remarkably tender-hearted in letters to his sons, making up affectionate nicknames and reporting that he was "acting as nurse to two wee guinea pigs."[48]

Have men been limited by cultural concepts of manhood? Of course, though even completely gender-neutral concepts of what it means to be a good person would be restrictive in some ways. Still, masculine roles run the gamut from warrior to pacifist, from businessman to poet to philanthropist, from the pursuit of power to lifelong service to the less fortunate.

Men as Victims: Facts and Myths

While men's liberation challenges the orthodoxy of women as an oppressed class, it shares key elements of "political correctness": the politics of identity that eclipse the notion of a human condition; antipathy to individualism and achievement; a tendency to view human experience as shaped by social conditioning; and hence a penchant for social engineering (Farrell wants government programs to "give men special outlets and special incentives to express their feelings").[49]

Even author Jack Kammer, whose book *Good Will Toward Men* urges both sexes to embrace self-reliance and optimism, writes that men "are in the most maximum security prison of all, the prison that convinces its inmates that they are right where they want to be"—echoing the radical feminist view satirized by Christina Hoff Sommers: women who believe they're not oppressed "actually confirm the existence of a system of oppression, for they 'show' how the system dupes women by socializing them to *believe* they are free."[50]

What emerges from all this is a male version of "victim feminism"—an apotheosis of the victim culture in which the pantheon of the oppressed is completed by the admission of straight white guys. High school football is "male child abuse." Circumcision is "violence against an infant boy," comparable to clitoridectomy in the Third World. Men's shorter life spans and higher mortality rates are "male gendercide."[51]

Like the claims of "victim feminists," who leap from the fact that adult rape victims are overwhelmingly women to the pronouncement that rape is at the core of the female condition, many "masculist" grievances are a muddled mix of truth and melodramatic exaggeration:

• *Men are "the suicide sex."* American men commit suicide four times as often as women; this gap has widened, from about 2.5 to 1 in 1970, due to a one-third drop in female suicide rates and a small increase for men. (The sex differential in suicide rates is smaller in most European nations.) Is that because women but not men have been freed from the oppression of traditional roles? It's a tempting interpretation; but in the 1920s, the ratio was even higher—six to one.[52]

This is not to say that sex roles have nothing to do with this gap. Male unemployment is far more likely to lead to suicide. Women's tendency, biological or cultural, to be more protective toward their bodies may act as a buffer. (Perhaps for the same reason, women have been far more likely to seek medically assisted suicide.) While gender deserves attention as a factor in suicide, it makes no sense to turn suicide into a symbol of men's "powerlessness": In the United States, whites kill themselves far more often than blacks.[53]

• *Men die young because of the lethal pressures of male roles and medical neglect.* The seven-year differential in life expectancy can't be biological, men's advocates say, because it was only a one-year gap in 1920. But using 1920 as a comparison point is misleading: the gap was three years in 1901 and shrank temporarily because of the flu pandemic. Besides, there *is* a biological explanation for the widening of the longevity gap: "The elimination of infection as the dominant cause of death," writes Andrew Kadar of the UCLA School of Medicine, "has boosted the prominence of diseases that selectively afflict men earlier in life." Male fetuses, which don't have much of a sex role, are more often spontaneously aborted. Women's protection, it seems, comes less from female roles than from female hormones.[54]

On the other hand, women get sick more often and are much more prone to nonfatal but painful afflictions such as rheumatoid arthritis, as well as disability and dementia in old age. Some researchers believe that when *active* years after sixty-five are compared, the sexes are roughly equal.[55]

Is men's higher mortality related to sex roles? Probably, in that men have had more freedom *and* faced more pressure to engage in high-risk behaviors. Men die in accidents nearly three times as often as women, though not so often as to have a large effect on average life expectancy. The difference in heart disease and cancer deaths is affected, but not entirely explained, by alcohol and tobacco use. Male emotional repression is an unlikely culprit: sex differences in self-expression are far too small to cause health problems for men. In any case, were stoicism fatal, the Japanese, who hold the current world record in longevity for both sexes, should be far down the list.[56]

And while medical research funding in recent years has been somewhat skewed toward women due to feminist health activism, there's little if any evidence that men's lower life expectancy results from medical neglect. One dramatic claim made to support this contention—the Index Medicus lists *twenty-three* articles on women's health for every *one* item on male health problems—comes from Farrell's misreading of calculations by a researcher who found a 1.2 to 1 ratio. Another activist cries bias because cancer, the leading cause of early death in women, gets more funding than heart disease, the leading cause of early death in men—a bizarre complaint, since men account for 60 percent of cancer deaths. The likely reason for the disparity is that cancer is a far more intractable problem. Between 1970 and 1989, cancer mortality rates stayed nearly constant, while male death rates from heart disease dropped by nearly 40 percent, barely making a dent in the longevity gap, since the same medical advances lowered women's death rates.[57]

• *Men's lives are treated as more "disposable."* There is surely some truth to this, as the fact that 1,300 men but only two hundred women died on the *Titanic* should remind us. But one needn't go all the way back to 1912. Watching the 1974 disaster film *The Towering Inferno,* about a group of people trapped in a burning skyscraper, I was struck by the fact that even the scoundrel who tried to use his position as the building owner's son-in-law to be rescued before the other men did not try to cut ahead of the women. (The price women pay is lack of agency: they merely scream while the men try to do something.) War deaths of women and children are seen as especially horrible, though old men are sometimes added to the list, suggesting that it's more a question of perceived helplessness than of the value of life.[58]

The warrior role also embodies male "disposability." For most of history, as Farrell occasionally admits, childbearing made women's lives just as "disposable"; in this century, technological progress has all but eliminated the dangers of childbirth in the industrial world while making war deadlier than ever (to civilians as well as combatants, one might add). And we are obviously very far from accepting women in combat, though modern Western societies have little tolerance for *any* large-scale war casualties, something "masculists" tend to underestimate.

"We don't call the one *million* men who were killed or maimed *in one battle* in World War I . . . a holocaust, we call it 'serving the country,'" writes Farrell. But the carnage of World War I was hardly seen as glorious. The most popular book about the war, Erich Maria Remarque's 1929 novel, *All Quiet on the Western Front,* portrayed it as a senseless horror. Men's advocates are also given to exaggerating America's indifference to men who fought in Vietnam: Farrell claims that evidence of surviving POWs was swept under the rug because Americans wanted to put the war behind and the missing soldiers were mere men. Meanwhile, *Washington Post* reporter Thomas Lippman writes that "fantastic notions" about missing U.S. servicemen alive in Vietnam "can never be dispelled, because they are too deeply rooted in some corners of the national psyche."[59]

Likewise, it's a fact that the most hazardous occupations are overwhelmingly male: 92 percent of workplace fatalities and 80 percent of serious on-the-job injuries are suffered by men. It is also true that women have not flocked into dangerous jobs—*and* that women who have taken such jobs often did not receive a warm welcome from men.

That said, Farrell's rhetoric about politicians protecting women from workplace bias but slashing workplace safety measures for coal miners and other men bears little resemblance to reality. (Fatalities in mining have been cut sevenfold since 1968.) Conservatives hostile to the Occupational Safety and Health Administration are no friends of the Equal Employment Opportunity Commission; liberals who champion sexual harassment laws have always fought for more workplace safety regulations. Besides, if we do too little to ensure worker safety, one could make just as good an argument that we do too little to ensure auto safety—even though, for every two men killed on the job, five women (and ten men) die in car accidents.[60]

There is a real tendency to play up female victimization—part chivalry, part gender politics, part damsel-in-distress titillation. Yet it hardly translates into indifference to male pain. ("Victim feminists" and "victim masculists" never sound more alike than when they insist that the suffering of their sex is not given its due.) The deaths of policemen or firemen, who risk their lives to protect others, have always been treated as especially tragic; whether the deaths of women in such jobs are viewed differently is debatable. When fourteen Forest Service firefighters died in a 1994 fire in Colorado, the four women were not singled out in media coverage. Nor was there any extra focus on the women victims of Long Island Railroad shooter Colin Ferguson. Perhaps women as victims get special treatment only when the crime can be somehow attributed to their sex.[61]

The real double standard is that afflictions visited on men are treated simply as a human tragedy, while afflictions visited on women often become a matter of gender politics, thanks in part to feminist watchdogs ready to protest any description of female victimization in gender-neutral terms. The "masculist" answer is to demand that men be treated more like women; when a safety official complains that corners are cut because of time pressures "and then people die," Farrell bristles, "No. And then *men* die."[62] But perhaps real progress in this respect would be to start treating women more like men.

It is easy to poke fun at male victimism, a stance likely to be dismissed as misogynist by the left and unmanly by the right. Yet it is ultimately a response to the "culture of complaint" in which, with major help from feminists, we are now enmeshed. If victimhood— transformed into "innocence," as Shelby Steele puts it in the context of race—is the way to gain a legitimate voice, one can hardly blame men for trying to claim their share of the moral high ground.

Even the absurd attempts to prove that women were never any more oppressed than men become understandable when one considers that many feminists still use the "centuries of oppression" as a stick to beat men. It is hard to disagree with Farrell when he says that the perception of men as having all the power and women as having none (which was never quite true and is ludicrous in the United States in the 1990s) has made us reluctant to question any expansion of female power and made male-bashing the only socially acceptable form of bigotry.

Do Men Need a Movement?
A men's movement comparable to feminism in influence and size is not likely. But if one tries to imagine such a thing, the prospect of two rival movements trying to outshout and outwhine each other must be rather dismaying. Nor is there any reason to believe that "masculism" would avoid these pitfalls. It is already a small-scale

mirror image of feminism, with its own pseudo-statistics (like the twenty-three-to-one ratio of articles on women's health to articles on men's health in medical journals) and even a few ideologues who argue that men must turn to their own gender for sexual gratification if they are to free themselves from the "sexual ruling class."[63]

Also like the women's movement, the men's movement attracts quite a few wounded people who seek to give their private grievances a political meaning and cultivate rage. A writer in one of the movement's leading publications, the *Liberator,* proclaimed soon after O. J. Simpson's arrest in 1994 that he hoped O. J. would go free even if he was guilty, since women have gotten away with killing their husbands and feminists have rallied to their side.[64]

"The focus on male as victim will simply deepen the culture of victimhood," says *Playboy*'s Asa Baber, who still thinks it's important for the male side of gender issues to be heard.[65]

Since men's problems often stem from overzealous attempts to correct real or perceived injustices toward women, developing a more critical attitude toward victim feminism would do more to help men than developing its male equivalent. Another way out of the victimhood trap is to stress what "masculists" like Farrell recognize in their better moments: men's and women's issues are often two sides of the same coin. (If only women have the option to stay home, only women will sometimes have to defend their choice to work.)

"Any movement which focuses only on the problems of one side is doomed to deteriorate into something that portrays the other side as the villain," says Alan Rubinstein. Given that historically, women were the "special case" while the rights and responsibilities of adult men were the human norm, the sex role transition had to begin with the women's movement. When women were denied access to higher education, careers, and politics, it would have been a tad laughable to argue that having to be the breadwinners was unfair to men. Today, even if women still face some barriers, it is hardly ridiculous to point out that having the option to raise children full time, or swap a higher-paying job for a more fulfilling one, is a real advantage.

Clearly a feminism that defines its mission as "solidarity with women" rather than fairness for everyone is likely to result in unfairness to men. And while "masculism" is not the answer, what Baber calls an "equal rights movement" that takes the rights and concerns of men seriously is essential. Such a movement must give the men's movement credit for several key points feminists have largely ignored:

- The evolution of gender roles must expand options for both sexes.
- Male privilege never meant that most men were free to do as they pleased, or that everything they did was for selfish reasons, or that women had a corner on suffering. The historical fact of male dominance does not negate the fact of male sacrifice, in wars or in work.
- In personal relationships, men and women have equally good reasons to complain about the other sex.
- Today, most gender issues are women's *and* men's issues—and if we don't take the male perspective into account, we miss half the picture.

CHAPTER TEN

The Conservative Mistake

In a speech to a women's club in 1938, British writer Dorothy Sayers, the mystery novelist best known as the creator of aristocratic sleuth Peter Wimsey, gave her own answer to the eternal question, "What on earth do women want?" It was, she said, simply to be accepted "as human beings": "not as an inferior class and not, I beg and pray all feminists, as a superior class—not, in fact, as a class at all, except in a useful context."[1]

Sixty years later, we are far from simply accepting women as human beings. Most feminists view women as a class whose presumed interests are to be given priority and see equality as a matter of convenience: women are as tough and aggressive as men when it comes to fighting wars or fires, but frail and helpless when it comes to domestic violence; as carnal as men when it comes to sexual freedom, but innocent and victimized in any sexual conflict. To some extent, this has also become the party line in the mainstream media.

The principal alternative to this party line comes from conservatives, including a number of conservative female voices that have emerged in recent years. But are conservatives prepared to accept women as human beings?

Pick the conservative response to the rise of female-owned businesses or the shrinking of the gender gap in wages:

1. That's great. Women's progress attests to the dynamic nature of capitalism and shows how ridiculous it is to talk about American women today as an oppressed group.
2. That's terrible. Women have been seduced or forced out of the home, leading the decline of the family, neglect of children, and the feminization of men.

Actually, it's either of the above. In 1992, Congressman Dick Armey, then ranking Republican on the Joint House Economic Committee, issued a glowing report on the rise in women's earnings in the Reagan-Bush era, calling the eighties "'the decade of the woman' economically." On the other hand, in his 1994 book *Dead Right,* conservative journalist David Frum suggests that Reagan policies that helped "goose the job market and thus entice women to work" may have escalated family breakdown.[2]

Sometimes conservative commentators note with satisfaction that as women enter business, they are increasingly drawn to the Republican message of self-reliance and less government. Yet businesswomen who read conservative magazines are likely to find themselves denigrated as selfish creatures whose marriages "are not so much unions as partnerships of two career paths" and who treat their children as "interchangeable units."[3]

Attachment to traditional roles can at times supersede the other values of the right. Some conservatives have praised critiques of women's entry into the marketplace that stem from an underlying aversion to the market. Family Research Council president Gary Bauer has denounced proposals to privatize Social Security because, unlike the current system, such plans would not be skewed in favor of stay-at-home wives. This traditionalism can also lead to bizarre contradictions. In the welfare reform debate, many conservatives spoke passionately about work as a source of self-worth: welfare mothers "don't want their dignity and pride sapped one more day," Republican political analyst Kellyanne Fitzpatrick told a conservative audience—two months after suggesting that the GOP could win female votes with tax credits to help mothers leave their jobs.[4]

Conservatism's relationship with "equity" and "gender" feminism is no less paradoxical. (Things were simpler a decade ago, when there were just feminists and antifeminists.) "Equity feminists," who reject the rhetoric of gender war and support Western cultural values, seem to have fared well on the right. Christina Hoff Sommers's

Who Stole Feminism? was excerpted in *National Review;* William F. Buckley and Judge Robert Bork have cited *Professing Feminism,* Daphne Patai and Noretta Koertge's equity feminist critique of women's studies. Yet Carol Gilligan's theory of a feminine morality, criticized by these authors, has been invoked by conservatives from Marilyn Quayle to social scientist James Q. Wilson as validating traditional views of the sexes. The Gilliganian doctrine of girls' crumbling self-esteem has resurfaced in some defenses of single-sex schools in the same political quarters where Sommers's critique of this myth was applauded.[5]

Sexual issues bring these tensions to a head. For the most part, the feminist war on sexual harassment and date rape has encountered much derision on the right; Katie Roiphe, who took on this crusade in *The Morning After,* received praise from George Will and Rush Limbaugh. Yet Roiphe's scorn for sexual protections for women rankled *Commentary* critic Carol Iannone, who saw neofeminist hysteria as unfortunate but prompted by a "rational reaction" to the collapse of these protections. Irving Kristol, the godfather of neoconservatism, had voiced even less qualified enthusiasm for the feminist backlash against "sexual liberation," siding with the professor who wanted a harassing reproduction of Goya's *The Naked Maja* out of her classroom.[6]

Asssailing the feminist effort to abolish sexual distinctions, conservatives often don't realize that they are fighting yesterday's radicalism. Justice Ruth Bader Ginsburg, a leading proponent of "formal equality," has been castigated by Phyllis Schlafly for her "extremist feminist concepts" and by feminist legal theorists for her "androcentric" and "dangerous" beliefs.

In *The American Spectator,* John Corry grouses that "the official newsroom ethos . . . no longer recognizes gender." He illustrates this with the 1991 *New York Times* story that dissected the past of William Kennedy Smith's alleged victim, Patricia Bowman, supposedly reflecting the assumption that women deserve no special consideration (hardly official feminist policy in rape cases). Corry's next example of sexual correctness in the media is the lack of outrage when Senator Bob Packwood was forced to turn over his diaries for evidence of sexual misconduct; had this been done to a woman, he notes, "Anna Quindlen, Cokie Roberts, and Ellen Goodman's wrath would be unspeakable." Conservative critics need to get their story straight: are they attacking "genderlessness" or gender bias?[7]

The Maverick Prophets of Patriarchy

Virtually no one on the right really opposes equal rights for women, says William Kristol, the Republican strategist and publisher of the *Weekly Standard:* "There's some dispute around the margins . . . women and the military, stuff like that."[8]

True, it's not often that one finds conservatives praising ancient Roman laws requiring adult women to have male guardians (which, says *Chronicles* editor Thomas Fleming, would protect the poor things from being conned by lawyers and mutual fund salesmen).[9] But consider this defense of "manliness" on the editorial page of the *Wall Street Journal* by Harvey Mansfield, Kristol's former professor at Harvard and a frequent contributor to the *Standard:*

> The protective element of manliness is endangered by women having equal access to jobs outside the home. Women who do not consider themselves feminists often seem unaware of what they are doing to manliness when they work to support themselves. They think only that people should be hired and promoted on merit, regardless of sex.[10]

Mansfield is also chagrined by the notion that husbands and wives are partners with equal authority, since "gentle" feminine authority should "defer to the manly sort": "This does not mean that men have to decide, only that they have to *appear* to decide."

The pro-patriarchy contingent is a visible presence in conservative ranks. Among the regular contributors to *National Review* are sociologist Steven Goldberg, who argues that male dominance is inevitable so women might as well relax and enjoy it, and George Gilder. In *Sexual Suicide* (1973), Gilder asserted that women control "the economy of eros"—access to sex—and, to level the playing field, men must control everything else; equal opportunity in the workplace is disastrous, because men's work must affirm male identity and because women's real task is "domesticating" men. With his *idée fixe* that equality threatens male sexual potency, Gilder is something of a maverick. Still, conservatives can no more disavow him than feminists can disavow Catharine MacKinnon.[11]

Conservatives were in no rush to disavow F. Carolyn Graglia's 1997 tome, *Domestic Tranquility: A Brief Against Feminism,* which rivals any radical feminist tract in shrill extremism and sheer nuttiness (it's telling that just about the only feminist Graglia likes is Andrea Dworkin). In fact, the book was an alternate main selection of the Conservative Book Club, whose male reviewer rather ominously stated that "when women cease to be women they must be dealt with." It also received high praise from such conservative luminaries as William Kristol, Midge Decter, and columnist Mona Charen.[12]

Graglia, who left a legal career in the 1950s to raise her children, has a point (though hardly an original one) when she charges that many feminists tried to make the housewife a "pariah." But her protestations that she wants only equal respect for all choices ring hollow, given her vicious caricature of nontraditional women as "male clones" whose marriages are like homosexual cohabitation. Healthy women, Graglia makes it clear, want domesticity—or would want it if it weren't for feminist bullying and socialization that has warped their feminine natures.[13]

The real irony is that while Graglia decries feminist calumnies against women at home as passive, mindless and "less than fully human," she evokes these very stereotypes. She writes that a homemaker "is appreciated for being, not doing" and reduces motherhood almost entirely to biology. Her ideal woman, purged of "striving" and "aspirations of her own," wallows in contentment like a bovine in a field of flowers (Graglia's actual metaphor). Her real objection to mothers' work outside the home, it seems, is not that it consumes too much time but that it requires too large a core of separate self and "keeps the woman's analytical mind racing." And that's a *bad* thing, because a woman who uses her brain too much endangers her sexual and motherly nature: "When a woman lives too much in her mind, she finds it increasingly difficult to live through her body."[14]

Graglia unabashedly celebrates feminine passivity and submission, even suggesting that female genital mutilation is merely a too "draconian" way to achieve the worthy goal of curbing female sexual assertiveness. And she is deeply moved by Andrea Dworkin's argument that sexual intercourse erases a woman's independent will and selfhood—if only Dworkin would understand that this is *good*.[15]

Full-time motherhood, of course, is in no way incompatible with equality. But is George Gilder's or F. Carolyn Graglia's vision of womanhood compatible with a view of women as human beings?

Both of them seem to place women outside the human condition. "Man is the only animal for whom his existence is a problem which he has to solve," wrote Erich Fromm, using "man" in the generic sense. For Gilder, however, this applies only to the male, who has no role "inscribed in his body" and must seek "external achievement" to duplicate the creative feat woman attains in giving birth. Gilder is echoed by Graglia: "Childbearing is what really counts, and only women can do it," while "men must do other things to justify their existence."[16]

As Cynthia Ozick noted, mocking the idea of childbearing as a creative achievement even before Gilder recycled this cliché, the creation of life is nature's miracle, not woman's.[17] Any female mammal is capable of this "feat." To say this is not to degrade motherhood but to protest its reduction to biology. And aren't those "other things" precisely what separates us from other animals? Aren't the traits of which Graglia's "awakened" woman is "emptied out"—the inviolate self, the will, the "questing, restless mind"—essential attributes of being human?

Graglia would no doubt reply that these are just Western prejudices. To uphold her vision of womanhood, she has to abandon the conservative defense of the West and attack Western culture for elevating the "masculine power of mental creation" over "female physiological gestation"—which, she charges, caused women to feel devalued and made them want to become "pseudo-males."[18]

Women's Work and the Nostalgic Temptation

Are conservatives saying that women, or at least mothers, should stay home? Most of them would probably argue that they only want women to be able to choose. In her 1989 book *Enemies of Eros,* Maggie Gallagher concedes that the opportunities opened by feminism have worked well for ambitious women like former U.N. ambassador Jeane Kirkpatrick, but adds that "there is no reason, while creating new avenues for female achievement, to tear down the social institutions that make it possible for women to devote themselves to the nurture of children."[19]

It sounds perfectly reasonable. Who could be against choice? Yet too often, as in the case of Graglia, validations of traditional womanhood segue into put-downs of the nontraditional kind. When, during the 1992 presidential race, Hillary Rodham Clinton dismissed questions about conflicts of interest in her law practice with the infamous "I could have stayed home and baked cookies" comment, a letter writer in the *Wall Street Journal* accused her of disparaging women at home—but quickly went on to disparage women who put their "selfish desires" ahead of "ensuring that the next generation of Americans does not consist solely of serial killers and drug addicts." Danielle Crittenden's review of Susan Chira's pro-working mother book *A Mother's Place* in *National Review* boils down to the charge that Chira is a bad mother because she wasn't happy at home with her kids. An article by David Gelernter in *Commentary* is straightforwardly titled "Why Mothers Should Stay Home."[20]

In many people's eyes, the *option* to stay home quickly becomes a duty. Besides, the champions of full-time motherhood want it to be more than a private choice. "When it becomes the social norm for both spouses to work," writes Gallagher, "both spouses soon have to work."[21]

The social norm of stay-at-home motherhood was contingent on the recognition of the male provider role, which legitimized discrimination in the workplace: a man, after all, had a wife and kids to support. In 1946, only a quarter of Americans agreed that "all women should have an equal chance with men for any job"; half believed that only those unfortunates who had to support themselves should be treated equally, with the rest saying that preference should *always* go to a man. Nearly half said that a married woman with no young children shouldn't be allowed to hold a job if her husband could support her.[22]

Today, a few traditionalists such as Rockford Institute president Allan Carlson openly argue that married women's entry into the workforce destroyed the "family wage" that enabled men to be sole breadwinners. Families may not literally need a second wage to survive, but it's hard to keep up with the Joneses on one salary when both Mr. and Ms. Jones bring home a paycheck. Besides, as F. Carolyn Graglia observes, when too many affluent, educated women choose to work, homemaking loses "prestige."[23]

Graglia also asserts (twisting Betty Friedan's words in *The Feminine Mystique*) that women who did choose careers in the 1950s enjoyed both respect and ample opportunities. Friedan did refer to the "removal of . . . legal, political, economic, and educational barriers" to women; but she was talking about *formal* barriers such as company policies that barred the hiring of married women, and she also wrote that informal discrimination and "anti-feminine prejudice in business and the professions" contributed to women's retreat to the home. And much of *The Feminine Mystique* is an account, unrefuted by Graglia, of the denigration of career women in the culture of the 1950s. In the movie *All About Eve,* Bette Davis as actress Margo Channing fretted that a woman with a career lost things, such as feminine helplessness, which she would need to get and hold a man ("Without that, you're not a woman. You're something with a French provincial office or a book full of clippings").[24]

In 1962, the year before *The Feminine Mystique* was published, the announcement by young Elizabeth Hanford—the future Elizabeth Dole—that she was going to Harvard Law School literally made her mother sick: "Don't you want to be a wife, mother and hostess for your husband?" wailed Mrs. Hanford.[25]

And yet the belief that jobs were liberating for women was on the rise. Graglia seems to blame Friedan for single-handedly luring women out of their happy homes; but could that have happened if her ideas had not fallen on fertile soil? Even Mills College president Lynn White, whose 1950 book *Educating Our Daughters* was Friedan's prime exhibit of the doctrine that women should be educated as future homemakers, sang a different tune when he discussed the older woman's need to return to work or school: "The right to work is like the right to vote: a necessary form of human expression in a democratic society." Ten years later, a book called *College for Coeds* still stressed the importance of homemaking but also decried the notion that "girls must choose between marriage and a career" and described women's employment in glowing terms: "By using their talents and skills . . . they are acquiring a sense of fulfillment. They come to realize their importance as individuals."[26]

Perhaps 1950s culture was not as monolithic as Friedan depicted it; perhaps it was pulled in opposite directions by tradition and modernity. Antifeminist *extraordinaire* Goldberg concedes that the modern economy tends to draw women into the "public arena."[27] So do modern cultural values. It was probably inevitable that once the sexes were recognized as equal, male domains would open to women, and "male" work, identified with human achievement, would give women higher status than homemaking, unless a stigma remained attached to female ambition outside the home.

An astute analysis of prefeminist tensions between women's old and new roles was offered by Allan Bloom:

> For a long time middle-class women, with the encouragement of their husbands, had been pursuing careers. It was thought they had a right to cultivate their higher talents instead of being household drudges. . . . But, with rare exceptions, both parties still took it for

granted that the family was woman's responsibility and that, in the case of potential conflict, she would subordinate or give up her career.[28]

If careers were the source of fulfillment, such an expectation was bound to seem unfair: "This arrangement was ultimately untenable, and it was clear in which way the balance would tip," Bloom concludes. This very arrangement seems to be the best traditionalists can offer.

Today, the two-career couple has become a norm even in conservative circles (though some ideologues of stay-at-home motherhood have taken to pretending that they don't really have careers: the biographical note with a 1998 *New York Times* op-ed by Lisa Schiffren identifies her as "a full-time mother of two and an occasional writer"). Despite some conservatives' wishful thinking, women are not going home en masse. Of course, there are millions of mothers who do stay home with their children. But full-time motherhood is increasingly seen as a temporary stage, during which many women maintain ties to their professional lives, rather than a vocation. In one college survey, only one in ten female students said they wanted to resume full-time work right after having a child—but only one in five (and, interestingly, 5 percent of the men) preferred not to work indefinitely.[29]

It is important to respect people's choices. Certainly, a parent who puts her (or his) children's well-being ahead of career success deserves respect. Still, my view is that it's not a good idea to have no serious pursuits outside the family—a job, study, or a substantial commitment to volunteerism—for an extended time. I think such pursuits are important for the same reason Graglia thinks they're bad: to maintain a core of self apart from the web of intimate relationships, to remain engaged in "doing" and not just "being." Moreover, there are dangers in treating parenthood too much like a career and trying to mold a child with the focused effort one would apply to a work project.

For most of history, women's roles did not revolve around—to quote Graglia—"personal relations with husband and children"; their work, while centered near the home (as was men's work), was economically indispensable. Perhaps no one, man or woman, can live by love alone. In *The Assault on Parenthood,* Dana Mack laments that in the last century, family life has been depicted as a tangle of "dysfunction" in which parents cripple their children's psyches. Is it a coincidence that this happened when women's role was reduced largely to regulating the emotional temperature of the family?[30]

Sexual Politics, Conservative Style

While most on the right would no doubt distance themselves from opposition to equal opportunity on the job, a sort of Gilderism lite has become something of a social conservative orthodoxy on sex. It goes like this: traditional constraints gave women the leverage to harness men into marriage until they were swindled by sexual liberation. "In the twinkling of an eye (a male eye), women abandoned standards of sexual conduct which had protected them from untempered male lust," laments columnist Mona Charen.[31]

This vision of male-female relations is strangely ahistorical, ascribing universality to twentieth-century courtship patterns: the woman withholds sexual favors until she has roped the man into "commitment." For most of history, men were hardly in a position to press for sex, since they were rarely alone with unmarried women. The bride and groom might never meet before the wedding; even in the West, unchaperoned dates are a modern phenomenon. Among peasants and the urban poor, the sexes mingled far more freely—and premarital sex was common. If a girl got in trouble, it was less her civilizing influence than that of her kinsmen's fists that harnessed the culprit into marriage.

We don't know which sex, at the dawn of history, was more responsible for the emergence of monogamy. If our hominid foremothers were like some female apes, they mated indiscriminately, giving most males an incentive to be nice to their young. Maybe, as infants became more helpless for a longer time, females grew more anxious for a steady mate; maybe males grew more anxious for assurance that the baby they invested in was theirs. Since they left no diaries, who domesticated whom must remain a matter of conjecture.[32]

But Gilder's image of Woman the Civilizer, restraining the base impulses of the male, has no millennia of wisdom behind it, only less than two hundred years of sentimentalism. More often, women were seen as wayward creatures to be controlled. It is a historical anomaly for unmarried girls to be trusted with guarding their chastity, a task typically left to male relatives and carried out through often brutal measures—from genital mutilation to seclusion to harsh penalties for straying. David Gelernter likens traditional sexual strictures to a zoo cage: "Men were fenced in. Women were protected." Yet surely women were the ones caged, even if it was partly for their safety.[33]

By the 1950s, these strictures had lost much of their bite. Still, even Barbara Dafoe Whitehead, who argues that sexual freedom subverted girls' power to coax boys toward commitment by doling out favors but withholding sex, notes that the old order had its perils. In a steady relationship, a girl could "give in" and risk a ruined reputation or a disastrous pregnancy.[34] Writer Anne Roiphe remembers her adolescence as a time of "sexual terror," not power: "Girls were trying to do two contradictory things at once, satisfy the boys and be good girls or else."[35]

True, at the height of the sexual revolution, when "nice girls don't" went out the window, many nice girls were made to feel stupid and uptight if they *didn't*. Feminists were not as blind to this as many conservatives charge. In the first issue of *Ms.* in 1972, Anselma Dell'Olio assailed the sexual revolution as part of "the chain of abuse laid on women throughout patriarchal history," fuming that "women have been liberated only from the right to say no to sexual intercourse with men" (from which, Dell'Olio assumed, most women got little pleasure).[36]

More recently, some women may have used the threat of disease to bail out of the sexual revolution. But there are others, like the college student who mourned the loss of sexual freedom to AIDS in a 1990 article and complained of being "locked" into monogamy (while her older boyfriend assured her that the "wild times" hadn't been that much fun). To her, the post-Pill, pre-AIDS period was a happy time when women were "making up for the experiences they had long been denied by society and biology."[37]

One need not embrace the sexual revolution's excesses to be disturbed by the paternalistic notion that women must be denied freedom for their own good. No less alarming is the cynicism of some traditionalist arguments about the leverage women lose when they abandon premarital chastity.

By having sex without marriage, says Charen, "women [gave] away their trump." Former Bush speechwriter Jennifer Grossman, one of a new crop of Generation X conservative female commentators, deplores the folly of women who "give it away," invoking the old nugget: "Why buy the cow when the milk is free?"[38]

The talk of "bargaining power" is especially ironic since conservatives are the ones who lambaste feminists for "defining relations between men and women in terms of power and competition"—

and radical feminists are the ones who liken marriage to prostitution, which suddenly sounds less outrageous when phrases like "giving it away" are bandied about. Grossman, who shared with *U.S. News and World Report* that she made her current boyfriend wait "until the seventh month" (proving that conservatives aren't immune to the virus of exhibitionism), is frankly concerned with market value more than moral values. Reviewing a biography of Pamela Harriman in the *Weekly Standard,* she sighs that feminism has made the "courtesan," who gains power through sexual wiles, passé. Her role models include an ex–Ziegfeld girl who "made one of her five husbands slide a check for a million dollars under the bedroom door before she would admit him to the bridal bed."[39]

Proponents of the Why Buy the Cow theory of sex and marriage would say that it isn't cynical but merely realistic—though I doubt that many men who make this claim would apply it to themselves and say: *I married my wife because it was the only way to get laid.*

But is it realistic? Despite the talk of male flight from marriage due to an abundance of free milk and the loss of masculine roles, 70 percent of single men in a 1990 poll hoped to marry (same as women). Traditionalists invoke the male-fear-of-commitment bromide; but even they sometimes admit that many women who gripe about it are themselves closet commitment-phobes.[40]

The next generation of young men may, in fact, be keener on marriage than their potential mates. Seventy-three percent of teenage girls surveyed in 1994 but only 61 percent of boys thought they could have happy lives if they didn't marry; 60 percent of the boys and 77 percent of the girls said that they could be happy if they got divorced.[41] Unlike Susan Faludi, I don't think that women are defecting from marriage or that such a defection would be anything to celebrate. My point is that "male flight" is to the sexual politics of the right what "woman abuse" is to the sexual politics of the left: a small kernel of fact surrounded by a vast myth.

Victim Antifeminism

In *Sexual Suicide,* George Gilder clearly saw men as the real victims of feminism. Later, however, feminism's conservative foes developed their own version of female victimhood. "Women today are being punished, and the most horrifying part is that we are being punished *for our virtues,*" Maggie Gallagher declares in her victim antifeminist manifesto, *Enemies of Eros.* Graglia wails that women have been "grievously injured" by the new order. The victimizers are not only feminists. More often than not, the finger is pointed at a more familiar villain: the male, who will be a pig if given half a chance and was given such a chance by feminism and the sexual revolution.[42]

From columnist Mona Charen to eminent social scientist James Q. Wilson, conservatives echo the party line that the liberalization of divorce has freed men to abandon wives and children. (To bolster their case, they often invoke feminist advocacy research on the abuse of women in divorce courts.) In a review of Gallagher's *The Abolition of Marriage*, Amherst professor Hadley Arkes assails "laws that withdrew, from men, the incentive to marry, while they removed, from women, the levers they once had to preserve their marriages" and talks about the woes of divorced women. Describing the harms of divorce in *National Review*, political scientist John DiIulio cites health data suggesting that men suffer most, yet claims that easy divorce is "a great bargain for sex-seeking, social-responsibility-shirking guys, and a near-total disaster for women." Actual statistics on who abandons whom, and surveys showing that women are more pro-divorce—in 1994, 59 percent of men and 73 percent of women said that unhappily married parents shouldn't stay together for the sake of the children—are ignored.[43]

Even men who stay married, it seems, have been given new license for piggery. In *Commentary*, David Gelernter opines that "the typical husband would always have been happy to pack his wife off to work" even if it hurt his children, had he not been restrained by the cultural norm that mothers belong at home, which "shelter[ed] the typical woman from the predatory interests of the typical man." Other conservatives, too, make this charge. Yet since the 1940s, women have been more in favor of wives' employment than men.[44]

Like their feminist counterparts, victim antifeminists are particularly obsessed with sexual victimization—one area where the two come close to converging. Gallagher's assertion that a woman who has no-strings sex is being exploited no matter how "enthusiastically" she consents rings uncannily similar to Andrea Dworkin's assertion that a woman in intercourse is being violated even if she begs for it. In *Commentary*, chronicling the "sexual wreckage" that liberation has inflicted on young women, Wendy Shalit relies on two classics of the endangered-girls genre, Mary Pipher's *Reviving Ophelia* and Peggy Orenstein's *Schoolgirls*, from which she gleans gruesome tales of teenagers starving or cutting themselves to escape relentless sexual pressures. (In fact, almost as many high school boys as girls—about one in four—name the pressure to have sex as a cause of stress.)[45]

The woman who has an abortion also evolves from murderess to victim: According to an article by Shalit in *National Review,* the real culprit is usually the selfish boyfriend who doesn't want to be burdened with a child. Graglia, like some pro-life activists, even compares abortion to rape.[46]

Perhaps it shouldn't come as a surprise that during the Clinton scandals in 1998, the President's conservative opponents were so quick to adopt the language of "victim feminism." Some referred to Clinton's sexual relationship with young White House intern Monica Lewinsky—not only consensual but instigated by Lewinsky, according to her own testimony—as a case of sexual harassment because of his superior status. Others even suggested that First Lady Hillary Clinton, who continued to stand by her man, was a classic victim of "battered woman syndrome" and was "emotionally battered."[47]

Like feminist myths of victimization, anti-feminist ones often contain partial truths. There are, indeed, harried mothers who are pressured by their husbands into bringing in a paycheck, women who are talked by their boyfriends into having abortions, and devoted wives who are dumped like used Kleenex. But there is always another side: women whose husbands resent their careers; women who believe they are entitled to a man's money even when they are not raising children; men who are devastated when their offspring is aborted; the male casualties of divorce.

A cynic might see the conservative woman-as-victim line as a clever strategy to avoid the appearance of defending male privilege. But there is something else. To many traditionalists, it is far more comforting to believe that women are weak creatures led astray by a few Lady Macbeths and exploited by men (who are at least granted moral agency) than to admit that women *choose* to have sex without commitment, leave marriages, have abortions, and put their children in someone else's care.

Paternalism, Left and Right

Conservatives and liberals differ on plenty of things when it comes to women's roles. They may disagree about mothers working outside the home. They may disagree on whether the fact that fewer girls win math scholarships or play basketball is a result of social injustice or natural differences. They may disagree on women in combat, which liberals see in terms of equal opportunity (without mentioning the inequality of male-only draft registration) and some conservatives describe, borrowing radical feminist terminology, as "violence against women." But they seem to agree that it should be a matter of special concern to protect innocent females from bad males and other bad things.[48]

Conservatives are candid about their belief that men are the rightful protectors of "women and children" and that women should be spared such unpleasantness as danger on the frontlines or abusive training at military schools. Indeed, they accuse feminists of taking away women's protections in such areas as divorce and child custody, often making naive assumptions about the extent of the feminists' commitment to gender neutrality.[49] Feminists and liberals profess to be appalled by these patronizing attitudes—and then demand a myriad of special protections whose paternalism is only slightly camouflaged.

Conservative and liberal politicians easily join forces to be chivalrous, often taking the lead from female colleagues who believe that their mandate is to represent the interests of women. They will rush to women's defense when medical authorities advise limiting mammograms before the age of fifty. They will pass legislation requiring minimum hospital stays for procedures that happen to be unique to women—not only childbirth, which at least involves the welfare of the baby, but mastectomy, which is hardly any more "special" than prostatectomy or surgery for colon cancer. They will pass the Violence Against Women Act, oblivious to its underlying assumption that sexual and physical abuse of women and girls is part of a campaign of patriarchal terrorism.[50]

At other times, conservatives and liberals may be on opposite sides of an issue, but each side will invoke the interests of women. Those who advocate repealing no-fault divorce laws, or creating the option of a "covenant marriage" more difficult to dissolve, invoke impoverished abandoned wives; opponents raise the specter of women trapped in abusive marriages. Except for an occasional nod to the perspectives of fathers' groups or to wronged husbands, there is no mention of the possibility that men may have legitimate interests.[51]

On *The NewsHour* on PBS, author Barbara Dafoe Whitehead and commentator David Gergen talked about ways to encourage stable families without "stigmatizing the women" who leave bad marriages, and about tensions between the negative impact of divorce on children and its positive effect on the happiness of adults. Yet as Whitehead noted in passing, this positive effect is far from equally distributed: 80 percent of divorced women but only about half of the men say that they are better off after the divorce. Had it been the other way, it's hard to imagine that there would have been no discussion of how divorce was making many men happy at women's expense.[52]

Meanwhile, *New Republic* writer Hannah Rosin challenges a conservative activist's claim that restoring fault "gives the woman back some power" when her husband wants out, by pointing out that "in up to 65 percent of the cases, it's the woman who asks to get out of the marriage." But her conclusion is that *good* divorce reform would make it even easier for wives to leave, guaranteeing them a share of the husband's paycheck if he earns more: in other words, ensure that a woman can renege on the marriage contract yet keep all of its benefits.[53]

On both sides, there seems to be an agreement—narcissistic on the part of women, paternalistic on the part of men—that women's problems are uniquely deserving of attention and women's interests are uniquely legitimate. Bad things matter more when they happen to good women.

The strange convergence of radical feminism and patriarchal conservatism—and the alienation of both ideologies from real life—was exposed by the war of words between the National Organization for Women and Promise Keepers in 1997. NOW reacted as if the evangelical men's movement were about to establish a theocracy *á la* Margaret Atwood's *The Handmaid's Tale,* in which women were not allowed to work or read; delegates at the NOW convention even voted down an amendment to the anti–Promise Keepers resolution recognizing "men's genuine and appropriate needs to bond with each other and their families." Meanwhile, NOW's conservative critics acted as if only antimale, antifamily radicals could find anything objectionable about a group that exhorted men to be responsible husbands and fathers—ducking the Promise Keepers' rhetoric about men "taking back" family leadership.[54]

Even if leadership doesn't mean ruling with an iron fist but looking out for one's family, this implies that women, like children, are under the benevolent stewardship of men; declarations that husband

and wife are equal but he has the last word smack of Orwellian Newspeak. Nor is it a mainstream view: only 15 percent of Americans endorse the notion of male leadership in the family. Indeed, many men drawn to Promise Keepers by the message of personal renewal and responsibility describe their own marriages in strikingly egalitarian terms.[55]

On the other side, there is NOW's doublespeak about men being involved in the family as equal partners. Is this the same NOW that compares divorced fathers who want equal rights to batterers?[56]

Promise Keepers and their feminist foes share the belief that most social ills are men's fault and that women suffer endless wrongs at the hands of men (though they may not always define these wrongs in the same way). On a CNN talk show, a minister affiliated with Promise Keepers was asked why the movement addressed its message only to men. He explained that it was because "men are the main culprits of most of the wrong and evil in American society today," from crime to immorality and alcoholism. Eleanor Smeal of the Fund for the Feminist Majority remarked that what he said "sounds reasonable and fine"; she was just wary of his solutions.[57]

A *Ms.* reporter who went to a Promise Keepers rally "in drag" noted that the focus on male abusiveness, which clearly appealed to her, was based on the belief that "the ultimate responsibility for the world—for men's and women's lives both—is men's." Yet the feminists who deny women's capacity for abusiveness and their share of blame for male-female conflicts are really saying the same thing, just not as coherently.[58]

Reflecting on the idealization of the female world by "difference feminists" like Carol Gilligan, political scientist Diana Schaub wrote, "What we desperately need is a feminism leavened by an honest and hearty dollop of misogyny." It's a shocking thing to say, a seeming contradiction in terms. But Schaub is right—if "misogyny" means a rejection of the belief in women's special goodness and innocence, of the notion that women's suffering has a special claim to our sympathy and attention.[59]

In Search of a New Paradigm
The past thirty years' changes in women's lives are here to stay. They are rooted in core American values, from self-reliance to finding one's own place in life rather than having it assigned at birth. The

female version of the American dream now includes a good job as well as marriage, kids, and the house with the picket fence.

Like other social shifts, these changes come at a price and create confusion over issues even more basic than work versus family. How much equality do we want, given that women *are* physically the weaker sex? We may cringe at the inclusion of women in "women and children first"; but in the tragic sinking of a Swedish ferry in 1994, when people were largely on their own, most survivors were young men.[60] In other circumstances, from a fire to a robbery, women's survival may depend on men's greater strength. (Fear of losing this protectiveness may be one reason many self-sufficient women cling to vestiges of the male provider role.) Can we respect female independence and encourage women and girls to test their strength and bravery while recognizing that women sometimes need male protection? Can a culture torn between traditional chivalry, neofeminist paternalism, and equality hammer out a social contract that respects physical differences between the sexes without victimizing men or infantilizing women?

We're confused, too, about balancing equality and difference in the mating game. Some women turn to crutches like *The Rules* with their promise of "time-tested secrets." But in a feminist age, an attempt to recreate the rules of old-fashioned femininity is likely to turn into grotesque parody. The cold, Machiavellian underside of the coy damsel's act is laid bare; all the talk of love cannot hide the fact that love's got nothing to do with it. With their warnings that the "*Rules* girl" takes no emotional risks and their explicit view of men as "the adversary," *The Rules* belong squarely in the gender-war camp. That some conservatives have praised this amoral guide as a reaffirmation of old-fashioned femininity bespeaks either cynicism or desperation in the search for signs of a return to tradition.[61]

Some of our problems are simply the growing pains of transition. The sexual terrors that lead some girls to seek refuge in verbal-consent codes may have less to do with the delusion that male and female sexual needs are identical, as conservative critic Carol Iannone argues, than with a patchwork quilt of old and new norms: a culture in which aggressive female sexuality is celebrated yet a girl can still be branded a slut.[62]

Likewise, the feminist obsession with independence that, as Elizabeth Powers writes in *Commentary*, has robbed many women of the "spiritual enterprise" of building a life with another person is a leftover from an era when marriage required women, but not men, to surrender their separate identities and goals. As "peer marriage" becomes the norm, more women embark on this enterprise without the fear of losing themselves (even if Powers virtually refuses to recognize such marriages as real unions). A 1997 study of dual-career couples by the Catalyst research group found that these spouses were anything but roommates with separate lives: most spoke of constant, mutual "re-examination of decisions, priorities, and strategies for balancing career and home responsibilities."[63]

There are unquestionably those who would like to go back, though they may not realize what they would have to give up. Wendy Shalit, whose articles express deep unease about women's loss of traditional protections, quotes Rousseau: "The more women want to resemble [men], the less they will govern them, and then men will truly be the masters." I wonder if Shalit is familiar with Rousseau's other views—for example, that the sole purpose of women's education should be to teach them to please men.[64]

Social conservatives have raised important questions about the decline of civility, the divisiveness of radical feminism, and particularly the effects on children of precocious sexuality, family breakdown, and parental self-seeking. One need not be a reactionary to share such concerns. But this critique is undercut when conservatives insist on rigid sex-specific standards, or start venting psychosexual anxieties about unfeminine women, unmanly men, and "the liberation of women . . . from natural distinctions."[65]

If curtailing careers is something only *mothers* are expected to do, many ambitious women will perceive talk about "family values" as a personal attack, and some men will feel that they are denied the choices women have. If sexual morality means that women must deny their desires because men can't be expected to curb theirs, many women will resent it—while men get the dubious message that they can't be faulted for availing themselves of a sexual opportunity. And, bad as it is for conservatives to take a censorious tone toward women who breach traditional boundaries, arguing that every deplorable trend that has benefited men at women's expense makes things worse, contributing to a climate in which women's interests are pitted against men's.

In fact, the case against the "divorce culture" would be far stronger if it looked honestly at female responsibility for marital breakup and at the plight of abandoned husbands—just as the argument against sexual permissiveness would be stronger and less divisive if it didn't paint men as kids in the candy store of casual sex.

(Yes, 60 percent of sexually active teen girls wish they had waited longer, but so do nearly half of the boys.) One of the best critiques of the sexual revolution I have read, a 1983 essay by writer and psychotherapist Peter Marin, did not set up a men-against-women framework but argued that both had been hurt by the separation of sex from emotion. Marin wrote of men and women who "had slept with so many people that they found themselves frigid or unresponsive beside those whom they genuinely loved," and others for whom liberation had turned into disillusionment. The only distinction he made was to say that "men are less articulate, feel less justified than women in their public complaints."[66]

A "family values" crusade would be much more convincing if it recognized the variety of individual temperament and circumstance. The argument that the family is not disintegrating but evolving can be used to rationalize clearly unhealthy trends such as the rise in unwed motherhood; but it makes a lot of sense with regard to the two-income couple (which may even revive the extended family as more grandparents get involved in child rearing). It's unconscionable for a leading conservative intellectual like Norman Podhoretz to vilify fathers who take on a "mothering" role by equating them with men who desert their children.[67]

One conservative who has tried to transcend the traditionalist-versus-feminist dichotomy, Christian radio producer Nancy Pearcey, chides the Gilderites who would restore the ideology of "separate spheres" and female moral superiority. Men, she writes, can be good husbands and fathers only if they believe that "marital love and fidelity are not alien standards imposed on men, but central to the male character." Pearcey also predicts that the Information Age will bring more jobs home for both sexes, restoring something of the preindustrial norm of father presence in the home.[68]

Conservatives shouldn't stake their hopes on a comeback of traditional roles, and certainly not on the vogue for sex difference. "Difference feminists" don't want to restore domesticity; they want to establish a "caring" state and promote the "feminization of society"—the replacement of rational discourse by emoting and psychobabble—that conservatives rightly deplore (if only they didn't keep suggesting that this is a normal "feminine" frame of mind). The "New Victorians" want to punish male sexuality, not to promote female virtue.[69]

If conservatives have valid issues, feminists have real accomplishments. They deserve credit for helping break down the barriers of discrimination in the public arena; for making gender neutrality an accepted legal principle; for challenging stereotypes about women's nature. Thanks to them, achievement and ambition are no longer considered unfeminine and women are expected to make something of themselves, not just marry. Thanks to them, most of us believe that both parents can nurture young children.

But feminism as we know it is bankrupt. In some areas, it has promoted the dogma of "fifty-fifty" equality that ignores the fact that men and women tend to differ in a number of interests and preferences, not to mention physical ability. On other issues, it has made a mockery of its own principles of gender neutrality in the name of protecting women. It has not only failed to condemn but in many instances has actively promoted antimale sexism and gender antagonism. It has fostered the "abuse excuse" and less than equal accountability for women. It has endorsed a massive intrusion of the state and its bureaucracies into the personal lives of men and women.

Many debates between conservatives and feminists turn into a clash of two equally limited and unsatisfying ideologies. When it comes to gender in the armed forces, one side invokes the barbarism of subjecting women to the dangers of battle and the need to preserve traditional sexual distinctions; the other side insists that physical differences between the sexes don't matter and all sexual conflicts in the military are men's fault.[70]

Unfortunately, even feminists who have tried to transcend the mentality of victimhood and gender antagonism—Betty Friedan, Wendy Kaminer, Carol Tavris, Naomi Wolf—have often succumbed to "oppression myths," or failed to overcome the tendency to focus on women's problems. Meanwhile, the young conservative women whose lives represent the triumph of "equity feminism" rarely speak out against the prominence of patriarchal ideology on the right.

A conservatism that came to terms with women's (and men's) new roles would have much to contribute to the discussion of the issues of the day. So would a feminism that repudiated victimhood, gender warfare, and a knee-jerk alliance with the left. But to be relevant to the lives of millions of men and women living in a time of change and trying to find their own imperfect balance between the modern and the traditional, both movements must give up the identity politics of gender and see men and women as human beings—a vision missing from our public discourse today.

Where Do We Go from Here?

In the five years since I began to think of this book, there have been many skirmishes in the gender wars. Some of its excesses have been ridiculed. But for every sign of a return to sanity, there are several signs that the culture of gender polarization is alive. And maybe it's wrong to talk about a "return." In many ways, the attitudes perpetuating gender warfare are holdovers from the past, albeit in a twisted form—such as sentimental protectiveness toward women, or the tendency to see men and women as defined by their sex.

Traditional sex roles will continue to appeal to many men and women, whether for religious reasons or as an anchor in a world of uncertainty. These people deserve respect. As a society, however, it is unlikely that we can go back to the past; nor should we. And the "moderate" solution of grafting women's new rights and roles onto more traditional ideals of womanhood creates a new set of problems. It can leave women painfully torn between two worlds. It can allow them to gain male rights and keep female advantages, while leaving men with fewer options.

In some form, masculine and feminine archetypes, and some of the external trappings and rituals of gender, will always be with us; life would be poorer without them. But when it comes to our essential relationship to the world, our moral reasoning, our duties to ourselves, our families and our society, we should not be defined by sex. We must move toward a culture in which men and women are seen first and foremost as human beings with equal rights and equal responsibilities.

Too many countries around the world still deny women the basic rights of adult members of society (though it's worth remembering that men's lot in these countries usually is not too enviable either). Globally, the fight for women's rights is far from over. Is there anything left for a women's movement to do in America? Many arguments often given for the continued need for feminism—from the "epidemic" of violence against women to the neglect of women's health—don't hold up. There is, of course, room for efforts to bring girls and young women into areas where they are still underrepresented: technology, sports, chess. But when linked to adversarial, victim-oriented feminism, these initiatives may do more harm than good. (The idea of teenage girls' magazines focused on something other than fashions, boys, and Hollywood is a laudable one; but "alternative" magazines that dwell on the perils facing girls under patriarchy aren't much of an improvement.) Institutions from workplaces to schools need to be prodded into doing more to accommodate working parents.[1]

But the concept of feminism or of a women's movement remains too closely linked to the concept of women's advantage, of taking the woman's side. If we do need a movement, it should be an equal rights movement—not a National Organization for Women, but a National Organization for Gender Equality, even if it doesn't make for quite as catchy an acronym. Such a movement would not ask, "Is it good for women?" but, "Does it bring the sexes closer together?" It would stress flexible options for both sexes. It would stigmatize male-bashing just as antifemale slurs have already been stigmatized—and not just for men's sake: if women are allowed to get away with bigotry, it means that they are not being taken as seriously.

As for an agenda for an equal rights movement and for all of us, here are a few modest proposals:

1. *When making judgments that involve gender, try a mental exercise reversing the sexes.* Would a book called *Maybe She's Just a Bitch* (rather than *Maybe He's Just a Jerk*) be displayed in bookstores? Would we laugh at a movie about men taking revenge on their ex-wives? Would we condemn a female politician for divorcing her first husband? Would we condemn a male parent for working long hours?

2. *Condemn women behaving badly as much as men behaving badly.* In addition to judging men's and women's actions by a single standard, it's important to recognize that men and women often have different patterns of behavior, bad as well as good. Women are less likely to desert their children but more likely to alienate them from the other

parent. Men are more likely to dump a spouse who is not young or attractive enough; women, to dump a spouse who is not rich or successful enough. Men are more likely to use their power in the workplace to pressure women for sex; women, to use sex as a weapon. Typically female bad behavior should be stigmatized as much as typically male bad behavior.

3. *Stop politicizing women's (or men's) personal wrongs.* When it comes to manipulating, betraying, controlling, and otherwise mistreating each other, each sex generally gives as good as it gets. To frame these collisions in terms of gender oppression ensures that we get only one side of the story.

4. *Stop applying a presumption of sexism to every conflict involving a woman.* If a veteran female prosecutor was repeatedly interrupted in court by suggestions from her male boss (who had not prosecuted a case in years) until she quit the case and her job, it would undoubtedly be another shocking episode in the annals of a male-dominated judiciary. Such an incident did happen—but it involved two *male* prosecutors in a high-profile Florida trial, and it got little attention except as a setback to the case. There *can* be such a thing as human conflict with no gender politics involved.[2]

5. *Get the facts straight.* The media should not rely uncritically on information supplied by advocacy groups, even if they fight for good causes. (Gender issues aside, it's about time we recognized that ideological zeal can be as strong an incentive to bend the truth as the profit motive.) Professional groups, such as the American Medical Association, should think twice before endorsing questionable statistics on things like domestic violence as a cause of injury to women.

6. *Get over our obsession with gender differences and recognize that the sexes are neither fundamentally different nor exactly the same.* Why does it matter if two-thirds of women entrepreneurs but "only" 56 percent of men like to weigh all the options carefully before making a decision? Why should a "diversity awareness" session at the Citadel turn into a lesson in stereotyping as a speaker from a women's college informs cadets that "boys compete and girls negotiate"? And why, on the other hand, should we assume that all abilities, pursuits, and choices have to be distributed fifty-fifty between women and men?[3]

I would also suggest—with some apprehension, since the last thing we need is another "politically correct" taboo—that we turn a more critical eye on stale clichés about men and women (mostly about men) in popular culture. Do we really believe that when a woman mentions to her boyfriend that they have been together for six months, the typical man's response is to recall that his car needs an oil change?[4]

7. *Take gender politics out of the war on domestic violence.* The media should take a serious look at intimate violence by women, and popular culture should stop treating it as amusing. Police and the courts should enforce the law fairly for both sexes, and counseling programs should demand that women, like men, take responsibility for their actions (and not blame it on "psychological provocation"). Hearings in Congress and state legislatures on gender bias in domestic violence policies would be a good idea. The government, and major charities such as United Way or the Young Women's Christian Association, should also reexamine their connections to the battered women's movement with its radical ideology. At a minimum, taxpayer money allocated for domestic violence should not go *exclusively* or *primarily* to organizations that espouse a view of battering as patriarchal oppression, and these organizations should not be permitted to dictate policy.

Finally, we should recognize our limitations—that is, the unfortunate fact that, short of totalitarian intervention in private life, we are not going to end domestic violence completely.

8. *Reconsider the redefinition of rape.* Rape and sexual assault laws need to be revised to clarify the concepts of force and consent. Statutes should make it clear that while force does not require active resistance, it does require coercion that prevents the victim from ending physical contact with the assailant or puts her in reasonable fear of injury. If some version of "no means no" is legislated, it should spell out that the law does not apply to non-threatening verbal persuasion or nonforcible physical overtures. The litmus test should be whether the victim could have avoided sex without risking physical harm. Nor can the alleged victim's behavior be made irrelevant to the defendant's guilt: it is relevant in many other crimes, including homicide. And the rape shield law, meant to end the pernicious practice of suggesting that an "unchaste" woman was not a deserving victim, should not be used to make legitimate issues of credibility off-limits because they have to do with sex.

Rape and sexual assault prevention programs in colleges and schools have become hotbeds of amorphous definitions of rape. A comprehensive review of these programs is in order. If nothing else, no federal money should go to educational programs that blur the distinctions between sexual assault and nonviolent sexual pressure or manipulation, or encourage women to abdicate responsibility for unwanted but unforced sexual encounters. The term "date rape" should be kept out of the debate about proper sexual norms.

9. *Tighten the definition of sexual harassment.* It is appropriate for the law to be concerned with quid pro quo, sleep-with-me-or-you're-fired job-related sexual extortion and with illegal sexual acts in the workplace or in school—rape, fondling, indecent exposure. If we are to have civil liability for verbal harassment by supervisors or coworkers (and there are certainly egregious cases in that category), the plaintiff should have to show *intent* to abuse. Evidence of a "hostile environment" should require some actual hostility, just as a libel suit requires evidence of malice or recklessness. Employers have every right to establish stricter policies encouraging civility and to fire workers who pester others. But they should not have to fear lawsuits if they do not allow the hypersensitive to set the rules for everyone.

Perhaps, as Justice Scalia noted in *Harris,* the courts cannot do much better than they have, given the vague language of the law. One problem is that Title VII of the 1964 Civil Rights Law was meant to deal with sex discrimination, not sexual misconduct on the job. A new law may be part of the solution. Political scientist Ellen Frankel Paul argues for dropping the sex discrimination aspect and making sexual harassment a state tort, similar to intentional infliction of emotional distress. Feminists for Free Expression, an anticensorship group concerned about "sanitizing workplace speech in defense of women workers," has formulated a definition of hostile environment requiring "physical abuse" or "a pattern of targeted and/or intentional verbal abuse."[5]

10. *Presume that fathers and mothers are equal as parents, whether or not they play similar roles.* One cannot affirm a woman's right to shut the father out of her children's lives (assuming that he is not a sociopath) and at the same time encourage fathers to be more involved. For divorced parents, joint legal and (where possible) some form of joint physical custody should be the norm, unless there is evidence that one parent is unfit or poses a danger to the other parent. Fathers of children born out of wedlock should be encouraged to take on a parental role as well. If we are going to force unmarried

fathers to take financial responsibility for their children, we should take steps to ensure that those who want to be more than wallets have an opportunity to be real fathers—including an equal voice in adoption decisions. Deliberate acts to prevent a man from knowing of his child's existence should be criminalized as fraud.

11. *Encourage women to change their inegalitarian expectations of men to the same extent that we have encouraged men to change their inegalitarian expectations of women.* This does not mean that all or even half of successful women have to "marry down," or that all couples should divide child rearing fifty-fifty. But high-achieving women whose husbands who have taken primary responsibility for the home would not be bad role models for the young and ambitious. One worthy enterprise for the gender equality movement would be to hold discussions on balancing work and family in high schools and colleges. These workshops should not force either traditional or nontraditional views on young people (particularly if they have any connection to public funds). They should simply help clarify the costs and benefits of various arrangements and help girls and boys make realistic assessments of their choices and the consequences.

12. *In politics, stop treating women as an interest group and acting as if women's claims were more legitimate than men's.* One can hardly imagine a president or a member of Congress talking about what he or she has done for *men.* This would be understandable if women as a group were worse off than men. But this is not the case—certainly not in some areas where politicians have touted their actions on women's behalf, such as spending on health. An equally alarming trend is political intervention on women's behalf, in personal disputes related to gender conflicts, such as Rebecca Hansen's charges that the air force retaliated against her for filing a sexual harassment complaint or Dr. Elizabeth Morgan's quest to return to the United States despite her ongoing defiance of a court order to allow her ex-husband to see their daughter, after her charges of sexual abuse against him were found to be unsubstantiated.[6]

As long as women's voting patterns and political interests remain somewhat different from men's, attempts to seek the "women's vote" will continue. Nevertheless, just as most politicians today would recognize that they have a moral responsibility not to appeal to racial or ethnic bigotry, they should recognize that they have a moral responsibility not to contribute to gender polarization.

This twelve-step program may not take us to the Promised Land. Given the emotional complexities and conflicts that surround sexual and familial intimacy, some male-female tensions will always remain. But at least we will be able to look fairly and compassionately at both sides of these conflicts; at least we will not exaggerate them by turning them into political causes or squander our resources on trying to regulate personal interactions between men and women. Then, perhaps, we can get on to the more important business of trying to make life better for all of us—women, men, and our children.

Introduction

1. Christopher Lasch, "The Comedy of Love and the *Querelle des Femmes:* Aristocratic Satire on Marriage," in Christopher Lasch (Elisabeth Lasch-Quinn, ed.), *Women and the Common Life* (New York: W. W. Norton, 1997), p. 5.

2. "That 'I Do' Could Come with a Word of Warning," *Seattle Times,* February 17, 1995, p. B2. Films and books: see Alex Kucszynki, "Between the Sexes, It's World War III Out There," *New York Times,* July 19, 1998. Garofalo: ABC, *Politically Incorrect,* March 4, 1998. "Angry": Renée Graham, "Enough Is Enough, They Say," *Boston Globe,* April 29, 1992, p. 43.

3. ABC News Forum, *Men, Sex and Rape,* American Broadcasting Co., May 5, 1992.

4. Susan Faludi, *Backlash: The Undeclared War Against American Women* (New York: Crown, 1991), p. xxiii.

5. See Susan Friedman, "The Politics of Feminist Epistemology," *Democratic Culture,* fall 1994, p. 21. Judith Lorber, letter to the editor, *New York Times Magazine,* November 2, 1997, p. 16 ("double standards"); Catharine A. MacKinnon, "Liberalism and the Death of Feminism," in Dorchen Leidholdt and Janice G. Raymond (eds.), *The Sexual Liberals and the Attack on Feminism* (New York: Pergamon Press, 1990), p. 5.

6. See, e.g., Joan M. Shaughnessy, "Gilligan's Travels," *Law and Inequality,* November 1988, p. 12; Martha Chamallas, "Feminist Constructions of Objectivity: Multiple Perspectives in Sexual and Racial Harassment Litigation," *Texas Journal of Women and the Law* 1, 1992, pp. 131, 125.

7. Naomi Wolf, *Fire with Fire: The New Female Power and How It Will Change the 21st Century* (New York: Random House, 1994), p. xvii.

8. *Time*/CNN poll, *Time,* March 9, 1992, p. 54. In 1995, 11 percent of adults of both sexes described themselves as "strong feminists" and another 30 percent as "feminists." Women's Equality Poll 1995, Peter Y. Harris Research Group, April 1995.

9. Quindlen: see, e.g., Anna Quindlen, "Time to Tackle This," *New York Times,* January 17, 1993, p. E17 ("The greatest public health threat for many

American women is the men they live with"); "Little Big Woman," *New York Times,* February 2, 1992 (to find politicians who don't sleep around and know about real life, "look for a woman"). Women's magazines: Dianne Hales, "What Doctors Don't Know About Women's Bodies," *Ladies Home Journal,* February 1997, p. 50; Andrea Rock, "Unequal Justice," *Ladies Home Journal,* April 1995, p. 106; "America's Most Sexist Judges," *Redbook,* February 1994, p. 83; Rita Baron-Faust, "Why Doctors Mistreat Women," *Redbook,* May 1989, p. 114; Ellen Neuborne, "Hating Hillary," *Mademoiselle,* July 1996, p. 20.

10. Karen S. Peterson, "Political Correctness Goes Too Far, Not Far Enough," *USA Today,* February 2, 1994, p. 10D (three our of four women ages sixteen to twenty-nine agreed that it's offensive for a man to "talk to a female co-worker or fellow student about her sexual attractiveness); Yankelovich Clancy Shulman for *Time*/CNN, in Nancy Gibbs, "When Is It Rape?" *Time,* June 3, 1991, p. 50 (40 percent of women agree that it's rape if a man argues a woman into sex). Roseanne: Elinor Burkett, *The Right Women: A Journey into the Heart of Conservative America* (New York: Scribner, 1997), p. 250. See also John Lahr, "Dealing with Roseanne," *New Yorker,* July 17, 1995, p. 42.

11. *Redbook:* Jeanie Kasindorf, "Inside the Mind of a Rapist," *Redbook,* January 1993, p. 77; "a woman's distrust . . .": Linda Wayne (Syracuse University), Women's Studies List, (wmst-l@umdd.umd.edu), April 26, 1997. Poll: "Women's Opinion of Men Falls as Expectations Climb," *San Diego Union-Tribune,* April 26, 1990, p. A3; Gary Langer, "Women Find Men Mean, Oversexed, Lazy," *Bergen Record,* April 26, 1990, p. A1.

12. Mill: John Stuart Mill, *The Subjection of Women,* in Alice S. Rossi (ed.), *The Feminist Papers* (New York: Bantam Books, 1973), p. 208; Harriet Taylor Mill, "Enfranchisement of Women," in Alice S. Rossi (ed.), *Essays on Sex Equality* (Chicago: University of Chicago Press, 1970), pp. 108–110. Betty Friedan, *The Feminine Mystique* (New York: Dell, 1963), pp. 260–262.

13. Susan Faludi, "Let's Separate the Women (Hillary) from the Girls (Monica, Linda, Paula)," *New York Observer,* February 2, 1998, p. 1. "Faux feminists": Susan Faludi, "I'm Not a Feminist, But I Play One on TV," *Ms.,* March–April 1995, pp. 30–39.

14. Catharine A. MacKinnon, *Feminism Unmodified* (Cambridge: Harvard University Press, 1987), p. 102.

15. Karen Lehrman, *The Lipstick Proviso: Women, Sex & Power in the Real World* (New York: Anchor/Doubleday, 1997), pp. 5, 198.

16. See Carol Gilligan, "For Many Women, Gazing at Diana Was Gazing Within," *New York Times,* September 9, 1997, p. C4; Jane Gross, "Diana's Death Resonates with Women in Therapy," *New York Times,* September 13, 1997, p. 1.

17. Men haven't changed: Jon Tevlin, "Why Women Are Mad as Hell," *Glamour,* March 1992, p. 265; Lehrman, *The Lipstick Proviso,* pp. 134, 200; Katha Pollitt, "Dear Susan B. Anthony: Three Contemporary Responses," *New York Times,* July 18, 1998, p. B9; Katie Roiphe, "The Independent Woman (and Other Lies)," *Esquire,* February 1997, pp. 84–87.

18. Jessica Morgan, "Feminism Does Not Preclude Using Feminine Charms," *Daily Bruin,* July 15, 1996.

19. Warren Farrell, *The Myth of Male Power: Why Men Are the Disposable Sex* (New York: Simon & Schuster, 1993), p. 358.

20. "More for women": Wolf, *Fire with Fire,* p. 138. Elizabeth Wurtzel, *Bitch: In Praise of Difficult Women* (New York: Doubleday, 1998), p. 30. Osias: A. J. Benza and Michael Lewittes, "Static over WOR Show," *New York Daily News,* July 16, 1996, p. 18; Linda Barnard, "Sex Sells, and She Knows It," *Toronto Sun,* August 29, 1996, p. 69. Newspaper editor: Kathy Bishop, "Sexy Women Get the Power," *New York Post,* April 23, 1997, p. 13.

21. Ellen Fein and Sherrie Schneider, *The Rules: Time-Tested Secrets for Capturing the Heart of Mr. Right* (New York: Warner Books, 1996).

22. Definitions of abuse: see, e.g., Lisa Pohlmann, Skeek Frazee, and Merril Cousin, *Information Guide for Abused Women in Maine* (Augusta: Maine Division, American Association of University Women, 1988, and the Maine Coalition for Family Crisis Services, 1988–1991), p. 8; "Family Violence: Support for Battered Women," (Hyannis, Mass.: Independence House, undated). Sexual harassment: Ruth Shalit, "Romper Room," *New Republic,* March 29, 1993, p. 14.

23. Janet Radcliffe Richards, *The Sceptical Feminist,* 2d ed. (London: Penguin Books, 1980), p. 31.

24. Conservative claims: see, e.g., F. Carolyn Graglia, "The Breaking of the Women's Pact," *Weekly Standard,* November 11, 1996, pp. 29–33. Employers' attitudes: National Manpower Council, *Womanpower* (New York: Columbia University Press, 1957), p. 89; Valerie Kincade Oppenheimer, "The Sex-Labeling of Jobs," in Martha T. S. Mednick et al. (eds.), *Women and Achievement: Social and Motivational Analyses* (New York: Wiley, 1975), pp. 318–319; public attitudes: Roper Poll (for *Fortune* magazine), April 1946. College admissions: K. Patricia Cross, "Women as New Students," in Mednick et al., *Women and Achievement,* pp. 351–353. Fear of success: Matina Horner, "Fail: Bright Women," *Psychology Today* 3, November 1969, pp. 33–38.

25. Deborah L. Rhode, *Speaking of Sex: The Denial of Gender Inequality* (Cambridge, Mass.: Harvard University Press, 1997), p. 44 (charge against "dissident feminists"). Pollitt, "Dear Susan B. Anthony."

Chapter 1. Men Are from Earth, Women Are from Earth

1. Dorothy L. Sayers, "The Human-Not-Quite-Human," in Dorothy L. Sayers, *Are Women Human?* (Grand Rapids, Mich.: William B. Eerdmans Publishing Co., 1971), p. 37 (originally in Dorothy L. Sayers, *Unpopular Opinions,* 1947).

2. Michael D. Lemonick, "Daddy's Little Girl: Is Women's Intuition Inherited from the Father?" *Time,* June 23, 1997, p. 59.

3. David H. Skuse et al., "Evidence from Turner's Syndrome of an Imprinted X-Linked Locus Affecting Cognitive Function," *Nature,* June 12, 1997, pp. 705–708.

4. *London Mirror,* June 12, 1997, p. 2; Orbach, quoted in Tim Radford, "Genes Say Boys Will Be Boys and Girls Will Be Sensitive," *Guardian,* June 12, 1997, p. 1.

5. Skuse et al., "Evidence from Turner's Syndrome of an Imprinted X-

Linked Locus," p. 706. In another study, the gap in social competence is even smaller, with four boys for every five girls high in social skills. Peter J. LaFreniere and Jean E. Dumas, "Social Competence and Behavior Evaluation in Children Ages 3 to 6 Years: The Short Form (SCBE-30)," *Psychological Assessment* 8, 1996, pp. 369–377.

6. Danielle Crittenden, "Yes, Motherhood Lowers Pay," *New York Times,* August 22, 1995. Letters: Peggy Tarvin, "Baby Doll Syndrome," *New York Times,* August 28, 1995, p. A14; John K. Wilson, "Women's 76 Percent," *New York Times,* September 4, 1995, p. 18.

7. Barbara Kantrowitz, "Men, Women, and Computers," *Newsweek,* May 16, 1994, pp. 48–55. Joe Klein, "Socket Moms," *New Yorker,* April 13, 1998, pp 28–32; Ken Auletta, "In the Company of Women," *New Yorker,* April 20, pp. 72–79. Chess: Bruce Weber, "Chess's Problematic Endgame," *New York Times,* December 19, 1996, p. B1. Sports: George Vescey, "Blaze Left Her Mark in Garden," *New York Times,* January 8, 1997, p. B11. Architecture: Jill Jordan Sieder, "A Building of Her Own," *U.S. News and World Report,* October 14, 1996, p. 68.

8. Thomas B. Edsall, "1994's Female Nonvoters Will Support Clinton at Polls, Emily's List Survey Says," *Washington Post,* April 12, 1996, p. A19, and *Times Mirror* poll, October 31, 1995.

9. See, e.g., Robert Wright, "Feminists, Meet Mr. Darwin," *New Republic,* November 28, 1994, p. 46.

10. Angus Phillips, "Battle Lines Were Drawn on Women's Challenge; Sailor Tells of 'Terrible Rivalry' Aboard Boat," *Washington Post,* November 11, 1993, p. B2. See also Mark Starr, "A New Crew Rocks the Boat," *Newsweek,* January 16, 1995, pp. 70–71.

11. O'Toole and Imanishi-Kari: Daniel J. Kevles, "The Assault on David Baltimore," *New Yorker,* May 27, 1996, p. 94. High school girl: Norimitsu Onishi, "The Courts, and Not Grades, May Decide a High School's Valedictorian," *New York Times,* June 12, 1996, p. B5.

12. Peter Marks, "Give Two Hugs and Call Him in the Morning," *New York Times,* January 29, 1997, p. C9.

13. Vivian Gornick and Barbara K. Moran (eds.), *Woman in Sexist Society: Studies in Power and Powerlessness* (New York: Basic Books, 1971); Carol Gilligan, *In a Different Voice: Psychological Theory and Women's Development* (Cambridge, Mass.: Harvard University Press, 1982), p. 12.

14. See Gilligan, *In a Different Voice,* pp. 26, 54. For critiques, see Anne Colby and William Damon, "Listening to a Different Voice: A Review of Gilligan's *In a Different Voice,*" *Merrill-Palmer Quarterly* 29, 1983, p. 475; Lawrence J. Walker, "Sex Differences in the Development of Moral Reasoning: A Critical Review," *Child Development* 55, 1994, pp. 677–691; Stephen J. Thoma, "Estimating Gender Differences in the Comprehension and Preference of Moral Issues," *Developmental Review* 6, 1986, pp. 165–180; Judith G. Smetana, Melanie Killen, and Elliot Turiel, "Children's Moral Reasoning About Interpersonal and Moral Conflicts," *Child Development* 62, 1991, pp. 629–664.

15. Feminist critiques: Zella Luria, "A Methodological Critique," *Signs* 11,

1986, pp. 316–321, and Ketayun H. Gould, "Old Wine in New Bottles: A Feminist Perspective on Gilligan's Theory," *Social Work* 33, 1988, pp. 411–415. Lindsy Van Gelder, "Carol Gilligan: A Leader for a Different Kind of Future," *Ms.,* January 1984, pp. 37, 101. Academic feminism and the "different voice": Mary F. Belenky, Blythe M. Clinchy, Nancy R. Goldberger, and Jill M. Tarule, *Women's Ways of Knowing* (New York: Basic Books, 1986); for a critique, see Daphne Patai and Noretta Koertge, *Professing Feminism: Cautionary Tales from the Strange World of Women's Studies* (New York: Basic Books, 1994).

16. Judy Mann, "Womanthink," *Washington Post,* October 13, 1982, p. C1; Ellen Goodman, "A Little List of Reading for the Beach," *Boston Globe,* August 3, 1982, and "A Political Gender Gap," *Boston Globe,* October 19, 1982; "*Time* 25," *Time,* June 17, 1996.

17. Henry Allen, "The Professor's Conversation Piece," *Washington Post* national weekly edition, March 30–April 5, 1992, p. 9. Some feminists have accused Tannen of whitewashing male dominance. See, e.g., Aki Uchida, "When 'Difference' Is 'Dominance': A Critique of the 'Anti-Power-Based' Cultural Approach to Sex Differences," *Language in Society* 21, 1992, pp. 547–568.

18. Deborah Tannen, "I'm Sorry, I Won't Apologize," *New York Times Magazine,* July 21, 1996, p. 34; Deborah Tannen, *You Just Don't Understand* (New York: Ballantine, 1990) pp. 24–25.

19. Tannen, *You Just Don't Understand,* pp. 150, 151, 267.

20. Ibid., pp. 52, 53, 24.

21. See Deborah Tannen, "And Rarely the Twain Shall Meet," *Washington Post* national weekly edition, January 9–15, 1995, p. 25; Amy Sheldon, "Preschool Girls' Discourse Competence: Managing Conflict," in Mary Bucholtz, Kyra Hall and Birch Moonwomon (eds.), *Locating Power:* Proceedings of the Second Berkeley Women and Language Conference (Berkeley, Calif.: Berkeley Women and Language Group, 1993), pp. 529–539.

22. Gilligan: quoted in Van Gelder, "Carol Gilligan," p. 40. Robert Wright, "Feminists, Meet Mr. Darwin," *New Republic,* November 28, 1994, p. 44.

23. Robert Wright, *The Moral Animal: The New Science of Evolutionary Psychology* (New York: Pantheon, 1994); David Buss, *The Evolution of Desire: Strategies of Human Mating* (New York: Basic Books, 1994); Matt Ridley, *The Red Queen: Sex and the Evolution of Human Nature* (New York: Macmillan, 1993); Steven Pinker, *How the Mind Works* (New York: W. W. Norton, 1997).

24. Wright, "Feminists, Meet Mr. Darwin," p. 44; Ridley, *The Red Queen,* p. 263; Kingsley R. Browne, "Sex and Temperament in Modern Society: A Darwinian View of the Glass Ceiling and the Gender Gap," *Arizona Law Review* 37, 1995, pp. 973–1106; Sarah Blaffer Hrdy, *The Woman That Never Evolved* (Cambridge, Mass.: Harvard University Press, 1982), pp. 96–130.

25. Thomas Nagel, *The Last Word* (New York: Oxford University Press, 1997), p. 131.

26. Natalie Angier, "Does Testosterone Equal Aggression? Maybe Not," *New York Times,* June 20, 1995, p. A1; Anne Campbell, Steven Muncer, and Josie Odber, "Aggression and Testosterone: Testing a Bio-Social Model," *Aggressive Behavior* 23, 1997, pp. 229–238.

27. Sheri A. Berenbaum and Melissa Hines, "Early Androgens Are Related to Childhood Sex-Typed Toy Preferences," *Psychological Science* 3, 1992, pp. 203–206; Melissa Hines and Francine R. Kaufman, "Androgen and the Development of Human Sex-Typical Behavior: Rough-and-Tumble Play and Sex of Preferred Playmates in Children with Congenital Adrenal Hyperplasia (CAH)," *Child Development* 65, 1994, pp. 1042–1053; Sheri A. Berenbaum and Elizabeth Snyder, "Early Hormonal Influences on Childhood Sex-Typed Activity and Playmate Preferences: Implications for the Development of Sexual Orientation," *Developmental Psychology* 31, 1993, pp. 31–42. Girls with twin and older brothers: Brenda A. Henderson and Sheri A. Berenbaum, "Sex-Typed Play in Opposite-Sex Twins," *Developmental Psychobiology* 31, 1997, pp. 115–123.

28. Sharon Begley, "Gray Matters," *Newsweek,* March 27, 1995, p. 50; Ruben C. Gur et al., "Sex Differences in Regional Cerebral Glucose Metabolism During a Resting State," *Science* 267, 1995, pp. 528–531.

29. *Time,* January 20, 1992; *Newsweek,* March 27, 1995; "Boys and Girls are Different," ABC, February 1, 1995.

30. "Biodenial": Daphne Patai and Noretta Koertge, *Professing Feminism* (New York: Basic Books, 1994), p. 135. Anne Fausto-Sterling, "How Many Sexes Are There?" *New York Times,* March 12, 1993, p. A29. See also Anne Fausto-Sterling, *Myths of Gender: Biological Theories About Women and Men* (New York: Basic Books, 1985), pp. 219–220, and Michael Janofsky, "Coaches Concede That Steroids Fueled East Germany's Success in Swimming," *New York Times,* December 3, 1991, p. B15. Pressure on women scientists: ABC, "Boys and Girls Are Different"; Begley, "Gray Matters."

31. ABC, "Boys and Girls Are Different"; see also Browne, "Sex and Temperament," p. 1053.

32. Susan Goldberg and Michael Lewis, "Play Behavior in the Year-Old Infant: Early Sex Differences," *Child Development* 40, January 1969, pp. 21–31; Candice Feiring and Michael Lewis, "Sex and Age Differences in Young Children's Reactions to Frustration: A Further Look at the Goldberg and Lewis Subjects," *Child Development* 50, 1979, pp. 848–853.

33. Role of biology: Cindy L. Raymond and Camilla Persson Benbow, "Gender Differences in Mathematics: A Function of Parental Support and Student Sex Typing?" *Developmental Psychology* 22, 1986, p. 28; David C. Geary, "Sexual Selection and Sex Differences in Mathematical Abilities," *Behavioral and Brain Sciences* 19, 1996, pp. 229–284. Cultural factors: Kimberly A. Updegraff et al., "Gender Roles in Marriage: What Do They Mean for Girls' and Boy's School Achievement?" *Journal of Youth and Adolescence* 25, 1996, pp. 73–88; Jacquelynne S. Eccles et al., "Gender Role Stereotypes, Expectancy Effects, and Parents' Socialization of Gender Differences," *Journal of Social Issues* 46, 1990, pp. 183–201.

34. Making fun of feminists: Betsy Hart, "Kids' Big Gender Gap at Christmas," *Rocky Mountain News,* December 23, 1995, p. 47A. Letters to Santa: "Dear Santa," *Times-Picayune,* December 22, 1994, p. 1H; Mike Padgett, "Dear Santa. . . : Kids' Letters Seek Gifts of the Heart," *Arizona Republic,* December 23, 1994, p. 1; Ben Uhlmann, "Dear Santa," *(Madison, Wisc.) Capital Times,*

December 22, 1994, p. 1A; "Children Deliver Their Holiday Wish to Santa Claus," *(Lakeland, Fla.) Ledger,* December 14, 1995, p. D10; "Letters to Santa," *Stuart (Fla.) News/Port St. Lucie News,* December 18, 1996, pp. A3, A4, A7, A11–13; Converging toy preferences: Chris Reidy, "Wish Lists Confuse Elves: This Year, Young Girls Are Asking Santa for Action Toy over Dress-Up Dolly," *Boston Globe,* December 18, 1995, p. 1; *PR Newswire,* November 1, 1995. Beanie Babies: Jane Eisner, "Beanie-Mania Has Valuable Lessons for Young and Old Alike," *Dallas Morning News,* May 11, 1997, p. 5J.

35. Catherine S. Manegold, "Home Is Where the Soap-Box Derby Rolls," *New York Times,* May 26, 1992, p. B4; Rex Redifer, "Derby Day Gets Hopes Racing," *Indianapolis Star,* July 8, 1995, p. A1; James A. Merolla, "Island Girl, 10, in Ohio for Soapbox Derby," *Providence (R.I.) Journal-Bulletin,* August 8, 1996, p. 1D.

36. Tannen, *You Just Don't Understand,* p. 256; Campbell Leaper, "Influence and Involvement in Children's Discourse: Age, Gender, and Partner Effects," *Child Development* 62, 1991, pp. 797–911.

37. Tannen, *You Just Don't Understand,* p. 130; Elizabeth Joan Aries, "Verbal and Nonverbal Behavior in Single Sex and Mixed-Sex Groups: Are Traditional Sex Roles Changing?" *Psychological Reports* 51, 1982, pp. 127–134 (the students had been asked to discuss an ethical dilemma).

38. Browne, "Sex and Temperament," pp. 1074–1075, n. 702; Alice H. Eagly and Steven J. Karau, "Gender and the Emergence of Leaders: A Meta-Analysis," *Journal of Personality and Social Psychology* 60, 1991, pp. 685–710.

39. Deborah Blum, *Sex on the Brain: The Biological Differences Between Men and Women* (New York: Viking, 1997), pp. 66–67. Research: Nancy Eisenberg and Randy Lennon, "Sex Differences in Empathy and Related Capacities," *Psychological Bulletin* 94, 1983, pp. 100–131; Julie Larrieu and Paul Mussen, "Some Personality and Motivational Correlates of Children's Prosocial Behavior," *Journal of Genetic Psychology* 14, 1986, pp. 529–542; Jo Ann M. Farver and Wendy Husby Branstetter, "Preschoolers' Prosocial Responses to Their Peers' Distress," *Developmental Psychology* 30, 1994, pp. 334–341.

40. Janet Shibley Hyde and Elizabeth Ashby Plant, "Magnitude of Psychological Gender Differences," *American Psychologist* 50, 1995, pp. 159–161; see also Alice H. Eagly, "The Science and Politics of Comparing Women and Men," *American Psychologist* 50, 1995, pp. 145–158.

41. Patrice M. Miller, Dorothy L. Danaher, and David Forbes, "Sex-Related Strategies for Coping with Interpersonal Conflict in Children Aged Five and Seven," *Developmental Psychology* 22, 1986, pp. 543–548.

42. See, e.g., Tsai-Yen Chung and Steven R. Asher, "Children's Goals and Strategies in Peer Conflict Situations," *Merrill-Palmer Quarterly* 42, 1996, pp. 125–147.

43. Physical versus indirect aggression: Nicki R. Crick and Monique Mosher, "Relational and Overt Aggression in Pre-school," *Developmental Psychology* 33, 1997, pp. 579–588. Diane Carlson Jones, "Dominance and Affiliation as Factors in the Social Organization of Same-Sex Groups of Elementary School Children," *Ethology and Sociobiology* 5, 1984, pp. 193–202.

44. Betty Black, "Negotiating Social Pretend Play: Communication Differences Related to Social Status and Sex," *Merrill-Palmer Quarterly* 38, 1992, pp. 212–232.

45. Laura A. McCloskey and Lerita M. Coleman, "Difference Without Dominance: Children's Talk in Mixed- and Same-Sex Dyads," *Sex Roles* 27, 1992, pp. 241–257; see also Willard W. Hartup et al., "Conflict and Friendship Relations in Middle Childhood: Behavior in a Closed-Field Situation," *Child Development* 64, 1993, pp. 445–454.

46. William R. Charlesworth and Claire Dzur, "Gender Comparisons of Preschoolers' Behavior and Resource Utilization in Group Problem Solving," *Child Development* 58, 1987, p. 199.

47. Andrew Ahlgren, "Sex Differences in the Correlates of Cooperative and Competitive School Attitudes," *Developmental Psychology* 19, 1983, pp. 881–888.

48. Joan L. Duda, "Relationship Between Task and Ego Orientation and the Perceived Purpose of Sport Among High School Athletes," *Journal of Sport and Exercise Psychology* 11, 1989, pp. 318–335.

49. David Stimpson et al., "The Caring Morality and Gender Differences," *Psychological Reports* 69, 1991, p. 412.

50. Rae Carlson, "Sex Differences in Ego-Functioning: Exploratory Studies of Agency and Communion," *Journal of Consulting and Clinical Psychology* 37, 1971, pp. 267–277; Jo Keroes, "But What Do They Say? Gender and the Content of Student Writing," *Discourse Processes* 13, 1990, pp. 243–257; Anne T. Greeley and Howard E. A. Tinsley, "Autonomy and Intimacy Development in College Students: Sex Differences and Predictors," *Journal of College Student Development* 29, 1988, pp. 512–520. See also Dan P. McAdams et al., "Sex and the TAT: Are Women More Intimate Than Man? Do Men Fear Intimacy?" *Journal of Personality Assessment* 52, 1988, pp. 397–409; Candace B. Adams et al., "Young Adults' Expectations About Sex-Roles in Midlife," *Psychological Reports* 69, 1991, pp. 823–829.

51. Temperament: Sophia Bezirganian and Patricia Cohen, "Sex Differences in the Interaction Between Temperament and Parenting," *Journal of the American Academy of Child and Adolescent Psychiatry* 31, 1992, pp. 790–801. "Angry/defiant" children: Amanda W. Harrist, "Subtypes of Social Withdrawal in Early Childhood: Sociometric Status and Social-Cognitive Differences Across Four Years," *Child Development* 68, 1997, pp. 278–294. Small differences in compliance: Robert Cairns et al., "Growth and Aggression," *Developmental Psychology* 23, 1989, pp. 230–330. Gail Crombie and Dolores Gold, "Compliance and Problem-Solving Competence in Girls and Boys," *Journal of Genetic Psychology* 150, pp. 281–291; Thomas G. Power et al., "Compliance and Self-Assertion: Young Children's Responses to Mothers Versus Fathers," *Developmental Psychology* 30, 1994, pp. 980–989.

52. Beverly I. Fagot and Richard Hagan, "Observations of Parent Reactions to Sex-Stereotyped Behaviors: Age and Sex Effects," *Child Development* 62, 1991, pp. 617–628.

53. Kathryn Dindia and Mike Allen, "Sex Differences in Self-Disclosure: A Meta-Analysis," *Psychological Bulletin* 112, 1992, pp. 106–124; Kim Gale Dolgin

and Nozomi Minowa, "Gender Differences in Self-Presentation: A Comparison of Flatteringness and Intimacy in Self-Disclosure to Friends," *Sex Roles* 36, 1997, p. 371.

54. Women's magazines: George Simpson, "Why Men Don't 'Share' with Other Men," *Cosmopolitan,* December 1990, p. 80; Kevin Cook, "The Buddy System," *Cosmopolitan,* February 1995, p. 43. Study: Steve Duck and Paul H. Wright, "Reexamining Gender Differences in Same-Sex Friendships: A Close Look at Two Kinds of Data," *Sex Roles* 28, 1993, pp. 709–727. See also Harry T. Reis et al. "Sex Differences in the Intimacy of Social Interaction: Further Examination of Potential Explanations," *Journal of Personality and Social Psychology* 48, 1985, pp. 1204–1217; Rosemary C. Veniegas and Letitia Anne Peplau, "Power and the Quality of Same-Sex Friendships," *Psychology of Women Quarterly* 21, 1997, pp. 279–297.

55. Lynne R. Davidson and Lucile Duberman, "Friendship: Communication and Interactional Patterns in Same-Sex Dyads," *Sex Roles* 8, 1982, pp. 809–822.

56. J. T. Ptacek, Ronald E. Smith, and John Zanas, "Gender, Appraisal, and Coping: A Longitudinal Analysis," *Journal of Personality* 60, 1992, pp. 747–769; see also J. T. Ptacek, Ronald E. Smith, and Kenneth L. Dodge, "Gender Differences in Coping with Stress: When Stressor and Appraisal Do Not Differ," *Personality and Social Psychology Bulletin* 20, 1994, pp. 421–430; Steven E. Hobfoll et al., "Gender and Coping: The Dual-Axis Model of Coping," *American Journal of Community Psychology* 22, 1994, pp. 49–82.

57. In one study, men and women who read several cry-for-help scenarios and chose from several responses were more inclined to offer empathy than advice, though the preference was stronger in women. Elaine S. Belansky and Ann K. Boggiano, "Predicting Helping Behaviors: The Role of Gender and Instrumental/Expressive Self-Schemata," *Sex Roles* 30, 1994, pp. 647–661. In two other studies, women and men held very similar views of "problem-solving" and "nurturant" responses. Mark A. Barnett and Richard J. Harris, "Peer Counselors and Friends: Expected and Preferred Responses," *Journal of Counseling Psychology* 31, 1984, pp. 258–261; Margaret M. Fahey, "Instrumental and Expressive Behavior Styles: Differences in Male and Female Perceptions of Empathic Responding (Instrumental Behavior)" (Ph.D. dissertation, Kent State University, 1990).

58. "Sex is fine": Marty Klein and James R. Petersen, "*Playboy*'s College Sex Survey," *Playboy,* October 1996, p. 64 (the survey was distributed by professors at several colleges; students did not know that it was for *Playboy*). Sex and love: Michael E. Mills, "Gender Differences Predicted by Evolutionary Theory Are Reflected in Survey Responses of College Students" (paper presented at the Fourth Annual Meeting of the Human Behavior and Evolution Society conference, July 1992, Albuquerque, New Mexico).

59. Quoted in Guy Garcia, " ♀ = Coy Banter, ♂ = Nude Blondes," *New York Times,* October 23, 1994, p. H17.

60. Ibid.

61. Leslie Bennetts, "You Are What You Read," *Ladies Home Journal,* May 1996, p. 132. Orgasms: Judith Schwartz, "Can You Have a Better Orgasm?"

Redbook, November 1994, p. 96; Judith Newman, "How I Learned to Have an Orgasm," *Redbook,* March 1995, p. 82; Gail Hoch, "Sexual Satisfaction Guaranteed: The Secrets of Highly Orgasmic Women," *Redbook,* November 1996, p. 98; Hugo Lindgren, "Promiscuous with a Purpose," *Elle,* November 1996, p. 152. Adultery: Martha Moffett, "To Cheat or Not to Cheat?" *Cosmopolitan,* April 1995, p. 82; Mike Sager, "To Cheat or Not to Cheat: Advice for the Sorely Tempted," *GQ,* September 1996, p. 184. See also "The Affair," *Mirabella,* March–April 1996, p. 76; "The White-Hot Love Affair," *Woman's Own,* December 1994.

62. Maureen Dowd, "Men Behaving Badly," *New York Times,* September 29, 1996, p. E15; Jerry Adler, "Adultery: A New Furor over an Old Sin," *Newsweek,* p. 60.

63. Robert T. Michael, John H. Gagnon, Edward O. Laumann, and Gina Kolata, *Sex in America: A Definitive Survey* (Boston: Little, Brown, 1994), p. 236.

64. Russell Knoth, Kelly Boyd, and Barry Singer, "Empirical Tests of Sexual Selection Theory: Predictions of Sex Difference in Onset, Intensity, and Time Course of Sexual Arousal," *Journal of Sex Research* 24, 1988, pp. 73–89.

65. Howard Ehrlichman and Rosalind Eichenstein, "Private Wishes: Gender Similarities and Differences," *Sex Roles* 26, 1992, p. 399.

66. Mills, "Gender Differences Predicted by Evolutionary Theory."

67. Russell D. Clark and Elaine Hatfield, "Gender Differences in Receptivity to Sexual Offers," *Journal of Psychology and Human Sexuality* 2, 1989, pp. 39–55. In the follow-up study, when the fictitious sexual partner was a friend of a friend, 5 percent of the women accepted. Single bars: see, e.g., Edward S. Herold and Dawn-Marie K. Mewhinney, "Gender Differences in Casual Sex and AIDS Prevention: A Survey of Dating Bars," *Journal of Sex Research* 30, 1993, pp. 36–42.

68. Martin Fiebert and Lisa M. Tucci, "Sexual Coercion: Men Victimized by Women," *Journal of Men's Studies* 6, 1998, pp. 127–134.

69. Michael et al., *Sex in America,* p. 150.

70. Wright, "Feminists, Meet Mr. Darwin," p. 37.

71. Wright, *The Moral Animal,* p. 88.

72. David M. Buss, "Conflict Between the Sexes: Strategic Interference and the Evocation of Anger and Upset," *Journal of Personality and Social Psychology* 56, 1989, pp. 733–747. Other study: Dean M. Busby and Susan V. Compton, "Patterns of Sexual Coercion in Adult Heterosexual Relationships: An Exploration of Male Victimization," *Family Process* 36, 1997, pp. 81–94.

73. The numbers of subjects who find emotional infidelity more distressing vary greatly: 40 percent of men and 83 percent of women (David M. Buss et al., "Sex Differences in Jealousy: Evolution, Physiology, and Psychology," *Psychological Science* 3, 1992, pp. 251–255); 53 percent of men and 88 percent of women (Christine R. Harris and Nicholas Christenfeld, "Gender, Jealousy, and Reason," *Psychological Science* 7, 1996, pp. 363–366); 50 percent of men and 75 percent of women and 42 percent of men and 62 percent of women (two samples in David A. DeSteno and Peter Salovey, "Evolutionary Origins of Sex Differences in Jealousy?" *Psychological Science* 7, 1996, pp. 367–372). Considering divorce: Mills, "Gender Differences Predicted by Evolutionary Theory." These surveys mostly

involve unmarried college students. In a large survey of married couples, more men (12 percent) than women (9 percent) said they would not be bothered if their spouse had an occasional sexual fling. Philip Blumstein and Pepper Schwartz, *American Couples* (New York: William Morrow & Co., 1983), p. 254.

74. Wright, *The Moral Animal*, pp. 71, 139; Arlette Greer and David Buss, "Tactics for Promoting Sexual Encounters," *Journal of Sex Research* 31, 1994, p. 187.

75. Concerns about violence and disease: Herold and Mewhinney, "Gender Differences in Casual Sex."

76. High-status women valuing male attractiveness: Jill Neimark, "The Beefcaking of America," *Psychology Today,* November–December 1994, p. 32. Dowry: see Peter Gay, *The Tender Passion* (Oxford: Oxford University Press, 1986), p. 102. Abramson: Joe Morgenstern, "Killer in the Courtroom," *Playboy,* October 1994, p. 114; Thatcher: Beatrix Campbell, "The Path to Power," *New Statesman and Society,* June 23, 1995, p. 45. Boy toys: William Stadiem, "For the Hollywood Divorcée Who Has Everything: A Studly New Bimboy," *Cosmopolitan,* April 1995, p. 180.

77. Wright, *The Moral Animal*, pp. 81, 74.

78. Men are far more likely to find sex with a stranger or casual acquaintance at least somewhat satisfying, but few see it as very satisfying. Mills, "Gender Differences Predicted by Evolutionary Theory." On fantasy see, e.g., Bing Hsu et al., "Gender Differences in Sexual Fantasy and Behavior in a College Population: A Ten-Year Replication," *Journal of Sex and Marital Therapy* 20, 1994, pp. 103–118; Cindy M. Meston et al., "Ethnic and Gender Differences in Sexuality: Variations in Sexual Behavior Between Asian and Non-Asian University Students," *Archives of Sexual Behavior* 25, 1996, pp. 33–57. On sexual urges see, e.g., Knoth, Boyd, and Singer, "Empirical Tests of Sexual Selection Theory" (among college students, 14 percent of men and 7 percent of women said that sexual arousal bothers them enough to interfere with their studies several times a day, while 34 percent of men and 16 percent of women said this occurred once a day).

79. Michael et al., *Sex in America,* p. 148.

80. Janet S. Hyde, "Meta-Analysis and the Psychology of Gender Differences," *Signs* 16, 1990, p. 64. Hyde believes that whether differences in spatial ability are of biological origin is an open question.

81. Arianna Stassinopoulos, *The Female Woman* (New York: Random House, 1973), p. 101. Accountants: U.S. Department of Labor, Bureau of Labor Statistics: Employed persons by detailed occupation, sex, race, and Hispanic origin, 1993 annual averages.

82. "Girls Seek Equal Use of All Fields for Softball," *New York Times,* May 10, 1998, p. 26; Craig L. Hymowitz, "Losers on the Level Playing Field; How Men's Sports Got Sacked by Quotas, Bureaucrats and Title IX," *Washington Post,* September 24, 1995, p. C5; Walter Olson, "Title IX from Outer Space," *Reason,* February 1998, pp. 50–51.

83. Abby Goodnough, "The Perks of Equality," *New York Times,* December 16, 1996, p. B1.

84. March Peyser, "A Tragedy Yields Insight into Gender," *Newsweek,* March

24, 1997, p. 66; Mark Starr and Debra Rosenberg, "She's Breaking the Ice," *Newsweek*, March 24, 1997, p. 67.

85. England: Robert Matthews, "Taller and Wider Women Match Men in Arrogance," *London Sunday Telegraph*, July 21, 1996; Fred Brock, "Taking Hold of the Purse Strings, and Holding Their Own," *New York Times*, October 20, 1996, p. 8F. Gambling: Joyce Hoffman, "Women and Gambling," *Washington Post Magazine*, February 10, 1985, p. 10 (the proportion of women among problem gamblers has risen from 5 percent in 1975 to 33 percent in 1986); Joseph Hraba and Gang Lee, "Gender, Gambling and Problem Gambling," *Journal of Gambling Studies* 12, 1996, pp. 83–101. Substance abuse: Ronald Kotulak, "Women Narrow Gender Gap in Drug, Alcohol Abuse," *Chicago Tribune*, June 6, 1996, p. 1.

86. Biology and behavior: Begley, "Gray Matters," p. 54; Celia L. Moore, "Another Psychobiological View of Sexual Differentiation," *Developmental Review* 5, 1985, pp. 18–55; Blum, *Sex on the Brain*, pp. 121–122, 282. Modeling same-sex behavior: Browne, "Sex and Temperament," pp. 1051, 1064.

87. Alice H. Eagly, "The Science and Politics of Comparing Women and Men," *American Psychologist* 50, 1995, pp. 145–158 at 152.

88. Browne, "Sex and Temperament," p. 1098. Browne cites an article by David Popenoe ("Parental Androgyny," *Society*, September–October 1993, p. 5) asserting that "role-reversed" couples have a high rate of marital dissatisfaction and instability. But Popenoe cites no sources.

89. Margaret Brinig, "Why Can't a Woman Be More Like a Man?" (manuscript on file with author); 1990–1991 data from the Arlington, Virginia, County Clerk's Office.

90. "Each sex . . .": Browne, "Sex and Temperament," p. 1084, quoting Joseph E. Garai and Amram Scheinfeld, "Sex Differences in Mental and Behavioral Traits," *Genetic Psychology Monographs* 77, 1968. ADHD: see G. Pascal Zachary, "Male Order: Boys Used to Be Boys, But Do Some Now See Boyhood as a Malady?" *Wall Street Journal*, May 2, 1997, p. A1. Performing arts and student government: U.S. Department of Education, National Center for Education Statistics, *Digest of Education Statistics 1993*, Table 142.

91. Wright, "Feminists, Meet Mr. Darwin," p. 44; Ellen Galinsky, James T. Bond, Dana E. Friedman, *The Changing Workforce* (New York: Families and Work Institute, 1993), p. 28 (managers' perceived understanding of family problems).

92. Belenky et al., *Women's Ways of Knowing*, p. 55.

93. Catherine Keller, "Feminism and the Ethic of Inseparability," in Barbara H. Andolsen et al. (eds.), *Women's Consciousness, Women's Conscience* (San Francisco: Harper & Row, 1985), p. 250.

94. Gilligan treats women students' desire to model themselves on Stephen in James Joyce's *Portrait of the Artist as a Young Man* as "self-deprecation" (*In a Different Voice*, pp. 156–157). In *Women's Ways of Knowing*, women who prefer a "universal systematic methodology" to knowledge based on personal experience are said to "mimic a masculine authority" (p. 221).

95. Remarks at a 1987 symposium on the curriculum, quoted in Roger Kimball, *Tenured Radicals* (New York: Harper & Row, 1990). For critiques of

"difference feminsm" as a throwback to old stereotypes of women, see, e.g., Carol
Tavris, *The Mismeasure of Woman* (New York: Simon & Schuster, 1992); Faye J.
Crosby, *Juggling* (New York: Free Press, 1993); Naomi Wolf, *Fire with Fire* (New
York: Random House, 1993); Christina Hoff Sommers, *Who Stole Feminism?*
(New York: Simon & Schuster, 1994); Daphne Patai and Noretta Koertge,
Professing Feminism (New York: Basic Books, 1994); René Denfeld, *The New
Victorians* (New York: Warner Books, 1995).

96. Belenky et al., *Women's Ways of Knowing,* pp. 5–6. Compare Lynn White,
Educating Our Daughters (New York: Harper & Brothers, 1950), p. 48. Peggy
McIntosh, "Curricular Re-Vision: The New Knowledge for a New Age," in
Educating the Majority: Women Challenge Tradition in Higher Education, ed. Carol
Pearson, Donna Shavlik, and Judith Touchton (New York: Macmillan, 1989), p.
404. For a critique of White's book, see also Betty Friedan, *The Feminine Mystique*
(New York: Dell, 1963), p. 151.

97. Lynn Snowden, "Why Won't the World Accept a Woman Who Can't
Commit?" *Glamour,* October 1995, p. 169.

98. Jay Segal, *The Sex Lives of College Students* (Wayne, Pa.: Miles Standish
Press, 1984), p. 193.

99. Steven Carter and Julia Sokol, *He's Scared, She's Scared* (New York: Dell,
1993), pp. xvi, 76.

100. "What the New Wife Will—and Won't Do," *Redbook,* September 1996
(survey conducted for *Redbook* by the Cyber Dialogue polling firm); survey of
men: Lucy Sanna, "If I Could Make a Suggestion . . . ," *Woman's Own,* May
1997, p. 11. Studies: see Andrew Christensen and James L. Shenk,
"Communication, Conflict, and Psychological Distance in Nondistressed, Clinic,
and Divorcing Couples," *Journal of Consulting and Clinical Psychology* 39, 1991, pp.
458–463.

101. Ellen Fein and Sherrie Schneider, *The Rules: Time-Tested Secrets for
Capturing the Heart of Mr. Right* (New York: Warner, 1996).

102. Poll: NBC Women's Poll, September 1997 (Hart-Teeter). Nancy Friday,
The Power of Beauty (New York: HarperCollins, 1996), p. 540.

Chapter 2. The Mommy Wars and the Daddy Track

1. Anne Barnard et al., "Lawyer's Friends Learn Death Was No Accident,"
Philadelphia Inquirer, May 4, 1997, p. A1.

2. William C. Rhoden, "In Swoopes's Family, a Merging of Dreams," *New
York Times,* August 18, 1997, p. C9.

3. U.S. Bureau of Labor Statistics, 1995 data.

4. Simone de Beauvoir, *The Second Sex* (New York: Vintage, 1989 [orig.
Knopf, 1952]), p. 252; Kate Millett, *Sexual Politics* (Garden City, N.Y.:
Doubleday, 1970), p. 158.

5. Betty Friedan, *The Feminine Mystique* (New York: Dell, 1963), pp. 330,
362.

6. Jong: quoted in Claudia Wallis, "Onward, Women!" *Time,* December 4,
1989, p. 85.

7. See, e.g., Laura Shapiro, "The Myth of Quality Time," *Newsweek,* May 12,

1997, pp. 62–71.

8. Dana Mack, *The Assault on Parenthood: How Our Culture Undermines the Family* (New York: Simon & Schuster, 1997), pp. 267–268, 22, 193–194.

9. Susan Baer, "Many a Harried Woman Longs for Stay-at-Home Role," *Baltimore Sun*, May 9, 1997, p. 1A.

10. Pew Research Center, *Motherhood Today—A Tough Job, Less Ably Done* (Washington, D.C., May 9, 1997). Headlines: *Arizona Republic*, May 9, 1997; *Bergen (N.J.) Record*, May 11, 1997.

11. 1990 Virginia Slims Opinion Poll (Roper Organization); Virginia Slims American Women's Poll 1995 (Roper).

12. Robert J. Samuelson, "The Two-Earner Myth," *Washington Post National Weekly*, January 27, 1997, p. 5.

13. *Time/CNN* poll (Yankelovich Clancy Shulman), February 1992 (80 percent agreed that "women have as much responsibility to support a family as men do"). Beverly H. Burris, "Employed Mothers: The Impact of Class and Marital Status on the Prioritizing of Family and Work," *Social Science Quarterly* 72, 1991, p. 55.

14. Virginia Slims Poll, 1995. Louis Genevie and Eva Margolies, *The Motherhood Report: How Women Feel About Being Mothers* (New York: Macmillan, 1987), pp. 382, 389–390, 398–404.

15. Terry McCarthy, "A Stunning Verdict," *Time*, November 10, 1997; Margaret Carlson, "Home Alone," *Time*, November 10, 1997; Terry McCarthy, "One Mother's Story," *Time*, November 24, 1997; Katha Pollitt, "Killer Moms, Working Nannies," *Nation*, November 24, 1997.

16. National Opinion Research Center, General Social Survey 1994 ("preschool child likely to suffer"); Virginia Slims American Women's Poll 1995.

17. Thomas E. Ricks, "Day Care for Infants Is Challenged by Research on Psychological Risks," *Wall Street Journal*, March 3 1987; Jay Belsky and David Eggebeen, "Scientific Criticism and the Study of Early and Extensive Maternal Employment," *Journal of Marriage and the Family* 53, 1991, pp. 1107–1110.

18. Richard Lacayo, "The Kids Are All Right: Day Care—A New Study Says It's Mostly Harmless, Sometimes Helpful and Less Important Than Home," *Time*, April 14, 1997, p. 76; See also Susan Chira, "Study Says Babies in Child Care Keep Secure Bonds to Mothers," *New York Times*, April 21, 1996, p. 1; Barbara Vobejda, "Day Care Study Offers Reassurance to Working Parents," *Washington Post*, April 4, 1997, p. A1. Studies: NICHD Early Child Care Research Network, "The Effects of Infant Child Care on Infant-Mother Attachment Security: Results of the NICHD Study of Early Child Care," *Child Development* 68, 1997, pp. 860–879; NICHD Early Child Care Research Network, "Child Care and Mother-Child Interaction at 24 and 36 Months," *Developmental Psychology*, forthcoming).

19. Other studies: see Michael E. Lamb et al., "Nonmaternal Care and the Security of Infant-Mother Attachment: A Reanalysis of the Data," *Infant Behavior and Development* 15, 1992, pp. 71–83. Alarmism: see, e.g., Maggie Gallagher, "Day Careless," *National Review*, January 24, 1998, pp. 37–43; Andrew Peyton Thomas, "A Dangerous Experiment in Child-Rearing," *Wall Street Journal*, January 8, 1998,

p. A8.

20. Studies: Ellen Galinsky et al., *The Study of Children in Family Child Care and Relative Care* (New York: Families and Work Institute, 1994); S. Helburn et al., *Cost, Quality, and Child Outcomes in Child Care Centers: Executive Summary* (Denver: University of Colorado, 1995); see also Susan Chira, "Care at Child Day Centers Is Rated as Poor," *New York Times,* February 7, 1995, p. A12. Citations by conservatives: Michael Kelly, "The Depressing Truths on the Day-Care Crisis," *New York Post,* January 14, 1998, p. 31; Gallagher, "Day Careless." NICHD study: NICHD Early Child Care Research Network, "Characteristics of Infant Child Care: Factors Contributing to Positive Caregiving," *Early Childhood Research Quarterly* 11, 1996, pp. 269–306.

21. Jay Belsky and David Eggebeen, "Early and Extensive Maternal Employment and Young Children's Socioemotional Development: Children of the National Longitudinal Survey of Youth," *Journal of Marriage and the Family* 53, 1991, pp. 1083–1098; Theodore N. Greenstein, "Maternal Employment and Child Behavioral Outcomes: A Household Economics Analysis," *Journal of Family Issues* 14, 1993, pp. 323–354; Toby L. Parcel and Elizabeth G. Menaghan, "Early Parental Work, Family Social Capital, and Early Childhood Outcomes," *American Journal of Sociology* 99, 1994, pp. 972–1009.

22. Theodore N. Greenstein, "Are the 'Most Advantaged' Children Truly Disadvantaged by Early Maternal Employment?" *Journal of Family Issues* 16, 1995, pp. 149–169; Martha J. Moorehouse, "Linking Maternal Employment Patterns to Mother-Child Activities and Children's School Competence," *Developmental Psychology* 27, 1991, pp. 295–303.

23. Pew Research Center, *Motherhood Today,* p. 11.

24. Maryse H. Richards and Elena Duckett, "The Relationship of Maternal Employment to Early Adolescent Daily Experience With and Without Parents," *Child Development* 65, 1994, pp. 225–236.

25. Susan Chira, "Parents Take Less of a Role as Pupils Age," *New York Times,* September 5, 1994, p. 6 (reporting on the study by Nicholas Zill and Christine Winquist Nord, "Running in Place: How American Families Are Faring in a Changing Economy and an Individualistic Society").

26. Schlessinger: see James K. Glassman, "A Moralist on the Air," *Weekly Standard,* May 6, 1996, pp. 35–48. Rosemond: see Beth Brophy, "Because I Said So! Parents Are Responding to John Rosemond's Tough Love," *U.S. News and World Report,* November 10, 1997, pp. 69–71.

27. Precocious tots: see Mona Charen, "Why I Hate 'Anti-Family' Feminists," *Atlanta Constitution,* October 4, 1994, p. A19. Children's responses: Martha Hemphill, "Having Their Say," *Atlanta Journal-Constitution,* April 25, 1996, p. E1. Daughters of professional women: Marylou Tousignant, "'Superwoman' Losing Hero Status: Some Gifted Girls Loath to Juggle Work, Family, U-Va. Study Shows," *Washington Post,* January 3, 1995, p. B1. College women: Judith S. Bridges and Claire Etaugh, "Black and White College Women's Maternal Employment Outcome Expectations and Their Desired Timing of Maternal Employment," *Sex Roles* 35, 1996, pp. 543–562. Young adults: cited in Reed Abelson, "When Waaa Turns to Why," *New York Times,* November 11, 1997, p. D1.

28. Joannie M. Schrof, "No Whining!" *U.S. News and World Report,* July 14, 1997, p. 54.

29. Ellen Galinsky, James T. Bond, and Dana E. Friedman, *The Changing Workforce* (New York: Families and Work Institute, 1993), pp. 25, 28, 80–81.

30. Arlie Hochschild (with Anne Machung), *The Second Shift* (New York: Avon, 1989). Time-use studies: John P. Robinson and Geoffrey Godbey, *Time for Life: The Surprising Ways in Which Americans Use Their Time* (University Park: Pennsylvania State University Press, 1997), p. 108.

31. Rhona Mahony, *Kidding Ourselves: Breadwinning, Babies, and Bargaining Power* (New York: Basic Books, 1995).

32. CNBC, *Equal Time,* May 28, 1997.

33. Karen Foerstel, "Leaving House for Home: Molinari's Hubby Quits Congress," *New York Post,* February 26, 1998, p. 3.

34. See Lynn Langway, "A New Kind of Life with Father," *Newsweek,* November 30, 1981, pp. 93–99; Amy Saltzman with Patrick Barry, "The Superdad Juggling Act," *U.S. News and World Report,* June 20, 1988, pp. 67–70.

35. Maggie Gallagher, "The Price of the New 'Equality,'" *New York Post,* April 27, 1998, p. 29; citing Peggy Orenstein, "Almost Equal," *New York Times Magazine,* April 5, 1998. Gallagher writes that in a typical day, the father's caretaking role consists of checking his son's backpack in the morning and measuring out a dose of ear medicine for his five-year-old daughter, and later taking spaghetti sauce out of the freezer so that his wife can make dinner. Gallagher forgets to mention that he also drops off his daughter at preschool, tidies up the house after coming home from his university classes, checks his son's homework, sets the table for dinner, reads to his daughter, and lines up the babysitter.

36. Norman Podhoretz, "Our Endangered Species: Fathers," *New York Post,* June 17, 1986, p. 51; David Blankenhorn, *Fatherless America* (New York: Basic Books, 1995), pp. 101–102; Mack, *The Assault on Parenthood,* pp. 262–263 (stay-at-home dads), 270 (emphasis on gender differences).

37. Blankenhorn, *Fatherless America,* pp. 101, 118–119, 199, 219. See also Don Feder, "Life Without Fathers," *Washington Times,* June 19, 1994, p. B4.

38. Gail F. Nelson and Alan Fogel, "Learning to Care: Boys Are as Nurturant as Girls, But in Different Ways," *Psychology Today,* January 1988, p. 38.

39. Primates: Louise Silverstein, "Primate Research, Family Politics, and Social Policy: Transforming 'Cads' into 'Dads,'" *Journal of Family Psychology* 7, 1993, pp. 267–282; Michael E. Lamb, "Biological Determinism Redux," *Journal of Family Psychology* 7, 1993, pp. 301–304. Responsiveness to infants: Phyllis W. Berman, "Are Women More Responsive Than Men to the Young? A Review of Developmental and Situational Variables," *Psychological Bulletin* 88, 1980, pp. 668–695. Children and infants: Judith E. Owen Blakemore, "Children's Nurturant Interactions with Their Infant Siblings: An Exploration of Gender Differences and Maternal Socialization," *Sex Roles* 22, 1990, pp. 43–57.

40. Joann S. Lublin, "Yea to That '90s Dad, Devoted to the Kids . . . But He's Out Again?" *Wall Street Journal,* June 13, 1995, p. A1; "High-Powered Fathers Savor Their Decisions to Scale Back Careers," *Wall Street Journal,* June 12, 1996, p. B1. On full-time fathers, see also Susan R. Pollack, "More Fathers Take a

Career Hit to Be Home for Their Kids," *Detroit News,* June 19, 1998.

41. Barbara Vobejda and D'Vera Cohn, "Today, a Father's Place Is in the Home," *Washington Post,* May 20, 1994, p. A1; Barbara Vobejda, "As Jobs Return, Dad Care Reverts to Day Care," *Washington Post,* April 24, 1996, p. A1; Lynne M. Casper, *My Daddy Takes Care of Me! Fathers as Care Providers,* U.S. Department of Commerce, Bureau of the Census, Current Population Reports P70-59 (September 1997).

42. Princeton Survey Research Associates/*Newsweek* poll, May 1996, and Jerry Adler, "Building a Better Dad," *Newsweek,* June 17, 1996, pp. 58–64. Other studies on fathers' contributions: see Galinsky, Bond, and Friedman, *The Changing Workforce,* pp. 54–55; L. Colette Jones and Judith A. Heerman, "Parental Division of Infant Care: Contextual Influences and Infant Characteristics," *Nursing Research* 41, 1992, pp. 228–234; Brent A. McBride and Gail Mills, "A Comparison of Mother and Father Involvement with Their Preschool Age Children," *Early Childhood Research Quarterly* 8, 1993, pp. 457–477; William T. Bailey, "A Longitudinal Study of Fathers' Involvement with Young Children: Infancy to Age Five Years," *Journal of Genetic Psychology* 155, 1994, pp. 331–339.

43. Blankenhorn, *Fatherless America,* pp. 113–114, 212–213. Poll: Lynn Smith and Bob Sipchen, "Two-Career Family Dilemma: Balancing Work and Home," *Los Angeles Times,* August 12, 1990, p. 1A. Actual versus preferred hours: Cynthia Costello and Barbara Kivimae Krimgold, eds., *The American Woman: 1996–97* (New York: W. W. Norton and the Women's Research and Education Institute, 1996), p. 157; Phyllis Moen and Donna I. Dempster-McClain, "Employed Parents: Role Strain, Work Time, and Preferences for Working Less," *Journal of Marriage and the Family* 49, 1987, pp. 579–590. Texas Instruments seminar: Associated Press, 1997.

44. Claudia Shuster, "First-Time Fathers' Expectations and Experiences," *Early Education and Development* 5, 1994, pp. 261–276.

45. Student surveys: Jean D. Manis et al., *Factors Affecting Choices of Majors in Science, Mathematics and Engineering at the University of Michigan* (Ann Arbor: University of Michigan Center for the Education of Women, 1989); Michael E. Mills, "Gender Differences Predicted by Evolutionary Theory Are Reflected in Survey Responses of College Students" (paper presented at the Fourth Annual Meeting of the Human Behavior and Evolution Society conference, July 1992, Albuquerque, N.M.).

46. Nancy Gibbs and Michael Duffy, "Desperately Seeking Lori," *Time,* October 14, 1996, p. 44; letters to the editor, *Time,* November 4, 1996, p. 4.

47. David Popenoe, "Parental Androgyny," *Society,* September–October 1993, pp. 5–12.

48. Blankenhorn, *Fatherless America,* pp. 219, 275, 313.

49. For a summary of research on fathers' positive influence on daughters, see Caryl Rivers, Rosalind Barnett, and Grace Baruch, "What a Father Can Teach a Girl," *Boston Globe,* February 26, 1980. Survey: Thomas G. Power and Josephine A. Shanks, "Parents as Socializers: Paternal and Maternal Views," *Journal of Youth and Adolescence* 18, 1989, pp. 203–220.

50. Mothers' influence: Anna L. von der Lippe, "Agency and Communion in

Three Generations of Women and Their Relation to Socialization," *Scandinavian Journal of Psychology* 26, 1985, pp. 289–304. Parents' expectations: Ellen Greenberger and Wendy A. Goldberg, "Work, Parenting, and the Socialization of Children," *Development Psychology* 25, 1989, pp. 22–35; Lawrence A. Kurdek and Mark A. Fine, "Mothers, Fathers, Stepfathers, and Siblings as Providers of Supervision, Acceptance, and Autonomy to Young Adolescents," *Journal of Family Psychology* 9, 1995, pp. 95–99. Interaction with children: see, e.g., Marc T. Frankel and Howard A. Rollins, Jr., "Does Mother Know Best? Mothers and Fathers Interacting with Preschool Sons and Daughters," *Developmental Psychology* 19, 1983, pp. 694–702; Thomas G. Power, "Mother- and Father-Infant Play: A Developmental Analysis," *Child Development* 56, 1985, pp. 1514–1524.

51. Blankenhorn, *Fatherless America,* p. 119 ("extra set of hands"), p. 277 ("primary caretaker" fathers, citing the findings of Kyle Pruett). "I'm doing things . . .": Shuster, "First-Time Fathers' Expectations and Experiences."

52. Father-child relationships: Paul R. Amato and Alan Booth, *A Generation at Risk: Growing Up in an Era of Family Upheaval* (Cambridge, Mass.: Harvard University Press, 1997), pp. 65, 134–135. Blankenhorn, *Fatherless America,* p. 281. One study Blankenhorn cites as proof that "among couples espousing androgynous norms, marital happiness drops with the arrival of children" seems to show the opposite: the greater the shift toward traditional roles, the less positively the wife evaluated the marriage, though the drop in satisfaction was especially pronounced for women who attributed fewer stereotypically feminine traits to themselves. Jay Belsky et al., "Sex Typing and Division of Labor as Determinants of Marital Change Across the Transition to Parenthood," *Journal of Personality and Social Psychology* 50, 1986, pp. 517–522.

For other research, see, e.g., Carolyn Pape Cowan and Philip A. Cowan, "Who Does What When Partners Become Parents: Implications for Men, Women, and Marriage," *Marriage and Family Review* 12, 1988, pp. 105–131; Francine M. Deutsch et al., "Taking Credit: Couples' Reports of Contributions to Child Care," *Journal of Family Issues* 14, 1993, pp. 421–437; Kirby Deater-Deckard and Sandra Scarr, "Parenting Stress Among Dual-Earner Mothers and Fathers: Are There Gender Differences?" *Journal of Family Psychology* 10, 1996, pp. 45–49; Shelley M. MacDermid et al., "Changes in Marriage Associated with the Transition to Parenthood: Individual Differences as a Function of Sex-Role Attitudes and Changes in the Division of Household Labor," *Journal of Marriage and the Family* 52, 1990, pp. 475–486.

53. Genevie and Margolies, *The Motherhood Report,* pp. 360–361.

54. Hochschild, *The Second Shift,* p. 11; Mahony, *Kidding Ourselves,* p. 6.

55. Divergences between men and women on traditional roles: see, e.g., Sampson Lee Blair, "Employment, Family, and Perceptions of Marital Quality Among Husbands and Wives," *Journal of Family Issues* 14, 1993, pp. 189–212; Paul R. Amato and Alan Booth, "Changes in Gender Role Attitudes and Perceived Marital Quality," *American Sociological Review* 60, 1995, pp. 58–66. Views on housework and child care: Virginia Slims American Women's Poll 1995.

56. Conservatives: e.g., Kingsley R. Browne, "Sex and Temperament in Modern Society: A Darwinian View of the Glass Ceiling and the Gender Gap,"

Arizona Law Review 37, 1995, p. 1097, n. 861. Genevie and Margolies, *The Motherhood Report,* pp. 358–359.

57. Alice M. Atkinson, "Fathers' Participation in Day Care," *Early Child Development and Care* 66, 1991, pp. 115–126; Cowan and Cowan, "Who Does What When Partners Become Parents," at p. 127. Sabotaging the father: see Sara Gable et al., "Marriage, Parenting, and Child Development: Progress and Prospects," *Journal of Family Psychology* 5, 1992, pp. 276–294. Laundry: Shannon Brownler and Matthew Miller, "Lies Parents Tell Themselves About Why They Work," *U.S. News and World Report,* May 12, 1997.

58. Beth Levine, "My Husband's Too Good a Dad," *Redbook,* July 1995, p. 156.

59. Sally Abrahms, "Do You Really Want Him to Be a Great Dad?" *Redbook,* June 1994, pp. 152–154; Thurston Clarke, "Fatherhood: How It Changes the Man—and His Marriage," *Glamour,* March 1995, p. 217.

60. Pepper Schwartz, *Peer Marriage: How Love Between Equals Really Works* (New York: Free Press, 1994), pp. 158–163.

61. Anne Roiphe, *Fruitful: A Real Mother in the Real World* (Boston: Houghton Mifflin, 1996). See also Susan Chira, *A Mother's Place* (New York: HarperCollins, 1998). Judy Mann, "Some Heartening News for Working Mothers," *Washington Post,* May 8, 1998, p. E3.

62. Sam Osherson: quoted in Abrahms, "Do You Really Want Him to Be a Great Dad?", p. 154; Genevie and Margolies, *The Motherhood Report,* p. 358.

63. Mahony, *Kidding Ourselves,* pp. 198, 216.

64. Women's preferences: Mills, "Gender Differences Predicted by Evolutionary Theory"; John M. Townsend and Laurence W. Roberts, "Gender Differences in Mate Preference Among Law Students: Divergence and Convergence of Criteria," *Journal of Psychology* 127, 1993, pp. 507–528. Katie Roiphe, "The Independent Woman (and Other Lies)," *Esquire,* February 1997, pp. 84–86.

65. "I Was Ashamed of My Husband's Job," *Good Housekeeping,* August 1991, p. 28.

66. Joseph B. White and Carol Hymowitz, "Broken Glass: Watershed Generation of Women Executives Is Rising to the Top," *Wall Street Journal,* February 10, 1997, p. A1.

67. Blankenhorn, *Fatherless America,* p. 217.

68. Jill Natwick Johnston, "Of Glass Ceilings and Sticky Floors," *Wall Street Journal,* May 10, 1996, p. A10.

69. Gloria Steinem, "A New Egalitarian Life Style," *New York Times,* August 26, 1971, p. 37.

70. Phyllis Chesler, *Mothers on Trial: The Battle for Children and Custody* (New York: McGraw-Hill, 1986), p. 153.

71. Gary L. Ackerman, "Men: Child-Care Leave for Fathers?" *Ms.,* September 1973, p. 118; John Leonard, "Fathering Instinct," *Ms.,* May 1974, p. 52; Kenneth Pitchford, "The Manly Art of Child Care," *Ms.,* October 1978, pp. 96–98; Alan Lupo, "Life with Alyssa," *Ms.,* February 1980, pp. 77–78; Sheila Weller, "My Father/My Self," *Ms.,* May 1981, p. 53; Letty Cottin

Pogrebin, "Big Changes in Parenting," *Ms.,* February 1982, pp. 41–46; Samuel Robinson, "One-on-One with My Daughter," *Ms.,* August 1984, p. 112; Jonathan King and Mark Shapiro, "My Father–Myself: Men Talk About What They Learned from Their Fathers," *Ms.,* September 1985, pp. 73–80; David Osborne, "Beyond the Cult of Fatherhood," *Ms.,* September 1985, pp. 81–84. Letty Cottin Pogrebin, *Family Politics: Love and Power on an Intimate Frontier* (New York: McGraw-Hill, 1983), p. 206.

72. Letty Cottin Pogrebin, "The Teflon Father," *Ms.,* September–October 1990, pp. 95–96.

73. Steinem: CNBC, *Equal Time,* September 17, 1997. Articles: Rosemary L. Bray, "Remember the Children," *Ms.,* September–October 1994, p. 38; John Paul Edge, "Paternal Legacy: How 'Normalized' Terror at Home Creates the Soldier," *Ms.,* May–June 1993, p. 84; Joy Harjo, "My Sister, Myself: Two Paths to Survival," *Ms.,* September–October 1995, p. 70; Patricia Bell-Scott, "The Artist as Witness: A Conversation with Sapphire," *Ms.,* March–April 1997, p. 78; Susan Jane Gilman, "A Michigan Judge's Ruling Punishes Single Mothers," *Ms.,* November–December 1994, p. 92.

74. Sara Ruddick, "Thinking About Fathers," in Marianne Hirsch and Evelyn Fox Keller (eds.), *Conflicts in Feminism* (New York: Routledge, 1990), pp. 224–225, 231. "Fathers" with a capital F is what Ruddick calls traditional fathers, who, in her view, don't do the children any good at all.

75. Mary Becker, "Maternal Feelings: Myth, Taboo and Child Custody," *Review of Law and Women's Studies* 1, 1992, p. 221.

76. Chesler, *Mothers on Trial,* pp. 35–36, 156, 153–155.

77. Nancy D. Polikoff, "The Deliberate Construction of Families Without Fathers: Is It an Option for Lesbian and Heterosexual Mothers?" *Santa Clara Law Review* 36, 1996, pp. 375–394; Susan Faludi, *Backlash: The Undeclared War Against American Women* (New York: Crown, 1994), p. 404.

78. Katha Pollitt, "Bothered and Bewildered," *New York Times,* July 22, 1993, p. A23; Katha Pollitt, "Are Women Morally Superior to Men?" *Nation,* December 28, 1992, p. 804.

79. Rosalind Rosenberg, *Divided Lives: American Women in the Twentieth Century* (New York: Hill and Wang, 1992), p. 100.

Chapter 3. Oppression Stories

1. Judy Mann, *The Difference: Growing Up Female in America* (New York: Warner Books, 1994), p. 276.

2. Anna Quindlen, "The Glass Half Empty," *New York Times,* November 22, 1990.

3. Peggy Orenstein, "The Schoolgirl Scandal," *Glamour,* October 1994, p. 244; Andrea Rock, "Unequal Justice," *Ladies Home Journal,* April 1995, p. 106; Rita Baron-Faust, "Why Doctors Mistreat Women," *Redbook,* May 1989, p. 114; "How to Enjoy the Battle of the Sexes," *New Yorker,* February 26–March 4, 1996, pp. 176–177 (for pay statistics see Cynthia Costello and Barbara Kivimae Krimgold, *The American Woman 1996–97* [New York: W. W. Norton/Women's Research and Education Institute, 1996], p. 68); Emily MacFarquhar, "The War

Against Women," *U.S. News and World Report,* March 28, 1994, pp. 42–48.

4. Survey by the Gallup Organization for *Newsweek,* October 10–11, 1991, in Karlyn H. Keene, "Exploring American Society: 'Feminism' vs. Women's Rights," *Public Perspective,* November–December 1991, p. 4; Susan Faludi, *Backlash: The Undeclared War Against American Women* (New York: Crown, 1994), pp. xvi, 458.

5. Laura Shapiro, "Why Women Are Angry," *Newsweek,* October 21, 1991, p. 41.

6. Faludi, *Backlash,* pp. 108, 40–41.

7. *New Yorker,* December 23, 1991, p. 108; Eleanor Clift, "Have We Come a Long Way, Baby?" *Washington Post Book World,* November 3, 1991, p. 3; see also Ellen Goodman, "The 'Man Shortage' and Other Big Lies," *New York Times Book Review,* October 27, 1991, p. 1.

8. Nancy Gibbs, "The War Against Feminism," *Time,* March 9, 1992, p. 52; Sylvia Nasar, "Women's Progress Stalled? Just Not So," *New York Times,* October 18, 1992, sec. 3, p. 1.

9. Joan Acocella, "The Politics of Hysteria," *New Yorker,* April 6, 1998, p. 75.

10. Faludi, *Backlash,* pp. 364, 366. For data see U.S. Department of Labor, Bureau of Labor Statistics, *Current Population Survey,* 1983–91 annual averages.

11. Faludi, *Backlash,* p. xvii. Crime rates: Timothy J. Flanagan and Kathleen Maguire (eds.), *Sourcebook of Criminal Justice Statistics 1991,* U.S. Department of Justice, Bureau of Justice Statistics (Washington, D.C.: U.S. Government Printing Office, 1991), p. 372, Table 3.127. M. Dwayne Smith and Ellen Kuchta, "Trends in Violent Crime Against Women, 1973–1989," *Social Science Quarterly* 74, 1993, pp. 28–29.

12. "Already small . . .": Faludi, *Backlash,* p. xvii. Tax reforms: "What Does Washington Have Against Two-Income Families?" *Forbes,* July 17, 1995, p. 37.

13. Barbara Gamarekian, "Women Are Liberating a Citadel of Male Power," *New York Times,* May 18, 1988, p. A24; Faludi, *Backlash,* p. 257.

14. Wilson: quoted in Phil Gailey, "Whither the Women's Movement?" *New York Times,* December 13, 1985. Judy Mann, "The Electables," *Washington Post,* November 7, 1986, p. B3; see also Susan Trausch, "Gains for Women Seen in Midterm Campaigns," *Boston Globe,* November 5, 1986. Numbers of female candidates and winners are from the Center for the American Woman in Politics, Eagleton Institute (New Brunswick, N.J.), 1992.

15. Margaret Carlson, "It's Our Turn," *Time,* fall 1990 special issue, p. 16; Maralee Schwartz, "Women Hold Their Own in Quest for State and Congressional Posts," *Washington Post,* November 8, 1990, p. A46.

16. Critiques of *Fatal Attraction:* see, e.g., Richard Cohen, "A New Stereotype: The Crazy Career Woman," *Washington Post,* October 6, 1987, p. A21; Linda Winer, "A Movie's Dangerous Message," *Newsday,* October 9, 1987. Baby boom: Faludi, *Backlash,* p. 131.

17. Faludi, *Backlash,* pp. 136–137, 116, 128; Janet Maslin, "Cinderella in a Business Suit," *New York Times,* December 21, 1988.

18. Faludi, *Backlash,* p. 148.

19. See Stanley Rothman, "Was There Ever a Backlash Against Women? The

Presentation of Gender in the Mass Media," in Rita J. Simon (ed.), *Neither Victim nor Enemy* (Lanham, Md.: University Press of America, 1995), pp. 131–151; David J. Atkin et al., "Ready for Prime Time: Network Series Devoted to Working Women in the 1980s," *Sex Roles* 25, 1991, p. 677. National Commission on Working Women: Judy Mann, "Women and Television," *Washington Post,* November 26, 1986, p. C3.

20. Faludi, *Backlash,* pp. 147, 153, 168.

21. Ibid., pp. 76, 82.

22. Eloise Salholz, "If You're a Single Woman, Here Are Your Chances of Getting Married," *Newsweek,* June 2, 1986, p. 54.

23. Susan Faludi, "Single at 30 . . . ," *Chicago Tribune,* December 21, 1986, p. X:19. See also William R. Greer, "Marriage Research Puts Three in Spotlight," *New York Times,* July 19, 1986, p. 52.

24. Faludi, *Backlash,* p. 99; Neil G. Bennett and David E. Bloom, "Why Fewer American Women Marry," *New York Times,* December 13, 1986, p. A27. For coverage of the Census study see, e.g., Spencer Rich, "The Marrying Kind; Women over 30 More Likely, New Study Says," *Washington Post,* January 14, 1987, p. D1; Thomas Palmer, "Study: Odds Not So Bad for Women Seeking Marriage," *Boston Globe,* January 14, 1987, p. 3. While Faludi makes much of the fact that newspapers gave Bennett and Bloom space to take on the Census demographers, she leaves out the fact that the main target of their article was the "spinster boom" media treatment of their study. They again stressed that lower marriage rates were largely a product of choice made possible by women's "economic and social independence."

25. Jane E. Gross, "Single Women: Coping with a Void," *New York Times,* April 28, 1987, p. A1.

26. Faludi, *Backlash,* p. 89.

27. Barbara Kantrowitz, "A Mother's Choice," *Newsweek,* March 31, 1986; Faludi, *Backlash,* p. 90.

28. Faludi, *Backlash,* p. 90; Barbara Kantrowitz, "The Real 'Mr. Moms,'" *Newsweek,* March 31, 1986, p. 52.

29. "Feminism's Next Step," *New York Times Magazine,* July 5, 1981, p. 14; Faludi, *Backlash,* p. 76.

30. Claudia Wallis, "Onward, Women!" *Time,* December 4, 1989, and Faludi, *Backlash,* p. x; Harry F. Waters and Janet Huck, "Networking Women," *Newsweek,* March 13, 1989, and *Backlash,* p. 146.

31. See, e.g., Ellen Goodman, "Smart Women Wise Up: Old-Maidhood Beats a Bad Marriage," *Los Angeles Times,* June 3, 1986; Georgie Anne Geyer, "'Why Don't You Get Married?' Shorthand for Curbing Woman's Function," *Los Angeles Times,* June 11, 1986; Nancy Shute, "Studying the Study," *Chicago Tribune,* January 25, 1987; Jane Wooldridge, "'Old Maids'? Not in the 1980s," *Miami Herald,* June 29, 1986, p. 1G; Connie Koenenn, "Return to Tradition? Ads That Call Women Happiest at Home Spark Wave of Protest," *Los Angeles Times,* December 26, 1988.

32. "She's Come a Long Way—Or Has She?" *U.S. News and World Report,* August 6, 1984 ("Or has she?" refers not to possible drawbacks of liberation but to

persisting inequities); Ann McGrath, "Living Alone and Loving It," *U.S. News and World Report*, August 3, 1987; Anita Shreve, "The Working Mother As Role Model," *New York Times Magazine*, September 9, 1984, p. 38; Beverly Beyette, "NOW's Birthday More Than a Nostalgia Trip," *Los Angeles Times*, November 23, 1986; Irene Sege, "NOW Notes Twenty Years of Feminism," *Boston Globe*, December 1, 1986, p. 2; Vivian Gornick, "Who Says We Haven't Made a Revolution?" *New York Times Magazine*, April 15, 1990; Leigh Behrens, "Standup Women: A Commanding Presence on the Late Night Landscape," *Chicago Tribune*, October 23, 1988; Julie Wheelock, "A New Driving Force in Auto Sales," *Los Angeles Times*, November 4, 1987; Juliet F. Brudney, "Attracting Women to New Fields," *Boston Globe*, March 8, 1984, p. 45; Eric Schmitt, "Female Entrepreneurs Thrive," *New York Times*, August 18, 1986, p. D1; Albert B. Crenshaw, "Women Own More Businesses," *Washington Post*, October 3, 1990, p. F1; "Mother's Workday" (editorial), *Boston Globe*, May 14, 1989, p. A34; "The Market for Mothers" (editorial), *New York Times*, May 13, 1984, p. E22.

33. Jean M. Twenge, "Attitudes Toward Women, 1970–1995: A Meta-Analysis," *Psychology of Women Quarterly* 21, 1997, pp. 35–51; Daphne Spain and Suzanne M. Bianchi, *Balancing Act: Motherhood, Marriage, and Employment Among American Women* (New York: Sage, 1996), pp. 181–183, Tables 7.1, 7.2.

34. See Maggie Gallagher, *Enemies of Eros: How the Sexual Revolution Is Killing Family, Marriage and Sex and What We Can Do About It* (Chicago: Bonus Books, 1989), p. 62; Jack Anderson, "Group Boosts Mothers Who Stay at Home," *Washington Post*, May 10, 1984, p. B23.

35. Laura Shapiro, "Why Women Are Angry," *Newsweek*, October 21, 1991, p. 41.

36. Expectations: U.S. Department of Labor National Longitudinal Survey, cited by Karlyn H. Keene and Everett C. Ladd, "American College Women: Educational Interests, Career Expectations, Social Outlook and Values" (paper prepared for the Women's College Coalition, 1990). Wage ratios: Costello and Krimgold, *The American Woman 1996–97*, p. 69.

37. American Bar Association Commission on Women in the Profession, *Unfinished Business: Overcoming the Sisyphus Factor* (Chicago: American Bar Association, 1995), pp. 10, 14, 25.

38. Deborah L. Rhode, *Speaking of Sex: The Denial of Gender Inequality* (Cambridge, Mass.: Harvard University Press, 1997), p. 152. Study: Joy A. Schneer and Frieda Reitman, "Effects of Alternate Family Structures on Managerial Career Paths," *Academy of Management Journal* 36, 1993, p. 838.

39. CNN & Company, May 24, 1998; Heather Maher, "Women's Salaries Still Fall Far Below Men's," ABCNews.com, June 12, 1998.

40. Betsy Morris, "Executive Women Confront Midlife Crisis," *Fortune*, September 18, 1995, p. 60.

41. Anne Conners and Norman Siegel, "School for Girls Only? No, That's Sex Discrimination," *New York Daily News*, November 19, 1997, p. 63. See also Clyde Haberman, "New All-Girls' School in Manhattan: Clamor in the 90's over an Old Idea," *New York Times*, September 6, 1996, p. B3.

42. See Thomas M. Smith, *The Educational Progress of Women* (Washington,

D.C.: U.S. Department of Education, National Center for Education Statistics, 1995); National Center for Education Statistics, *Digest of Education Statistics* (Washington, D.C.: U.S. Government Printing Office, 1997); Westinghouse Science Talent Search Science Service Database (Westinghouse Foundation, 1997); Gail Jones, "Gender Differences in Science Competitions," *Science Education* 75, 1991, pp. 159–167.

43. College data: National Center for Education Statistics. Older women returning to college: Gabrielle Lange, *AAUW Outlook,* spring 1997, p. 15. African-Americans: American Council on Education, *Minorities in Higher Education* (Washington, D.C., 1994). Advanced degrees: Mary Jordan, "College Women's Aspirations Top Men's," *Washington Post,* January 24, 1994, p. A9.

44. AAUW, *Shortchanging Girls, Shortchanging America* (Washington, D.C.: AAUW Educational Foundation, 1990), and *How Schools Shortchange Girls* (Washington, D.C.: AAUW Educational Foundation, 1992).

45. Christina Hoff Sommers, *Who Stole Feminism? How Women Have Betrayed Women* (New York: Simon & Schuster, 1994), pp. 163–164; retraction by the Sadkers, in Amy Saltzman, "Schooled in Failure?" *U.S. News and World Report,* November 7, 1994, pp. 88–93.

46. Jacquelynne Eccles and Phyllis Blumenfeld, "Classroom Experiences and Student Gender: Are There Differences and Do They Matter?" in Louise Cherry Wilkinson and Cora B. Marrett (eds.), *Gender Influences in Classroom Interaction* (New York: Academic Press, 1985), pp. 79–114; Linda Wilson Morse and Herbert M. Handley, "Listening to Adolescents: Gender Differences in Science Classroom Interaction," in Wilkinson and Marrett, *Gender Influences,* pp. 46–47. Claims that boys are given longer to answer: Myra and David Sadker, *Failing at Fairness: How America's Schools Cheat Girls* (New York: Scribner's, 1994), p. 58; Ellen Goodman, "The Course Is Sexism Education, and the Schools Are Flunking," *Boston Globe,* February 24, 1994, p. 15.

47. AAUW/Greenberg-Lake Full Data Report (Washington, D.C.: Greenberg-Lake, 1990). Critique: Sommers, *Who Stole Feminism?* pp. 137–156. For other studies, see Herschel D. Thornburg and Randy M. Jones, "Social Characteristics of Early Adolescents: Age Versus Grade," *Journal of Early Adolescence* 2, 1992, pp. 229–239; Scott J. Cienki and Charles I. Brooks, "Self-Esteem of High School Students as a Function of Sex, Grade, and Curriculum Orientation," *Psychological Reports* 64, 1989, pp. 191–194; Ann K. Mullis et al., "Cross-Sectional and Longitudinal Comparisons of Adolescent Self-Esteem," *Adolescence* 27, 1992, pp. 51–61; Richard M. Lerner et al., "Sex Differences in Self-Concept and Self-Esteem of Late Adolescents: A Time-Lag Analysis," *Sex Roles* 7, 1981, pp. 702–722; Karen E. Ablard and Carol J. Mills, "Implicit Theories of Intelligence and Self-Perceptions of Academically Talented Adolescents and Children," *Journal of Youth and Adolescence* 25, 1996, pp. 137–148. Even studies in which girls score lower in self-esteem find only a slight difference—e.g., Linda A. Jackson et al., "Gender and Self-Concept: A Reexamination of Stereotypic Differences and the Role of Gender Attitudes," *Sex Roles* 30, 1994, pp. 615–629.

48. Recognition of boys' problems: Kate Zernike, "Spotlight on Boys: Schools Not Meeting Needs, Studies Say," *Boston Globe,* January 6, 1997, p. A1; Kristina

Sauerwein, "Boy Trouble," *Los Angeles Times,* November 23, 1994, p. 3E. Girls' self-esteem: Jane E. Brody, "Girls and Puberty: The Crisis Years," *New York Times,* November 4, 1997, p. F9; Judy Mann, "A Perilous Age for Girls," *Washington Post,* October 10, 1997, p. E3; Melinda Sacks, "Growing Up Can Be Hell," *Chicago Tribune,* February 4, 1996. Government initiatives: Department of Health and Human Services press release, "HHS Awards $1 Million to Build Bright Futures for Young Girls," October 15, 1997. Estrich: CNN, *Crossfire,* December 26, 1996.

49. *Elusive Equality: The Experiences of Women in Legal Education* (Chicago: American Bar Association, 1996) ("Many students perceive law school as gender neutral. In fact, the experience of most students may be positive"). For women's complaints see pp. 8–10, 15–17, 63–64. Coverage: "ABA Report Finds Bias Against Women," *Los Angeles Times,* February 3, 1996, p. A4; Saundra Torry, "ABA Panel Finds Sex Bias in Law Schools," *Washington Post,* February 3, 1996, p. A3; "Women Still Encounter Sex Bias in Ranks of Nation's Law Schools," *Austin (Tex.) American-Statesman,* February 9, 1996, p. A1.

50. Judy Mann, "The Pharmaceutical Double Standard," *Washington Post,* May 22, 1998, p. E3; Amy Goldstein, "Viagra's Success Fuels Birth Control Debate: Are Health Insurers Favoring Men?" *Washington Post,* May 20, 1998, p. A1.

51. Joanne Jacobs, "Americans Viagra-vated over the Price of Sex," *San Jose Mercury News,* May 18, 1998, p. 7B; see also Goldstein, "Viagra's Success Fuels Birth Control Debate." Carly Simon: *Newsweek,* May 18, 1998, p. 21.

52. Ellen Goodman, "A Health-Research Bias," *Boston Globe,* June 21, 1990, p. 15; "Medical Bias?" (editorial), *San Francisco Chronicle,* July 29, 1991, p. A18; "Equal-Opportunity Killers" (editorial), *USA Today,* February 10, 1993, p. A10; Dianne Hales, "What Doctors Don't Know About Women's Bodies," *Ladies Home Journal,* February 1997, pp. 50–54. World News Sunday (ABC), May 22, 1994. Clinton: Amy Goldstein, "A Growing Chorus Against Breast Cancer," *Washington Post,* October 19, 1993, p. A1. Schroeder: quoted in Goodman, "A Health-Research Bias." For Shalala's comments see, e.g., Michael Posner, "Women and Depression Studied," *Philadelphia Daily News,* July 15, 1993.

53. Mary Lou Wright, "Killing Our Men," *Atlanta Journal-Constitution,* May 12, 1993, p. A13.

54. Andrew Kadar, "Sex-Bias Myth," *Atlantic Monthly,* November 1994, p. 17.

55. Heart attack death rates: *Statistical Abstracts of the United States,* 1992, Adjusted Death Rates by Cause (Table 117), p. 85. Rosenthal: Elisabeth Rosenthal, "Different But Deadly," *New York Times Magazine,* September 17, 1989, p. 120.

56. *Oprah,* October 26, 1994.

57. Critiques of male bias: see, e.g., Carol Tavris, *The Mismeasure of Woman* (New York: Simon & Schuster, 1992), p. 94. For the study, see "Final Report on the Aspirin Component of the Ongoing Physicians' Health Study," *New England Journal of Medicine* 321, 1989, pp. 129–135. Dr. Lynn Rosenberg: author's interview, October 11, 1994. Low-fat diet trial: "The Lipid Research Clinics Coronary Primary Prevention Trial Results," *Journal of the American Medical Association* 251, January 20, 1984, p. 352.

58. Framingham study: e.g., Helen B. Hubert et al., "Obesity as an Independent Risk Factor for Cardiovascular Disease: A 26-Year Follow-up of Participants in the Framingham Heart Study," *Circulation* 67, 1983, p. 968. Nurses' Health Study: Meir J. Stampfer et al., "A Prospective Study of Postmenopausal Estrogen Therapy and Coronary Heart Disease," *New England Journal of Medicine* 313, 1985, pp. 1044–1049; "Relative and Absolute Excess Risks of Coronary Heart Disease Among Women Who Smoke Cigarettes," *New England Journal of Medicine* 317, 1987, pp. 1303–1309; JoAnn Manson et al., "A Prospective Study of Aspirin Use and Primary Prevention of Cardiovascular Disease in Women," *Journal of the American Medical Association* 266, 1991. In *The Mismeasure of Woman* (p. 102), Carol Tavris wrongly implies that the nurses' study was undertaken to quell the outcry over the all-male doctors' study.

59. Study: Jerry H. Gurwitz et al., "The Exclusion of the Elderly and Women from Clinical trials in Acute myocardial Infarction," *Journal of the American Medical Association* 268, 1992, pp. 1417–1422. Research on sex differences: e.g., H. Bolooki et al., "Results of Direct Coronary Artery Surgery in Women," *Journal of Thoracic Cardiovascular Surgery* 69, 1975, pp. 271–277; L. S. Fisher et al., "Association of Sex, Physical Size, and Operative Mortality After Coronary Artery Bypass in the Coronary Artery Surgery Study (CASS)," *Journal of Thoracic Cardiovascular Surgery* 84, 1982, pp. 334–341.

60. Author's interview with Dr. Marcia Angell, October 14, 1994.

61. John Z. Ayanian and A. M. Epstein, "Differences in the Use of Procedures Between Men and Women Hospitalized for Coronary Heart Disease," *New England Journal of Medicine* 325, 1991, pp. 221–225; Daniel B. Mark et al., "Absence of Sex Bias in the Referral of Patients for Cardiac Catheterization," *New England Journal of Medicine* 330, 1994, pp. 1101–1106; Steven J. Bernstein et al., "The Appropriateness of Use of Cardiovascular Procedures in Women and Men," *Archives of Internal Medicine* 154, 1994, pp. 2759–2765. Unnecessary treatments: see, e.g., Nina A. Bickell et al., "Referral Patterns for Coronary Artery Treatment: Gender Bias or Good Clinical Judgment?" *Annals of Internal Medicine* 116, 1992, pp. 791–797. Female heart attack survivors tend to fare worse than men: in one study, 12 percent of women and 6 percent of men died within a year. But although age and coexisting illnesses did not fully account for this gap, neither did "bias": the men and women had received similar care. Jon Van, "Scientists Find Theories on Heart Disease in Women May Be Wrong," *Chicago Tribune,* November 18, 1990. Media reports: Gina Kolata, "Studies Say Women Fail to Receive Equal Treatment for Heart Disease," *New York Times,* July 25, 1991, p. A1; see also Tim Friend, "Women Lose Out on Heart Treatments," *USA Today,* November 13, 1991, p. A1.

62. Medical research "to the benefit of men": National Women's Health Network, fund-raising letter, 1994 (on file with author). Mortality rates: U.S. Bureau of the Census, *Statistical Abstract of the United States,* 1992, Table 117, p. 85.

63. Kent Jenkins, "Caucus Proposes Women's Medical Office," *Washington Post,* July 27, 1990, p. C3; Dr. Andrew G. Kadar, "The Sex-Bias Myth in Medicine," *Atlantic Monthly,* August 1994, pp. 66–70.

64. Stroke: see, e.g., D. T. Wade and Hewer R. Langton, "Stroke:

Associations with Age, Sex, and Side of Weakness," *Archives of Physical and Medical Rehabilitation* 67, 1986, pp. 540–545; Linda A. Hershey, "Stroke Prevention in Women: Role of Aspirin Versus Ticlopidine," *American Journal of Medicine* 91, 1991, pp. 288–292. Hypertension: Hypertension Detection and Follow-up Program Cooperative Group, "Five-year Findings of the Hypertension Detection and Follow-up Program," *Journal of the American Medical Association* 242, 1979; see also Jeremiah Stamler et al., "Background and Design of the New U.S. Trial on Diet and Drug Treatment of 'Mild' Hypertension," *American Journal of Cardiology* 59, 1987, pp. 51G–60G.

65. Richard G. Stevens et al., "Body Iron and the Risk of Cancer," *New England Journal of Medicine* 319, 1988, pp. 1047–1052; Leslie Laurence and Beth Weinhouse, *Outrageous Practices: The Alarming Truth About How Medicine Mistreats Women* (New York: Fawcett, 1994), p. 63.

66. Laurence and Weinhouse, *Outrageous Practices,* p. 3. Studies: e.g., N. H. Lauersen et al., "Danazol: An Antigonadotropic Agent in the Treatment of Pelvic Endometriosis," *American Journal of Obstetrics and Gynecology* 123, 1975, pp. 742–747.

67. Quoted in Hales, "What Doctors Don't Know About Women," p. 54.

68. Sally L. Satel, "There Is No Women's Health Crisis," *Public Interest,* winter 1998, p. 29.

69. Ruth B. Merkatz et al., "Women in Clinical Trials of New Drugs: A Change in Food and Drug Administration Policy," *New England Journal of Medicine* 294, 1993, pp. 293–296. Women were 69 percent of subjects in tests of anti-inflammatory drugs approved in 1988, 44 percent for cardiovascular drugs, and 30 percent for anti-ulcer drugs. See also Janice K. Bush, "The Industry Perspective on the Inclusion of Women in Clinical Trials," *Academic Medicine* 69, 1994, pp. 708–715.

70. Bush, "The Industry Perspective," p. 708. "Experimental subjects": feminist scholar Alice Dan, quoted in Laurence and Weinhouse, *Outrageous Practices,* pp. 74–75.

71. "Medical mal(e)-practice": Laurence and Weinhouse, *Outrageous Practices,* p. 51. Hysterectomies: Ibid., pp. 168, 173; see also Natalie Angier, "In a Culture of Hysterectomies, Many Question Their Necessity," *New York Times,* February 17, 1997, p. A1. HMO attempts to limit hysterectomies: Susan E. Reed, "Miss Treatment," *New Republic,* December 29, 1997, pp. 20–22 (cover title: "Do HMOs Hate Women?"). Urologists: Geoffrey Cowley, "To Test or Not to Test," *Newsweek,* December 27, 1993, p. 43.

72. Louis Harris and Associates, *Commonwealth Fund Survey of Women's Health* (New York: Commonwealth Fund, 1993). Media coverage: see Karen Brothers, "Women Don't Get Care," *Newsday,* July 15, 1993; Larry Lipman, "Women Feel Shut Out of Health Care," *Seattle Post-Intelligencer,* July 15, 1993; Annette Fuentes, "Health Care for Women Ailing: Study," *New York Daily News,* July 15, 1993; "One-Third of Women Lack Basic Health Care," *Atlanta Journal,* July 15, 1993.

73. Mammograms: CNBC, *Equal Time,* February 7, 1997; "Doctor Group Rejects Regular Prostate Testing," *Los Angeles Times,* March 15, 1997, p. 15.

74. See, e.g., Ellen K. Bertone, "Idea of Choice Must Inform Hysterectomy,"

letter to the editor, *New York Times,* February 24, 1997, p. A14.

75. John Schwartz, "Federal Women's Health Study Faulted," *Washington Post,* November 2, 1993, p. A10; Warren E. Leary, "Study of Women's Health Criticized by Review Panel," *New York Times,* November 2, 1993, p. A16.

76. CNN, *Crossfire,* December 26, 1996.

77. Hillary Clinton: Eric Pooley, "Reinventing Hillary," *Time,* December 2, 1996, p. 37; Kathleen Smith, "Assessing the First Lady" (letter to the editor), *Time,* December 23, 1996, p. 8. For charges of arrogance and hubris directed at Newt Gingrich see, e.g., David Gergen, "After Backstabbing, GOP Backs Gingrich, Sort of," *Los Angeles Times,* July 27, 1997; Dick Polman, "Is He a New Newt? Or Just a Modified Version?" *Philadelphia Inquirer,* May 3, 1998, p. Q10. Critiques of *Ally McBeal:* see Joyce Millman, "Foxy Lady," *Salon,* October 20, 1997; Ruth Shalit, "Canny and Lacy," *New Republic,* April 6, 1998, p. 27.

78. Robert Granfield, "Contextualizing the Different Voice: Women, Occupational Goals, and Legal Education," *Law and Policy* 16, January 1994, pp. 1–26. Rhode, *Speaking of Sex,* pp. 20, 1.

79. Witch-hunts: Tanice G. Foltz, book reviews, *Gender and Society* 9, 1995, pp. 514–515; Mervyn Rothstein, "Kelly McGillis," *Playbill,* July 1994, p. 42; Frank Rich, "Seen But Not Heard," *New York Times,* May 25, 1997, p. E11.

80. Flinn: "Uniform Treatment of Sexes at Issue in Adultery Case," *Orlando Sentinel,* May 22, 1997, p. 1A; Karen Foerstel, "Pilot Is Loose with Truth, Too: Air Force," *New York Post,* May 22, 1997, p. 12; Roger Angell, "Sins Like Flinn's," *New Yorker,* June 2, 1997, p. 4; Naomi Wolf on MSNBC, June 7, 1997. Court-martial data: "Military Double Standard? No, But a Lot of Confusion," *USA Today,* June 10, 1997, p. 12A.

81. Sheryl Gay Stolberg, "New Cancer Cases Decreasing in the U.S. as Deaths Do, Too; Drop Is First Since 1930s; But Minorities and Women Are Still Particularly at Risk—Black Men Fare Worst," *New York Times,* March 13, 1998, p. A1; see also Warren Farrell, "Wrong Conclusion" (letter to the editor), *New York Times,* March 18, 1998, p. A22.

82. Andrea Dworkin, *Life and Death: Unapologetic Writings on the Continuing War Against Women* (New York: Free Press, 1997), pp. 118, 132.

Chapter 4. The Myth of Gender Violence

1. Katha Pollitt, "Violence in a Man's World," *New York Times Magazine,* June 18, 1989, p. 18.

2. See, e.g., Al Guard, et al., "Stalker Kills Wall St. Woman Exec," *New York Post,* April 8, 1994, pp. 4–5; Murray Weiss, "A Tragic and All-Too-Common Pattern," *New York Post,* April 9, 1994, p. 2; Don Singleton, "Commish Eyes New Strategy," *New York Daily News,* April 9, 1994, p. 6.

3. Jack Peritz, "Spurned Woman Kills Ex-Lover," *New York Post,* September 21, 1993.

4. Jane Furse, "Slayer Ends Life," *New York Daily News,* April 9, 1994, p. 6.

5. Shooting: Tom Coakley, "Wife of Marine Flier from Boston Charged in Slaying of Daughters," *Boston Globe,* October 15, 1991, p. 23. Picket: Teresa M. Hanafin, "Pickets Slam Store's Sale of Videos Depicting Violence Against

Women," *Boston Globe,* October 15, 1991, p. 23. Dworkin: Andrea Dworkin, *Our Blood: Discourses and Prophecies on Sexual Politics* (New York: Harper & Row, 1976), p. 19.

6. *New York Times Book Review,* September 28, 1997, p. 23 (review); Deborah L. Rhode, *Speaking of Sex: The Denial of Gender Inequality* (Cambridge, Mass.: Harvard University Press, 1997), p. 96; Helen Neuborne: U.S. Senate, Committee of the Judiciary, *Women and Violence: Hearing on Legislation to Reduce the Growing Problem of Violent Crime Against Women (Part 1),* 101st Cong., 2d sess., 1990, pp. 107, 57–58.

7. Carol Lynn Mithers, "The War Against Women," *Ladies Home Journal,* October 1989, p. 137; David Nyhan, "Shhh . . . 14 Women Were Slaughtered," *Boston Globe,* December 10, 1989, p. A19; Richard Cohen, "Sex and Crime," *Washington Post Magazine,* December 31, 1989, p. W7; Joan Beck, "A Bill That Would Treat Rape with the Gravity It Deserves," *Chicago Tribune,* April 1, 1994, p. 13; Patt Morrison, "A Shot in the Dark," *Los Angeles Times Magazine,* March 22, 1992. Jonesboro: Miriam Zoll, "What About the Boys?", *Boston Globe,* April 23, 1998, p. A19; see also Jenny Stromer-Galley and Kate Kenski, "Gender May Hold Some Answers in Tragic Wave of School Killings," *Philadelphia Inquirer,* April 28, 1998. Anna Quindlen, "Time to Tackle This," *New York Times,* January 17, 1993, p. E17; Bob Herbert, "Wives and Batterers," *New York Times,* June 29, 1994, p. A23.

8. "The Beast: Is Manhood the Root of All Evil?" *New York,* April 22, 1996, p. 15.

9. "Mom Charged in Tot Death," *New York Newsday,* April 24, 1996, p. A23; Marjorie Valburn et al., "Mother Held in Stabbing Death of Son," *Philadelphia Inquirer,* March 16, 1996, p. B1; Rose Kim and Cham Lam, "Twisted Love: Suspect in Slay Plot Saw Beau's Daughter as Rival, DA Says," *New York Newsday,* February 5, 1996, p. A3; Al Baker, "Wife Is Held Without Bail: Gluzman Called a 'Flight Risk,'" *New York Newsday,* April 20, 1996, p. A4; Colin Poitras and Stacy Wong, "Griffin Guilty of Murder; She May Face Death Penalty," *Hartford Courant,* April 23, 1996, p. A1.

10. Judy Mann, "Our Culture as a Cause of Depression," *Washington Post,* December 7, 1990, p. B3.

11. Jill Radford, Introduction to Jill Radford and Diana E. H. Russell, *Femicide: The Politics of Woman Killing* (New York: Twayne/Macmillan, 1992), pp. 9–10.

12. Jane Caputi, *The Age of Sex Crime* (Bowling Green, Ohio: Bowling Green State University Popular Press, 1987); Deborah Cameron and Elizabeth Frazier, *The Lust to Kill: A Feminist Investigation of Sexual Murder* (New York: New York University Press, 1987). See also Eric W. Hickey, "The Etiology of Victimization in Serial Murder: A Historical and Demographic Analysis," in Steven A. Egger (ed.), *Serial Murder: An Elusive Phenomenon* (New York: Praeger, 1990) (about 30 percent of serial murderers have targeted only females and 21 percent only males).

13. Timothy J. Flanagan and Kathleen Maguire, *Sourcebook of Criminal Justice Statistics 1991,* U.S. Department of Justice Bureau of Justice Statistics (Washington, D.C.: U.S. Government Printing Office, 1992), Table 3.28, p. 282.

Lynching analogy: Catharine MacKinnon, "The Palm Beach Hanging," *New York Times*, December 15, 1991. Date rape of gay students: John L. Baier et al., "Patterns of Sexual Behavior, Coercion, and Victimization of University Students," *Journal of College Student Development* 32, 1991, p. 316. Male rape: A. Kaufman et al., "Male Rape Victims: Noninstitutionalized Assault," *American Journal of Psychiatry* 137, 1980, pp. 221–223; Flanagan and Maguire, *Sourcebook of Criminal Justice Statistics 1991*, Table 3.29, p. 283; Sam Roe and Nara Schoenberg, "Rape: The Making of an Epidemic," *Toledo (Ohio) Blade*, October 11, 1993, p. 5. The FBI does not compile data on sexual offenses against males, since it defines rape as forcible intercourse with a female. VAWA lawsuit: *Doe v. Hartz*, 970 Federal Supplement 1375, 1406–08 (N.D. Iowa 1997); No. 9703986, 1998 U.S. App. LEXIS 1918 (8th Circuit, January 26, 1998). See also Nina Bernstein, "Judge Upholds Law Making Gender-Motivated Crimes a Civil-Rights Violation," *New York Times*, July 10, 1997, p. A16.

14. Carolyn Kozma and Marvin Zuckerman, "An Investigation of Some Hypotheses Concerning Rape and Murder," *Personality and Individual Differences* 4, 1983, p. 23; Garfield A. Harmon, R. Glynn Owens, and Michael E. Dewey, "Rapists' Versus Non-Rapists' Attitudes Toward Women," *International Journal of Offender Therapy and Comparative Criminology* 39, 1995, p. 269; Robert A. Prentky et al., "Development of a Rational Taxonomy for the Classification of Rapists: The Massachusetts Treatment Center System," *Bulletin of the American Academy of Psychiatry and the Law* 13, 1985, p. 39.

15. Flanagan and Maguire, *Sourcebook of Criminal Justice Statistics 1991*, Table 2.28, p. 196. Patterns of fear of crime: interview with Mark Warr (University of Texas at Austin) by Katherine Dunn, January 19, 1994 (transcript provided to author).

16. [Pauline B. Bart and Eileen G. Moran,] "The Politics of Institutional Responses to Violence Against Women," in Bart and Moran (eds.), *Violence Against Women: The Bloody Footprints* (Newbury Park, Calif.: Sage, 1993), p. 148.

17. Anna Quindlen, "A Bias Crime," *New York Times*, May 6, 1990, p. E23; Lisa Heinzerling, "A New Way of Looking at Violence Against Women," *Glamour*, October 1990; Helen Neuborne in *Women and Violence*, Part I, p. 59; Linda McCabe, "Womanslaughter Is a Hate Crime," *Los Angeles Times*, December 6, 1991, p. B7; Timothy Clifford, "Rampage Suspects' Words Can Be Used Against Them," *New York Newsday*, February 24, 1990, p. 3; Emily Sachar, "Jogger's Testimony of Terror," *New York Newsday*, June 29, 1990, p. 3.

18. "The Citadel's Culture of Abuse" (editorial), *New York Times*, January 14, 1997, p. A14; Henry Eichel and Anna Griffin, "Citadel Announces Punishments: One Dismissed, 9 Disciplined in Hazing," *Charlotte (N.C.) Observer*, March 11, 1997, p. 1A.

19. Rick Reilly, "What Is the Citadel?" *Sports Illustrated*, September 14, 1992, p. 70.

20. War crimes: "It's about women and children being tortured and murdered," advertisement for the Court TV coverage of the Bosnian war crimes trial, *New York Times*, September 9, 1996, p. A12; James C. McKinley, Jr., "Dead Women and Children: The Toll of Ethnic Revenge," *New York Times*, July 6,

1996, p. 5. Concern about the sexual abuse of women in prison: see, e.g., Pierre Thomas, "Growing Female Inmate Population Facing Greater Assault Risk, Study Says," *Washington Post,* December 8, 1996, p. A18; "Law Bars Sex Between Guards, Inmates," *Buffalo News,* July 11, 1996, p. A6; David Josar, "Justice Department Sues State Over Conditions in 2 Prisons," *Detroit News,* March 11, 1997; Nina Siegal, "Locked Up in America: Slaves to the System," *Salon,* September 1, 1998. Rates of sexual abuse in prison: Cindy Struckman-Johnson et al., "Sexual Coercion Reported by Men and Women in Prison," *Journal of Sex Research* 33, 1996, pp. 67–76 (22 percent of male and 7 percent of female respondents reported sexual assault by either staff or other inmates). Perception of crimes: Katherine C. Kormos, Dean C. White, and Charles I. Brooks, "Sex Differences in Rated Seriousness of Crimes," *Psychological Reports* 70, 1992, pp. 867–870; Ferrel Christensen, *The Other Side of Sexism,* Educational Series No. 1 (Edmonton, Alberta: MERGE [Movement to Establish Real Gender Equality] 1992), p. 11.

21. "High Murder Rate for Women on the Job," *New York Times,* October 3, 1993.

22. Magda Lewis, "Interrupting Patriarchy: Politics, Resistance, and Transformation in the Feminist Classroom," *Harvard Educational Review* 60, November 1990.

23. Rates of violent crime by women: Kathleen Maguire and Ann L. Pastore (eds.), *Sourcebook of Criminal Justice Statistics 1995,* U.S. Department of Justice, Bureau of Justice Statistics (Washington, D.C.: U.S. Government Printing Office, 1995), p. 406, Table 4.8; Rita J. Simon and Jean Landis, *The Crimes Women Commit, the Punishments They Receive* (Lexington, Mass.: Lexington Books, 1991), p. 46.

24. Assaults on women by women: Ronet Bachman, *Violence Against Women: A National Crime Victimization Survey Report,* U.S. Department of Justice/Bureau of Justice Statistics, NCJ-145325 (Washington, D.C.: U.S. Government Printing Office, January 1994), p. 5. Crime rates in New York: Deborah R. Baskin and Ira B. Sommers, *Casualties of Community Disorder: Women's Careers in Violent Crime* (New York: Westview Press/HarperCollins, 1998), pp. 22–23. Feminist views of female criminals: see, e.g., Meda Chesney-Lind, *The Female Offender: Girls, Women and Crime* (Thousand Oaks, Calif.: Sage, 1997). Similarity of male and female motives: Baskin and Sommers, *Casualties of Community Disorder,* pp. 103–126. Girl gangs: Andrea Jones, "'They Get Right in Your Face': Are Girls Turning Meaner?" *Utne Reader,* July–August 1994, pp. 54–55; Murray Weiss and Bill Hoffman, "Three Girls Busted in Park Ave. 'Gang' Slash," *New York Post,* October 2, 1997; Philip Messing et al., "Latest Slash Attack Has 'Bloods' Written All over It," *New York Post,* October 8, 1997; Philip Messing and Larry Celona, "Girls' Fight over Boys Turns into Bloody Subway Slashing," *New York Post,* November 13, 1997.

25. Mary B. Harris, "Sex and Ethnic Differences in Past Aggressive Behaviors," *Journal of Family Violence* 7, 1992, pp. 85–102.

26. Sarah Ben-David, "The Two Facets of Female Violence: The Public and Private Domains," *Journal of Family Violence* 8, 1993, pp. 345–359; male and female aggression: Ross D. Parke and Ronald G. Slaby, "The Development of

Aggression," in Paul H. Mussen and E. Mavis Hetherington (eds.), *Handbook of Child Psychology, Vol. 4: Socialization, Personality, and Social Development* (New York: Wiley, 1983), pp. 547–641.

27. United Press International, "NOW Opens National Convention in Boston," July 2, 1993.

28. Murray A. Straus and Richard J. Gelles, "Societal Change and Change in Family Violence from 1975 to 1985 as Revealed by Two National Surveys," *Journal of Marriage and the Family* 48, 1986, pp. 465–479; Murray A. Straus and Glenda Kaufman Kantor, "Change in Spouse Assault Rates from 1975 to 1992: A Comparison of Three National Surveys in the United States" (paper presented at the 13th World Congress of Sociology, Bielefeld, Germany, July 19, 1994).

29. Mildred Daley Pagelow, "'Battered Men' Syndrome Is a Myth,'" *Los Angeles Times*, July 3, 1994; Jack C. Straton, "Husband Battering Statistics Misleading," *Oregonian*, September 6, 1994; "What About Battered Men?" National Coalition Against Domestic Violence news release, Denver, Colo. July 20, 1994; Lynn Hecht Schafran, letter to the editor, *U.S. News and World Report,* February 19, 1996.

30. Early findings and interpretation: Murray A. Straus, "Victims and Aggressors in Marital Violence," *American Behavioral Scientist* 23, 1980, pp. 681–704. 1985 survey: Jan E. Stets and Murray A. Straus, "Gender Differences in Reporting Marital Violence and Its Medical and Psychological Consequences," in Murray A. Straus and Richard J. Gelles, *Physical Violence in American Families* (New Brunswick, N.J.: Transaction, 1990), pp. 151–165.

31. Martin S. Fiebert, "References Examining Assaults by Women on Their Spouses/Partners," *Sexuality and Culture* 1, 1997, pp. 273–286. See also Amy A. Ernst et al., "Domestic Violence in an Inner-City ED," *Annals of Emergency Medicine* 30, 1997, pp. 190–197.

32. Daniel Saunders, "Who Hits First and Who Hurts Most? Evidence for the Greater Victimization of Women in Intimate Relationships" (paper presented at the 41st Annual Meeting of the American Society of Criminology, Reno, Nevada, November 1989); Demie Kurz, "Physical Assaults by Husbands: A Major Social Problem," in Richard J. Gelles and Donileen R. Loseke (eds.), *Current Controversies in Family Violence* (Newbury Park, Calif.: Sage, 1993), pp. 88–103; Martin D. Schwartz and Walter S. Dekeseredy, "The Return of the 'Battered Husband Syndrome' Through the Typification of Women as Violent," *Crime, Law and Social Change* 20, 1993, p. 254. Study: L. Kevin Hamberger, "Female Offenders in Domestic Violence: A Look at Their Actions in Context" (paper presented at the meeting of the American Psychological Association, San Francisco, August 19, 1991).

33. Dina Vivian and Richard Heyman, "Marital Violence in Clinic Couples: Typologies Based on a 'Contextualized/Gender Sensitive' Assessment" (paper presented at the Fourth International Family Violence Research Conference, University of New Hampshire, July 1995); Michele Cascardi and Dina Vivian, "Context for Specific Episodes of Marital Violence: Gender and Severity of Violence Differences," *Journal of Family Violence* 10, 1995, pp. 265–293. Recent survey: see Patricia G. Tjaden and Nancy Thoennes, "The Prevalence and

Consequences of Intimate Partner Violence: Findings from the National Violence Against Women Survey," paper presented at the American Society of Criminology 49th Annual Meeting, San Diego, Calif., November 1997, and Murray A. Straus, "The Controversy over Domestic Violence by Women: A Methodological, Theoretical, and Sociology of Science Analysis," paper presented at the Claremont Symposium on Applied Social Psychology on Violence in Intimate Relationships, Claremont Graduate University, Claremont, Calif., February 1998.

34. Ronet Bachman, *Violence Against Women: A National Crime Victimization Survey Report* (Washington, D.C.: U.S. Department of Justice/Bureau of Justice Statistics, 1994), p. 6. In this survey, men accounted for about 8 percent of the victims of spousal violence.

35. Ronet Bachman and Linda E. Saltzman, *Violence Against Women: Estimates from the Redesigned Survey,* Bureau of Justice Statistics Special Report, U.S. Department of Justice, NCJ-154348 (Washington, D.C.: U.S. Government Printing Office, August 1995), pp. 3, 8.

36. Mildred Daley Pagelow, "The 'Battered Husband Syndrome': Social Problem or Much Ado About Little?" in N. Johnston (ed.), *Marital Violence,* Sociological Review Monograph, 31 (London: Routledge & Kegan Paul), p. 185.

37. Feminist claims: Pagelow, "'Battered Husband Syndrome,'" p. 188; Lynda M. Carson, "Can Women Be Batterers?" *Coalition Reporter* (New Jersey Coalition for Battered Women), November 1997. Lesley A. Gregorash, "Family Violence: An Exploratory Study of Men Who Have Been Abused by Their Wives" (master's thesis, University of Calgary, 1993); Philip W. Cook, *Abused Men: The Hidden Side of Domestic Violence* (Westport, Conn.: Praeger, 1997); Janet R. Johnston and Linda E. G. Campbell, "A Clinical Typology of Interparental Violence in Disputed-Custody Divorces," *American Journal of Orthopsychiatry* 63, 1993, p. 196.

38. Anson Shupe, William A. Stacey, and Lonnie R. Hazlewood, *Violent Men, Violent Couples* (Lexington, Mass.: Lexington Books, 1987); Anson Shupe, William A. Stacey, and Lonnie R. Hazlewood, *The Violent Couple* (Westport, Conn.: Praeger, 1994), pp. 13, 53, 55.

39. Author's interview with Lonnie Hazlewood, August 16, 1995.

40. Cook, *Abused Men,* pp. 110–119, and Richard J. Gelles, "Research and Advocacy: Can One Wear Two Hats?" *Family Process* 33, 1994, pp. 93–95. The article is R. M. McNeely and Gloria Robinson-Simpson, "The Truth About Domestic Violence: A Falsely Framed Issue," *Social Work* 32, 1987, pp. 485–490.

41. Irene Frieze: Scott Sleek, "Sorting Out the Reasons Couples Turn Violent," *APA Monitor* 29, April 1998. Janet Johnston: author's interview, September 28, 1994.

42. Carson, "Can Women Be Batterers?" Studies: Diane R. Follingstadt et al., "Sex Differences in Motivations and Effects in Dating Violence," *Family Relations* 40, January 1991, pp. 51–57; Cascardi and Vivian, "Context for Specific Episodes of Marital Violence."

43. Author's interview with Wendy Kaminer, February 25, 1994.

44. Stets and Straus, "Gender Differences in Reporting Marital Violence," pp. 151–165; Lisa D. Brush, "Violent Acts and Injurious Outcomes in Married

Couples: Methodological Issues in the National Survey of Families and Households," in Pauline B. Bart and Eileen Geil Moran (eds.), *Violence Against Women: The Bloody Footprints* (Newbury Park, Calif.: Sage, 1993), pp. 240–251; "Physical Violence and Injuries in Intimate Relationships," *Morbidity and Mortality Weekly Report* 45, September 6, 1996 (16 percent of female and 7 percent of male victims seek medical attention for injuries); Barbara J. Morse, "Beyond the Conflict Tactics Scale: Assessing Gender Differences in Partner Violence," *Violence and Victims* 10, 1995, pp. 251–272 (in 1992, 13 percent of men involved in partner violence and 20 percent of women reported some injury, while 2 percent of men and 2.3 percent of women reported seeking medical care). Justice Department study: Michael R. Rand, *Violence-Related Injuries Treated in Hospital Emergency Departments,* U.S. Department of Justice, Bureau of Justice Statistics Special Report (Washington, D.C.: U.S. Government Printing Office, August 1997).

45. Lesbian battering: Achy Obejas, "Women Who Batter Women," *Ms.,* September–October 1994, p. 53. Reena Sommer: author's interview, September 1995. Divorcing/separated couples: Janet R. Johnston, "Gender, Violent Conflict and Mediation," *Family Mediation* 3, 1993, pp. 9–13; assault with hot liquids: Mary Jeanne Krob et al., "Burned-and-Battered Adults," *Journal of Burn Care and Rehabilitation* 7, 1986, pp. 529–531; F. J. Duminy and D. A. Hudson, "Assault Inflicted by Hot Water," *Burns* 19, 1993, pp. 426–428.

46. Mark Gerson, "Race, O.J. and My Kids," *New Republic,* April 24, 1995, p. 28.

47. Marjorie Valbrun et al., "Mother Held in Stabbing Death of Son," *Philadelphia Inquirer,* March 16, 1996, p. B1.

48. Psychological harm: Vivian and Heyman, "Marital Violence in Clinic Couples"; Dina Vivian and Jennifer Langhinrichsen-Rohling, "Are Bi-Directionally Violent Couples Mutually Victimized? A Gender-Sensitive Comparison," *Violence and Victims* 9, 1994, pp. 107–124. "Women live in fear": Ellen Pence, quoted in Tamar Lewin, "Battered Men Sounding Equal-Rights Cry," *New York Times,* April 20, 1993, p. A12. Studies: Neil S. Jacobson et al., "Affect, Verbal Content, and Psychophysiology in the Arguments of Couples with a Violent Husband," *Journal of Consulting and Clinical Psychology* 62, 1994, p. 986; Johnston and Campbell, "A Clinical Typology of Interparental Violence in Disputed-Custody Divorces," p. 195.

49. Morse, "Gender Differences in Partner Abuse," p. 268.

50. Pagelow, "'Battered Husband Syndrome,'" p. 194.

51. Author's interview with Don C., December 1996. Details of his story were confirmed by his coworkers and by Carole Danner, who runs a counseling group he has attended.

52. Lenore Walker, *The Battered Woman* (New York: HarperCollins, 1979), p. xv. Pamphlets: *Family Violence: Support for Battered Women* (Hyannis, Mass.: Independence House, 1994); *Information on Domestic Violence* and *Dating Violence: Breaking Patterns,* Jersey Battered Women's Service; *What Can I Do About Domestic Violence?* Radio Shack/National Crime Prevention Council/National Sheriffs' Association brochure; *You Have the Right to be Free from Abuse,* Westchester (New

York) Coalition of Family Violence Agencies. See also Chittenden County (Vermont) Domestic Violence Protocol, Chittenden County Domestic Violence Task Force, October 1996, p. 18.

53. Associated Press, June 12, 1996.

54. Maguire and Pastore, *Sourcebook of Criminal Justice Statistics 1995,* pp. 354–355, Table 3.127.

55. Doug Brown, "Wife-Battering: Normal for Many," *Los Angeles Times,* June 20, 1985, p. V:1 (Lenore Walker); Coramae Richey Mann, "Getting Even? Women Who Kill in Domestic Encounters," *Justice Quarterly* 5, 1988, pp. 33–51.

56. Al Baker, "Through the Heart: Husband Dies of Stab Wounds," *New York Newsday,* January 24, 1997, p. A3.

57. "Claims of Physical Abuse Didn't Hold Up in Trials of Some Women," *Columbus (Ohio) Dispatch,* January 27, 1991, p. 5F. Sexual jealousy as a male motive for killing. See, e.g., Russell P. Dobash et al., "The Myth of Sexual Symmetry in Marital Violence," *Social Problems* 39, 1992, pp. 71–91.

58. Female violence: John Leo, "Monday Night Political Football," *U.S. News and World Report,* January 8, 1996; Judith Sherven and Jim Sniechowski, "Women Are Responsible, Too," *Los Angeles Times,* June 21, 1994; Armin Brott, "The Facts Take a Battering," *Washington Post,* National Weekly Edition, August 8–14, 1994. Focus on violence against women and dubious claims: Jane E. Brody, "Each Year, Six Million American Women Become Victims of Abuse Without Ever Leaving the House," *New York Times,* March 18, 1992, p. C12; Mary E. Miller, "Domestic Violence: Not Just a Women's Issue," *Charlotte (N.C.) News and Observer,* May 24, 1994; Barbara Vobejda, "Experts Say Allegations Underscore Familiar Elements of Spouse Abuse," *Washington Post,* June 19, 1994; Jill Smolowe, "When Violence Hits Home," *Time,* July 4, 1994.

59. "95 percent": Jon Anderson, "Ending the Madness," *Chicago Tribune,* February 4, 1994; Don Colburn, "Domestic Violence: AMA President Decries 'A Major Public Health Problem," *Washington Post,* Health Section, June 28, 1994. Media coverage: Cook, *Abused Men,* pp. 44–46.

60. Michelle Trappen, "When Love Turns to Rage," *Oregonian,* June 27, 1994, p. C1; Lynn Elber (Associated Press), "Hartman's Friends Say Couple Had Problems," *Philadelphia Inquirer,* May 30, 1998.

61. Female domestic violence arrests: John Johnson, "A New Side to Domestic Violence," *Los Angeles Times,* April 27, 1997, p. A1; Leef Smith, "Increasingly, Abuse Shows Female Side," *Washington Post,* November 18, 1997, p. B1; Mareva Brown, "Arrests of Women Soar in Domestic Violence Cases," *Sacramento Bee,* December 7, 1997, p. A1.

62. CNN, *Crossfire,* July 22, 1994.

63. Doherty: J. D. Reed, "A Life on the Edge," *People,* June 14, 1993, pp. 90–96; policeman: Patt Morrison, "When Women Abuse Their Spouses," *Los Angeles Times,* June 30, 1991, p. B13.

64. Margery D. Rosen, "He Hit Me," *Ladies Home Journal,* April 1996, p. 16; *MacNeil/Lehrer NewsHour,* June 23, 1994; Wayne Parry, "Mother Accused of Killing Two Tots by Setting Car Afire," *Asbury Park (N.J.) Press,* February 23, 1994, p. A1.

65. Author's interview with Lisa LeBelle, June 21, 1995.

66. Author's interview with Pat F., January 10, 1998.

67. Patricia Pearson, *When She Was Bad: Violent Women and the Myth of Innocence* (New York: Viking, 1997), p. 232.

68. Abigail Van Buren, "Good Husband Picks Up a Bad Habit," *Chicago Tribune*, May 26, 1995.

69. "Power relationships": Evan Stark and Anne Flitcraft, *Women at Risk: Domestic Violence and Women's Health* (Newbury Park, Calif.: Sage, 1996), p. 16. L. Kevin Hamberger and Theresa Potente, "Counseling Heterosexual Women Arrested for Domestic Violence: Implications for Theory and Practice," *Violence and Victims* 9, 1994, pp. 125–137.

70. Walker, *The Battered Woman*, p. 98. Dawn Rogers, letter to the editor, *Detroit News*, May 1, 1997.

71. Letter from Kathy M. Durgin and Jane Baldwin-LeClair, Jersey Battered Women's Service, to Ann Scucci, Esq., June 8, 1995 (on file with author).

72. Kathleen Neumeyer, "Hell Hath No Fury," *Ladies Home Journal*, March 1991; Susan Lehman, "A Woman Scorned," *Mirabella*, September 1991; Stephanie Savage, "Women Who Kill and the Made-for-TV Movie: The Betty Broderick Story," in Alice Myers and Sara Wight (eds.), *No Angels: Women Who Commit Violence* (San Francisco: HarperCollins/Pandora, 1996), p. 124.

73. Watt Espy, quoted in Tom W. Kuncl, "South Carolina Child-Killer Could Join Other Mothers on Death Row," *Washington Times*, November 14, 1994. Susan Smith: see Judy Mann, "Susan Smith: How Killers Are Made," *Washington Post*, July 28, 1995, p. E3; Jack Hitt, "Susan Smith's Judgment Day," *Washington Post*, June 25, 1995, p. C5 (stressing Smith's molestation by her stepfather as a teen). Compare to Mary McGrory, "A Child's Right to Life," *Washington Post*, November 8, 1994, p. A2 (Smith's act as "raw evil").

74. Homicides: John M. Dawson and Patrick A. Langan, *Murder in Families*, U.S. Department of Justice/Bureau of Justice Statistics (Washington, D.C.: U.S. Government Printing Office, July 1994), p. 3. Child abuse: Joan Ditson and Sharon Shay, "Use of a Home-Based Microcomputer to Analyze Community Data from Reported Cases of Child Abuse and Neglect," *Child Abuse and Neglect* 8, 1984, pp. 503–509; Richard J. Gelles, "Child Abuse and Violence in Single-Parent Families: Parent Absence and Economic Deprivation," *American Journal of Orthopsychiatry* 59, 1989, p. 492, U.S. Department of Health and Human Services, *Child Maltreatment 1996: Reports from the States to the National Child Abuse and Neglect Data System* (Washington, D.C.: U.S. Government Printing Office, 1998).

75. Author's interview with Kristian Miccio, July 6, 1993. Parry, "Mother Accused of Killing Two Tots by Setting Car Afire" (Montalvo); Lizette Alvarez, "The Life and Love of a Single Father," *New York Times*, November 29, 1995, p. B1 (Eliza Izquierdo).

76. Evan Stark and Anne Flitcraft, "Women and Children at Risk: A Feminist Perspective on Child Abuse," *International Journal of Health Services* 18, 1988, pp. 108, 114; Jane Gross, "Seeing Rise in Child Abuse, Hospitals Step in to Try to Stop the Battering," *New York Times*, April 5, 1994, p. A18; Carla Riera and Enedelia Obregon, "Violence Against Children at Crisis Level, Report Says," *Austin (Tex.) American-Statesman*, April 26, 1995, p. A1.

77. Beth Frerking, "Killer Dads," *Atlanta Journal Constitution,* December 3, 1995, p. F1; Beth Frerking, "The Heinous Happens All the Time; Hard-to-Fathom Union Murders Are Not Isolated Events," *Atlanta Journal-Constitution,* November 13, 1994, p. D2; "Why Do Moms Kill Their Children?" *Sarasota Herald-Tribune,* February 13, 1995, p. 5B. Khoua Her: Rosalind Bentley and H. J. Cummins, "Why Do Mothers Kill Their Children?" *Minneapolis Star-Tribune,* September 5, 1998; Heron Marquez Estrada, "St. Paul Mother Charged with Murder," *Minneapolis Star-Tribune,* September 9, 1998.

78. Sara Ruddick, "Preservative Love and Military Destruction: Some Reflections on Mothering and Peace," in Joyce Trebilcot (ed.), *Mothering: Essays in Feminist Theory* (Totowa, N.J.: Rowman and Allanheld, 1984); quoted in Phyllis Chesler, *Mothers on Trial: The Battle for Children and Custody* (New York: McGraw-Hill, 1986), p. 58.

79. Labeling male killers: Pollitt, "Violence in a Man's World." Susan Smith: Frank Rich, "The Mother Next Door," *New York Times,* November 13, 1994, p. E15; see also Susan Bullington Katz, "Susan Smith—She's Too Close to Us," *New York Newsday,* November 16, 1994, p. A37.

80. R. Emerson Dobash and Russell P. Dobash, *Violence Against Wives: A Case Against the Patriarchy* (New York: Free Press, 1979), p. 57.

81. National Woman Abuse Prevention Project, *Domestic Violence: Understanding a Community Problem* (Washington, D.C., 1993), p. 12 (pamphlet). Nancy Montgomery, "Out of Control: Why Men Hurt Women," *Seattle Times,* May 6, 1991, p. A1. See also Lynda Gorov, "Male Sense of 'Owning' Women Blamed in Abuse," *Boston Globe,* March 7, 1993, Metro Section, p. 1.

82. See Elizabeth Pleck, "Criminal Approaches to Family Violence, 1640–1980," in Lloyd Ohlin and Michael Tonry, eds., *Family Violence,* vol. 11, *Crime and Justice: A Review of Research* (Chicago: University of Chicago Press), pp. 19–57.

83. Poll: Murray A. Straus, Glenda Kaufman Kantor, and David W. Moore, "Change in Cultural Norms Approving Marital Violence from 1968 to 1994" (paper presented at the annual meeting of the American Sociological Association, Los Angeles, August 7, 1994). See also Rodney Stark and James McEvoy III, "Middle-Class Violence," *Psychology Today* 4, 1970, pp. 107–112. Neil Jacobson, "Rewards and Dangers in Researching Domestic Violence," *Family Process* 33, 1994, p. 82. On the prevalence of wife beating, see Donald G. Dutton, "Patriarchy and Wife Assault: The Ecological Fallacy," *Violence and Victims* 9, 1994, pp. 167–182.

84. Violence during pregnancy: H. Amaro et al., "Violence During Pregnancy and Substance Use," *American Journal of Public Health* 80, 1990, pp. 575–579 (3 percent); Jacquelyn C. Campbell et al., "Correlates of Battering During Pregnancy," *Research in Nursing and Health* 15, 1992, pp. 219–226 (7 percent); "Physical Violence During the 12 Months Preceding Childbirth," *Morbidity and Mortality Weekly Report,* March 4, 1994, pp. 132–137 (6 percent). Injuries: Rand, "Violence-Related Injuries"; National Center for Health Statistics, *National Hospital Ambulatory Medical Care Survey: 1992 Emergency Department Summary,* Vital and Health Statistics, Series 13, No. 125 (Hyattsville,

Md.: National Center for Health Statistics), March 1997, p. 34. See also Jean Abbott et al., "Domestic Violence Against Women: Incidence and Prevalence in an Emergency Department Population," *Journal of the American Medical Association* 273, 1995, pp. 1763–1767 (1.7 percent of women in urban emergency rooms injured by a partner).

85. Elizabeth M. Schneider, "Particularity and Generality: Challenges of Feminist Theory and Practice in Work on Woman-Abuse," *New York University Law Review* 67, 1992, p. 543; Lesbian violence: Gwat-yong Lie and Sabrina Gentlewarrier, "Intimate Violence in Lesbian Relationships: Discussion of Survey Findings and Practice Implications," *Journal of Social Service Research* 15, 1991, pp. 41–59; Lettie Lockhart et al., "Letting Out the Secret: Violence in Lesbian Relationships," *Journal of Interpersonal Violence* 9, 1994, pp. 469–492. Bisexual women: Gwat-yong Lie et al., "Lesbians in Currently Aggressive Relationships: How Frequently Do They Report Aggressive Past Relationships?" *Violence and Victims* 6, 1991, pp. 121–135. Explanations of lesbian violence: Barbara Hart, "Lesbian Battering: An Examination," in Kerry Lobel (ed.), *Naming the Violence: Speaking Out About Lesbian Battering* (Seattle, Wash.: Seal Press, 1986); Karen W. Saakvitne and Laurie A. Pearlman, "The Impact of Internalized Misogyny and Violence Against Women on Feminine Identity," in Ellen P. Cook (ed.), *Women, Relationships and Power* (Alexandria, Va.: American Counselling Association, 1993), pp. 247–274; Coleman, "Lesbian Battering," 141, 149.

86. See, e.g., Lenore Walker, *The Battered Woman Syndrome* (New York: Springer, 1984), p. 171, Table 11.

87. National Public Radio, *Fresh Air* with Terry Gross, November 7, 1994.

88. One "fact" cited as evidence that batterers are not out of control, that "men often beat women in parts of their bodies where bruises won't show" ("Myths and Facts About Domestic Violence," Domestic Violence Project, Ann Arbor, Mich., 1991), may not be a fact at all: most studies find that injuries to the face and neck are most common in battered women. See, e.g., Anne Steward Helton et al., "Battered and Pregnant: A Prevalence Study," *American Journal of Public Health* 77, 1987, pp. 1337–1339; Bruce Rounsaville and Myrna Weissman, "Battered Women: A Medical Problem Requiring Detection," *International Journal of Psychiatry in Medicine* 8, 1977–1978, pp. 191–202.

89. Poverty: Murray A. Straus, "Social Stress and Marital Violence in a National Sample of American Families," in Straus and Gelles, *Physical Violence in American Families,* p. 196; "Physical Violence During the 12 Months Preceding Childbirth," *Morbidity and Mortality Weekly Report;* Ronet Bachman, *Violence Against Women: A National Crime Victimization Survey Report* U.S. Department of Justice/Bureau of Justice Statistics, NCJ-145325 (Washington, D.C.: U.S. Government Printing Office, January 1994), p. 7; Lawrence Sherman, *Policing Domestic Violence* (New York: Free Press, 1992), p. 345. Substance abuse: Glenda Kaufman-Kantor and Murray A. Straus, "The 'Drunken Bum' Theory of Wife Beating," in Straus and Gelles, *Physical Violence in American Families,* pp. 203–224; *Missouri Court Personnel Newsletter* 8, fall 1995, p. 5. Personality disorders: Donald G. Dutton and Andrew J. Starzomski, "Borderline Personality in Perpetrators of Psychological and Physical Abuse," *Violence and Victims* 8, 1993,

pp. 327–337. Violent women: Shupe, Stacey, and Hazlewood, *Violent Men, Violent Couples,* p. 56.

90. Dutton, "Patriarchy and Wife Assault," p. 177; Schneider, "Particularity and Generality," p. 547.

91. Ann Jones, "Crimes Against Women: Media Part of the Problem for Masking Violence in the Language of Love," *USA Today,* March 10, 1994, p. 9A ("What happens . . ."); Ann Jones, "Where Do We Go from Here?" *Ms.,* September–October 1994, p. 57 (research on batterers). Andrea Dworkin, *Life and Death: Unapologetic Writings on the Continuing War Against Women* (New York: Free Press, 1997), p. 118.

92. "Beauty Queen Is Convicted of Reduced Charges in Attack," *New York Times,* November 23, 1994, p. A21.

93. Patricia Davis, "Death Sought for Two Women," *Washington Post,* September 29, 1997, p. B1.

94. Feminist concerns: Kurz, "Physical Assaults by Husbands," p. 99; Pagelow, "The Battered Husband Syndrome"; Claire M. Renzetti, "On Dancing with a Bear: Reflections on Some of the Current Debates Among Domestic Violence Theorists," *Violence and Victims* 9, 1994, pp. 195–200. Politicians' speeches: see, e.g., *Congressional Record,* October 4, 1994.

95. Hamberger and Potente, "Counseling Heterosexual Women," p. 129.

Chapter 5. Legislating the Gender War
1. Author's interviews with Susan Finkelstein and John L., August 1997.
2. Author's interview with Renée Ward, July 21, 1994.
3. John Heilemann, "The Crusader," *New Yorker,* February 24–March 3, 1997, p. 125 (Charlotte Watson); Susan Schechter, "The Future of the Battered Women's Movement," in Frédérique Delacoste and Felice Newman (eds.), *Fight Back! Feminist Resistance to Male Violence* (Minneapolis, Minn.: Cleis Press, 1981), p. 94.
4. Susan Schechter, *Women and Male Violence: The Visions and Struggles of the Battered Women's Movement* (Boston: South End Press, 1982), p. 248 (shelter worker); Susan Schechter, keynote address at the Second Annual Texas Council on Family Violence Conference, October 19–21, 1983, Austin, Texas, p. 6. Schechter, "The Future of the Battered Women's Movement," p. 94.
5. Pamela Johnston, "Attack from the Right," in Delacoste and Newman, *Fight Back!* p. 90.
6. Ibid., pp. 89, 91.
7. Author's interviews with Dyan Kirkland, July 18, 1994, February 15, 1995.
8. Author's interview with Barbara Raye, September 2, 1995.
9. Author's interviews with Trenna Perkins, July 18, 1994, and Eve Lipchik, July 8, 1994; see also Eve Lipchik, "Spouse Abuse: Challenging the Party Line," *Networker,* May–June 1991, p. 59.
10. Author's interview with Janice Dimmit, February 4, 1997. North Carolina: Correspondence between the North Carolina Governor's Crime Commission and the Violence Against Women Committee (May 1998) and other documents on file with author. Hawaii: excerpts from the investigative report cited in Kerry

Lobel, "Battered Women's Programs Under Attack," *Coalition Reporter* (New Jersey Coalition for Battered Women), summer 1994, pp. 12–13.

11. Sara R. Epstein, Glenda Russell, and Louise Silvern, "Structure and Ideology of Shelters for Battered Women," *American Journal of Community Psychology* 16, 1988, pp. 345–367.

12. *NCADV Voice,* spring 1991, p. 19; Lisa Pohlmann et al., *Information Guide for Abused Women in Maine* (Augusta: Maine Division, American Association of University Women, 1988, and Maine Coalition for Family Crisis Services, 1988–1991), p. 11; Transition House (Cambridge. Mass.) brochure, 1996; Andrea Dworkin, "Freedom Now," in *Life and Death: Unapologetic Writings on the Continuing War Against Women* (New York, Free Press, 1997), pp. 152–168.

13. Virginia Goldner, "Making Room for Both/And," *Networker,* March–April 1992, pp. 60, 61.

14. Claire M. Renzetti, "The Poverty of Services for Battered Lesbians," *Journal of Gay and Lesbian Social Services* 4, 1996, pp. 61–68; Claire M. Renzetti, *Violent Betrayal: Partner Abuse in Lesbian Relationships* (Newbury Park, Calif.: Sage, 1992) (survey of lesbians).

15. Goldner, "Making Room for Both/And," pp. 59–60.

16. Susan Schechter, *Guidelines for Mental Health Practitioners in Domestic Violence Cases* (Washington, D.C.: National Coalition Against Domestic Violence, 1987) p. 16. No essay defending joint counseling: Richard J. Gelles, "Research and Advocacy: Can One Wear Two Hats?" *Family Process* 33, 1994, pp. 93–95. Studies on joint counseling: K. Daniel O'Leary, "Physical Aggression in Intimate Relationships Can Be Treated Within a Marital Context Under Certain Circumstances," *Journal of Interpersonal Violence* 11, 1996, pp. 450–452; Stephen J. Brannen and Rubin Allen, "Comparing the Effectiveness of Gender-Specific and Couples Groups in a Court-Mandated Spouse Abuse Treatment Program," *Research on Social Work Practice* 6, 1996, pp. 405–424.

17. Lipchik, "Spouse Abuse"; author's interview with Lonnie Hazlewood, August 16, 1995.

18. Goldner, "Making Room for Both/And," p. 60.

19. See Kay Longcope, "Sarah Buel: From Child Laborer to Harvard Law School," *Boston Globe,* February 8, 1988, p. 12. Buel is also the originator of the now thoroughly debunked claim, based on a misinterpretation of statistics from the March of Dimes, that the battering of pregnant women causes more birth defects than all medical causes combined. See Christina Hoff Sommers, *Who Stole Feminism?: How Women Have Betrayed Women* (New York: Simon & Schuster, 1994), p. 14.

20. Author's interview with James Fagan, October 5, 1995.

21. Michigan Judicial Institute Regional Judicial Seminar on Domestic Violence, "Domestic Violence and Domestic Relations" and "Myths and Facts About Domestic Violence" (1991). See also Massachusetts Trial Court Judicial Institute, "Domestic Violence: Improving the Court's Response" (October 1994, April 1995).

22. Seminars: University of Cincinnati press release, May 14, 1997. Grant: Press release from the Domestic Violence Coordinating Council of Hamilton

County, October 6, 1996. Book: Dee L. R. Graham with Edna I. Rawlings and Roberta K. Rigsby, *Loving to Survive: Sexual Terror, Men's Violence, and Women's Lives* (New York: New York University Press, 1994), pp. xiv, 85.

23. Marilyn Garateix, "On Patrol Against Domestic Violence: Ft. Lauderdale Counselor Goes to Scene of Crime," *Miami Herald,* November 1, 1993, p. 1A.

24. Stacey, Hazlewood, and Shupe, *The Violent Couple,* pp. 132–137 (Austin FVDN); materials from EMERGE and RAVEN on file with author. Author's interview with Glenna Auxier, July 25, 1995.

25. EMERGE counselor David Adams mentioned the last of these incidents at the Fourth International Family Violence Research Conference (Durham, N. H., July 1995). The "physical violence" section of the EMERGE "Violent and Controlling Behavior Checklist" includes "standing over her," "banging the table," and "outshouting."

26. "Violent and Controlling Behavior Checklist" (EMERGE); "Batterers' Counseling and Intervention," workshop at the Massachusetts Trial Court Judicial Institute Domestic Violence Education Project, April 12, 1995 (list of abusive behaviors and "excuses"); "Men Being Battered," intviol-l@uriacc.uri.edu (Intimate Violence Research and Practice Issues List), April 13, 1995 (Jeff Sutter).

27. Margaret Carlson, "Preventable Murders," *Time,* October 16, 1995, p. 64.

28. Booklet: Pohlmann et al., *Information Guide for Abused Women in Maine,* p. 11; Miccio: author's interview, July 6, 1993; Stasi: *Daily News,* May 15, 1995, p. 4.

29. Elizabeth Pleck, "Criminal Approaches to Family Violence, 1640–1980," in Lloyd Ohlin and Michael Tonry (eds.), *Family Violence,* vol. II: *Crime and Justice* (Chicago: University of Chicago Press, 1989), pp. 19–57.

30. *State v. Oliver* (North Carolina, 1874), quoted in Del Martin, *Battered Wives* (New York: Pocket Books, 1983), p. 33. Police captain: quoted in Pleck, "Criminal Approaches," p. 31.

31. Lawrence W. Sherman, *Policing Domestic Violence* (New York: Free Press, 1992), p. 26.

32. Nan Oppenlander, "Coping or Copping Out," *Criminology* 20, 1982, pp. 460–461.

33. Sherman, *Policing Domestic Violence,* pp. 38–42 (citing other studies).

34. Kathleen J. Ferraro, "Cops, Courts, and Woman Battering," in Pauline B. Bart and Eileen G. Moran (eds.), *Violence Against Women: The Bloody Footprints* (Newbury Park, Calif.: Sage, 1993), p. 171. See also Daisy Quarm and Martin Schwartz, "Domestic Violence in Criminal Court: An Examination of New Legislation in Ohio," *Women and Politics* 4, 1984, pp. 29–46.

35. Sherman, *Policing Domestic Violence;* on the debate in the Wisconsin legislature see p. 136.

36. Author's interview with Christopher Pagan, July 2, 1997.

37. Author's interview with Pete S., August 1995.

38. Susan Yocum, "Police Can't Prevent Domestic Killing," *Los Angeles Times,* October 4, 1989, p. II:7.

39. Author's interview with "Sally Gilmore," May 1997.

40. "Enlist Manning Against Spouse Abuse" (editorial), *Seattle Times,* November 4, 1996, p. B4; Peter Lewis, "Manning Pleads Guilty in Domestic Abuse," *Seattle Times,* November 4, 1996, p. B1.

41. See "Judge Defends Slap on Wrist in Abuse Case" (AP), *Chattanooga Free Press,* January 19, 1996; Mitch Albom, "Whose Justice Was It in Abuse Case?" *Detroit Free Press,* January 21, 1996, p. 1E; Ellen Goodman, "The Envelope, Please . . .," *Boston Globe,* August 25, 1996, p. D7.

42. Women denied equal protection: e.g., Paul Reidinger, "Unequal Protection: Do the Police Ignore Domestic Violence?" *ABA Journal,* March 1989, p. 102. New York bill: Joyce Purnick, "Politics Stalling Family Violence Bills," *New York Times,* June 27, 1996, p. B3.

43. California bill: Greg Lucas, "Accused Batterers Can't Pay to Erase Charges Under New Law," *San Francisco Chronicle,* June 10, 1997, p. A20; gun law: James Bovard, "Disarming Those Who Need Guns Most," *Wall Street Journal,* December 23, 1996.

44. Ferraro, "Cops, Courts, and Woman Battering," p. 171. Judicial conferences: see, e.g., Massachusetts Trial Court Judicial Institute, First Annual Conference on Domestic Violence, September 22, 1994. See also Catherine S. Manegold, "Making Abuse a Crime a Spouse Can't Forgive," *New York Times,* May 1, 1994, p. 18E. Warren Moon: Bruce Nichols, "Football Star Acquitted on Spouse-Abuse Charge," *Washington Post,* February 23, 1996, p. A4.

45. Ann Baker, "Jury Finds Law Prof Not Guilty in Assault," *St. Paul Pioneer Press,* January 28, 1995, p. 1B; "Judge May Dismiss Erlinder Domestic Abuse Case," *St. Paul Pioneer Press,* January 27, 1995, p. 6C; "Law Professor's Trial to Begin," *St. Paul Pioneer Press,* January 25, 1995, p. 1B.

46. James W. Dolan, "Women Twice Abused: By Lovers and the Courts," *Boston Globe,* July 10, 1993, p. 11.

47. Ferraro, "Cops, Courts, and Woman Battering," p. 173 ("women are the best experts"); see also Jan Hoffman, "When Men Hit Women," *New York Times Magazine,* February 16, 1992, p. 26, and Manegold, "Making Spouse Abuse a Crime a Spouse Can't Forgive." Study: "David Ford and M. J. Regolie, "The Preventive Impact of Policies for Prosecuting Batterers," in Eve S. Buzawa and Carl G. Buzawa (eds.), *Domestic Violence: The Changing Criminal Justice Response* (Westport, Conn.: Auburn House, 1992), pp. 181–208.

48. Baker, "Jury Finds Law Prof Not Guilty in Assault."

49. Russ Bleemer, "N.J. Judges Told to Ignore Rights in Abuse TROs," *New Jersey Law Journal* 140, April 24, 1995.

50. Russ Bleemer, "Judge Rebuked by AOC on TRO Training," *New Jersey Law Journal* May 8, 1995; "King Ousts District Court Judge MacNichol," *Portland Press Herald,* August 30, 1997.

51. "The Tragedies of Domestic Violence: A Qualitative Analysis of Civil Restraining Orders in Massachusetts," Office of the Commissioner of Probation, Massachusetts Trial Court, October 12, 1995.

52. Author's interview with Elaine Epstein, September 21, 1995.

53. Paul King: "Educating Judges" (editorial), *Boston Globe,* November 17, 1986, p. 16, and Eileen McNamara, "'No Quick Fix' in Abuse Case, Judge

Rules," *Boston Globe,* November 13, 1986, p. 1; Elaine M. Epstein, "Speaking the Unspeakable," *Massachusetts Bar Association Newsletter* 33, June–July 1993, p. 1.

54. Miriam Goldstein Altman, "Litigating Domestic Abuse Cases Under Ch. 209A," *Massachusetts Lawyers Weekly,* October 23, 1995, p. B6. Fagan: transcript, Commonwealth of Massachusetts, District Court Department, Taunton Division, September 21, 1995. In that case, the judge vacated the restraining order due to the distant relationship between the plaintiff and the defendant (she had been married to his brother for a few weeks two years earlier), and to the woman's admission that he had never made threats but only "start[ed] arguments."

55. Ruling: *Commonwealth v. Gordon,* 553 N.E. 2d 915, 1990. Questions about fear: David C. Grossack and Patrick Flynn, "Legislation to Reform the Abuse-Prevention Law," *Massachusetts Lawyers Weekly,* April 17, 1995, p. 11.

56. See Alison Bass, "The War on Domestic Abuse," *Boston Globe,* September 25, 1994, p. 1; "Dismissing Domestic Abuse" (editorial), *Boston Globe,* September 27, 1994.

57. "Restraining Orders: Use and Abuse" (editorial), *Massachusetts Lawyers' Weekly,* September 27, 1993, p. 10; Heather Anderson, "Pay Up or Shut Up," *North Shore (Boston, Mass.) Weekly,* January 21, 1996.

58. This account is based on court and police records and affidavits by Robert Byers, as well as interviews with court officers in 1996. A brief summary of the case also appeared in Grossack and Flynn, "Legislation to Reform the Abuse-Prevention Law."

59. Suggestion on detecting impostors: see Kendall Anderson, "Abuse in the System," *Dallas Morning News,* May 12, 1998. Michael Grunwald, "Accused Had Said He Was Abused: Two Restraining Orders Were Issued Against Ex-Girlfriend," *Boston Globe,* February 15, 1995, p. 17.

60. Flynn: John Laidler, "Political Notebook," *Boston Globe North Weekly,* October 11, 1992. Criminal records of defendants: Andrew Klein, "Reabuse in a Population of Court-Restrained Male Batterers After Two Years: Development of a Predictive Model" (Ph.D. dissertation, Northeastern University, 1994), pp. 40–48.

61. Four to 5 percent of the charges are false: Lisa Kosan, "Senate Candidate Decries Use of Restraining Orders," *Peabody (Mass.) Times,* August 10, 1992, p. B1.

62. Author's interview with Barbara Gray, October 13, 1995. See also Kosan, "Senate Candidate Decries Use of Restraining Orders."

63. Arnold Rutkin, "From the Editor," *Family Advocate* 18, winter 1996.

64. *Corrente v. Corrente,* 281 N.J. Super. 243 (App. Div. 1995, reversed); *Murray v. Murray,* 267 N.J. Super. 406, 410 (App. Div. 1993, reversed); Susan K. Livio, "Courts Give Fewer Restraining Judgments," *Asbury Park (N.J.) Press,* February 12, 1996, p. A1; Susan K. Livio, "Domestic Argument Cases in Top Court," *Asbury Park (N.J.) Press,* February 4, 1997, p. A1.

65. David H. Dunlap, "The Adult Abuse Act: Theory v. Practice," *UMKC Law Review* 64, 1996, p. 686.

66. Documents and correspondence on file with author.

67. Flynn McRoberts, "Chaney Case Leaves Trail of Wreckage, Hope,"

Chicago Tribune, March 17, 1993, p. 1NW.

68. Terry Wilson, "Stalking Law Sees First Conviction; Man Gets Two-Year Sentence for Terrorizing Girlfriend," *Chicago Tribune,* November 25, 1992, C:3; Jacquelyn Boyle and Lawrence Patrick III, "Law Brings Hundreds of Stalking Complaints; Number of Cases Startles Authorities," *Detroit Free Press,* August 2, 1993, p. 1A; "Woman Convicted of Stalking Charge," *Boston Globe,* July 1, 1994, p. 27.

69. The Georgia law specifies that no "overt threat of death or bodily injury" has to be made (official Code of Georgia Annotated, 16-5-90 [1993]). See also D.C. Act 10–46 in the Council of the District of Columbia, 1993 D.C. ALS 53, and 1993 Pa. ALS 28. Councilman: Judy Bailey, "'Lovesick' Official Accused of Stalking," *Atlanta Journal-Constitution,* June 12, 1993, p. B2. The councilman had to resign his post and was sentenced to one year's probation and a fine after pleading no contest to a stalking charge. "Metro in Brief," *Atlanta Journal-Constitution,* September 15, 1993, p. D2.

70. Charles Mount, "Richmond Stalking Suspect Can't Get Fair Trial, Lawyer Says," *Chicago Tribune,* June 12, 1993, p. NW5.

71. Curtis Lawrence, "First Stalking Trial Results in Acquittal," *Chicago Tribune,* December 19, 1992, p. NW5; Lynn Van Mattre, "Wheaton Man Found Not Guilty in Stalking," *Chicago Tribune,* April 5, 1995, Metro Section, p. 1. O'Reilly: quoted in Eric Zorn, "In Stalking, the Law Sometimes Crosses the Line," *Chicago Tribune,* October 5, 1995, Metro Section, p. 1.

72. Zorn, "In Stalking, the Law Sometimes Crosses the Line."

73. New Jersey case: *State v. L.C.,* App. Div. 1995 (reversed); Wisconsin mother: Sherman, *Policing Domestic Violence,* p. 121. Female arrests: Leef Smith, "Increasingly, Abuse Shows Female Side," *Washington Post,* November 18, 1997, p. B1.

74. Lynda M. Carson, "Can Women Be Batterers?" *Coalition Reporter* (New Jersey Coalition for Battered Women), November 1997, p. 13 ("if women are violent . . . "); Sherman, *Policing Domestic Violence,* pp. 254–255.

75. Author's interviews with Sally Goldfarb, July 1993, and with "Deborah Beck," February 1997. "Cucumber Assault Gets Hungry Husband in a Pickle" (UPI), *Washington Times,* August 23, 1996.

76. Commonwealth of Massachusetts, Governor's Commission on Domestic Violence, "Uniform Enforcement Standards for Prosecutors and Police," 1994, Addendum II, "Domestic Violence Investigation Training" pp. 13–14.

77. Holly Maguigan, "Battered Women and Self-Defense: Myths and Misconceptions in Current Reform Proposals," *University of Pennsylvania Law Review* 140, 1991. Texas case: *Williams v. State,* 70 S.W. 756, 757–758 (Tex. Crim. App. 1902). 1940s and 1950s cases: Maguigan, "Battered Women and Self-Defense."

78. For a review and critique of Lenore Walker's research, see David L. Faigman and Amy Wright, "The Battered Woman Syndrome in the Age of Science," *Arizona Law Review* 39, 1997, pp. 68–114.

79. Elson case: Faye Fiore, "A Battered Wife Wins Acquittal in Women Claiming 'Battered Woman Syndrome,' Who Are Not Isolated: Murder Case," *Los Angeles Times,* December 26, 1989, p. B1. David Simon and William F. Zorzi,

Jr., "Case Histories Reveal Troubling Questions About Circumstances of the Crimes," *Baltimore Sun,* March 17, 1991, p. 6A.

80. Murder case: George Lane, "Psychogenic Amnesia Suffered by Peggy Saiz, Witness Claims," *Denver Post,* October 8, 1993, p. B5. Rate of success for the "battered woman" defense: Faigman and Wright, "The Battered Woman Syndrome in the Age of Science," p. 113.

81. See, e.g., Nancy Gibbs, "Till Death Do Us Part," *Time,* January 18, 1993, p. 38; Joseph C. Nunes, "Show Mercy: Clemency Project Takes Up Cause of Battered Women," *Chicago Tribune,* September 12, 1993, WomanNews Section, p. 1; "Compassion—On a Case-by-Case Basis," *Los Angeles Times,* January 18, 1993, p. B6.

82. Patrick A. Langan and John M. Dawson, "Spouse Murder Defendants in Large Urban Counties," U.S. Department of Justice, Bureau of Justice Statistics, NCJ-153256 (Washington, D.C.: Government Printing Office, September 1995), pp. iv, 16, 22. Smaller studies from other areas have shown differences that may be less dramatic but still unmistakably favor women. See, e.g., Todd Richssin and Jon Schmid, "When Abuse Turns to Homicide," *New York News and Observer,* July 3, 1994, p. 1A.

83. See "Claims of Physical Abuse Didn't Hold Up in Trials of Some Women," *Columbus (Ohio) Dispatch,* January 27, 1991, p. 5F; "Murder Defense Is Used in Theft," *Boston Globe,* December 16, 1997, p. D8 (rearrests). June Briand: Raymond Hughes, "Briand Fiction," *(Claremont, N.H.) News Leader,* November 26, 1996; Lois R. Shea, "N.H. Pardons Woman in Husband's Slaying," *Boston Globe,* December 5, 1996, p. B4; Nancy West, "Briand Says Friend Told Her to Kill Husband," *The Manchester (N. H.) Union Leader,* November 3, 1996.

84. Jeff Benkoe, "Woman Sentenced to a Day in Jail," *New York Newsday,* December 1, 1987, p. 22.

85. Elayne Clift, "A Stalker? Or Misunderstood?", *Christian Science Monitor,* June 26, 1998, p. 15; Katherine Shaver and Michael E. Ruane, "Five-Week Aron Case Ends in Mistrial," *Washington Post,* March 31, 1998, p. A10.

86. George Lardner Jr., "How Kristin Died," *Washington Post,* National Weekly Edition, January 4–10, 1993, pp. 8–12.

87. Douglas J. Besharov, "Overreporting and Underreporting Are Twin Problems," in Gelles and Loseke, *Current Controversies in Family Violence,* p. 265.

88. Richard Gelles, remarks at National Family Violence Research Conference, July 1995; Sherman, *Policing Domestic Violence,* pp. 231–238; verbal communication from Dr. David Gremillion, July 1995.

89. John Laidler, "Political Notebook," *Boston Globe North Weekly,* October 11, 1992; see also Kosan, "Senate Candidate Decries Use of Restraining Orders."

90. Studies: Janice Grau et al., "Restraining Orders for Battered Women: Issues of Access and Efficacy," *Women and Politics* 4, 1984, pp. 13–28; Andrew R. Klein, "Re-Abuse in a Population of Court-Restrained Male Batterers After Two Years: Development of a Predictive Model," in Eve S. Buzawa and Carl G. Buzawa (eds.), *Do Arrests and Restraining Orders Work?* (Thousand Oaks, Calif.: Sage, 1996), pp. 192–213; Adele Harrell and Barbara E. Smith, "Effects of

Restraining Orders on Domestic Violence Victims," in Buzawa and Buzawa, pp. 214–242.

91. Eric Zorn, "A Seminar in Divorce, Down-and-Dirty Style," *Chicago Tribune,* November 4, 1988, 2:1. 105th Congress, 2d Session, H. R. 3514, Bill to Prevent Violence Against Women, and for Other Purposes, March 19, 1998. See also Susan Sarnoff, "The Institutionalization of Misinformation: VAWA II," *Women's Freedom Network Newsletter,* July/August 1998, p. 1.

Chapter 6. Sex Crimes, Political Crimes

1. James Anderson, "Confessions of a Mad Dog Rapist in Prison," *SAFAR (Society Against False Accusations of Rape) Newsletter,* October–November 1995.
2. Katha Pollitt, "Men, Women and the Question of Consent," *Washington Post,* National Weekly Edition, June 3–9, 1996, p. 36.
3. See, e.g., Mim Udovitch, "Give 'Em Enough Rape," *Village Voice,* July 13, 1993, p. 18.
4. Martha Bellisle, "Wrongfully Jailed Man Earns Degree," Associated Press, May 24, 1998.
5. See Eric Salter and Andrew Blankstein, "Deputy's Wife Recants Statements That Her Husband Had Raped Her," *Los Angeles Times,* February 12, 1997, p. B4; Timothy Williams, "Deputy Held on Rape Charges Is Exonerated," *Los Angeles Times,* April 11, 1997, p. B1.
6. See Vivian Berger, "Man's Trial, Woman's Tribulation: Rape Cases in the Courtroom," *Columbia Law Review* 77, 1977, pp. 2–103; Susan Estrich, "Rape," *Yale Law Journal* 95, 1986, pp. 1087–1184.
7. Linda A. Fairstein, *Sexual Violence* (New York: William Morrow, 1993), p. 127; see also Estrich, "Rape," pp. 1105–1132.
8. See Leigh Bienen, "Rape III—National Developments in Rape Reform Legislation," *Women's Rights Law Reporter* 6, 1980, p. 203. On resistance see, e.g., *State v. Harris,* 70 N.J. Super. (1961), and *People v. Nash,* 261 Cal. App. 2d (1968).
9. For a summary of rape reform efforts see Bienen, "Rape III." Berger, "Man's Trial, Woman's Tribulation," p. 32 ("sacrificing . . ."); interview with criminal lawyer Rikki Klieman in Jack Kammer, *Good Will Toward Men* (New York: St. Martin's Press, 1994), pp. 153–162.
10. Catharine MacKinnon, *Feminism Unmodified: Discourses on Life and Law* (Cambridge, Mass.: Harvard University Press, 1987), p. 82.
11. *Acquaintance Rape* (Baltimore: American College Health Association, 1992).
12. "When She Says No, It's *Always* Rape," *The Thistle,* November 4, 1992; Alison Bell, "Date Rape," *'Teen,* July 1997, p. 70.
13. Ann Landers, "If Woman Is Drunk, It Might Be Rape," *Detroit Free Press,* December 17, 1995, p. 2G.
14. Susan Jacoby, "Common Decency," *New York Times Magazine,* May 19, 1991, p. 22.
15. Author's interviews with Virginia MacKay-Smith, March 1993, and Kathryn Geller Myers, June 3, 1994.
16. Robin Warshaw, *I Never Called It Rape* (New York: Harper Perennial, 1994), p. xxiv; Charlene L. Muehlenhard and Jennifer L. Schrag, "Nonviolent

Sexual Coercion," in Andrea Parrot and Laurie Bechhofer (eds.), *Acquaintance Rape: The Hidden Crime* (New York: Wiley, 1991), pp. 122–123.

17. *San Francisco Examiner,* February 7, 1991, p. A1. For the specifics of the survey see Joanne Jacobs, "Just Say 'No' to Unwanted Sex," *San Jose Mercury News,* May 29, 1989, and Lisa Koven and Rick St. John, "Sexual Assault at Stanford," *Stanford Review,* summer 1992.

18. Donald P. Baker, "Talk on Sexual Violence Stirs Campus," *Washington Post,* April 26, 1996, p. C3; Brooke A. Masters, "Alleged Date Rape Is College's Topic A: William and Mary Campus Is Divided on Student's Public Accusation," *Washington Post,* April 27, 1992, p. B1; Nancy Gibbs, "The Clamor on Campus," *Time,* June 3, 1991, pp. 54–55.

19. Author's interview with Gillian Greensite, December 13, 1993; see also Gillian Greensite, "Acquaintance Rape Clarified," *Freeing Our Lives,* winter 1992.

20. Jason Vest, "The School That Put Sex to the Test: At Antioch, a Passionate Reaction to Consent Code," *Washington Post,* December 3, 1993, p. G1; Deborah Sullivan, "Date Rape Allegation Ignites a Furor at Pomona College," *Los Angeles Times,* May 21, 1994, p. B1.

21. Katha Pollitt, "Not Just Bad Sex," *New Yorker,* October 4, 1993, p. 222; Lois Pineau, "Date Rape: A Feminist Analysis," in Leslie Francis (ed.), *Feminism, Philosophy, and the Law* (University Park, Pa.: Princeton University Press, 1996), p. 22; Ellen Goodman, "Behind the Sexual Liberation Struggle," *Boston Globe,* October 28, 1993. Subverting female passivity: Naomi Wolf, *Fire with Fire: The New Female Power and How It Will Change the 21st Century* (New York: Random House, 1993), p. 193; Eric Fassin, "Playing by the Antioch Rules," *New York Times,* December 26, 1993, p. E11.

22. "Activate the policy": "Quotables," *Chicago Tribune,* March 1, 1994, Perspective Section, p. 19; letting go: Blanche Vernon, "Sex Q&A," *Mademoiselle,* May 1997, p. 93. Pollitt, "Men, Women and the Question of Consent."

23. Charlene L. Muehlenhard and Lisa C. Hollabaugh, "Do Women Sometimes Say No When They Mean Yes? The Prevalence and Correlates of Women's Token Resistance to Sex," *Journal of Personality and Social Psychology* 54, 1988, pp. 872–879; Lucia O'Sullivan and Elizabeth R. Allgeier, "Disassembling a Stereotype: Gender Differences in the Use of Token Resistance," *Journal of Applied Social Sciences* 24, 1994, pp. 1035–1055.

24. *Glamour,* January 1995 (survey by BKG Youth Inc.)

25. See, e.g., Cindy Struckman-Johnson, "Forced Sex on Dates: It Happens to Men, Too," *Journal of Sex Research* 24, 1988, pp. 234–241; Susan B. Sorenson et al., "The Prevalence of Adult Sexual Assault: The Los Angeles Epidemiologic Catchment Area Project," *American Journal of Epidemiology* 126, 1987.

26. *Facts on Rape* (Hackensack, N.J.: Bergen County Rape Crisis Center, 1992) ("life-threatening"); Richard S. Orton, "Date Rape: Critiquing the Critics," *Journal of Sex Research* 31, 1994, p. 149.

27. Bernice R. Sandler, "Ten Reasons to Obtain Verbal Consent for Sex," *About Women on Campus,* winter 1994.

28. Estrich, "Rape," p. 1182.

29. *Rusk v. State,* 43 Md. App. 476, 406 A.2d 624, 626 (1979).

30. *People v. Barnes,* 721 P.2d 110 (Cal. 1986).

31. A detailed account of the case is found in *Commonwealth of Pennsylvania v. Robert Berkowitz,* 609 A.2d 1338 (Pa. Superior Court, 1992).

32. *Commonwealth v. Berkowitz,* 641 A.2d 1161 (Pa. 1994). See also Emilie Lounsberry, "Court: 'No' Is Not Enough in Rape Cases," *Philadelphia Inquirer,* June 2, 1994, p. A1; Steve Marshall, "Ruling That Rape Must Be Forced Is Criticized," *USA Today,* June 3, 1994, p. 3A; Dale Russakoff, "Where Women Can't Just Say 'No'; Pennsylvania Supreme Court Rules Force Is Needed to Prove Rape," *Washington Post,* June 3, 1994.

33. "I did . . .": Associated Press, June 3, 1994. Resistance to rape: see, e.g., P. A. Marchbanks et al., "Risk of Injury from Resisting Rape," *American Journal of Epidemiology* 132, 1990, pp. 540–549; Janice M. Zoucha-Jensen and Ann Coyne, "The Effects of Resistance Strategies on Rape," *American Journal of Public Health* 83, 1993, pp. 1633–1634. Susan Estrich, "Rape: A Question of Force," *USA Today,* August 11, 1994.

34. John L. Kennedy, "'No Means No' Sexual Assault Law Sent to Gov. Ridge," *Pennsylvania Lawyers' Weekly,* March 27, 1995, p. 3. *People v. Schmidt,* Colo. App., 885 P.2d 312, 1994.

35. *In re M.T.S.,* 609 A.2d 1266 (N.J. 1992). The account of the case is based on appellate briefs from the case. Katha Pollitt later scoffed at the notion that a court made up of "one woman and six middle-aged men" had been "corrupted by radical feminism" (Pollitt, "Not Just Bad Sex"); but the ruling cited such radical feminist authors as Diana Russell, who regards rape as a "logical expression" of normal masculinity and a means of keeping women "in their place" (see Diana E. H. Russell, *The Politics of Rape: The Victim's Perspective* [New York: Stein and Day, 1975], pp. 256, 265).

36. Berger, "Woman's Trials, Man's Tribulations"; Note, "The Rape Corroboration Requirement: Repeal Not Reform," *Yale Law Journal* 81, 1972. Legal changes: Estrich, "Rape," p. 1137.

37. Estrich, "Rape," pp. 1172, 1175.

38. Bob Egelko, "State High Court OK's Telling Jury It May Take Rape Victim's Word," *Sacramento Bee,* May 8, 1992, p. B7; Jerome H. Skolnick, "Here, the Odds Are with Women," *Los Angeles Times,* December 15, 1991 (conviction rate).

39. *Michigan v. Ivers,* State of Michigan Court of Appeals, unpublished opinion, December 2, 1997.

40. MacKinnon, *Feminism Unmodified,* p. 5; Joseph D. Grano, "Free Speech v. the University of Michigan," *Academic Questions,* spring 1990, pp. 13–14.

41. Dan Morain, "Woman Recants Rape Tale," *Los Angeles Times,* August 20, 1991. "Many bristle . . .": see, e.g., Addei Fuller and Ann McGettigan, "Falsely Accused: What Does a Rapist Look Like?" *Seattle Times,* February 4, 1990.

42. Rate of false reports: see, e.g., Judith Gaines, "Rape Case Accusation Found False," *Boston Globe,* June 30, 1991, p. 33; Nancy Montgomery, "False Reports of Rape Are Rare But Costly, Alarming; Victims May Be Afraid to Reveal Assaults," *Seattle Times,* January 24, 1995, p. B3. Feminist arguments: see, e.g., Deborah Rhode, *Speaking of Sex: The Denial of Gender Inequality* (Cambridge,

Mass.: Harvard University Press, 1997), p. 125. Unfounding procedures: Stephen Buckley, "Unfounded Reports of Rape Confound Area Police Investigators," *Washington Post,* June 27, 1992, p. B1.

43. Buckley, "Unfounded Reports of Rape"; Eugene J. Kanin, "False Rape Allegations," *Archives of Sexual Behavior* 23, 1994, pp. 81–92.

44. Polygraphs: Frank Langfitt, "Md. Police Polygraph Some Rape Victims," *Baltimore Sun,* August 29, 1993; Doris Sue Wong, "SJC Ruling Prohibits Lie Detector Evidence," *Boston Globe,* December 12, 1989.

45. See, e.g., E. J. Kanin, "Male Aggression in Dating-Courtship Relations," *American Journal of Sociology* 63, 1957, pp. 197–204. Motives for "crying rape": Kanin, "False Rape Allegations," pp. 85–86, 89.

46. Kanin, "False Rape Allegations," p. 90; author's interview with Eugene Kanin, January 3, 1996. Other estimates: Christy Scattarella, "Was It Rape? False Reports Raise Fears That Police Won't Believe Real Victims," *Seattle Times,* October 21, 1991, p. A1; Jeanne C. Marsh, Alison Geist, and Nathan Caplan, *Rape and the Limits of Law Reform* (Boston: Auburn House, 1982), p. 103.

47. "The old myths . . .": Susan Estrich, "Sex, Dates and Criminal Rape," *Miami Herald,* November 17, 1991.

48. *Geraldo Rivera,* CBS, March 27, 1997.

49. Fairstein, *Sexual Violence,* p. 142.

50. Ibid., pp. 217–222.

51. Alice Vachss, *Sex Crimes* (New York: Random House, 1993), p. 111 (not a "good victim"); Gary LaFree, *Rape and Criminal Justice: The Social Construction of Rape* (Belmont, Calif.: Wadsworth, 1989), pp. 216, 218–219.

52. Estrich, "Sex, Dates and Criminal Rape."

53. Peter Hermann, "Woman's Past Is Told to Hart Jury," *Baltimore Sun,* June 21, 1991; "Alleged Victim Suicidal During Breakup, Psychiatrist Says," *Baltimore Sun,* June 27, 1991; "Arundel Broker Found Not Guilty in Rape Case," *Baltimore Sun,* July 4, 1991.

54. Mary P. Johnson, "Uphold Victims' Rights," *Baltimore Sun,* July 17, 1991.

55. All information on the Anderson case comes from the records of the Marion County Courthouse, Oregon (Case 86C20495, 1989; copies on file with author) and from a videotape of the trial.

56. See Laura Italiano, "Accuser Called Kitty-Litter Loon," *New York Post,* September 25, 1997; Brooke A. Masters and Mandy Stadtmiller, "Did Albert Have the Best Defense?" *Washington Post,* September 27, 1997; Richard Cohen, "A Case That Should Not Have Come to Trial," *Washington Post,* September 25, 1997; *Rivera Live,* CNBC, September 25, 1997.

57. John Sullivan, "Defense in Sex Case Says Court Let Accuser Lie," *New York Times,* March 24, 1998, p. B5; Andrea Peyser, "Life's Experiences Leave You Clueless About 'Cyberbabes,'" *New York Post,* April 16, 1998; Steve Dunleavy, "Wacko Wetzel Left Cybersex Lawyer Defenseless," *New York Post,* May 30, 1998.

58. Great American TV Poll #1 (Princeton Survey Research Associates), January 1991.

59. See Berger, "Man's Trial, Woman's Tribulation"; J. Alexander Tanford

and Anthony J. Bocchino, "Rape Victim Shield Laws and the Sixth Amendment," *University of Pennsylvania Law Review* 128, 1980, pp. 544–602; Pamela J. Fisher, "*State v. Alvey:* Iowa's Victimization of Defendants Through the Overextension of Iowa's Rape Shield Laws," *Iowa Law Review* 76, 1991, pp. 835–870; Lisa M. Dillman, "*Stephens v. Miller:* Restoration of the Rape Defendant's Sixth Amendment Rights," *Indiana Law Review* 28, 1994.

60. Jodi Enda, "Was Retarded Girl's Yes a No?" *Philadelphia Inquirer,* February 1, 1993; "Three Convicted in Glen Ridge Rape Trial," *Philadelphia Inquirer,* March 17, 1993; "Advocates for Retarded See Double Edge of N.J. Rape Verdict," *Philadelphia Inquirer,* March 21, 1993. Bill: Marjorie Balbrun, "Whitman Signs New Domestic-Abuse Laws," *Philadelphia Inquirer,* August 12, 1994.

61. On the multiple personality disorder controversy, see Paul McHugh, "Witches, Multiple Personalities, and Other Psychiatric Artifacts," *Nature Medicine* 1, 1993, p. 113.

62. "New Questions Raised in Wisconsin Rape Case," *Chicago Tribune,* November 25, 1990; Robert Imrie, "New Trial in 46-Personality Rape Case in Doubt," *St. Paul Pioneer Press,* December 8, 1990, p. 15A.

63. Robert Imrie (Associated Press), "Court Upholds Sexual Assault Conviction, Sentence," *St. Paul Pioneer Press,* June 1, 1995, p. 3B.

64. *State v. Steadman* (Wisc. Court of Appeals, District III, No. 94-2789-CR, May 31, 1995; unpublished).

65. Mark Bowles: Buckley, "Unfounded Reports of Rape." James Liggett: Jolayne Houtz, "Rape Puzzle Broke Apart with Last Piece; Charges Dropped Against Man," *Seattle Times,* January 14, 1992, p. B1.

66. U.S. Senate, Judiciary Committee, *The Response to Rape: Detours on the Road to Equal Justice,* May 1993, pp. 52–53.

67. U.S. Department of Justice, Bureau of Justice Statistics, *Tracking Offenders 1988* (Washington, D.C.: Government Printing Office, June 1991), p. 2; *The Response to Rape,* p. 65.

68. Vachss, *Sex Crimes,* pp. 278, 141, 146–147.

69. Michele Salcedo, "Ex-Cop's Plea Deal," *New York Newsday,* October 9, 1996; Sheryl McCarthy, "Sometimes, Even the 'Victim' Can Be Suspect," *New York Newsday,* October 14, 1996.

70. Jason Wolfe with Barbara Walsh, "State Tried Jailer Despite Case Riddled with Holes," *Maine Sunday Telegraph,* January 21, 1996, p. 1A. The Maine state legislature later agreed to pay O'Malley $150,000 in compensation. See "Wronged Jail Guard Awarded $150,000," *Portland Press Herald,* June 4, 1997.

71. Phyllis C. Richman, "This Is Not a Love Story: What One Date Rape Case Tells Us About Men, Women and Washington," *Washington Post,* November 21, 1993, p. C1.

72. Elinor J. Brecher, "The Whole Story," *Miami Herald,* November 26, 1989 (Sunday magazine), p. 10.

73. Tom Dubocq and Laurie Grossman, "Jurors Steadfast About Controversial Rape Verdict," *Miami Herald,* October 21, 1989, p. 1BR; Jim King, "Gwinnett Jurors Find Lord Guilty of Attempted Rape," *Atlanta Constitution,* March 30, 1990, p. E2.

74. Brecher, "The Whole Story."

75. "Rape Victims' Dress Not for Trial Evidence," *Miami Herald,* May 8, 1990.

76. Chip Brown, "Austin Jury Takes Two Hours to Convict 'Condom Rapist,'" *Houston Post,* May 14, 1993, p. A1.

77. Stuart Taylor, Jr., "Mike Tyson Deserves a Rematch," *American Lawyer,* May 1992, p. 28 (Taylor acknowledged Tyson's "history of brutal conduct toward women" and cautioned, "Maybe he deserves to be [in jail]. But not on the basis of this trial"); George P. Fletcher, *With Justice for Some: Victims' Rights in Criminal Trials* (Reading, Mass.: Addison Wesley, 1995), pp. 126–131.

78. Fletcher, *With Justice for Some,* p. 131.

79. Associated Press, "Five Tyson Jurors Have Doubts About Guilt," *St. Paul Pioneer Press,* March 26, 1995, p. 15C; Ron Borges, "Dershowitz: R.I. Court Ruling Should Help Free Tyson," *Boston Globe,* June 26, 1992, p. 69.

80. *Burden of Proof,* CNN, September 29, 1997.

81. On Steinem's involvement, see, e.g., Debbie Nathan and Michael Snedeker, *Satan's Silence: Ritual Abuse and the Making of a Modern American Witch Hunt* (New York: Basic Books, 1995), p. 242. For more on feminism and recovered memories see Mark Pendergrast, *Victims of Memory* (Hinesburg, Vt.: Upper Access Books, 1995). Herman: Judith L. Herman, "The Abuses of Memory," *Mother Jones,* March–April 1993, pp. 3–4.

82. *People v. Barnes,* 721 P.2d 110 (Cal. 1986), p. 122; Margaret T. Gordon, "Rape and the Benefit of Belief," *Chicago Tribune,* April 24, 1985; Fletcher, *With Justice for Some,* p. 131.

Chapter 7. Sexual McCarthyism

1. See, e.g., Jill Lawrence, "Air of Sexual McCarthyism Chills the Nation's Capital," *USA Today,* September 18, 1998, p. A1.

2. Secret files: *Docket Report* (Washington, D.C.: Center for Individual Rights), August 1995. Policies on workplace romances: Stuart Silverstein, "New Rules of Office Romance," *Los Angeles Times,* September 23, 1998, p. A1.

3. David I. Grossvogel, *Dear Ann Landers: Our Intimate Dialogue with America's Best-Loved Confidante* (Chicago: Contemporary Books, 1987), p. 153. Nineteenth- and early twentieth-century accounts of sexual coercion of working women: see, e.g., Jan Lambertz, "Sexual Harassment in the Nineteenth-Century English Cotton Industry," *History Workshop Journal* 19, 1985, pp. 29–61; Ann Farnsworth-Alvear, "The Mysterious Case of the Missing Men: Gender and Class in Early Industrial Medellin," *International Labor and Working-Class History* 49, 1996, pp. 73–92. Sherlock Holmes: Arthur Conan Doyle, "The Problem of Thor Bridge," in *The Complete Sherlock Holmes* (Garden City, N.Y.: Doubleday, 1930), p. 1061. Harassment as "violence against women": Louise F. Fitzgerald, "Sexual Harassment: Violence Against Women in the Workplace," *American Psychologist* 48, 1993, pp. 1070–1076.

4. Joe Sapia, "Sexual Harassment Policy May Be Overdue," *Asbury Park (N.J.) Press,* January 30, 1994, p. AA2; Emily Bliss, "Princeton Student Dining Hall Workers Experience Sexual Harassment," *Daily Princetonian,* January 12, 1998.

5. Virginia Slims American Women's Poll 1995 (Roper Organization, conducted in November–December 1994).

6. "Eye of the beholder": Susan Strauss (with Pamela Espeland), *Sexual Harassment and Teens: A Program for Positive Change* (Minneapolis: Free Spirit Publishing, 1992), pp. 46, 56.

7. "Too Many Guys Just Don't Get It," *New York Newsday*, October 10, 1991, p. 78.

8. Nancy Gibbs, "Office Crimes," *Time*, October 21, 1991, p. 52; Ellen Goodman, "Honk If You Believe Anita," *Boston Globe*, October 17, 1991, p. 17.

9. Joyce Slater, "'Hey, Sweet Thing!': For Women, Little Change," *USA Today*, October 11, 1991, p. 10A; Kim Masters, "Taking It Personally," *Washington Post*, October 11, 1991, p. D5.

10. Tannen: Gigi Anders, "Sexual Harassment: The Meanings of It All," *Washington Post*, October 11, 1991, p. D5. "Pedestal": Virginia Postrel, "Don't Put Women Back on Pedestals," *Los Angeles Times*, October 11, 1991; see also Sarah J. McCarthy, "Cultural Fascism," *Forbes*, December 9, 1991, p. 116; Cathy Young, "Sexual Harassment and Rhetorical Overkill," *New York Newsday*, October 22, 1991, p. 99.

11. Christopher Hitchens, "The Wrong Questions," *Washington Post Book World*, November 9, 1997, p. X4.

12. Ellis Henican, "No Laughing Matter at TA: 'Stupid' Joke by Bus Boss Proves as Funny as a Flat Tire," *New York Newsday*, January 30, 1992, p. 3; Nat Hentoff, "Sexual Harassment by Speaker Phone," *Washington Post*, March 14, 1992, p. A23.

13. "Legislator in Albany Says Colleagues Harassed Her," *New York Times*, January 12, 1993; Nicholas Goldberg, "Apology Made to Hill for Remark," *New York Newsday*, January 13, 1993; "Hill Should Fight Sex Harassment by Reporting It" (editorial), *New York Newsday*, January 27, 1993. (Hill, who is black, also charged that in 1989, an assemblyman whose advances she rejected yelled racial insults at her. But the culprit was never identified, and one may wonder why Hill didn't go public right away: sexual harassment may not have been a big deal then, but racial slurs surely were. Most of the attention focused on the other two offenses, to which the culprits confessed.) Judith Gaines, "Truth in Such Cases Often Elusive," *Boston Globe*, January 23, 1993; Frank Phillips, "Ex-MCAD Chief Cleared of Harassment," *Boston Globe*, June 22, 1993.

14. Anita F. Hill, "The Dismal Reality Remains," *Newsweek*, September 18, 1995, p. 34.

15. Rhode, *Speaking of Sex*, p. 98 (incidents not "isolated examples"); see also Fitzgerald, "Sexual Harassment," pp. 1070–1071. Survey: Karen K. Gard, "The Manager's Role in Stopping Unwanted Sexual Attention," *Public Manager: The New Bureaucrat*, March 22, 1996, p. 41.

16. Pollitt: *Heads Up* (with Michael Kinsley), CNN, June 25, 1994; Estrich and Smeal: *CNN & Co.*, May 10, 1994. As some commentators noted, Jones's allegations were not only better corroborated than Hill's but more serious (Stuart Taylor, Jr., "Her Case Against Clinton," *American Lawyer*, November 1996, p. 57).

17. *Equal Time,* CNBC, January 13, 1997; Susan Estrich, "Hostile Environment: It's a Case of the Powerless vs. the Powerful," *Los Angeles Times,* October 13, 1991, p. M1.

18. Surveys: e.g., Margot Slade, "Law Firms Begin Reining in Sex-Harassing Partners," *New York Times,* February 25, 1994, p. A19; "Responding to Harassment," *Washington Post,* March 13, 1996, p. A19.

19. See Fred Strebeigh, "Defining Law on the Feminist Frontier," *New York Times Magazine,* October 6, 1991, p. 31.

20. *Williams v. Saxbe,* 413 F. Supp. 654 (D.D.C. 1976) (first legal victory for concept of sexual harassment); EEOC Guidelines on Discrimination Because of Sex, 29 C.F.R. sec. 1604.11 (1980).

21. Mary Battiata, "Mechelle Vinson's Tangled Trials," *Washington Post,* August 11, 1986, and "Mechelle Vinson's Long Road to Court," *Washington Post,* August 12, 1986. Settlement: author's interview with Patricia Barry, March 13, 1996.

22. *Meritor Savings Bank v. Vinson,* 477 U.S. 57 (1986), p. 68. See also Philip Hager, "Sex Harassment Suits Not Tied to Money Upheld," *Los Angeles Times,* June 20, 1986, p. 1.

23. Quoted in Tamar Lewin, "Sexual Harassment in the Workplace: A Grueling Struggle for Equality," *New York Times,* November 9, 1986, p. F12.

24. Ellen Frankel Paul, "Sexual Harassment As Sex Discrimination: A Defective Paradigm," *Yale Law and Policy Review* 8, 1990, pp. 333–364.

25. Seattle Human Rights Department, *Building for Equality* (Seattle, Wash., 1996), p. 1.

26. Stephen Henderson, "America Re-Examines the Issues," *Chicago Tribune* (*Internet Tribune* edition), May 23, 1996 (quoting Monica Ballard).

27. Ginsburg: *Harris v. Forklift Systems, Inc.,* 114 S. Ct. 367 (1993) (Ginsburg, J., concurring), p. 372. Norton: quoted in Leah Beth Ward, "Zaring Suit Puts Gender-Based Remarks on Trial," *Cincinnati Enquirer,* February 26, 1995, p. E1. "Kid sister test": Ronald M. Green, "The 'Kid Sister' Test for Harassment," *New York Times,* August 23, 1998, p. BU13. Green adds that the test is "not gender-specific," but it's hard to imagine anyone getting worked up at the thought of a kid brother having to hear sexual banter at the office.

28. Jeffrey Rosen, "Men Behaving Badly," *New Republic,* December 29, 1997, p. 18; see also Joan Biskupic, "Justices Hear Harassment Case," *Washington Post,* December 4, 1997, p. A25. For other cases of this type see *Goluszek v. Smith,* 697 F. Supp. (N.D. Ill. 1988); see also L. M. Sixel, "Wrongs Without Remedy: Federal Laws Offer Little Relief from Same-Sex Harassment," *Houston Chronicle,* September 17, 1995, Business Section, p. 1.

29. Decisions rejecting the view that Title VII covers sexual harassment: *Corne v. Bausch & Lomb,* 390 F. Supp. 161 (D. Ariz. 1975). Harassment lawsuits under tort and contract law: *Monge v. Beebe Rubber,* 316 A.2d 529 (N.H. 1974), *Miller v. Bank of America,* 418 F. Supp. 233 (1976). MacKinnon: Catharine A. MacKinnon, *Sexual Harassment of Working Women* (New Haven, Conn.: Yale University Press, 1979), p. 88.

30. Eugene Volokh, "How Harassment Law Restricts Free Speech," *Rutgers*

Law Review 47, 1995, p. 563; Eugene Volokh, "What Speech Does 'Hostile Work Environment' Harassment Law Restrict?" *Georgetown Law Journal* 85, 1997, pp. 627–648. See also Kingsley R. Browne, "Title VII as Censorship: Hostile-Environment Harassment and the First Amendment," *Ohio State Law Journal* 52, 1991, p. 481, and Nadine Strossen, "Regulating Workplace Sexual Harassment and Upholding the First Amendment—Avoiding a Collision," *Villanova Law Review* 37, 1992, p. 757.

31. Pamphlet: U.S. Department of Labor, *Sexual Harassment: Know Your Rights* (Washington, D.C.: U.S. Government Printing Office, 1994). *Esquire* incident: Mary Huhn, "*Esquire* Reader May Be Facing Dismissal over Possession," *New York Post,* September 4, 1997; Jerry Weatherhogg, "LOTT Worker in Esquire Uproad Fired," *The Olympian,* November 7, 1997, p. C1.

32. Charles Looney, director of the EEOC New England office, quoted in Gibbs, "Office Crimes," p. 53.

33. Keven Willey, "Kyle Should Think Again about That Lawsuit," *Arizona Republic,* February 11, 1998, p. B2.

34. Art Buchwald, "The Harass Poll," *Washington Post,* November 17, 1983, p. C1.

35. Virgil L. Sheets and Sanford L. Braver, "Perceptions of Sexual Harassment: Effects of a Harasser's Attractiveness" (paper presented at the conference of the Western Psychological Association, Phoenix, Ariz., 1993).

36. *Harris v. Forklift Systems, Inc.,* 113 S. Ct. 1382, 122 L.Ed.2d 758 (1993).

37. *Harris v. Forklift Systems, Inc.,* 1994 U.S. Dist. LEXIS 19928; "Sex Harassment Case Settled," *Washington Post,* February 10, 1995, p. A2; Aaron Epstein, "Can Words Alone Spell Illegal Sexual Harassment?" *Miami Herald,* October 10, 1993, p. 1K.

38. David G. Savage, "Irritation or Harassment? High Court to Decide," *St. Louis Post Dispatch,* October 12, 1993, p. 11B.

39. Karin Miller, "Supreme Court—Sexual Harassment," Associated Press, October 10, 1993.

40. Ninth Circuit Court: *Ellison v. Brady,* 924 F.2d 872 (9th Cir. 1991) at 879, n. 12.

41. Seventh Circuit case: *Baskerville v. Culligan Int'l. Co.,* 50 F.3d 428 (7th Cir. 1995). *Oncale v. Sundowner Offshore Services Inc.,* No. 95-568 (U.S. March 4, 1998).

42. Walter Olson, "Have the Harassment Rules Changed?" *Wall Street Journal,* April 6, 1998.

43. *Hall v. Gus Construction Co., Inc.,* 842 F.2d 1010 (8th Cir. 1988).

44. UPI, "Sex Harassment Judgement Is Upheld," January 4, 1996. The details of the case are from Brief of Appellant, *Zaring v. Black,* U.S. Court of Appeals for the Sixth Circuit, March 25, 1996.

45. The account of *Kimzey v. Wal-Mart* is based on briefs filed with the U.S. Court of Appeals for the Eighth Circuit (No. 95-4219, Cross-Appeal 95-4220). Sexual harassment suits over nonsexual abusive behavior by bosses: see, e.g., *Montandon v. Farmland Industries, Inc.,* 116 F.3d 355 (1997).

46. Michael A. Verespej, "New-Age Sexual Harassment," *Industry Week,* May 15, 1995, p. 64; Phillip M. Perry, "Avoid Costly Lawsuits for Sexual Harassment,"

Law Practice Management, April 1992, p. 18. See also Barry A. Harstein and Thomas M. Wilde, "The Broadening Scope of Harassment in the Workplace," *Employee Relations Law Journal* 19, 1994, p. 648. "Seinfeld" verdict: Marshall H. Tanick, "No Rhyme or Reason for 'Seinfeld' firing," *National Law Journal,* August 18, 1997, p. A19. 1998 rulings: Joan Biskupic, "Supreme Court Draws Line on Harassment," *Washington Post,* June 27, 1998, p. A1; Liza Mundy, "Liability, Not Labels," *Washington Post,* June 27, 1998, p. A1.

47. Cheryl Johnson, "The Latest in Offensive Workplace Items? A New Yorker Cartoon," *Minneapolis Star Tribune,* January 18, 1994; Abigail Van Buren, "'Dog Named Sex' Wags Its Tale for Fresh Laughs," *St. Paul Pioneer Press,* April 7, 1995, p. 2E; *Cardin v. VIA Tropical Fruits, Inc.,* 7 Fla. L. Weekly Fed. D456 (1993) (see more on this court case below).

48. Government agency policies: for a summary see Volokh, "What Speech Does 'Hostile Work Environment' Harassment Law Restrict?" Corporate policies: Joann S. Lublin, "Companies Try a Variety of Approaches to Halt Sexual Harassment on the Job," *Wall Street Journal,* October 11, 1991, p. B1

49. Hatten's board game: author's interview with Chuck Hatten, April 19, 1996, and Daryl Strickland, "Board Game Helps Workers Learn Do's, Don'ts of Sexual Harassment," *Seattle Times,* March 1, 1996, p. E1. Harassment training: Julia Lawlor, "Stepping over the line," *Sales and Marketing Management,* October 1995, p. 90; Deborah Duenes and Francine Hermelin, "Sexual Harassment Inc.," *Working Woman,* October 1994, p. 9.

50. Rhode, *Speaking of Sex,* pp. 97–98. For the story of the graduate student, see Nat Hentoff, "A 'Pinup' of His Wife," *Washington Post,* June 5, 1993, p. A21.

51. Silva case: Anthony Flint, "Issues of P.C. Not Always Clear," *Boston Globe,* January 30, 1994, p. 37. Silva, who was suspended because he refused to get counseling, sued the university and was eventually reinstated. Professor penalized for being too friendly: Linda Chavez, "Sexual Harassment: One Case Gone Awry," *USA Today,* August 23, 1995, p. 11A (Professor James Maas at Cornell); sex-related essay topics: R. M. O'Neill, "Protecting Free Speech When the Issue Is Sexual Harassment," *Chronicle of Higher Education,* September 13, 1996, pp. B3–B4. Lyman: Dean Solov, "Ex-USF Student Says Professor's Punishment Too Lenient," *Tampa Tribune,* August 20, 1997.

52. See Duff Wilson, "Aide Goes Public in Ombudsman Beef," *Seattle Times,* September 10, 1996, p. B1; David Schaeffer, "Ombudsman Is Fired," *Seattle Times,* October 22, 1996. Krull sued and later collected a $450,000 settlement: Dave Birkland and Kery Murakami, "Fired Ombudsman to Receive $450,000 from King County," *Seattle Times,* January 13, 1998, p. B2.

53. *Pierce v. Commonwealth Life Insurance Co.,* 825 F. Supp. 783 (Ky., 1993).

54. Alex Michelini, "Male Teller Can't Bear Nudie Pix," *New York Daily News,* January 16, 1995.

55. Margot Slade, "Sexual Harassment: Stories from the Field," *New York Times,* March 27, 1994, pp. E1, E6.

56. See, e.g., Pamela Warrick, "The Buss Fuss," *Los Angeles Times,* September 27, 1996; Julia Prodis, "Stealing Kisses," Associated Press, September 27, 1996.

57. Nina J. Easton, "The Law of the School Yard," *Los Angeles Times*

Magazine, October 2, 1994, p. 16; Ruth Shalit, "Romper Room," *New Republic,* March 29, 1993, p. 14 (quote from Sue Sattel).

58. Mary Jordan, "Sex Harassment Complaints Starting in Grade School; Taunts, Intolerance on the Rise, Survey Finds," *Washington Post,* June 2, 1993, p. A1.

59. Same-sex harassment: Nina J. Easton, "The Law of the School Yard," *Los Angeles Times Magazine,* October 2, 1994, p. 16. Training materials: *Boys and Girls Getting Along: Teaching Sexual Harassment Prevention* (St. Paul: Minnesota Department of Education, 1993); *Project RAP: Relationships and Power* (Trenton, N.J., 1994).

60. AAUW, *Hostile Hallways: The AAUW Survey on Sexual Harassment in America's Schools* (Washington, D.C.: American Association of University Women, 1993), and Jordan, "Sex Harassment Complaints Starting in Grade School."

61. Celebration of Our Work conference, Institute for Research on Women, Douglass College/Rutgers University, May 1993.

62. *Boys and Girls Getting Along,* pp. 23, 65.

63. Frank Ahrens, "Coach Flynn's Toughest Race," *Washington Post,* September 8, 1998, p. B1.

64. MacKinnon, *Sexual Harassment of Working Women,* p. 1; "Responding to Harassment," *Washington Post,* March 13, 1996 (survey of federal workers); Associated Press, "Study: Many Women Doctors Harassed," *Chicago Tribune,* December 23, 1993, p. 19.

65. L. A. Winokur, "The Sexual-Harassment Debates," *Progressive,* November 1993, p. 37.

66. Catharine A. MacKinnon, "Sexuality, Pornography, and Method: Pleasure Under Patriarchy," *Ethics* 99, 1989, pp. 314–346 (on feminist theory). MacKinnon has also written that "heterosexuality . . . institutionalizes male sexual dominance and female sexual submission" (*Toward a Feminist Theory of the State* [Cambridge, Mass.: Harvard University Press, 1989], p. 113).

67. Kathryn Abrams, "Gender Discrimination and the Transformation of Workplace Norms," *Vanderbilt Law Review* 42, 1989, p. 1205. Abrams concedes that "many women hold positive attitudes about uncoerced sex" but seeks to "balance" this with a reference to Andrea Dworkin's *Intercourse,* summarized as, "Sexual intercourse is inherently coercive and contributes inevitably to the subordination of women" (p. 1209, note 94).

68. "Pornography": Abrams, "Gender Discrimination and the Transformation of Workplace Norms," p. 121. Abrams citation: *Robinson v. Jacksonville Shipyards,* 760 F. Supp. 1486 (M.D. Fla. 1991), p. 1542.

69. Martha Chamallas, "Feminist Constructions of Objectivity: Multiple Perspectives in Sexual and Racial Harassment Litigation," *Texas Journal of Women and the Law* 1, 1992, p. 126; Susan Estrich, "Sex at Work," *Stanford Law Review* 43, 1991, p. 860: "I would have no objection to rules which prohibited men and women from sexual relations in the workplace, at least with those who worked directly for them." Compare Estrich on MSNBC's *Internight,* January 26, 1998, discussing Bill Clinton's alleged affair with White House intern Monica Lewinsky: "As a matter of good practice, don't mess with people who work for you. But it's not against the law." Flirting tips: "How to Make an Impact on a Man,"

Cosmopolitan, February 1989, p. 177.

70. Patti A. Giuffre and Christine L. Williams, "Boundary Lines: Labeling Sexual Harassment in Restaurants," *Gender and Society* 8, 1994, p. 379.

71. Ibid., p. 397.

72. See *Robinson v. Jacksonville Shipyards* and *Ellison v. Brady,* 924 F.2d 872, 879 (9th Cir. 1991); *Cardin* v. *VIA Tropical Fruits.*

73. Ellen Goodman, "Crichton's 'Disclosure' Incomplete," *Boston Globe,* December 18, 1994, p. 83 (see also Abrams, "Gender Discrimination," pp. 1188–1189); Dianne Hales and Dr. Robert Hales, "Can Men and Women Work Together?" *Parade,* March 20, 1994, p. 10 ("would you tell another guy . . ."); Christine Bertelson, "A Simple Test for Harassment," *St. Louis Post-Dispatch,* September 6, 1994, p. B1 (the "mom" test); Toni Bryan, "Sexual Harassment: You Don't Have to Take It," *Cosmopolitan Life After College,* fall–winter 1994, p. 101.

74. Ellison: *Ellison v. Brady,* 924 F.2d 872 (9th Cir. 1991), p. 879. After Ellison refused to go out for drinks with coworker Sterling Gray, he handed her a note saying, "I cried over you last night . . . I could not stand to feel your hatred for another day," and later confronted Ellison in a hallway and demanded that she talk to him. He then wrote her several bizarre, obsessive letters.

75. Beth Milwid, *Working with Men* (New York: Berkeley Books, 1990), p. 124 (originally published as *What You Get When You Go for It* [Dodd, Mead, 1987]).

76. Malcolm Gladwell, "The Healy Experiment," *Washington Post* (Magazine), June 21, 1992, pp. 9–10. The resulting tensions eventually forced Healy to leave the school.

77. Milwid, *Working with Men,* p. 126.

78. Kingsley R. Browne, "Title VII as Censorship: Hostile-Environment Harassment and the First Amendment," *Ohio State Law Journal* 52, 1991, p. 491 (men's views of women colleagues); Hales and Hales, "Can Men and Women Work Together?" (Susan Webb); Abrams, "Gender Discrimination and the Transformation of Workplace Norms," p. 1209.

79. Carol Brooks Gardner, *Passing by: Gender and Public Harassment* (Berkeley: University of California Press, 1995), pp. 1–2, 178. Cynthia Grant Bowman, "Street Harassment and the Informal Ghettoization of Women," *Harvard Law Review* 106, 1993, p. 517.

80. Mark Lorando, "New Study: Sexual Harassment on Sitcoms Suggests Some Producers Just Don't Get It," *New Orleans Times Picayune,* January 5, 1995, p. E1; "On Television: Sex Harassment Is Routine, Study Says," *Atlanta Constitution,* December 26, 1994, p. C9.

81. Ellen Goodman, "Running a Light in the Harassment Zone," *Boston Globe,* July 4, 1993, p. A23.

82. Conservatives: see, e.g., Irving Kristol, "Reflections on Love and Family," *Wall Street Journal,* January 7, 1992, p. A10.

83. *Swentek v. USAir,* 830 F.2d 552 (1987).

84. Author's interview, November 4, 1994.

85. "Nurses Sue Ex-Boss over Bawdy Jokes," *San Francisco Chronicle,* March

31, 1993, p. A19.

86. Bill Turque, "The Class of '92: Housebroken," *Newsweek,* November 29, 1993, p. 32 (Margolies-Mezvinsky); Mark Thompson, "A Political Suicide," *Time,* May 13, 1996 (Blanchard); Elizabeth Kolbert, "An Open Mike, A Loudmouth Live, and Thou . . .," *New York Times,* September 26, 1993, p. E2 (radio talk show hosts).

87. Verespej, "New-Age Sexual Harassment" (male complaints), *Washington Post,* March 13, 1996, p. A16; Rebecca A. Thacker and Stephen F. Gohmann, "Male/Female Differences in Perceptions and Effects of Hostile Environment Sexual Harassment: 'Reasonable' Assumptions?" *Public Personnel Management* 22, 1993, pp. 461–472 (federal workers); AAUW, *Hostile Hallways.*

88. Differences overstated: Thacker and Gohmann, "Male/Female Differences in Perceptions and Effects of Hostile Environment Sexual Harassment." Robert Wright, "Feminists, Meet Mr. Darwin," *New Republic,* November 28, 1994, pp. 34–46.

89. "Mark Jennings and LaShawn Howell, "Uh, Girls Aren't the Only Ones Getting Hassled," *Washington Post,* July 25, 1993, p. C3.

90. David Thomas, *Not Guilty: The Case in Defense of Men* (New York: William Morrow, 1993), p. 136.

91. Jay Segal, *The Sex Lives of College Students* (Wayne, Pa.: Miles Standish Press, 1984), p. 286.

92. *Zowayyed v. Lowen Company, Inc.,* 735 F. Supp. 1497 (1990).

93. Molly Haskell, "Managing Your Sexuality," *Working Woman,* August 1994, p. 31.

94. See, e.g., Bruce Avolio, Jane Howell and John Sosik, "A Funny Thing Happened on the Way to the Bottom Line" (paper presented at the 1996 meeting of the Society of Industrial and Organizational Psychology, San Diego); see also Associated Press story by Dave Ivey, September 1, 1996.

95. Verne Gay, "Old Yeller," *George,* May 1998, p. 97. Kirk Johnson, "Office Romance: Love On Line at Speed of Light," *New York Times,* March 26, 1994.

96. Eloise Salholz, "Did America 'Get It'?" *Newsweek,* December 28, 1992, p. 22 (Andrea Sankar); "For Water Cooler Paramours, Ties That (Legally) Bind," *New York Times,* February 22, 1998, p. WK7.

97. Alex Kuczynski, "In Offices, an Excuse to Mention S*x," *New York Times,* February 1, 1998, p. ST1.

98. "Unusual interest": Philip Hillen, the top civilian executive of the Army's Military Traffic Management Command, was fired in 1985 for allegedly harassing five female employees. In one instance, the woman "said he had taken an unusual interest in her career and looked at her in a sexually suggestive way." Greg Pierce, "Court: Agencies Are Free to Define Sexual Harassment," *Washington Times,* April 26, 1994, p. A7.

99. See, e.g., Goodman, "Running a Light in the Harassment Zone."

Chapter 8. Men and Their Children

1. Joan Beck, "A Chilling Message to Working Moms," *Chicago Tribune,* March 16, 1995. See also Eileen McNamara, "Working Moms: Guilty," *Boston Globe,* March 4, 1995; Robin Abcarian, "As Standards Go, This One's a Double,"

Los Angeles Times, March 8, 1995; Anna Quindlen, "Done in by Day Care," *New York Times,* July 30, 1994.

2. Judith Regan, "An Open Letter to Mr. Clark," *Newsweek,* March 13, 1995, p. 57; *This Week with David Brinkley,* ABC, March 5, 1995.

3. Susan Chira, *A Mother's Place: Taking the Debate About Working Mothers Beyond Guilt and Blame* (New York: HarperCollins, 1998), pp. 186–187; LynNell Hancock, "Putting Working Moms in Custody," *Newsweek,* March 13, 1995, p. 54 (Clark); Paul Duggan, "Old Assumptions Die on the Custody Battlefield," *Washington Post,* August 24, 1994, p. A1 (Prost).

4. Stephanie Abarbanel, "The Day-Care vs. Grandma Custody Battle," *Good Housekeeping,* February 1995. See also Jacquelynn Boyle, "Maranda's Dad Says the Point Is Just Her," *Detroit Free Press,* August 5, 1994.

5. *Ireland v. Smith,* Opinion of the Court, Macomb County Circuit Court, Michigan, June 27, 1994.

6. Alice Hector: Melody Petersen, "The Short End of Long Hours: A Female Lawyer's Job Puts Child Custody at Risk," *New York Times,* July 18, 1998, p. D1. New York case: *Lenczycki v. Lenczycki,* 543 M/U/S2d 724 (A.D.2 Dept. 1989). See also *re the Marriage of Leopondo,* 106 Illinois Appellate Court, Third Judicial Circuit 444, 435 N.E.2d 1312, aff'd (1983).

7. Karen Winner, *Divorced from Justice: The Abuse of Women and Children by Lawyers and Judges* (New York: Regan Books/HarperCollins, 1996); 1996 National NOW Conference Resolutions, *National NOW Times,* October 1996. See also Teresa M. Hanafin, "Fathers' Rights Advocates Will Fast," *Boston Globe,* November 5, 1991, p. 65; Marian Henriquez Neudel, "Do You Think Mothers 'Automatically' Get Custody? Think Again," *Chicago Tribune,* August 22, 1994.

8. Phyllis Chesler, *Mothers on Trial: The Battle for Children and Custody* (New York: McGraw-Hill, 1986), pp. 80–81. Most of the sixty women were recruited through Chesler's newspaper ad or referred by lawyers, psychologists, or women's centers. Obviously, women dissatisfied with the outcome of their cases would have been much more likely to participate. Many were lesbians; this doesn't mean they should have lost custody, but it does suggest that these were not typical cases.

9. For mixed reviews of *Mothers on Trial,* see, e.g., Wendy Kaminer, "Worst-Case Scenarios," *New York Times Book Review,* January 5, 1986, and Carol Rinzler, "Family Fights: Who Gets the Kids?" *Washington Post,* February 2, 1986. Witch-trial parallel: Chesler, *Mothers on Trial,* pp. 308–331. For citations of Chesler's figures, see Kay Longcope, "Phyllis Chesler Makes Her Custody Case," *Boston Globe,* February 6, 1986; Sharon Johnson, "The Odds on Custody Change," *New York Times,* March 17, 1986; Leslie Berger, "Money a Potent Factor in Thomas Custody Case," *Los Angeles Times,* October 20, 1993, p. A1. Weitzman: Lenore J. Weitzman and Ruth B. Dixon, "Child Custody Awards: Legal Standards and Empirical Patterns for Child Custody, Support and Visitation After Divorce," *University of California–Davis Law Review* 12, 1979, pp. 473–521; Lenore J. Weitzman, *The Divorce Revolution: The Unexpected Social and Economic Consequences for Women and Children in America* (New York: Free Press, 1986), p. 233. See also Andree Brooks, "Mothers Defending Rights of Custody," *New York Times,* February 26, 1983, p. 48. Massachusetts Gender Bias Study: Report of the

Gender Bias Study of the Supreme Judicial Court (Boston: Commonwealth of Massachusetts, 1989), p. 62. Citations in the media: see, e.g., D'Vera Cohn, "For Women, Work Gains Can Mean Home Losses," *Washington Post,* August 26, 1994; Susan Chira, "Custody Fight in Capital: A Working Mother Loses," *New York Times,* September 20, 1994; Susan Weiner, "Irreconcilable Differences: Parenting Is More Than a Battle of the Sexes," *Chicago Tribune,* September 30, 1994; Lisa Genasci, "Increasingly, Working Mothers Lose in Custody Fights," *Los Angeles Times,* January 20, 1995; McNamara, "Working Moms: Guilty."

10. Report of the Gender Bias Study, p. 57.

11. Weitzman, *The Divorce Revolution,* pp. 232–234. Gender Bias Study data: Amy Koel et al., "A Comparison of Joint and Sole Legal Custody Agreements," in E. Mavis Hetherington and Josephine D. Arasteh, eds., *Impact of Divorce, Single-Parenting, and Stepparenting on Children* (Hillsdale, N.J.: Erlbaum, 1988), p. 78. The Gender Bias Study (p. 62) refers simply to cases in which "the father sought custody."

12. Virgil Sheets and Sanford Braver, "Gender Differences in Satisfaction with Divorce Settlements," *Family Relations* (in press), and Sanford L. Braver and William A. Griffin, "Involving Fathers in the Post-Divorce Family" (paper presented at the Conference on Father Involvement, National Institute of Child Health and Human Development, Bethesda, Md., October 1996).

13. Wendy Reiboldt and Sharon Seiling, "Factors Related to Men's Award of Custody," *Family Advocate* 15, 1993, pp. 42–45.

14. Eleanor E. Maccoby and Robert H. Mnookin, *Dividing the Child* (Cambridge, Mass.: Harvard University Press, 1992), pp. 104–105, 149–150.

15. Ed Hayward, "Abusers Would Be Denied Custody Under Gov's Bills," *Boston Herald,* February 14, 1997, p. 4. Legal Aid attorney: Beth A. Levy, "Courts Should Curtail Abusive Fathers' Visits" (letter to the editor), *New York Times,* September 11, 1995.

16. See *In re the marriage of Jeanine Nevers and David Nevers,* Brief of Appellee/Cross-Appellant, No. 94 D 1605, Appellate Court of the State of Illinois, Second Judicial District, pp. 39, 44; Brief of Appellant.

17. "Putting Kids in the Middle" (editorial), *Atlanta Constitution,* February 19, 1996, p. A10 ("though 90 percent of custody goes to women, that's largely because most men don't want it . . ."). Desire for custody: Maccoby and Mnookin, *Dividing the Child,* pp. 99–102. The self-reported mean rating of the importance attached to the custody outcome was 8.4 for fathers and 8.8 for mothers.

18. Maccoby and Mnookin, *Dividing the Child,* p. 102; Douglas R. Page, "The Fitness Factor," *Family Advocate,* winter 1993, p. 47. In a survey in Vermont, 40 percent of male attorneys and 26 percent of female attorneys said that they "often" or "sometimes" discouraged male clients from filing for custody because of bias in the courts. *Gender and Justice: Report of the Vermont Task Force on Gender Bias in the Legal System* (1991), pp. 105–106.

19. Eric D. Turner, "Do's and Don't for Fathers Seeking Custody," *Family Advocate* 15, 1993, pp. 50–54 (moving out). Legal representation: Reiboldt and Seiling, "Factors Related to Men's Award of Custody," p. 44 (84 percent of wives

and 63 percent of husbands were represented by an attorney); Maccoby and Mnookin, *Dividing the Child,* p. 108; Gay C. Kitson, *Portrait of Divorce* (New York: Guilford Press, 1992), p. 241. For claims that women do not have the resources for legal representation, see, e.g., Report of the Gender Bias Study, pp. 20, 63. On husbands' payment of legal costs see Page, "The Fitness Factor." The Massachusetts Gender Bias Study acknowledges that Legal Aid usually represents only "primary caretakers" (read mothers) in custody disputes (p. 21).

20. Report of the Gender Bias Study, pp. 59–63; Deborah Rhode, *Speaking of Sex: The Denial of Gender Inequality* (Cambridge, Mass.: Harvard University Press, 1997), p. 190.

21. Deborah Eisel, "Can Fathers Be 'Mothers'? What Lawyers and Mental Health Professionals *Really* Think About Fathers and Custody," *Family Advocate,* winter 1993, pp. 62–67; Philip W. Cook, *Abused Men: The Hidden Side of Domestic Violence* (Westport, Conn.: Praeger, 1997), p. 66 ("get a regular job"); Jane Young, "The Fathers Also Rise," *New York,* November 18, 1985, p. 72 (Judge Huttner).

22. See, e.g., Rhode, *Speaking of Sex,* p. 182; Lorraine Dusky, *Still Unequal: The Shameful Truth About Women and Justice in America* (New York: Crown, 1996), p. 355; Nancy Polikoff, "Child Custody Disputes: Exploding the Myth That Mothers Always Win," in Irene Diamond (ed.), *Families, Politics and Public Policy: A Feminist Dialogue on Women and the State* (New York: Longman, 1982); Weitzman, *The Divorce Revolution,* pp. 225, 310–318; Maggie Gallagher, *Enemies of Eros: How the Sexual Revolution Is Killing Family, Marriage, and Sex and What We Can Do About It* (Chicago: Bonus Books, 1989), p. 207.

23. Maccoby and Mnookin, *Dividing the Child,* pp. 102, 156–157. See also Jed H. Abraham, "'The Divorce Revolution' Revisited: A Counter-Revolutionary Critique," *Northern Illinois University Law Review* 9, 1989, p. 282, and Margaret F. Brinig and Michael V. Alexeyev, "Trading at Divorce: Preferences, Legal Roles and Transaction Costs," *Ohio State Journal of Dispute Resolution* 8, 1993, pp. 279–297.

24. Scott Altman, "Lurking in the Shadow," *Southern California Law Review* 68, 1995, pp. 493–543. Other research: Sheets and Braver, "Gender Differences in Satisfaction with Divorce Settlements."

25. Author's interview with Al Manning, August 8, 1996.

26. Altman, "Lurking in the Shadow," p. 503; Rhode, *Speaking of Sex,* p. 182.

27. Massachusetts father: author's interview with E.H., July 15, 1996. Georgia case: *Gaffron v. Harrison,* Fulton County Superior Court Docket E-2692, December 17, 1993, hearing; see "Failure in Fulton," *Voices for Children* (Children's Rights Council of Georgia), October–December 1993.

28. The account of this case is based on legal briefs and trial transcripts in the case. State of Michigan, Circuit Court for the County of Ingham, File No. 89-66580-DM.

29. *New York Times,* June 4, 1990, p. A18.

30. Karen S. Schneider, "Daddy Meanest," *People Weekly,* September 4, 1995, p. 40.

31. Adding nuance: See, e.g., Michael Mariott, "Fathers Find That Child

Support Means Owing More Than Money," *New York Times,* July 20, 1992; William Claiborne, "Support Program Helps 'Deadbeat Dads' Find Jobs," *Washington Post,* February 11, 1994, p. A3; Jason DeParle, "Welfare Overhaul Initiatives Focus on Fathers," *New York Times,* September 3, 1998, p. A1. Clinton: Edward Walsh, "Clinton Stance Bolsters Group's Crusade to Enforce Child Support," *Washington Post,* January 3, 1993, p. A3. "Fathers Are Parents, Too," *Atlanta Journal-Constitution,* June 29, 1993, p. A12.

32. See Kitson, *Portrait of Divorce,* pp. 93, 123, and Lynn Gigy and Joan B. Kelly, "Reasons for Divorce: Perspectives of Divorcing Men and Women," *Journal of Divorce and Remarriage* 18, 1992, pp. 174–175. See also Maccoby and Mnookin, *Dividing the Child,* p. 95; Sanford Braver, Marnie Whitley, and Christine Ng, "Who Divorced Whom? Methodological and Theoretical Issues," *Journal of Divorce and Remarriage* 20, 1993, p. 1.

33. Weitzman, *The Divorce Revolution,* pp. 310–318, 258–259.

34. See, e.g., Katharine Webster, "Divorce Statistics Were Wrong," *Atlanta Constitution,* May 17, 1996, p. A6. Weitzman's statistic had been cited in hundreds of stories in the press, 250 law review articles, and at least 24 cases in state appellate and supreme courts. Delia M. Rios, "New Evidence Splits from Widely Used Divorce Research," *Oregonian,* April 21, 1996. For earlier critiques of *The Divorce Revolution,* see Saul D. Hoffman and Greg J. Duncan, "What Are the Economic Consequences of Divorce?" *Demography* 25, 1988, p. 641; Abraham, "'The Divorce Revolution' Revisited."

35. Lisa Cornwell, "Divorce Costly to Men, Study Says," *Columbus Dispatch,* July 26, 1994; *Journal (Akron, Ohio),* July 17, 1994, p. B1. The study was conducted by Gene Pollock and Atlee Stroup, College of Wooster, Ohio.

36. Sanford Braver, "The Economic Impact of Divorce on Mothers and Fathers" (presentation at the conference of the Children's Rights Council, Arlington, Va., October 25, 1997).

37. Braver, "The Economic Impact of Divorce"; see also *Estimates of Expenditures on Children and Child Support Guidelines,* U.S. Department of Health and Human Services, 1990, pp. 2–6 ("per capita expenditures 'estimates' are likely to overestimate the true level of expenditures on children").

38. Bruce Walker, "Deadbeat Dads? Look Closer," *Christian Science Monitor,* August 16, 1996, p. 18.

39. See Cheryl Weitzstein, "'Bogus Number' Inflates Payment Problem," *Washington Times,* May 13, 1994. For use of the $34 billion figure, see, e.g., Anthony M. DeStefano, "Child-Support Deadbeats Abound," *New York Newsday,* August 15, 1995, p. A14.

40. See Gordon H. Lester, *Child Support and Alimony,* Current Population Reports, Series P-60, No. 173 (Washington, D.C.: Bureau of the Census, September 1991). In one survey, nearly a quarter of the mothers with no support award said that they didn't want support; 15 percent said the father couldn't pay. See Government Accounting Office, *Interstate Child Support: Mothers Receive Less Support from Out-of-State Fathers* (Washington, D.C.: Government Accounting Office, January 1992), p. 19. Unwed fathers' resources: see Steven A. Holmes, "Low Wage Fathers and the Welfare Debate," *New York Times,* April 25, 1995, p. A12.

41. Spencer Rich, "50% Falling Short on Child Support," *Washington Post,* October 11, 1991, p. A8. Fathers' reports: Freya L. Sonenstein and Charles Calhoun, *The Survey of Absent Parents Pilot Result* (Washington, D.C.: U.S. Department of Health and Human Services, July 1988). The survey was commissioned by the Department of Health and Human Services but terminated after a pilot study. See also Sanford L. Braver et al., "Noncustodial Parents' Report of Child Support Payments," *Family Relations* 4, 1991, pp. 180–185 ("self-serving and 'ex-spouse-bashing'" reports).

42. See Ron Haskins, "Child Support: A Father's View," in Alfred Kahn and Sheila Kamerman, *Child Support: From Debt Collection to Social Policy* (Newbury Park, Calif.: Sage, 1988), p. 306; Jessica Pearson and Nancy Thoennes, "Supporting Children After Divorce: The Influence of Custody on Support Levels and Payments," *Family Law Quarterly* 22, 1988, p. 333; Braver et al. "Noncustodial Parents' Report of Child Support Payments," p. 182. Payments reduced by mutual agreement: H. Elizabeth Peters et al., "Enforcing Divorce Settlements: Evidence from Child Support Compliance and Award Modifications," *Demography* 30, 1993, pp. 719–730. Welfare fraud: e.g., *In the interest of Marissa S., a minor child,* District Court, 231st Judicial District, Tarrant County, Tex., 1996, case records on file with author.

43. GAO, *Interstate Child Support,* p. 19.

44. Pearson and Thoennes, "Supporting Children After Divorce"; Braver et al., "Non-Custodial Parents' Reports"; David Chambers, *Making Fathers Pay: The Enforcement of Child Support* (Chicago: University of Chicago Press, 1979); Judi Bartfeld and Daniel R. Meyer, "Are There Really Deadbeat Dads? The Relationship Between Ability to Pay, Enforcement, and Compliance in Nonmarital Child Support Cases," *Social Service Review* 68, 1994, pp. 219–235; "Family Matters," *Dallas Morning News,* April 20, 1996 "Most wanted" lists: see, e.g., *The Support Report* (Virginia Department of Social Services), January 1993.

45. Elaine Sorensen, "A Little Help for Some 'Dead-beat' Dads," *Washington Post,* November 15, 1995, p. A25.

46. Kathleen Smith, "Fathers Fight for the Right to See Their Kids," *Bucks County (Pa.) Midweek,* February 8, 1995, p. 8A. See also Bill Maxwell, "'Deadbeat' Isn't Always the Word," *St. Petersburg Times,* June 2, 1996, p. 1D.

47. Lester, *Child Support and Alimony* (census data); Sanford Braver, remarks at the conference of the Children's Rights' Council, Bethesda, Md., March 1995; Joyce Arditti and Katherine R. Allen, "Understanding Distressed Fathers' Perceptions of Legal and Relational Inequities Post-Divorce," *Family and Conciliation Courts Review* 31, 1993, p. 469 ("I don't mean power").

48. Sanford L. Braver et al., "A Longitudinal Study of Noncustodial Parents: Parents Without Children," *Journal of Family Psychology* 7, 1993, pp. 21, 20.

49. Debra Umberson and Christine L. Williams, "Divorced Fathers: Parental Role Strain and Psychological Distress," *Journal of Family Issues* 14, 1993, p. 392.

50. Joyce A. Arditti, "Factors Related to Custody, Visitation, and Child Support for Divorced Fathers: An Exploratory Analysis," *Journal of Divorce and Remarriage* 17, 1992, pp. 34, 39.

51. Author's interview, July 15, 1996.

52. See Barbara Sullivan, "Locking Dad Out," *Chicago Tribune,* February 1, 1989; Mara Rose Williams, "Cut Off from Their Children," *Atlanta Constitution,* February 20, 1994.

53. Neil Chethik, "Law Backs the Right to Parental Visits," *Detroit Free Press,* May 28, 1995, p. 2J.

54. Claims by women's advocates: in Maureen Downey, "Parents at War over Custody, Cash," *Atlanta Constitution,* September 25, 1989, p. B1; Lewin, "Father's Vanishing Act"; Rhode, *Speaking of Sex,* p. 188. Jensen: *In the Matter of the Adoption of Matthew Stephen Jensen and Jacob Paul Jensen,* No. L-80-087, Court of Appeals, Sixth Appellate District, Lucas County, Ohio (slip opinion), January 23, 1981. See also D. C. Burch, "Gerri Stacks the Deck," *Paper (Toledo, Ohio),* May 19, 1995. Complaints by mothers and fathers: Jessica Pearson, "Gender Differences in Visitation Complaints" (presentation at the annual conference of the Association of Family and Conciliation Courts, Montreal, Canada, May 17–20, 1995); Sanford H. Braver et al., "Frequency of Visits by Divorced Fathers: Differences in Reports by Fathers and Mothers," *American Journal of Orthopsychiatry* 61, 1991, pp. 448–454. Adult children's reports: Glynnis Walker, *Solomon's Children: Exploding the Myths of Divorce* (New York: Arbor House, 1986), p. 83. Mothers' reports: Braver et al., "Frequency of Visits by Divorced Fathers"; J. A. Fulton, "Parental Reports of Children's Post-Divorce Adjustment," *Journal of Social Issues* 35, 1979, pp. 126–139; Judith S. Wallterstein and Joan B. Kelly, *Surviving the Breakup: How Children and Parents Cope with Divorce* (New York: Basic Books, 1980), p. 125.

55. In one survey, the wife's failure to spend the money of the children was the one excuse for not paying child support, besides unemployment, that divorced men recognized as valid. Haskins, "Child Support: A Father's View," p. 306. Legal fees: Sullivan, "Locking Dad Out," quoting Edward Nichols, social worker and founder of Fathers' Advocacy, Information and Referral ("supporting their attorneys"); Gruber: documents on file with author.

56. Earlier data: Frank F. Furstenberg et al., "Paternal Participation and Children's Well-Being After Marital Dissolution," *American Sociological Review* 52, 1987, pp. 695–701. Recent data: Judith A. Seltzer and Yvonne Brandreth, "What Fathers Say About Involvement with Children After Separation," *Journal of Family Issues* 15, 1994; Maccoby and Mnookin, *Dividing the Child,* p. 176.

57. Leslie Simon, "What Makes Poppa Run?" (presentation at the 1995 annual conference of the Association of Family and Conciliation Courts, Montreal, Canada, May 17–20, 1995). Survey: Geoffrey L. Greif, "When Divorced Fathers Want No Contact with Their Children: A Preliminary Analysis," *Journal of Divorce and Remarriage* 23, 1995, pp. 75–85.

58. Chesler, *Mothers on Trial,* p. 219. Effects of divorce on men: A. M. Zeiss et al., "Sex Differences in Initiation of and Adjustment to Divorce," *Journal of Divorce* 4, 1980; Catherine K. Riessman and Naomi Gerstel, "Marital Dissolution and Health: Do Males or Females Have Greater Risk?" *Social Science and Medicine* 20, 1985, pp. 627–635; H. S. Friedman et al., "Psychosocial and Behavioral Predictors of Longevity," *American Psychologist* 50, 1995, pp. 69–78.

59. Debra Umberson and Christine L. Williams, "Divorced Fathers: Parental

Role Strain and Psychological Distress," *Journal of Family Issues* 14, 1993, p. 396; Joyce A. Arditti, "Factors Related to Custody, Visitation, and Child Support for Divorced Fathers: An Exploratory Analysis," *Journal of Divorce and Remarriage* 17, 1992, pp. 23–42.

60. Pearson, "Gender Differences in Visitation Complaints." Nonresident mothers are somewhat less likely to complain about visitation denial, and custodial fathers somewhat less likely to complain that the mother doesn't exercise visitation.

61. *Debra Pascale v. James Pascale*, Supreme Court of New Jersey, A-91/92–94 (July 10, 1995).

62. Author's interviews with Joan Entmacher and James Pascale, July 1995.

63. Fathers' groups: Thom Weidlich, "Dads' Rights Advocates Come of Age," *National Law Journal*, March 13, 1995 (10,000 estimate). The 50,000 estimate comes from men's rights activist and newsletter publisher Rod Van Mechelen (June 18, 1996). Author's interview with Phil Gagliano, August 21, 1996.

64. See, e.g., Weidlich, "Dads' Rights Advocates Come of Age"; Hallye Jordan, "Mr. Mom Goes to Sacramento," *Los Angeles Daily Journal*, July 18, 1994.

65. Rich Zubaty, *Surviving the Feminization of America* (Tinley Park, Ill.: Panther Press, 1993). Activists with no personal gripes: see, e.g., post on the Fathers' Rights and Equality Exchange list, October 10, 1994 (FREE.L@vix.com, on file with author). Second wives: Sonia Nazario, "Not with My Husband's Money You Don't!" *Los Angeles Times Magazine*, December 3, 1995.

66. Author's interview with Robin Welch, August 12, 1996.

67. See Anne P. Mitchell, "The Maternal Bond," *American Journal of Family Law* 9, 1995, pp. 125–133. Margaret Wuwert: author's interview, August 24, 1996.

68. Joanne Schulman and Valerie Pitt, "Second Thoughts on Joint Child Custody: Analysis of Legislation and Its Implications for Women and Children," *Golden Gate University Law Review* 12, 1982, pp. 538–571. Mary Becker, "Maternal Feelings: Myth, Taboo, and Child Custody," *Review of Law and Women's Studies* 1, 1992, p. 203; see also Mary Becker, "Judicial Discretion in Child Custody: The Wisdom of Solomon?" *Illinois Bar Journal* 81, 1993, p. 657.

69. Becker, "Maternal Feelings," pp. 201–203, 199; Mary E. Becker, "The Politics of Women's Wrongs and the Bill of 'Rights': A Bicentennial Perspective," *University of Chicago Law Review* 59, 1992, pp. 484–485 (churches).

70. 1996 National NOW Conference Resolutions, *National NOW Times*, October 1996. Feminist groups have claimed that in mediation, women are intimidated into giving away too much. However, in a California study of mediation, 16 percent of mothers and 23 percent of fathers felt that "the other parent had an unfair advantage" ("Client Evaluations of Mediation Services: Perspectives of Mothers and Fathers, 1993," Family Court Services, Administrative Office of the Courts, San Francisco, 1995). Ireland: CNN, *Crossfire*, February 2, 1996. Opposition to "Mrs. Doubtfire" bill: see, e.g., National Organization for Women, "Urgent Message from California State Coordinator Elizabeth Toledo," California Action Center, September 9, 1994 letter to California State Assembly from the American Association of University

Women, March 17, 1994 (on file with author).

71. Polikoff, quoted in Berger, "Money a Potent Factor in Thomas Custody Case"; Sally Goldfarb in Jan Hoffman, "Divorced Fathers Make Gains in Battles to Increase Rights," *New York Times,* April 26, 1995, p. A1; Tammy Bruce, "Marcia Clark's Dilemma," *Los Angeles Daily News,* March 7, 1995; U.S. Senate, Committee on the Judiciary, *Hearings on Legislation to Reduce the Growing Problem of Violent Crime Against Women,* 101st Cong., 2d sess., December 11, 1990, Part 2, p. 177 (Sarah Buel).

72. E.g., December 12, 1995, hearing of the New York State Senate Committee on Children and Family (Father's Rights Association–Capital District Regional Chapter Newsletter, January 1996).

73. Report of the Gender Bias Study, p. 35.

74. For a summary of legal developments in this area, see Tonya M. Zdon, "Putative Fathers' Rights: Striking the Right Balance in Adoption Laws," *William Mitchell Law Review* 20, 1994, pp. 929–966.

75. Martha Shirk, "Unwed Youth Fought Years for His Baby," *St. Louis Post Dispatch,* February 13, 1994, p. 1A.

76. Ellen Warren, "Love, Fear Stirred Adoptive Parents to Act," *Chicago Tribune,* August 20, 1993, p. 1; Aidan Gilbert, letter to the editor, *Chicago Tribune,* August 4, 1997, p. 10.

77. Ronald K. Henry, "'Primary Caretaker': Is It a Ruse?" *Family Advocate,* summer 1994, pp. 53–54.

78. Janet R. Johnston et al., "Ongoing Postdivorce Conflict: Effects on Children of Joint Custody and Frequent Access," *American Journal of Orthopsychiatry* 49, 1989, pp. 576–592. Level of conflict postdivorce: Maccoby and Mnookin, *Dividing the Child,* p. 238 (a quarter of divorced couples were "conflicted" and about 10 percent reported high hostility). See also Christopher H. Schmitt, "Research Transformed into Weapon for Custody: In Divorce Wars, Facts Are Flexible, Children Hostages," *San Jose Mercury News,* February 18; 1989; Sandra G. Boodman, "Joint Custody Proving No Panacea for Children," *Washington Post,* September 12, 1995, p. A1.

79. Conflating joint physical and legal custody: e.g., William N. Bender, "Joint Custody: The Option of Choice," *Journal of Divorce and Remarriage* 21, 1994, pp. 115–131. Studies of joint physical custody chosen by mutual agreement: see Judith B. Grief, "Fathers, Children, and Joint Custody," *American Journal of Orthopsychiatry* 49, 1979, pp. 311–319; Virginia M. Shiller, "Joint Versus Maternal Custody for Families with Latency Age Boys: Parent Characteristics and Child Adjustment," *American Journal of Orthopsychiatry* 56, 1986, pp. 486–489. Only about 5 percent of divorced couples nationwide have joint residential custody.

80. Joint legal custody: Marjorie Linder Gunnoe and Sanford L. Braver, "The Effects of Joint Legal Custody on Family Functioning, Controlling for Factors That Predispose a Joint Award," *Child Development* (forthcoming). Judith A. Seltzer, "Father by Law: Effects of Joint Legal Custody on Nonresident Fathers' Involvement with Children" (paper presented at the Conference on Father Involvement of the National Institute of Child Health and Human Development, Bethesda, Md., October 10–11, 1996). Joint physical custody: Marsha Kline et al.,

"Children's Adjustment in Joint and Sole Physical Custody Families," *Developmental Psychology* 25, 1989, pp. 430–438; Jessica Pearson and Nancy Thoennes, "Custody After Divorce: Demographic and Attitudinal Patterns," *American Journal of Orthopsychiatry* 60, 1990, pp. 233–249; Christy M. Buchanan et al., "Adolescents and Their Families After Divorce: Three Residential Arrangements Compared," *Journal of Research on Adolescence* 2, 1992, pp. 261–291. Child support: Pearson and Thoennes, "Supporting Children After Divorce," p. 330; Joyce A. Arditti, "Differences Between Fathers with Joint Custody and Noncustodial Fathers," *Journal of Orthopsychiatry* 62, 1992, pp. 187–195. Relitigation: Frederick W. Ilfeld, Holly Z. Ilfeld, and John R. Alexander, "Does Joint Custody Work? A First Look at Outcome Data of Relitigation," *American Journal of Psychiatry* 139, 1982, pp. 62–66; Diane K. Shrier et al., "Levels of Statisfaction of Fathers and Mothers with Joint or Sole Custody Arrangements," *Journal of Divorce and Remarriage* 10, 1991, pp. 163–169.

81. "More Good News About Divorce," *Washington Post,* January 25, 1998.

82. *Freeland v. Freeland,* 92 Wash. 482, 159 p. 698 (1916).

83. What to tell daughters: Petersen, "The Short End of Long Hours" (quoting Alice Hector's colleague, Joseph P. Clock). Relocation: see, e.g., Larry Speer, "Court Affirms Divorced Mother's Right to Relocate," *Los Angeles Times,* July 2, 1992, p. B1 (quoting ACLU attorney John Davidson: "It is not within the court's power to order people where they can or cannot live").

84. Dear Abby, "Move Tough on Divorcing Dad," *New York Post,* July 7, 1998, p. 20.

85. Regan, "An Open Letter to Mr. Clark." See also Beck, "A Chilling Message to Working Moms."

86. Blankenhorn, *Fatherless America,* p. 3.

Chapter 9. Are Men Victims Too?

1. Ted Honderich (ed.), *The Oxford Companion to Philosophy* (Oxford, England: Oxford University Press), p. 528 (essay by Ferrel Christensen).

2. Peter Maass, "A Conference, a Joke, a New Look at Sexism," *Washington Post,* July 27, 1996, p. A1; CNN, *Capital Gang,* July 27, 1996.

3. Sam Howe Verhovek, "As Woman's Execution Nears, Texas Squirms," *New York Times,* December 31, 1997, p. A1. Earlier analysis: see, e.g., Ted Gest, "A House Without a Blueprint," *U.S. News and World Report,* July 8, 1996, pp. 41–42.

4. "U.S. Elderly Suicide Rate Up," *Chicago Tribune,* January 11, 1996, p. 2. In 1984, the *Los Angeles Times* ran an article about suicide and elderly men: Gloria Kaufman Koenig, "Helping No. 1 Suicide . . . Risk Elderly Men," *Los Angeles Times,* November 13, 1984, p. V1. See also *Statistical Abstracts of the United States 1993,* Table 137, "Suicide Rates by Sex, Race, and Age Group: 1970 to 1990."

5. In 1990, the suicide rate per 100,000 for white males ages fifteen to nineteen was 19.3; for white females in the same age group, 4.0; for black males, 11.5; for black females, 1.9. *Statistical Abstracts of the United States 1993,* Table 137, "Suicide Rates by Sex, Race, and Age Group: 1970 to 1990."

Women get "more severe sentences": Lorraine Dusky, *Still Unequal: The*

Shameful Truth About Women and Justice in America (New York: Crown, 1996), p. 265. Women serve out longer portions of sentences: "Reform Sought in Legal System to Cut Sex Bias," *Miami Herald,* October 6, 1989, p. 2B; "Bias in the Courts" (editorial), *Boston Globe,* June 25, 1989, p. 82; Allan R. Gold, "Sex Bias Is Found Pervading Courts," *New York Times,* July 2, 1989; Fawn Germer, "Gender Bias Still Taints Colorado's Courts," *Rocky Mountain News,* April 23, 1993, p. 6A; "Even in Prison, Men Get Better Treatment Than Women" (editorial), *Glamour,* March 1994, p. 80.

According to a 1989 Bureau of Justice Statistics study, male offenders were more than twice as likely as women charged with similar crimes to be incarcerated for more than a year. *The Prosecution of Felony Arrests, 1986,* U.S. Department of Justice, Bureau of Justice Statistics, NCJ-113248 (Washington, D.C.: Government Printing Office, June 1989). In Pennsylvania in 1986, male aggravated assault defendants were 33 percent more likely to be convicted than women; among those convicted, men were 80 percent more likely to be incarcerated. Men charged with robbery were 33 percent more likely to be convicted and 30 percent more likely to be imprisoned. Similar patterns were found in New York and California. See Rita J. Simon and Jean Landis, *The Crimes Women Commit, the Punishments They Receive* (Lexington, Mass.: Lexington Books, 1991), pp. 71–75, 82–84. In Colorado in 1990, men's sentences were 35 to 65 percent longer. Curtis Eichelberger, "Gender Bias Alive and Well in Court Sentencing System," *Rocky Mountain News,* April 10, 1995, p. 4D. Even when factors besides gender—severity of offense, prior convictions—are taken into account, women are more likely to have the charges dismissed or to receive a light sentence. See, e.g., *Sentencing Outcomes in 28 Felony Courts in 1985,* U.S. Department of Justice, Bureau of Justice Statistics, NCJ-105743 (Washington, D.C.: U. S. Government Printing Office, July 1987).

6. Katha Pollitt, "Killer Moms, Working Nannies," *Nation,* November 24, 1997, p. 9; Blaine Raden, "Danish Mother Free to Take the Child Home; Father Faces Trial in Stroller Case," *Washington Post,* May 17, 1997. Amy Klein, "Father Gets 8 Years in Montgomery Abuse Case," *Washington Post,* February 28, 1998, p. B1.

7. Time/CNN/Yankelovich Clancy Shulman poll, February 1992 (telephone poll of 1,250 adults).

8. See, e.g., Trip Gabriel, "Call of the Wildmen," *New York Times Magazine,* October 14, 1990, p. 36; Jon Tevlin, "Of Hawks and Men: A Weekend in the Male Wilderness," *Utne Reader,* November–December 1989, p. 50; Robert Bly and Keith Thompson, "What Men Really Want: An Interview with Robert Bly," *New Age,* May 1982, p. 30.

9. See Donna Minkowitz, "In the Name of the Father," *Ms.,* November–December 1995, pp. 64–71.

10. E-mail post from Rod Van Mechelen, June 18, 1996.

11. Author's interviews with Sean Gralton, February 12 and June 25, 1996. See also "Spreading the Word" (editorial), *Daily Free Press* (Boston University), September 28, 1994; Jessica Collins, "New Group Looks at Men's Point of View," *Daily Free Press,* September 26, 1994, p. 1.

12. Author's interview with Mike Arst, March 1, 1994.

13. Author's interview with Alan Rubinstein (not his real name), June 24, 1996. Some of this material also comes from a letter (on file with author) and e-mail messages.

14. Jeffrey Seeman, "Feminism and the Male Stereotype," *Egalitarian*, April 1994, p. 7.

15. Tina Brown, speech at the annual meeting of the American Newspaper Publishers Association, May 1991, printed in *Media Report to Women*, winter 1991–1992, p. 6; Rebecca Pepper Sinkler, "Look Back in Pleasure," *New York Times Book Review*, April 6, 1997, p. 31; Jeff Giles, "Swimming with Sharks," *Newsweek*, August 4, 1997 ("an exposé of sexism"); Sheryl Connelly, "'Men' at Work As Jerks," *New York Daily News*, August 3, 1997. British press: Amelia Gentleman, "New Man Shown to Be a Dirty Rat," *Guardian*, July 29, 1998; Linda Grant, "Honestly, I Don't Hate Them, but Why Are Men Like That?" *Guardian*, July 21, 1998. See also David Aaronovitch, "Spare Me and My Fellow Men from the New Orthodoxy: Female Good, Male Bad," *Independent*, May 14, 1998.

16. "Last Laugh," *Psychology Today*, September–October 1993, pp. 16–17. Books: see Alex Kuczynski, "Between the Sexes, It's World War III Out There," *New York Times*, July 19, 1998; Anita Liberty, *How to Heal the Hurt by Hating* (New York: Ballantine, 1998). Alex Witchel, "Gone, Perhaps, But No Less Chatty," *New York Times*, February 22, 1998.

17. Copy of printout on file with author. See also Jane Gross, "Now Look Who's Taunting; Now Look Who's Suing," *New York Times*, February 26, 1995, p. E1.

18. Cornell: Barbara Krauss, judicial administrator, Cornell University, "To the Cornell Community and Other Interested Persons," November 18, 1995 (statement on file with author); Associated Press, "Students Sorry About E-Mail," November 15, 1995. University of Maryland: "UM Men Protest 'Potential Rapist' Label," *Baltimore Sun*, May 7, 1993, p. 9A; "'Potential Rapists,' Part II," *Washington Times*, May 13, 1993, p. G2.

19. Judy Markey, "Male-Bashing," *Redbook*, May 1993, p. 105.

20. Karen Lehrman, *The Lipstick Proviso: Women, Sex and Power in the Real World* (New York: Doubleday, 1997), pp. 3, 134.

21. Cindy Chupack, "Shopping for a Boyfriend," *Glamour*, September 1996, p. 208. See also Snowden, "Why Won't the World Accept a Woman Who Can't Commit?" and Louise Bernikow, "The Oh, So Dependent Man," *Cosmopolitan*, December 1995, p. 138.

22. Katie Roiphe, "Adultery's Double Standard," *New York Times Magazine*, October 12, 1997, pp. 54–55. See also Martha Duffy, "Fractured Fairy Tales," *Time*, March 11, 1996, pp. 46–54; Sue Arnold, "What Does Charles See in Camilla?" *Chatelaine*, August 1993, pp. 50–54; Katy Kelly, "Princess for the Post-Feminist Generation," *USA Today*, September 2, 1997, p. 20A; Mark Stuart Gill, "The Phone Stalkers," *Ladies Home Journal*, September 1995, p. 82 (harassing phone calls).

23. Carol Scibelli, "Did the Abandoned Bride Read the Signs?" *New York Newsday*, December 15, 1997, p. A26; NBC, *Today* Show, November 25, 1997;

Frank Rich, "Four Weddings and a Runaway," *New York Times,* May 5, 1994, p. A27.

24. Dr. Joyce Brothers, "A Prostitute's No Stranger to Danger," *New York Daily News,* April 9, 1998, p. 78.

25. Welfare reform debate: see, e.g., Jason DeParle, "Better Work Than Welfare: But What If There's Neither?" *New York Times Magazine,* December 18, 1994, p. 42; John McCormick and Evan Thomas, "One Family's Journey from Welfare," *Newsweek,* May 26, 1997, p. 28.

26. Warren Farrell, *The Myth of Male Power* (New York: Simon & Schuster, 1993), p. 52.

27. Families and Work Institute/Whirlpool Foundation, *Women: The New Providers,* (May 1995).

28. MSNBC, *Newschat,* October 22, 1997.

29. Catherine Kohler Riessman, *Divorce Talk: Women and Men Make Sense of Personal Relationships* (New Brunswick, N.J.: Rutgers University Press, 1990), p. 52 (doctor).

30. Ann Landers, *New York Newsday,* March 10, 1994, p. 94, May 23, 1994, p. B14.

31. Women reenergized by a stay at home: see, e.g., Elizabeth Fox-Genovese, *"Feminism Is Not the Story of My Life": How Today's Feminist Élite Has Lost Touch with the Real Concerns of Women* (New York: Doubleday, 1996), p. 256. Regina A. Rochford, "A Gift from Mom in Her New Career," *New York Times,* May 12, 1996, p. F13.

32. Jean Gonick, "Who Pays for Dinner?" *New Woman,* August 1993, p. 55.

33. See, e.g., 1993 Yankelovich poll, in Richard Morin, "The Manly Man Returns—and He Is Sensitive Too," *Philadelphia Inquirer,* September 7, 1993, p. A19; Louie E. Ross and A. Clarke Davis, "Black-White College Student Attitudes and Expectations in Paying for Dates," *Sex Roles* 35, 1996, pp. 43–53; Janet Shibley Hyde et al., "Fathers and Parental Leave," *Journal of Family Issues* 14, 1993, pp. 616–641; Hart-Teeter Poll/NBC Women's Study, September 20–22, 1997.

34. Michael Pakenham, "Are You a Victim Yet? If Not, Get in Line," *Baltimore Sun,* June 18, 1995, p. 4F.

35. See, e.g., Alex Beam, "Men's Lib, Born Again," *Boston Globe,* October 18, 1993, p. 13.

36. Women less oppressed: see, e.g., Roy U. Schenk, *The Other Side of the Coin: Causes and Consequences of Men's Oppression* (Madison, Wisc.: Bioenergetics Press, 1982).

37. Farrell, *The Myth of Male Power,* pp. 42–66.

38. Marilyn French, *The War Against Women* (New York: Summit, 1992).

39. Simone de Beauvoir, *The Second Sex* (New York: Vintage, 1989), p. 480; Farrell, *The Myth of Male Power,* p. 96.

40. Schenk, *The Other Side of the Coin,* p. 28.

41. Farrell, *The Myth of Male Power,* pp. 85, 91.

42. Author's interview with Ferrel Christensen, March 5, 1994.

43. Kathy Chen, "Equal Opportunity Isn't a Big Concern for Mosuo Women," *Wall Street Journal,* August 30, 1995, p. A1.

44. Betty Friedan, *The Feminine Mystique* (New York: Dell, 1963), p. 301.

45. Farrell, *The Myth of Male Power,* p. 105.

46. Neil Chethik, "A New Baby Boy Is a Chance for Men's Emotions to Thrive," *Detroit Free Press,* December 19, 1993, p. 2H.

47. Poll: Yankelovich, Skelly and White, Monitoring Attitudes of the Public '78 poll, June 1978 (self-control was considered important by over 90 percent). Emotional repression: "Repress Yourself," *Psychology Today,* September–October 1997, p. 12; Emily Nussbaum, "Good Grief! The Case for Repression," *Lingua Franca,* October 1997, pp. 48–51.

48. Carol Tavris, *The Mismeasure of Woman* (New York: Simon & Schuster, 1992), p. 247. Theodore Roosevelt: Thomas Mallon, *The American Spectator,* December 1995, p. 72 (reviewing *A Bully Father: Theodore Roosevelt's Letters to His Children,* edited by Joan Paterson Kerr).

49. Farrell, *The Myth of Male Power,* p. 371.

50. Jack Kammer, *Good Will Toward Men* (New York: St. Martin's Press, 1994) pp. xvii–xviii; Sommers, *Who Stole Feminism?* p. 96.

51. Farrell, *The Myth of Male Power,* pp. 362, 221–223 (Farrell refers to clitoridectomy as "circumcising the hood of the female clitoris," even though it usually involves the removal of the entire clitoris, and sometimes part of the labia). "Gendercide": Raj Kumar Singh, "Why a Men's Movement?" *Backlash!* March 1995.

52. "Suicide sex": Farrell, *The Myth of Male Power,* p. 164. Statistics: Adjusted Death Rates by Cause, 1970 to 1989, *Statistical Abstracts of the United States,* 1992, p. 85. David Lester, "The Sex Distribution of Suicides by Age in the Nations of the World," *Social Psychiatry and Psychiatric Epidemiology* 25, 1990, pp. 87–88. 1920s: U.S. Department of Commerce, Bureau of the Census, *Historical Statistics of the United States: Colonial Times–1970,* Bicentennial Edition, pt. 2, ser. A24–25 and H981–982.

53. Colin Pritchard, "Suicide, Unemployment and Gender in the British Isles and European Economic Community (1974–1985): A Hidden Epidemic?" *Social Psychiatry and Psychiatric Epidemiology* 23, 1988, pp. 85–89; Bijou Yand et al., "Suicide and Unemployment: Predicting the Smoothed Trend and Yearly Fluctuations," *Journal of Socio-Economics* 21, 1992, pp. 39–41.

54. U.S. Department of Commerce, Bureau of the Census, *Social Indicators III* (Washington, D.C.: U.S. Government Printing Office, December 1980), p. 96. Andrew Kadar, "The Sex-Bias Myth in Medicine," *Atlantic Monthly,* August 1994, p. 70; William R. Hazzard, "Biological Basis of the Sex Differential in Longevity," *Journal of the American Geriatrics Society* 34, 1986, pp. 459, 468 (hormones). One hundred thirty to 170 boys are conceived for every 100 girls, but the ratio at birth is only 106 to 100.

55. Deborah L. Wingard, "The Sex Differential in Morbidity, Mortality and Lifestyle," *Annual Review of Public Health, 1984,* p. 445; Alan J. Silman, "Why Do Women Live Longer and Is It Worth It?" *British Medical Journal* 294, 1987, p. 1311.

56. Alcohol and tobacco use: Wingard, "The Sex Differential," pp. 433–458. Emotional expression: Kathryn Dindia and Mike Allen, "Sex Differences in Self-

Disclosure: A Meta-Analysis," *Psychological Bulletin* 112, 1992, p. 118.

57. Farrell, *The Myth of Male Power*, p. 189. See Steven Collins, letter in *Forbes*, April 11, 1994. After Collins's correction, the 23:1 figure still appears in the paperback edition of *The Myth of Male Power* and in the rhetoric of men's activists. See, e.g., James Novak, "The Feminist Attack on Men's Health," *Men's Advocate*, March 1994, p. 10; David Dinn, "Saving Males," letter to the editor, *Indianapolis Star*, January 17, 1996. Heart disease versus cancer; Ian Wilson, *Men's Health: A Cause for Concern* (Washington, D.C.: Men's Health Network, 1993), p. 18; "Death Rates, by Selected Causes and Selected Characteristics: 1970 to 1989," *Statistical Abstracts of the United States 1993*, p. 85.

58. Titanic: see Christine Montgomery, "Still Women, Children First?" *Washington Times*, February 4, 1998, p. 68.

59. Farrell, *The Myth of Male Power*, pp. 29, 148–149. MIAs: Thomas W. Lippman, "Prisoners of Lore: Why the Myth of Vietnam POW-MIAs Won't Die," *Washington Post*, April 25, 1993, p. C5.

60. Farrell, *The Myth of Male Power*, pp. 121, 234. Fatalities in mining: "Discontented Labor," *Charlotte (N.C.) Observer*, July 2, 1995, p. 2C. See also Frank Swoboda, "GOP Bills on OSHA Face Veto by Clinton," *Washington Post*, February 20, 1996, p. C1. Car accidents: *Statistical Abstracts of the United States, 1993*, p. 89 (Table 122, "Death Rates from Accidents and Violence: 1970 to 1989"; Table 123, "Deaths and Death Rates from Accidents, by Type: 1970 to 1989").

61. Tillie Fong et al., "They Came to Fight the Fire," *Rocky Mountain News*, July 10, 1994; see, e.g., Joe Haberstroh and Letta Tayler, Railroad Shooting: "Getting on with Life," *New York Newsday*, February 12, 1995, p. A4.

62. Feminist watchdogs: see, e.g., Jenny Stromer-Galley and Kate Kenski, "Gender May Hold Some Answers in Tragic Wave of School Killings," *Philadelphia Inquirer*, April 28, 1998 ("The news media have described the Jonesboro [schoolyard shooting] victims as 'children' and 'teachers,' not specifically girls and women"). Farrell, *The Myth of Male Power*, p. 119.

63. See Schenk, *The Other Side of the Coin*, pp. 116–117.

64. Raj Kumar Singh, "Gender Justice: Why I'm Rooting for O.J.," *Liberator*, September 1994, p. 27.

65. Author's interview with Asa Baber, April 8, 1994.

Chapter 10. The Conservative Mistake

1. Dorothy L. Sayers, "Are Women Human?" in Dorothy L. Sayers, *Are Women Human?* (Grand Rapids, Mich.: William Eerdmans Publishing Co., 1971), pp. 32–33.

2. "Relative Income Gains of Women: An Historical Perspective," prepared for Rep. Richard K. Armey (R-TX), Joint Economic Committee (October 1992); David Frum, *Dead Right* (New York: Basic Books, 1994), p. 66.

3. Elizabeth Powers, "A Farewell to Feminism," *Commentary*, January 1997, p. 29.

4. Harvey Mansfield, "Backlasch: The Trouble with Feminism," *Weekly Standard*, April 14, 1997, p. 31 (reviewing *Women and the Common Life* by

Christopher Lasch). Gary L. Bauer, "Save Social Security, Save Our Families," *New York Times*, January 23, 1997. Welfare reform: Concerned Women of America meeting, broadcast on C-Span July 19, 1996; Kellyanne Fitzpatrick, "Beyond the Gender Gap," *Wall Street Journal*, May 17, 1996.

5. Citations of *Professing Feminism:* William F. Buckley, "The Women's Movement: More and More Frazzled," *New York Post*, December 12, 1994; Robert H. Bork, *Slouching Toward Gomorrah* (New York: HarperCollins, 1996), pp. 195–196. Gilligan: Marilyn Quayle, "Workers, Wives and Mothers," *New York Times*, September 11, 1992, p. A35; James Q. Wilson, *The Moral Sense* (New York: Free Press, 1993), pp. 179–181; Maggie Gallagher, *Enemies of Eros: How the Sexual Revolution Is Killing Family, Marriage and Sex and What We Can Do About It* (Chicago: Bonus Books, 1989), pp. 40–41 (see also Christina Hoff Sommers, *Who Stole Feminism? How Women Have Betrayed Women* [New York: Simon & Schuster, 1994], pp. 151–152, and Daphne Patai and Noretta Koertge, *Professing Feminism: Cautionary Tales from the Strange World of Women's Studies* [New York: Basic Books, 1994], pp. 161, 166). Girls' schools: see, e.g., Anita K. Blair, "Cutting Our Noses," *Women's Quarterly*, winter 1996, p. 8

6. Roiphe: Rush Limbaugh, *See, I Told You So* (New York: Pocket Star Books, 1993), pp. 205–207; George F. Will, "Gothic Feminism," *Washington Post*, October 24, 1993, p. C7; Carol Iannone, "Sex and the Feminists," *Commentary*, September 1993, p. 52. Irving Kristol, "Reflections on Love and Family," *Wall Street Journal*, January 7, 1992, p. A10. (The *Naked Maja* episode was widely ridiculed as "political correctness" gone mad; see, e.g., Sommers, *Who Stole Feminism?* pp. 270–271.) See also Charlotte Allen, "Penthouse Pest: Why Porn Crusader MacKinnon Is Right," *Washington Post*, November 28, 1993, pp. C1–C2.

7. See "Ruth Bader Ginsburg's Feminist World View," *Phyllis Schlafly Report*, July 1993; Mary Becker, "Prince Charming: Abstract Equality," *Supreme Court Review*, 1987, pp. 201, 207, 224. John Corry, "Out You Go!" *American Spectator*, January 1994.

8. Quoted in James Atlas, "The Counter-Counterculture," *New York Times Magazine*, February 12, 1995, p. 54.

9. Thomas Fleming, "The Truth About Patria Potestas," *Family in America* 10, December 1996, p. 4.

10. Harvey Mansfield, "Why a Woman Can't Be More Like a Man," *Wall Street Journal*, November 3, 1997, p. A22.

11. George F. Gilder, *Sexual Suicide* (New York: Quadrangle/New York Times, 1973); George Gilder, "End Welfare Reform as We Know It," *American Spectator*, June 1995, pp. 24–27. Male sexual inadequacy: Gilder, *Sexual Suicide*, p. 134; Gilder, "Still Different," *National Review*, November 30, 1984, pp. 48–49;

12. F. Carolyn Graglia, *Domestic Tranquility: A Brief Against Feminism* (Dallas: Spence, 1997); Mona Charen, "How Feminism Steered Women into Unhappiness," *St. Louis Post Dispatch*, May 18, 1998.

13. Graglia, *Domestic Tranquility*, pp. 378–379 (equal respect), 44 (male clones), 29 (homosexual comparison), 247, 332–334, 342–343.

14. Ibid., pp. 119, 139 (feminist stereotypes), 94 ("being, not doing"), 85, 373

(biology), 340 ("striving"), 339 (bovine), 378 (the mind).

15. Ibid., p. 259 (passivity), 207–213 (genital mutilation), 338–343 (Dworkin).

16. Erich Fromm, *Man for Himself* (New York: Fawcett, 1975 [original edition: Holt, Rinehart & Winston, 1947]), p. 49; Gilder, *Sexual Suicide,* pp. 18, 24; Graglia, *Domestic Tranquility,* p. 156 ("child-bearing").

17. Cynthia Ozick, "Women and Creativity: The Demise of the Dancing Dog," in Vivian Gornick and Barbara K. Moran (eds.), *Woman in Sexist Society: Studies in Power and Powerlessness* (New York: Basic Books, 1971), p. 438.

18. Graglia, *Domestic Tranquility,* pp. 40–41.

19. Gallagher, *Enemies of Eros,* p. 150.

20. Kimm Ellen Edwards, letter to the editor, *Wall Street Journal,* March 26, 1992; Danielle Crittenden, "The Good Mother," *National Review,* July 20, 1998; David Gelernter, "Why Mothers Should Stay Home," *Commentary,* February 1996, pp. 25–28.

21. Gallagher, *Enemies of Eros,* p. 139.

22. Roper Poll, April 1946, in *Fortune,* August 1946, pp. 5–14.

23. Allan C. Carlson, "What Happened to the 'Family Wage'?" *Public Interest,* spring 1986, p. 10; see also Paul Adam Blanchard, "Insert the Word 'Sex': How Segregationists Handed Feminists a 1964 'Civil Rights' Victory Against the Family," *Family in America,* March 1998. Graglia, *Domestic Tranquliity,* p. 80.

24. Graglia, *Domestic Tranquility,* p. 115; Betty Friedan, *The Feminine Mystique* (New York: Dell, 1963), pp. 60–61.

25. Richard Stengel (with Amy Blackman and Elizabeth Larson), "Liddy Makes Perfect," *Time,* July 1, 1996.

26. Lynn Mills, *Educating Our Daughters: A Challenge to the Colleges* (New York: Harper & Brothers, 1950), p. 122; Leo C. Muller and Ouida Gean Muller, *College for Coeds* (New York: Pitman, 1960), p. 12.

27. Steven Goldberg, "Can Women Beat Men at Their Own Game?" *National Review,* December 27, 1993, p. 32.

28. Allan Bloom, *The Closing of the American Mind* (New York: Simon & Schuster, 1987), pp. 127–128.

29. Lisa Schiffren, "Candice Bergen vs. Murphy Brown," *New York Times,* June 12, 1998, p. A21; see also Lisa Schiffren, "Family First," *Wall Street Journal,* March 19, 1998. College survey: Michael E. Mills, "Gender Differences Predicted by Evolutionary Theory Are Reflected in Survey Responses of College Students" (paper presented at the 4th Annual Meeting of the Human Behavior and Evolution Society conference, July 1992, Albuquerque, N.M.).

30. Mack, *The Assault on Parenthood,* pp. 29–53.

31. Mona Charen, "Paying the Dues for the Sexual Revolution," *New York Newsday,* January 22, 1990, p. 46.

32. For fascinating theories on the sexual habits of our ancestors, see Helen E. Fisher, *Anatomy of Love* (New York: W. W. Norton, 1992), pp. 129–159.

33. Gelernter, "Why Mothers Should Stay Home," p. 27.

34. Barbara Dafoe Whitehead, "The Failure of Sex Education," *Atlantic Monthly,* p. 74.

35. Anne Roiphe, *Fruitful: A Real Mother in the Modern World* (Boston:

Houghton Mifflin, 1996), p. 128.

36. Anselma Dell'Olio, "The Sexual Revolution Wasn't Our War," *Ms.*, spring 1992, p. 104. Charen lists "the stupidity of embracing the sexual revolution" among the reasons she has not embraced feminism. Mona Charen, "Why I Hate 'Anti-Family' Feminists," *Atlanta Journal-Constitution*, October 4, 1994.

37. Karla Vermeulen, "Growing Up in the Shadow of AIDS," *New York Times*, September 30, 1990.

38. Charen, "Paying the Dues for the Sexual Revolution"; Jennifer Grossman: ABC, *Politically Incorrect*, April 30, 1997; David Whitman, "Was It Good for Us?" *U.S. News and World Report*, May 19, 1997, p. 58.

39. Ruth Wisse, in "On the Future of Conservatism: A Symposium," *Commentary*, February 1997, p. 42 (feminism and power); Whitman, "Was It Good for Us?" (Grossman on her boyfriend); Jennifer Grossman, "In Praise of Courtesans," *Weekly Standard*, November 4, 1996, p. 34.

40. Maggie Gallagher, *The Abolition of Marriage: How We Destroy Lasting Love* (Washington, D.C.: Regnery Gateway, 1996), p. 87; Virginia Slims Poll 1990.

41. *New York Times*/CBS News Poll; see Tamar Lewin, "Poll of Teen-Agers: Battle of the Sexes on Roles in Family," *New York Times*, July 11, 1994, pp. A1, B7.

42. Gilder, *Sexual Suicide*, pp. 104, 260. Gallagher, *Enemies of Eros*, p. 69; Graglia, *Domestic Tranquility*, p. 197.

43. Mona Charen, "Keeping Promises, Saving Society," *Atlanta Constitution*, June 20, 1995; James Q. Wilson, "The Family-Values Debate," *Commentary*, April 1993, pp. 24–32. Citing advocacy research: Gallagher, *Enemies of Eros*, pp. 196, 206; Graglia, *Domestic Tranquility*, pp. 299–301. Hadley Arkes, "Finding Fault with No-Fault," *Wall Street Journal*, April 16, 1996; John J. DiIulio, Jr., "Deadly Divorce," *National Review*, April 7, 1997. Poll on divorce: General Social Survey (National Opinion Research Center), 1994.

44. Gelernter, "Why Mothers Should Stay Home," p. 28. See also Gallagher, *Enemies of Eros*, pp. 45–46; Andrew Peyton Thomas, "A Dangerous Experiment in Child-Rearing," *Wall Street Journal*, January 8, 1998. Polls: Fortune poll, 1946 (Roper); General Social Survey 1993.

45. Gallagher, *Enemies of Eros*, pp. 260–261; Andrea Dworkin, *Intercourse* (New York: Free Press, 1987), p. 133. Wendy Shalit, "Daughters of the (Sexual) Revolution," *Commentary*, December 1997, pp. 42–45. Girls and boys: *Commonwealth Fund Survey of the Health of Adolescent Girls* (New York: Commonwealth Fund/Louis Harris and Associates, 1997).

46. Wendy Shalit, "Whose Choice?" *National Review*, May 18, 1998; Graglia, *Domestic Tranquility*, p. 192. See also Daphne de Jong, "Legal Abortion Exploits Women," in Bonnie Szumski (ed.), *Abortion: Opposing Viewpoints* (St. Paul, Minn.: Greenhaven Press, 1986), p. 164.

47. Monica Lewinsky as victim of "sexual harassment": see, e.g., Linda Chavez, "Monica Lewinsky Is in Need of Some Sisterly Support Yet the Feminists Remain Silent," *Philadelphia Inquirer*, January 28, 1998; David Norcross, former general counsel to the Republican National Committee, on *Burden of Proof*, CNN, August 7, 1998. Hillary Clinton as victim of "battered women's syn-

drome": e.g., Bay Buchanan, *Larry King Live,* CNN, August 21, 1998.

48. Combat as "violence against women": see, e.g., Center for Military Readiness, *CMI Notes,* September 1997, pp. 4, 6.

49. E.g., Kate O'Beirne, *Capital Gang,* CNN, March 29, 1997.

50. Charles Krauthammer, "Play-Doctors on the Hill," *Washington Post,* February 14, 1997, p. A21, and Raymond Hernandez, "D'Amato Goes to Albany, and a Law on Mastectomy Stays Is Born," *New York Times,* January 23, 1997, p. B9.

51. See, e.g., Michael McManus, "Voters Should Care About Divorce Reform," *Detroit News,* September 19, 1996, p. A11; Connie Koenenn, "A Move to Crack Down on Breakups," *Los Angeles Times,* February 22, 1996, p. E1; Karen S. Peterson, "Saying 'No' to the Notion of No-Fault Divorce," *USA Today,* January 15, 1996, p. 1D. Acknowledgment of fathers: "Bill to End No-Fault Divorce in Florida Would Make It Harder to Break Up," *New York Times,* December 29, 1996, p. 19; Barbara Vobejda, "Critics, Seeking Change, Fault 'No-Fault' Divorce Laws for High Rates," *Washington Post,* March 7, 1996, p. A3.

52. *The NewsHour with Jim Lehrer,* PBS, February 24, 1997.

53. Hanna Rosin, "Separation Anxiety," *New Republic,* May 6, 1996, p. 16.

54. NOW resolution: Sally Satel, "NOW's Time Is Past," *Wall Street Journal,* July 11, 1997, p. A14. Conservative critics: see, e.g., Laura Ingraham, "Men Who Can Do Nothing Right," *New York Times,* July 10, 1997, p. A23; Joseph Perkins, "Promise Keepers' Goal: Racial, Marital Harmony," *New York Post,* October 3, 1997, p. 29. See also John D. Spalding, "Bonding in the Bleachers: A Visit to the Promise Keepers," *Christian Century,* March 6, 1996, p. 260.

55. Fox News-Opinion Dynamics Poll, October 1997 (Associated Press, October 4, 1997). Egalitarian relationships: see, e.g., Lee Moriwaki and Carol Ostrom, "Men's Convention to Draw 64,000 to the Kingdome," *Seattle Times,* July 2, 1995, p. A1.

56. See, e.g., "Promise Keepers Conference in UT's Stadium Has 35,000," *Chattanooga Free Press,* June 7, 1997, p. A7 (quoting local NOW leader Jeanne Kerwin).

57. CNN, *TalkBack Live,* October 3, 1997.

58. Donna Minkowitz, "In the Name of the Father," *Ms.,* November–December 1995, p. 69.

59. Diana Schaub, "Girls Just Wanna Have Fun," *Public Interest,* fall 1997, p. 122.

60. Thomas Ginsberg, "On Ferry, a Stark Battle for Survival," *Philadelphia Inquirer,* September 30, 1994, p. A3.

61. Ellen Fein and Sherrie Schneider, *The Rules: Time-Tested Secrets for Capturing the Heart of Mr. Right* (New York: Warner, 1995), p. 82. Conservative praise: Suzanne Fields, "What Pamela Harriman Knew," *Washington Times,* November 14, 1996, p. A19; Graglia, *Domestic Tranquility,* p. 252.

62. *Time*/CNN poll, in Nancy Gibbs, "How Should We Teach Our Children About Sex?" *Time,* May 24, 1993, p. 63.

63. Powers, "A Farewell to Feminism." Study: Catalyst, *Two Careers, One*

Marriage: Making It Work in the Workplace (New York: Catalyst, 1997), Executive Summary.

64. Wendy Shalit, "A Ladies' Room of One's Own," *Commentary,* August 1995, p. 34.

65. Unmanly men and unfeminine women: see, e.g., Mansfield, "Why Can't a Woman Be More Like a Man?"; Noemie Emery, "The Androgyny Party," *Commentary,* June 1993, pp. 49–50. "Natural distinctions": William Kristol, "On the Future of Conservatism," *Commentary,* February 1997, p. 32.

66. Tamar Lewin, "Boys Are More Comfortable with Sex Than Girls, Study Finds," *New York Times,* May 18, 1994. Peter Marin, "A Revolution's Broken Promises," *Psychology Today,* July 1983, pp. 51–57.

67. Norman Podhoretz, "Our Endangered Species: Fathers," *New York Post,* June 17, 1986.

68. Nancy Pearcey, "Rediscovering Parenthood in the Information Age," *Family in America,* March 1994.

69. "Feminization": see, e.g., Christopher Caldwell, "The Feminization of America," *Weekly Standard,* December 29, 1996. Irving Kristol, "The Feminization of the Democrats," *Wall Street Journal,* September 9, 1996.

70. See, e.g., Danielle Crittenden, "This Is the Army, Mrs. Jones," *Women's Quarterly,* summer 1997; Linda Bird Francke, *Ground Zero: The Gender Wars in the Military* (New York: Simon & Schuster, 1997).

Epilogue

1. Associated Press, April 12, 1997.

2. Val Ellicott and Christine Stapleton, "Prosecutor Quits in Burning Trial; Lawyer Blasts 'Inept' Handling of Case," *Palm Beach Post,* August 31, 1993, p. 1A; see also Frank Cerabino, "Victim's Getting Burned a 2nd Time by Judicial System," *Palm Beach Post,* September 2, 1993, p. 1B.

3. CNN Morning News, April 23, 1997.

4. Dave Barry, "Male Junk: An Anthropological and Historiographic Guide to Guys," *Washington Post,* May 7, 1995.

5. Ellen Frankel Paul, "Sexual Harassment As Sex Discrimination: A Defective Paradigm," *Yale Law & Policy Review,* v. 8, No. 2, 1990, pp. 333–364. Paul's model tort (p. 362) would define harassment as "sexual propositions incorporating overt or implicit threats of reprisal" or sexual conduct "so persistent and offensive that a reasonable person would find it extreme and outrageous." Liability would require intent or recklessness and "economic detriment and/or extreme emotional distress" to the victim. The employer would be liable if he was notified of the harassment and took no action, or provided no complaint mechanism.

6. See Peter Boyer, "Admiral Boorda's War," *New Yorker,* September 16, 1996, p. 68 (Rebecca Hansen); Paul Butler, "Taking Lessons from Elizabeth Morgan," *Legal Times,* June 8, 1998, p. 24.

ACKNOWLEDGMENTS

In the five years that I spent working on this book, many people had a part in making it possible. My literary agents, Glen Hartley and Lynn Chu, provided invaluable aid, encouragement, and advice from the start. My original editor at The Free Press, Adam Bellow, steered me wisely through the first draft of the manuscript; his successor, Elizabeth Maguire, guided me firmly yet sensitively through its final stages. Both made excellent suggestions that helped make the book what it is. Edith Lewis capably oversaw the copyediting and production.

The Earhart Foundation's grants enabled me to focus on this book and do the necessary research. Above all, I am grateful to Anthony Sullivan and David Kennedy for their confidence in this project.

Special thanks are due those who read all or parts of the work in progress and offered comments: Christina Hoff Sommers, Daphne Patai, Lawrence Mintz, John Fund, Ferrel Christensen, Michael Mills, Susan Sarnoff, Sally Satel, Eugene Volokh, Kay Schwarzberg, Jayne Tear, Kathleen Neville, Mark Pendergrast, Deborah Weiss.

The Cato Institute provided vital research assistance; in particular, I'd like to thank Jeremy Hildreth, Diana Brickell, Scott Cosenza, and other Cato interns for their work. Valuable research services were also performed by Beth Bangert, then a graduate student at American University.

Many men and women agreed to be interviewed for this book, often sharing deeply personal experiences, whether under their own names or anonymously. I deeply appreciate their time and their trust.

In the often arduous process of research and information gathering, I had the help of many well-wishers. Dr. David Gremillion supplied a wealth of data on domestic violence research and gender issues in medicine. Anne Mitchell, Stuart Miller, David Usher, and Ron Henry were excellent sources on divorce and child custody issues. Betty Duffey alerted me to important cases involving charges of sexual assault. Jack Kammer introduced me to the men's and fathers' movement. Barry Dank's Academic Sexual Correctness e-mail list was a goldmine of information on sexual harassment law and policy. Martin Morse Wooster has been an impressive one-man volunteer clipping service. Other sources were Michael Weiss, Sara Flohr, Timothy Smith, James Gregory, Malcolm George, Armin Brott, Katherine Dunn, Katherine Kersten, David Levy, Rikki Klieman, R.L. McNeely, Philip Cook, Reena Sommer, Richard Gelles, Eugene Narrett, Patrick Flynn, David Boaz, Karlyn Keene Bowman, Carole Danner, Tom Rettberg, Raymond Hughes, Judith Kleinfeld, Sarah McCarthy, David Dunlap, Richard France, Brian Carnell, and David Fontes.

For their friendship and support, I would like to thank John Koroly, Stephan and Abigail Thernstrom, Tama Starr, Michael Fumento, Alan Kors, Rita Simon, and Andrew Kaufman.

To William Vesterman, a wonderful teacher and my first mentor, I shall always be grateful for helping me find my way as a writer and for his continuing support. I am also thankful for the encouragement I have received from newspaper and magazine editors who have published my work during these years: Virginia Postrel, Richard Burr, Mike Leary, John Timpane.

To my parents, Alexander and Marina Young, I owe more than words can ever express. From them I have learned the values that lie at the foundation of this book: that every person should be treated as an individual; that the complexities of life cannot be tailored to fit any ideology; that it is unseemly and ignoble to defend the interests of the group to which you belong not because these interests are just, but because the group is your own.

Finally, no expression of gratitude would be complete without a mention of my colleagues who have challenged politically correct orthodoxies on gender and championed a vision of relations between women and men based on individual freedom, equal rights, and equal responsibilities: Christina Hoff Sommers, Daphne Patai, Karen Lehrman, Rene Denfeld, Katie Roiphe, David Thomas, Jean Bethke Elshtain, Elizabeth Fox-Genovese, Asa Baber, Donna Laframboise, Patricia Pearson, Nadine Strossen, Mark Pendergrast, Kate Fillion, Joan Kennedy Taylor, Armin Brott, and others. They are my models of intellectual integrity and courage. Thanks to them, even when we don't agree on everything, I know that I am not a lone maverick but part of a movement — part of what I hope is the movement of the future.